Bigos 60

POLISH
COOKBOOK

To compensate
for the first
Christmas away
from West Oak
with love
Daddy.
17/12/89

ZOFIA CZERNY

POLISH
COOKBOOK

PAŃSTWOWE WYDAWNICTWO EKONOMICZNE
WARSZAWA

Translated from Polish by
Christina Cękalska
May Miller

Illustrated by
Czesław Wielhorski

Photographs by
Janusz Czarnecki
Jerzy Proppe
Jan Styczyński

Edited by
Zofia Kozłowska
Zofia Surzycka-Mliczewska

Copyright © 1961, 1975
Państwowe Wydawnictwo Ekonomiczne
ul. Niecała 4a
00-098 Warszawa

First edition 1961
Revised edition 1975

*Printed and bound in Yugoslavia
by Mladinska knjiga — Ljubljana*

CONTENTS

FOREWORD

The Polish cuisine has its own ancient traditions, and its specialities which distinguish it from the cuisine of other countries. It has, of course, undergone the influence of European culinary art. However, it can easily be noticed that dishes deriving from other countries are prepared, in Poland, in a somewhat different way, mostly with the addition of typically Polish condiments, such as mushrooms, dill, marjoram, caraway etc.

The "Polish Cookbook" is dedicated to all those who should like to enrich their menu either with typically Polish dishes, or with dishes known also in other countries, but prepared in a Polish way. The author, Mrs. Zofia Czerny, proposes in her book about 1200 recipes for appetizers, soups, additions to soups, vegetarian dishes, meats, fish, sauces, cakes, desserts, and beverages. With the use of the above recipes, a menu for every day and a festive occasion can be composed, containing different dishes, from the simplest ones, to those demanding a special knowledge of the "arcana" of the cuisine, from potato soup to loin of venison. In the first place, however, it gives the possibility to learn the traditional ways of preparing such popular Polish dishes as: dill pickles (ogórki kwaszone), beet soup (barszcz), black soup (czarnina), hunter's dish of meat, cabbage and sauerkraut (bigos), tripe à la Warsaw (flaki pó warszawsku), filled dumplings (pierogi), pullets à la Polonaise (kurczęta po polsku), carp in Polish sauce (karp w sosie polskim), Polish yeast cake (baba), poppy-seed roll (makowiec), Easter short cake (mazurek), bison-grass vodka (żubrówka) and many others.

The recipes included in the "Polish Cookbook" are mostly calculated for 5 persons, with the exception of dishes which are usually being served for a reception, such as: pâtés, galantines, turkey, goose etc, as well as all the recipes for cakes.

Presenting the book to our readers, we wish them success in cooking and good appetite.

The Editors

TABLE OF MEASUREMENTS

Notice: **1 cup water = 1/4 quart**

Product	Measure	Weight in oz.	Weight in grams
Flour, Cereals, Dried Peas and Beans, Sugar			
Baking powder	3 tsp.	0.35	10
Barley, pearl	2 tbs.	0.98	28
Barley, pearl	1/2 cup	3.5	100
Bread crumbs	3/8 cup	1.26	36
Beans dried, medium	1/2 cup	3.5	100
Flour, potato	1 cup	4.48	128
Flour, white	1 1/2 tbs.	0.52	15
Flour, white	1 cup	3.85	110
Groats	2 1/2 tbs.	0.98	28
Macaroni, uncooked	1 cup	3.5	100
Noodles, uncooked	1 1/2 cup	3.5	100
Oats, rolled	1 1/3 cup	3.5	100
Peas dried	1/2 cup	3.5	100
Rice, uncooked	1/2 cup	3.5	100
Spaghetti	3/4 cup	3.5	100
Sugar, granulated	1 tsp.	0.14	4
Sugar, granulated	1 tbs.	0.45	13
Sugar, granulated	1/2 cup	3.5	100
Dairy products			
Butter	1 tbs.	0.49	14
Butter	7 tbs.	3.5	100
Butter	1 cup	7.91	226
Cottage cheese	1/2 cup	3.5	100
Cottage cheese	6 tbs.	3.5	100
Cream, sour 20%	1 tbs.	0.52	15
Cream, sweet 20% and 40 %	1/2 cup	3.5	100
Milk	1 cup	8.4	240
Fats			
Fat back with cracklings	1 tbs.	0.52	15
Lard	7 tbs.	3.5	100
Margarine	7 tbs.	3.5	100
Oil	1 tbs.	0.49	14
Oil	1/2 cup	3.6	103
Vegetables			
Asparagus	15 med. stalks	35.3	1 000
Beet	1 medium	4.2	120
Cabbage	1 small	35.3	1 000
Cabbage	medium	53.0	1 500
Carrot, cooked	5/8 cup	3.5	100

Product	Measure	Weight in oz.	Weight in grams
Carrot, raw	small	2.8	80
Carrot, raw	medium	3.5 —5.25	100—150
Cauliflower	medium	17.6	500
Cauliflower	large	35.3	1 000
Celery root (celeriac)	medium	0.52— 7.0	150—200
Celery root (celeriac)	large	8.75—10.5	250—300
Cucumber or pickle	medium	3.5 — 4.2	100—120
Cucumber or pickle	large	4.2 — 7.0	120—200
Leek, with leaves	medium	3.5	100
Leek, without leaves	medium	2.1 — 2.8	60— 80
Mixed vegetables, grated, raw, average	1/2 cup	3.5	100
Onion	small	1.4	40
Onion	medium	1.75— 2.1	50— 60
Onion	large	3.5	100
Paprika	1	3.5	100
Parsley	small	2.8	80
Parsley	large	4.2 — 5.25	120—150
Peas, green, shelled	3/4 cup	3.5	100
Pumpkin, grated	1/2 cup	3.5	100
Sauerkraut	2/3 cup	3.5	100
Spinach, cooked	1/2 cup	3.5	100
Tomato	medium	3.5	100
Tomato	large	5.25— 6.30	150—180
Tomato, pulp	1/2 cup	3.5	100

Fruit

Product	Measure	Weight in oz.	Weight in grams
Apple	medium	3.5 — 4.2	100—120
Apple	large	5.25	150
Bilberries	2/3 cup	3.5	100
Blueberries	2/3 cup	3.5	100
Cherries (sweet and morello)	15	3.5	100
Cranberries	2/3 cup	3.5	100
Currants	1/2 cup	3.5	100
Gooseberries	1/2 cup	3.5	100
Lemon or orange juice	1/2 cup	3.5	100
Pear	small	3.5	100
Pear	large	5.25	150
Raspberries	1 cup	3.5	100
Wild strawberries	2/3 cup	3.5	100

Dried fruits and nuts

Product	Measure	Weight in oz.	Weight in grams
Almonds, shelled, grated	1/4 cup	1.0	29
Almonds, shelled, grated	3/4 cup	3.5	100
Dates, dried	14	3.5	100
Figs, dried	18	3.5	100
Hazelnuts, shelled	8—10	0.52	15
Prunes, dried	12	3.5	100
Raisins	3/4 cup	3.5	100
Walnuts, shelled and grated	1 cup	2.97	85

Miscellaneous

Product	Measure	Weight in oz.	Weight in grams
Gelatin (powdered)	1 tsp.	0.1	3
Gelatin (powdered)	10 tbs.	3.5	100
Honey	5 tbs.	3.5	100
Yeast (compressed)	1 cake	0.35	10

COLD AND HOT APPETIZERS

COLD APPETIZERS

SPREADS FOR BREAD AND CANAPÉS

Cottage Cheese or Bryndza (Sheep Cheese) with Paprika

*2 1/2 cups bland cottage cheese or sheep cheese * 3 tbs. butter * salt * paprika*

Cream butter in bowl. Add cheese and cream into smooth paste. Add salt and paprika to taste.

Cream Cheese with Tomato Paste

*2 1/2 cups white cream cheese * 2 tbs. thick tomato paste * salt * paprika*

Cream cheese in bowl. Add salt and paprika, and cream thoroughly with tomato paste.

Fermented Cheese

Crumble cottage cheese in bowl. Leave in covered bowl for 24 hours in warm place so that cheese ferments.
Mix cheese well with a spoon or fork. Add salt. Caraway seeds may be added too.

Sautéed Cottage Cheese

*2 lb. cottage cheese * 2 tbs. butter * 2 egg yolks * salt * caraway seeds*

Crumble pressed cottage cheese in bowl. Cover and let stand 1 to 3 days in warm place until the cheese ferments. Mix and cream cheese every day. When the cheese begins to pull, place in pan and cook short while: melt butter in pot, place cheese and sauté on small flame mixing constantly until cheese melts.
Season with salt, add caraway seeds. Egg yolks may be added to hot cheese. Add egg yolks and stir vigorously. Pour seasoned hot cheese on deep plate and cool. Serve with bread. The hot cheese may be spread on bread.

Cottage Cheese with Caraway Seeds and Sour Cream

*2 1/2 cups bland cottage cheese * 1/2 cup sour cream * 1 tsp. caraway seeds * salt*

Cream cheese. Add sour cream and mix well. Add salt and caraway seeds to taste. Serve on lettuce leaves.

Cottage Cheese with Chives and Sour Cream

*2 1/2 cups bland cottage cheese * 1/2 cup sour cream * 3 tbs. young scallion greens or chives * salt*

Rinse chives and chop.
Cream cheese and add sour cream to form thin paste.
Combine with chives and salt. Place on lettuce leaves arranged on a platter. Serve on dessert plates.

Cottage Cheese with Chives and Radishes

*2 1/2 cups bland cottage cheese * 1/2 cup sour cream * 10 radishes * 2 tbs. chives * salt*

Rinse chives and chop.
Rinse radishes and cut together with leaves.

Cream cheese and combine with sour cream, radishes, chives and salt. Place on lettuce leaves and serve on salad plates.

Cottage Cheese with Radishes and Cucumbers

*2 1/2 cups bland cottage cheese * 5 radishes * 1 small cucumber * 1/2 cup heavy sour cream * 2 tbs. chives * salt*

Rinse radishes carefully and cut with leaves.
Rinse cucumber, peel and cut into small cubes. Rinse chives and chop.
Cream cheese and combine with sour cream, radishes and cucumber. Add salt. Place on lettuce leaves and serve on salad plates. Sprinkle with chives. Prepare just before serving.

Cottage Cheese with Tomatoes

*2 1/2 cups bland cottage cheese * 1/2 cup heavy sour cream * 1 small cucumber * 2 medium tomatoes * 2 tbs. chives * salt*

Rinse tomatoes and cut into small segments. Rinse cucumber, peel and cut into small cubes.
Cream cheese and combine with sour cream, tomatoes and cucumber. Add salt. Place on lettuce leaves and serve on salad plates. Sprinkle with chives. Prepare just before serving.

Cream Cheese with Kippers or Sprats

*2 1/2 cups white cream cheese * 2 tbs. butter or margarine * 1 kipper or 5 sprats * salt*

Remove heads, skin and tails from sprats and mash, together with bones, into paste. Remove skin from kipper and mash meat and soft roe into paste.
Cream butter. Add cheese, fish and salt. Place paste on lettuce leaves and serve on salad plates.

Bryndza (Sheep Cheese) with Sardines

*2 1/2 cups sheep cheese * 4 sardines with oil * paprika * salt*

Cream cheese in bowl. Add sardines and cream until smooth.
If mixture is too thick add some sardine oil gradually, creaming constantly until mixture becomes smooth and easy to spread.

Add paprika and salt to taste.
Place mixture on lettuce leaves or use as spread for canapés or for sandwiches.

Chive Butter

*7 tbs. butter * 2 tbs. chives * salt*

Rinse chives and chop very fine.
Cream butter in bowl adding chives gradually. Cream until smooth.
Scrape butter from sides of bowl and mix well. Place on plate and smooth out mixture. Let mixture cool until it sets.
Form rounds with cutter or balls.
Serve with rare meat.
May be used as spread for canapés.

Horse-Radish Butter

*7 tbs. butter * 2 tbs. horse-radish * salt*

Rinse horse-radish, peel and grate fine.
Cream butter in bowl and follow recipe for Chive Butter. Serve with boiled or sautéed fish, rare meat or use as spread for canapés.

Herring Butter

*1 herring (salted) * 7 tbs. butter*

Rinse herring, remove skin, fillet and clean, removing even small bones. Chop fine and cream into smooth paste.
Cream butter and follow recipe for Chive Butter. Serve with canapés, bread, baked potatoes, meat sauté or rare meat.

Kipper Butter

*1 kipper (with roe) * 7 tbs. butter * salt*

Remove skin and bones from kipper. Clean fish, remove filament from roe.
Cream kipper in bowl, add roe and cream together into smooth paste. Add salt.
Cream butter and follow recipe for Chive Butter.
Serve with canapés, bread or baked potatoes.

Ementhaler Paste

*3/4 cup soft, melted Ementhaler cheese * salt * paprika*

Cream cheese with spoon. Add salt to taste and a generous amount of paprika. Mix thoroughly. Use as spread for canapés.

Herring Paste

*1 herring (salted) * 5 oz. fat from boiled ham * 1/2 onion * pepper*

Rinse, slit and clean herring. Chop into fine smooth paste.
Grind ham fat.
Grate onion fine.
Combine all ingredients and cream. Add pepper to taste and let set. Serve with canapés, baked potatoes or rare meat.

Egg and Chive Paste

*3 eggs * 3 tbs. butter or margarine * chives * salt * heavy sour cream*

Cook hard-boiled eggs, cool in cold water and shell.
Chop whites fine and press yolks through fine sieve.
Rinse chives and chop.
Cream butter and add chives and egg yolks. Cream. Combine with egg whites and add salt.
If mixture is too thick add 1 to 2 spoons of sour cream.
Serve as spread for canapés.

Liver Paste

*7 oz. veal, pork or lamb liver * 1 egg yolk * mustard * salt * pepper * 1/2 herring * chives*

Remove liver membrane and veins and chop with knife.
Cream until fluffy.
Clean and chop herring.
Rinse chives and chop fine.
Combine liver with herring and cream. Add egg yolk, salt, mustard and pepper to taste.
Butter bread slices and spread with paste.
Sprinkle with chives.

CANAPÉS

How to Make Canapés

For canapés use long, narrow bread, rolls, or rectangular loaf.
Use white, rye, or whole-wheat bread. Do not use fresh bread.
Cut with a sharp knife into thin slices. Remove crust before cutting.
Cut into thin slices, particularly whole-wheat bread. Cut long bread into rounds.
Butter the bread. Butter may be combined with various foods like soft Ementhaler cheese and paprika, chives or herring.
Place desired food on buttered bread trying to form a design. When varieties of food are arranged garnish canapés paying attention to the combination of colors. Prepare each variety separately and arrange according to varieties on a tray or on large platters.
Keep (even for a short time) covered with a clean, damp napkin or plastics sheet as canapés dry out quickly and lose their fresh appearance.

Ingredients for Canapés

Cold meats sliced thin or ground ham left-overs.
Smoked tenderloin, sliced thin
'or **pâté** cut into thin squares or triangles.
Herring fillet divided into pieces. Sardines divided lengthwise into halves and quarters.
Smoked salmon sliced thin, divided into equal small pieces.
Cheese pastes with herring, eggs, butter, etc. (page 13—15).
Cheese, all varieties: bryndza (sheep cheese), Trappist cheese, Roquefort, Ementhaler, cut in thin slices. Cream and melted cheese.
Hard-boiled eggs, sliced or chopped.
Pickled carrots and mushrooms, orange agaric preserve, cut in strips.
Dill pickles, cut in slices or in halves.
Green parsley, chopped fine or in sprays, to arrange on platter.
Tomatoes, carrots and **cucumbers** unpeeled, cut in slices.
Radishes, sliced or whole and made into a rose to arrange on platter.
Lettuce to arrange on platter.
Mustard.

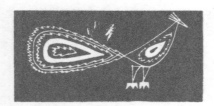

18

Recipes for Various Canapés

*2 long and narrow canapé rolls * butter*
I. *1 herring (salted) * chive butter * 1/2 dill pickle * pickled carrot*
II. *4 oz. smoked means * 2 hard-boiled eggs * mustard * green parsley *
* horse-radish * mayonnaise*
III. *4 oz. yellow cheese * 4 sardines * 2 hard-boiled eggs * cucumber slices * radishes*
IV. *2 hard-boiled eggs * 1 hard tomato (medium size) * mayonnaise *
* lettuce leaves*

Prepare canapé savories:
Soak herring, skin, fillet and cut each half into 3 parts.
Cook eggs, shell and cut each egg into five slices.
Remove rim from cheese and slice thin.
Remove skin from smoked meat and slice.
Prepare chive butter, etc.
Prepare garnish.
Cut bread or rolls into slices and butter.

Prepare various canapés:
I. Place one piece of herring flat, cover with chive butter, garnish with slices of dill pickle or pickled carrot.
II. Place one piece of smoked meat, dot with mustard and place on top one slice of egg. Garnish with green parsley, horse-radish and mayonnaise.
III. Arrange cheese slices on bread and garnish with sardines, egg and radishes or cucumber slices.
IV. Place egg slices on bread. Garnish with tomato slices, lettuce leaves and mayonnaise.
Arrange canapés on platters according to varieties.

HERRING APPETIZERS

Herring Rolls

*3 herrings (salted) * 1 small pickle * 2 firm tomatoes (medium size) *
* 2 eggs * 12 slices of onion * 3/4 cup mayonnaise*

Clean and soak herrings as described above. Remove skin and fillet.
Cut each fillet in half, lengthwise.
Roll each strip of fillet into tight rounds (four rounds out of each herring).
Cook eggs until hard, cool in cold water and shell. Cut each egg into 6 slices.
Cut pickle or tomatoes and onion into 12 slices.

Arrange herring rolls on glass salad dish in the following manner: place a slice of onion on a slice of pickle and then stand up each herring roll. Top with egg slice.
Each roll may be covered with a spoonful of mayonnaise.

Herrings in Sour Cream

*5 herrings (salted) * 1/2 cup onion (soaked in boiling water with vinegar or lemon juice) * 1 cup sour cream * green parsley * 1 tbs. sugar * 2 eggs*

Wash herrings, cut off heads and tails. Slit stomach and remove roe.
Place herrings in enameled dish and soak for few hours in water, or clean, fillet and soak in milk.
Squeeze herrings free of water or milk, skin and remove bones. Place two fillets together and cut diagonally into two pieces.
Cut onion into thin slices. Onion may be soaked in boiling water with lemon juice or vinegar. Drain after a while and press out water.
Mix sour cream with sugar.
Cover herrings with sour cream a few hours before serving. Arrange scalded or raw onion slices on top.
Serve with green parsley and hard-boiled eggs as garnish.

Herrings in Oil with Onion

*5 herrings (salted) * 3 tbs. mustard * 1/2 cup oil * bay leaf*

Prepare herrings and soak as described in recipe above.
Squeeze out water. Skin and fillet.
Cover each half of herring with mustard. Roll into whorls and arrange in a jar side by side.
Pour oil over herrings to cover them completely and place bay leaves on top. Cover with wax paper. Store in cool place.
Serve on a glass salad dish, piercing each piece with a toothpick.
Garnish with gherkins, pickled carrot vinaigrette and onion rounds.
Herring in oil may be stored for a week.
The herring oil may be used to make mayonnaise or for potato salad.

Herrings in Mayonnaise

*5 herrings (salted) * 1/2 cup mayonnaise with 1 egg yolk*

Wash herrings, cut off heads and tails. Clean and soak in cold water for 12 hours, changing water several times.

Remove herrings and squeeze out water. Skin and fillet. Remove bones without tearing meat.

Place two fillets together and arrange on a square, glass dish. Cut diagonally into two pieces.

Prepare mayonnaise with one egg yolk (see page 314). Season to taste and pour thick sauce over fillets.

Garnish with vegetables in season.

If not using prime, salted herring, use small, tender herrings salted in barrels.

When soaked and squeezed out, remove skin and place flat in a small container. Cover with milk for 2 or 3 hours. Remove from milk and squeeze out excess. Fillet and continue according to instructions given above. Herrings in sour cream may be prepared in the same way.

Herrings on Apple Salad

S a l a d: *2 medium apples (juicy) * 1 cup heavy sour cream * horse-radish to taste * 1 tbs. sugar * 3 herrings (salted) * * G a r n i s h: lettuce or savoy cabbage leaves * tomato or carrot slices * green leek slices*

Rinse herrings and remove roe. Cut off heads and tails. Soak for a few hours.

Skin and fillet. Place two fillets together again. Cut each herring diagonally into two pieces.

Rinse apples, pare and grate coarsely. Add horse-radish, sour cream and sugar. Mix.

Arrange lettuce or 'savoy cabbage leaves on four sides of a square salad dish. Place apple salad in salad dish. Pat out evenly. Place pieces of herring on top. Garnish each piece of herring with tomato or carrot slice and round of green leek.

Pickled Herrings in Roe Sauce

*5 small, tender herrings from barrel (roe) * 1/2 cup water * vinegar to taste * 2 bay leaves * allspice * herring roe * 1 medium onion * 1 tsp. sugar * 10 slices of gherkin * 10 slices of carrot*

Soak herrings a day ahead. Change water several times. On following day fillet in halves.

Prepare stock. Bring water to the boil and add vinegar to taste. Add allspice, bay leaves and onion. Press roe through sieve and combine with cooled stock. Add sugar to taste.

Roll halves of herrings into whorls, placing into centers onion from stock, slices of carrot, gherkin or cucumber. Pin herrings with toothpicks. Place in jar side by side.

Cover herrings with cold stock and place bay leaves on top.

Cover with wax paper and store in cool place.

Serve with baked potatoes or bread.

Herrings in Vegetables

*10 raw, unsalted herrings * 1 cup oil * 1 medium carrot * 1 medium parsley * 1/2 medium celery root * 2 medium onions * 4 bay leaves * all-spice *salt * 3 tbs. vinegar*

Clean herrings, fillet and salt.

Wash vegetables in water, clean and cut into slices. Place in pot and cover with small amount of water and part of the oil. Simmer vegetables in this liquid on slow fire together with seasoning. Cool.

Heat remaining oil, sauté herrings and place in jar: one layer of herring to one layer of vegetables. Sprinkle with vinegar.

Cover with oil from sauté pan and store in cool place.

EGG APPETIZERS

Eggs in Mayonnaise

*5 eggs * 3/4 cup mayonnaise * G a r n i s h: tomato or carrot slices * * slices of pickle or cucumber * slices of leek cut across * lettuce leaves * * orange agarics salted or in vinegar * mushrooms in vinegar*

Cook hard-boiled eggs. Cool and peel. Arrange on rectangular plate and pour sauce over them. Garnish with vegetables in season. Garnish plate with lettuce leaves cut in half lengthwise and arrange along sides of the plate.

Eggs in Cold Sauces

*5 eggs * 1/2 recipe of horse-radish sauce with mustard or tartare sauce (see page 314, 315)*

Prepare as above.

Garnish with vegetables in season.

Eggs Stuffed with Mustard

*5 eggs * 1 oz. stale roll * 1/2 cup milk * 1/2 small onion * 3 1/2 tbs. butter * 1 tbs. mustard * salt * pepper * green parsley * 5 oz. bread * 1 oz. Ementhaler cheese*

Cook hard-boiled eggs, cool and peel.
Soak roll in milk. Squeeze out milk.
Lightly brown fine chopped onion in fat.
Cut eggs in half, remove yolks and set aside whites. Grind egg yolks with soaked roll and onion. Add mustard, salt and pepper to taste.
Fill egg white halves mixture, shape like whole egg.
Remove bread crust and cut into thin slices the length and width of an egg. Butter the slices.
Place filled eggs on bread slices and garnish with cheese and colorful vegetables in season.
Serve on a rectangular dish garnished on sides with lettuce leaves cut in half lengthwise.

Eggs Stuffed with Herring

*5 eggs * 1/2 small onion or chives * 1 herring (salted) * 1 oz. stale roll * 1/2 cup milk * 5 oz. bread * 1 1/2 tbs. butter*

Cook hard-boiled eggs, cool and peel.
Soak roll in milk and squeeze out.
Dice onion or chives.
Wash and chop herring.
Cut eggs lengthwise, remove yolks, set aside halved whites.
Grind all ingredients, mix.
Fill egg whites with mixture.
Shape like a whole egg.
Cut off crusts of bread, slice into squares to fit the egg, spread with butter.
Arrange eggs on the bread, garnish with colorful vegetables in season.
Serve on a rectangular platter, garnished with lettuce or cabbage leaves.

Eggs Stuffed with Smoked Fish

*5 eggs * 1 oz. stale roll * 1/2 cup milk * salt * paprika * 1 kipper * 1 cup mayonnaise*

Cook hard-boiled eggs, cool and peel.
Soak roll in milk and squeeze out.

Cut eggs lengthwise and remove yolks. Set aside halved whites.
Skin fish and remove meat.
Grind fish, egg yolks and roll. Add salt (if necessary) and paprika.
Fill egg whites with mixture shaping like a whole egg.
Arrange eggs on rectangular dish and pour mayonnaise over them. Garnish with colorful vegetables in season.

Eggs Stuffed with Ham

*5 eggs * 5 oz. fat ham or back bacon * 10 tbs. cooling meat aspic * 1 cup mayonnaise * some sour cream may be needed*

Cook hard-boiled eggs, cool and peel. Cut lengthwise. Remove yolks carefully and set aside white halves.
Grind ham and egg yolks. Mix well and thin with sour cream, if necessary.
Fill egg white halves with mixture, forming like whole eggs.
Arrange eggs on rectangular plate. Cooling meat aspic may be poured over them. Garnish with vegetables in season.
Serve with mayonnaise.

PÂTÉS

Pork Pâté

*1 lb. pork or veal liver * 1 lb. pork meat * 4 oz. jowl * 1 medium onion * 2 small, dried mushrooms * 3 oz. stale roll * salt * pepper * bay leaf * * grease for mold * 1 oz. fat back for mold*

Wash mushrooms in warm water. Rinse.
Rinse liver and remove membrane.
Rinse meat.
Place liver in boiling water, bring to a boil and drain.
Cut jowl into small pieces and sauté with chopped onion.
Sauté meat in jowl fat and onion. Add mushrooms, bay leaf and small amount of water. Stew until tender.
Place roll into meat sauce and soak.
Grind meat and cooked liver twice, together with mushrooms, roll and jowl. Mix well. Add salt and pepper to taste.
Grease pudding mold and line with slices of fat back. Place meat mixture in mold and press in with spoon. Cover mold. Place in boiling water.
Steam 3/4 of an hour. Remove, uncover and cool mold. Remove pâté and place on round plate.

Veal Pâté

*2 lb. veal * 1 herring (prime, tender) * 3 tbs. fat * 1/2 medium onion *
* 3 potatoes * 3 tbs. butter * 1/2 cup flour * 1/2 cup sour cream * 2 eggs *
* salt * pepper or paprika * nutmeg * grease for mold*

Rinse herring, soak, changing water several times.
Rinse meat, separate from bone, place in heated fat and brown on all sides.
Slice onion and add to meat. Add small amount of water and stew until tender in covered pot. Cool. Remove meat and press sauce through sieve.
Rinse potatoes, peel and cook. Cool.
Melt butter, add flour and brown lightly stirring constantly. Set aside.
Add sour cream to browned flour and mix in meat sauce. Bring to a boil, stirring constantly (sauce should be thick).
Squeeze herring out of water. Cut off head and tail, remove skin and bones. Grind herring, meat and potatoes 3 times. Place in browned flour sauce, add salt, pepper, nutmeg to taste. Add eggs and mix thoroughly.
Place meat mixture in greased mold and press in with spoon. Cover mold and place in boiling water. Cook 3/4 of an hour over a high flame. Remove and uncover mold.
When the pâté is slightly cooled unmold on round plate.
Serve warm or cold.

Chicken Pâté
(or other poultry)

*1 large chicken * 7 oz. mixed vegetables without cabbage * 5 oz. poultry
and veal liver * 1/2 cup butter or poultry fat * 2 oz. stale roll * 1 medium
onion * 1 egg * 2 egg yolks * salt * pepper * ginger * nutmeg * (chicken
broth) * butter to grease mold*

Rinse chicken and cook slowly until tender.
Remove and separate skin and bones.
Rinse liver and soak in lukewarm water.
Squeeze out water, remove membrane from veal liver and stew until half cooked with butter and chopped onion, sprinkling with broth. Do not brown onion or meat.
Cut roll into small cubes. Add to liver and simmer a short while. Remove from fire and cool.
Grind chicken meat, liver with sauce and roll three times through fine mesh. Add egg, egg yolks, salt and seasonings to meat mixture. Add broth until mixture is like soft butter. Knead well.

25

Grease round mold for pâté and place in meat. Press in with spoon, cover, place in boiling water and steam for 3/4 hour.

Remove mold, uncover and cool so that top of pâté does not dry out.

Before quite cool loosen with knife around edges. When cold remove pâté from mold.

Serve with mayonnaise or tartare sauce.

Goose Liver Pâté

*2 lb. goose livers * milk * 3 oz. fat back * 1 large onion * pinch of white pepper, nutmeg and allspice * 2 tbs. concentrated beef broth * salt*

Take livers from fattened geese, rinse and soak in milk for a few hours. Remove from milk and squeeze out. Dry in towel. Remove membrane.

Cover fat back with boiling water. Add salt to taste and cook until tender. Skim off fat from fat back while cooking. Fry cooked fat back to steam off water. Do not brown.

Cut onion into fine slices and add fat skimmed off water. Stew onion in fat without browning.

Drain steamed fat back and cut with sharp knife into thin slices. Divide into 2 parts.

In top of double boiler arrange layers of fat back with alternate layers of onion and liver. Sprinkle with well-ground seasonings and cover with second part of fat back. Sprinkle with broth. Cover and place over hot water. Cook 25 minutes over boiling water.

Remove from fire and cool. Grind and press mixture through sieve. Add salt to taste to pâté and cream. Place in porcelain dish pressing in firmly. Cover with thin layer of melted lard. Cover with wax paper and store in a cool, dry place. The pâté will keep a long time.

Remove lard from pâté before serving. Remove pâté and shape into cube. Freeze and cut with a sharp knife into 1/2 inch slices.

Pâté looks more effective served in aspic.

*1 lb. pâté * 4 cups concentrated beef broth * 3 to 4 tbs. gelatine*

Prepare 3 cups strong beef broth. Bring broth to a boil. Dissolve gelatine and place in cool place.

Form pâté into cube and cut into portions 2 by 1 1/2 inches.

Pour some setting aspic on bottom of a small rectangular mold, retaining the remainder. Stand up pieces of pâté in aspic and make them firm. Add aspic gradually waiting for it to set, and then pour in more and wait for it to set, and so on until the pâté is covered with aspic.

Before serving ease aspic around edges of mold with knife. Set mold in hot water for a short while. Unmold immediately.
Garnish with vegetables in season.

Hare Pâté

*1 lb. pork meat * 4 oz. fat back * 1 fore part of a hare and hare giblets * * 1 medium onion * bay leaf * 4 oz. stale roll * 2 eggs * salt * pepper * allspice * grease for mold * 1 oz. fat back for mold*

Rinse the pork and hare meat. Stew slowly with onion, bay leaf and fat back, covering with small amount of water.
Drain meat when tender and separate from bones.
Boil off excess water from sauce of meat.
Soak roll in meat sauce and grind with meat and fat back three times.
Mix well. Add salt, pepper and allspice to taste. Add eggs and knead well.
Place in pudding mold which has been greased and lined with stripes of fat back. Press firmly with spoon. Cook in steam on high flame for 45 minutes. Remove mold, uncover and dry in very hot oven.
Cool and remove from mold.

Codfish Pâté

*1 lb. codfish without head * 3 oz. fat back * 1 oz. celery root * 1 oz. parsley * 1 large onion * 2 oz. stale roll * 2 cups fish stock * 1 1/2 tsp. potato starch * 1/2 egg * salt * ginger * nutmeg * paprika * grease and bread crumbs for mold*

Clean codfish, remove skin and sprinkle with vinegar.
Cook stock with celery root, parsley and part of the onion. Drain off and add salt to stock. Cook fish in stock. Remove and drain off fish. Separate from bones.
Cut fat back and melt. Stew remainder of onion. Do not brown.
Soak roll in fish stock and squeeze out.
Grind fish with roll, vegetables from stock and stewed onion.
Add 1/2 egg and potato starch to fish mixture. Add seasoning to taste. Knead well.
Grease mold or pot and sprinkle with bread crumbs. Place fish mixture in mold and steam (or bake in pot).
Serve hot or cold.

MEAT APPETIZERS

Tartar Steak

*1 lb. beef without bone (loin) * salt * pepper * 2 medium onions * 4 tbs.
chopped mushrooms in vinegar * 5 tbs. chopped gherkins * 3 tbs. capers *
* 5 egg yolks * green parsley*

Rinse meat, grind and mash into a smooth paste together with salt and
pepper. Form 5 tall steaks and arrange on platter greased with oil. Make
a hollow in the center of each steak.

Chop onion and sprinkle with water and lemon so that onion does not
turn black.

Cut mushrooms and gherkins in fine cubes.

Place a raw egg yolk in the hollow in each steak, sprinkle with salt and
green parsley.

Place a portion of mushrooms, gherkins, capers and onion beside each
steak. Garnish plate with vegetables in season: lettuce and radishes or
cucumber or tomato slices.

Serve steak with oil.

Roast Beef

*2 lb. beef (roast beef) * 5 oz. vegetables without cabbage * 1/2 medium
onion * 1 1/2 tbs. oil * salt * 2 tbs. flour * 3 tbs. fat*

Rinse meat and marinate in vegetables, onion and oil for one or two
days before using (see page 183). Store in cool place.

Scrape oil and vegetables off meat with knife.

Sprinkle meat with salt and flour.

Heat fat in pot large enough to contain meat.

Place meat in pot and baste with fat.

Place in very hot oven and bake quickly so that blood appears, when meat
is pricked.

Remove from oven and cool.

Take off fat and cut meat into thin slices. Cut slantingly with a sharp
knife like carving ham.

Serve with gherkins, cold sauces, lettuce and tomato salad or cucumbers
in sour cream.

Roast Veal

*2 lb. veal (for roast) * salt * garlic * 3 tbs. fat*

Rinse meat and remove bones that are not lodged too deeply in flesh. When meat is separated from bone, roll it tight and tie with scalded string.
Crush garlic and salt. Rub into meat.
Melt fat in small roasting pan and brown meat in hot fat.
Place in oven and roast, baste frequently. When water has steamed off, sprinkle sauce with water so that it does not burn.
Roast for 1 hour. Remove from sauce and cool.
Remove sauce from sides of pan and sprinkle with water. Cook and pour on plate. Cool.
Cut cold meat into thin slices across the grain. Arrange on platter.
Remove fat from congealed sauce. Cut congealed sauce into small cubes and garnish meat.
Serve with cold sauces and fresh salads in season.

Roast Pork

*2 lb. pork (boned loin) * salt * 3 tbs. lard * 1 tsp. caraway seeds * 1 large onion * marjoram*

Rinse meat and sprinkle with salt.
Rinse caraway seeds.
Heat fat in small roast pan. Brown meat in fat and sprinkle with caraway seeds.
Place meat in oven and roast. Baste with sauce from pan bottom. Add water as it steams off.
Cut onion in slices and add to meat before it is fully cooked. Sprinkle meat with marjoram.
Roast until tender (about an hour). Remove and cool.
Cut cold roast into thin slices across the grain.

Cold Cuts

Cold cuts are an indespensable part of cold appetizers. Several varieties should be chosen (at least two) which differ in color, as for instance: ham, pâté, smoked tenderloin, roast beef and raw, dried, smoked sausage. Cold cuts should be sliced thin and symetrically. The skin should be removed. Larger slices should be cut in half. Large layers of fat, as on ham, should be cut off, leaving an edge of less than half an inch. The trimmed fat may be used to prepare paste for canapés.

Garnish plate with cold meats with an edge of lettuce, tomato slices, cucumber, etc., depending on the season. Serve with tartare sauce, or with sour cream, horse-radish and mustard sauces.

JELLIED APPETIZERS

Fish Stock (4 Cups)

*5 to 6 cups water * 1 medium onion * 2 oz. carrot * 2 oz. parsley * 2 oz. celery root * salt * bay leaf * allspice * 1 lb. fish left-overs (fins, bones, heads without gills, rinsed skin, backbones)*

Clean vegetables and cut into pieces. Cook together with salt and seasoning.

Add fish left-overs (backbones and bones, fins, skin and heads). Cook and drain off stock. Bring stock to a boil. (There should be 4 cups of liquid.)

If necessary, clear according to recipe given below.

How to Clear Aspic

*4 cups fish stock * 2 tbs. gelatine * 2 to 3 egg whites * 1 tbs. vinegar (6%)*

Soften gelatine in cold water for an hour. When it swells dissolve in a small amount of hot stock, stirring constantly. Cool remainder of stock and add raw egg whites and the dissolved gelatine and vinegar. Beat mixture thoroughly with an egg beater. Heat slowly, stirring constantly and bring to a boil.

When liquid has come to a boil remove from hot flame and leave to clear (about 30 minutes).

When the liquid is clear, skim off stock and drain liquid slowly, add gradually to sieve lined with a damp fine linen. When clearing a large amount of stock use a linen napkin tied by its four corners to the four legs of an upturned stool. The napkin must hang loosely so that the liquid does not spill over but drip slowly into a dish placed under it. The stock must be lukewarm when drained so that it does not coagulate when dripping through.

Chill the drained aspic mixture.

Fish Aspic Cups

*3 lb. fish (codfish, carp, tench, perch-pike, pike) * salt * 4 cups fish stock*

Clean fish, remove fins, skin, head and tail. Fillet, salt and set aside.
Prepare fish stock with vegetables and fish left-overs (see above).
Drain off stock and steam off to 4 cups. Bring stock to a boil. Divide
fillets into equal parts of 7 to 10 oz. each. Add pieces of fish gradually
to boiling stock. Cook slowly on a small flame (12 to 15 minutes). Remove
fish carefully. Remove bones holding meat with fingers so as not to
damage it.
Prepare molds or cups of one size. Wet bottom with setting aspic mixture
(fish stock). Garnish with vegetables in season. When garnish has set in
the aspic, add fish pieces and cover with cooling aspic. Chill.
Before serving, dip molds in boiling water and remove immediately.
Loosen aspic around edges with knife and place on plate.
Serve with lemon, vinegar, mayonnaise, tartare sauce.

Codfish Fillets in Aspic

*1 1/2 lb. codfish fillets * 5 cups water * 7 oz. mixed vegetables without
cabbage * salt * 2 tbs. gelatine*

Cut fillets into narrow pieces (3 to 5 oz.), roll and tie with a string.
Prepare vegetable stock. Cover vegetables with boiling water, salt and
cook 20 to 30 minutes.
Cook fillets, rolled with the outer side to the center, in the stock. Remove
carefully and place on plate. Steam off fish stock to 3 cups. Add gelatine
to fish stock and clear. Pour some setting aspic on the bottom of the platter.
When aspic becomes firm, arrange the fish on the platter.
Garnish with vegetables in season. Arrange garnish each portion of fish.
Pour setting aspic gradually over fish and garnish, taking care that the
garnish does not float to the top. Place almost set aspic on top of fish or
cover fish with chopped aspic.
Serve with cold sauces as for instance mayonnaise or tartare.

Pike or Codfish Galantine

*F i s h   m i x t u r e: 2 oz. stale roll * 1/2 cup milk * 1 large onion *
* 3 1/2 tbs. butter * 2 lb. pike * 1 egg * 1 tsp. sugar * salt * pepper *
* O m e l e t: 3/4 cooked spinach * 3 eggs * salt * 2 tbs. water * 1 1/2
tbs. butter for frying * S t o c k: 6 cups water * 7 oz. mixed vegetables*

31

*without cabbage * 1 medium onion * bay leaf * allspice * salt * A s p i c :
3 cups stock * 3 egg whites to clear aspic * 2 tbs. gelatine * 1 tbs. vinegar
(6⁰/₀)*

Soak roll in milk and squeeze out.
Slice onion and stew in butter. Do not brown.
Clean fish and fillet. Remove skin from fillets and grind half of the meat
with onion and roll. Add 1 raw egg, sugar, salt and pepper to mixture.
Knead well until mixture forms into one ball.
Prepare the omelet. Cook spinach in a large amount of water. Squeeze
out water and press through sieve. Separate egg whites from egg yolks.
Mix egg whites with spinach thoroughly.
Add salt to egg yolks and mix well adding 2 tbs. of water. Fry high omelet
on small skillet. Cool and cut into finger-width strips.
Cut remaining raw fish meat into finger-width strips.
Grease a cloth towel with butter. Place ground mixture on cloth and spread.
Place omelet strips and strips of fillet in rows on mixture. Roll galantine
tightly and roll in towel. Tie both ends of towel with string and tie the
galantine through center and across.
Prepare stock from vegetables. Cover galantine with boiling stock and cook
slowly on low flame for 45 minutes. When cooked, remove from fire and
cool galantine in stock.
Remove the galantine and take off the towel. Cut into slices 1/2 inch
thick.
Soften gelatine in cold water.
Pour galantine stock into pot and boil until 3 cups remain. Add softened
gelatine, mix and cool. Mix with vinegar and raw egg whites and heat
slowly until mixture boils. Remove from fire to clear.
When liquid is clear drain slowly through sieve lined with damp cloth.
Cool.
Arrange the galantine on a plate and garnish each portion. Cover with
cooling aspic. Serve with cold sauces.

Codfish Roll in Aspic

F i s h   m i x t u r e : *2 lb. codfish * 2 oz. stale roll * 1/2 cup milk * 3 tbs.
butter * 1/2 medium onion * 1 egg * salt * pepper * 1 tbs. potato starch *
S t o c k : 6 cups water * 7 oz. mixed vegetables without cabbage * 1 medium onion * bay leaf * allspice * salt * A s p i c : 3 cups stock * 2 tbs.
gelatine*

Prepare fish mixture as in recipe on page 274.
Spread fat on damp towel and sprinkle with flour.

Place fish mixture on towel and form into a roll. Roll in towel and tie both ends with string.

Cook stock with vegetables (and fish bones). Drain off stock and add salt. Bring stock to a boil and place roll into it. Cook on slow fire for one hour.

Remove stock with fish roll from fire and let cool. Remove fish roll and unroll carefully from towel when completely cooled. Place on plate.

Cut diagonal slices 1/2 inch thick. Arrange on plate. Add softened gelatine to 3 cups of stock, melt and stir. Garnish fish with vegetables in season and cover with cooling aspic or serve with cold sauces.

Jewish Pike Forcemeat in Aspic

F i s h   m i x t u r e: *2 1/2 lb. pike * 2 oz. stale roll * 1/2 cup milk * * 1 large onion * 3 1/2 tbs. butter * 1/2 egg * salt * pepper * nutmeg * * 1/2 cup water * S t o c k: 6 cups water * 7 oz. mixed vegetables without cabbage * fish backbone with bones and head * salt * bay leaf * allspice * * A s p i c: 3 cups stock * 2 tbs. gelatine * 3 egg whites to clear aspic * * 1 tbs. vinegar (6%)*

Remove scales from fish. Cut off fins and tail. Rinse fish. Make an incision around the head and without cutting the gullet clean fish, pulling in the direction of the gullet.

Remove skin cutting it carefully away from the meat with a sharp knife. Begin from incision made near the head.

Fold back skin and draw it off in the direction from the head to the tail.

Carefully cut away skin from the meat.

Cut fish off from skin at the tail, cutting through the backbone. Turn skin and set aside.

Fillet the fish.

Soak roll in milk and squeeze out.

Stew onion in butter. Do not brown.

Grind fish with roll and onion. Add 1/2 egg, salt and seasoning to mixture and knead well, adding 1/2 cup cold water.

Stuff skin of pike with the mixture. Do not press it in too tightly. Sew skin and place stuffed pike in oblong pot. Cover with cold water. Add pike's head, bones and vegetables to water. Add salt, allspice and bay leaf and cook in covered pot for one hour.

After fish is cooked, remove from fire and cool slowly in stock. When cold remove stuffed fish and cut in slightly diagonal slices 1/2 inch thick.

Bring 3 cups of fish stock to a boil, remove from fire and mix with softened gelatine. Clear with egg whites and drain. Cool.

Arrange sliced fish on long and narrow plate. Garnish sides of plate with colorful, cut vegetables. Cover fish with cooling aspic or dot with set aspic cut in cubes.

Serve with tartare or mustard sauce.

This dish may also be served with hot, horse-radish sauce.

Carp, Tench or Pike in Aspic

S t o c k: *2 1/2 lb. fish * 6 cups water * 7 oz. mixed vegetables without cabbage * fish backbone (plus heads if any) * 1 medium onion * * allspice * pepper * bay leaf * salt * A s p i c: 3 cups stock * 2 tbs. gelatine * 3 egg whites to clear aspic * 1 tbs. vinegar (6⁰/₀) * G a r n i s h: green parsley * green peas * 2 eggs * gherkins*

Clean fish and divide into two parts lengthwise, remove backbone only.

Prepare vegetable stock adding fish heads, backbones, onion and seasoning. Drain and pour into small pot. Salt.

Cut fish across into 2 inch pieces.

Cook fish in stock on slow fire, placing several pieces at a time in stock. Cook 10 to 15 minutes.

Remove large bones from fish, holding meat with fingers. Arrange fish on plate.

Dissolve gelatine and mix with 3 cups of fish stock. Clear stock with egg whites and chill.

Cook hard-boiled eggs. Cool, shell and cut in slices or pieces.

When aspic begins to set, garnish fish with vegetables, eggs, gherkins. Pour small amount of aspic over fish and let set. Pour small amount of aspic and let set again. Repeat 2 or 3 times.

Serve with vinegar or lemon or with cold sauces.

Codfish Balls on Mayonnaise Salad

F i s h   b a l l s: *1 1/2 lb. cleaned codfish without head * 2 oz. stale roll * * 1/2 cup milk * 1 medium potato * 1/2 medium onion * 2 1/2 tbs. fat * 1 1/2 tsp. potato starch * 1/2 egg * salt * pepper * ginger * * nutmeg * S t o c k: 6 cups water * 7 oz. mixed vegetables without cabbage * 1 medium onion * allspice * bay leaf * salt * pepper * fish backbone and bones * G a r n i s h: 1/2 recipe for mayonnaise salad (see page 44) * lettuce leaves * 2 hard-boiled eggs*

Clean codfish, fillet and remove skin.

Soak roll in milk and squeeze out.

Peel potato and cook.

Stew onion in fat. Do not brown.

Grind fish meat with roll, potato and onion. Combine mixture with 1/2 egg and potato starch and season to taste.

Cook stock with vegetables, seasoning and fish bones and drain off. Add salt. Shape 10 round balls out of fish mixture and throw into boiling stock. Cook slowly on small flame.

Prepare the mayonnaise salad (see page 44), set aside part of the mayonnaise before mixing salad.

Arrange separate portions of mayonnaise salad on lettuce leaves on a plate. Place balls on top and cover with mayonnaise.

Each portion may be covered with cooling aspic and garnished with hard-boiled eggs and vegetables in season.

Jewish Carp with Vegetables

*2 lb. carp * 6 cups water * 1 large onion * 1 medium carrot * 1 medium parsley * 3 oz. celery root * 2 tbs. sugar * salt * pepper * allspice * piece of bay leaf * 1 tbs. gelatine*

Shave off scales and clean and prepare fish according to page 273.

Cut fish across into slices 3/4 inch wide. Cut through the backbone, using scissors.

Clean vegetables, rinse and cut into slices and arrange on bottom of small pot.

Arrange pieces of fish on top of vegetables. Add salt, sugar and powdered seasoning. Place head, that has been cut lengthwise into two flat pieces, on vegetables and fish and cover with water.

Cover pot and cook fish on small flame about 1 hour. Do not stir.

Add water if liquid steams off during cooking, so that fish remains covered.

When the vegetables are tender pour off part of the stock and dissolve the gelatine. Stir and heat. Pour into the cooked fish and vegetables, bring to a boil and remove from fire.

Cool in the pot in which the fish has been cooked.

Jewish carp is served in the pot in which it has been cooked. Serve with vegetables on which the fish was arranged for cooking.

Serve with vinegar, tartare sauce or mayonnaise.

Greek Codfish or Carp

*3 lb. fish * 4 tbs. oil * small piece of celery root * 1 medium carrot * 1 medium parsley * 2 large onions * 3 tbs. thick tomato preserves * 1/2 bay leaf * salt * pepper * sugar * 1 tbs. mustard * vinegar to taste*

Clean fish and fillet. Do not remove skin. Cut across into portions 2 inches wide. Salt.

Heat oil and fry fish. Arrange on plate so that slices are close to each other.

Clean vegetables and cut into small cubes. Chop onion.

Place vegetables into hot oil and sauté. Add salt and seasoning. Sprinkle with water and cook until tender. Add tomato purée to the vegetables and vinegar and sugar to taste. The vegetables should contain only a small amount of stock.

Arrange vegetables on fish and cool.

Greek fish may be served hot or cold.

Marinated Codfish

*2 lb. codfish without head * 6 cups water * small piece of celery root * * 1 small carrot * 1 small parsley * 1 large onion * 3 tbs. vinegar * salt * * pepper * piece of bay leaf * allspice * 2 tbs. gelatine*

Clean codfish, remove membrane from stomach cavity.

Remove the skin and fillet. Cut fillets into equal portions. Clean vegetables, rinse. Add bones and skin of codfish and cook stock adding salt and seasoning. Drain off stock.

Place fish meat into boiling stock, add vinegar to taste and cook slowly on small flame (10 min.). Remove fish and arrange on salad dish.

Steam off stock to 3 cups and dissolve gelatine. Garnish fish with vegetables. Cover with liquid and chill.

Serve with vinegar, horse-radish in vinegar or with cold sauces.

Marinated Carp

*2 lb. carp * salt * 1 large onion * vinegar with water (4 cups water, 3 tbs. 6º/o vinegar) * allspice * bay leaf*

Clean fish. Remove head, fins and tail. Cut fish in half and cut each half into quite wide pieces. Salt the fish.

Bring to a boil the vinegar and water with onion, seasoning and salt. Place on small flame and place fish in liquid. Cook slowly.

Remove fish on plate with a draining spoon. (Cook head longer).
Add vinegar to taste to vinegar liquid, remove onion and steam off liquid to 3 cups. Cover fish with stock and chill.
Serve in round salad dish with salads or cold sauces.
The marinated fish covered with stock may be stored in cool place in a narrow stone pot or jar for 10 days.

Meat Aspic for Covering

*6 cups water * 1 lb. calf's bones (soft), calf's joints and knuckles * * allspice * salt * bay leaf * 1 small onion * 1 small parsley * 1 small carrot * 1 small piece of celery root * 2 tbs. gelatine * 1 tbs. vinegar (6%) * 3 egg whites to clear aspic*

Rinse bones and chop. Cover with water and cook slowly for 2 hours. Clean vegetables, rinse and add to bones. Add seasoning and cook. Drain off stock and skim off fat. Steam stock to 4 cups.
Add salt and vinegar to stock. Add dissolved gelatine. Clear aspic with egg whites and place in cool spot. Pour when aspic begins to set.

Aspic without Gelatine

*8 cups water * 3 lb. calf's joints and knuckles * 1 small parsley * 1 small piece of celery root * 1 small carrot * 1 small onion * salt * bay leaf * * allspice * 2 tbs. vinegar * 1 tbs. thick tomato preserves * 3 egg whites to clear aspic*

Rinse bones, chop and cover with water. Add salt and cook under cover on medium flame about 4 hours.
When the bones are almost cooked add cleaned vegetables and seasoning. Cook until very tender.
Drain stock through cheese cloth. There should be 4 cups of stock. If necessary steam or add to make up necessary amount. Add vinegar and stir in tomatoes for color. Clear with egg whites and chill. Pour over food when aspic begins to set.

Aspic made from Poultry Legs

*6 cups water * 1 lb. poultry legs * 1 medium onion * 1 small carrot * * 1 small parsley * 1 small piece of celery root * bay leaf * allspice * salt*

Scald legs in several waters. Be careful not to keep them in boiling water too long because doing so makes them difficult to skin. Clean each

portion by removing claws and skin. Remove skin from knee joint toward claws.

Rinse legs, chop and cover with cold water. Add salt to taste and cook slowly.

Clean vegetables and add to poultry legs before they are ready. Add seasoning. Cook until very tender.

Drain liquid and if necessary clear and use as aspic or mix with left-over cooked meat and chill in mold or separate molds.

Meat Aspic with Calf's and Pork Knuckles

*6 cups water * 2 calf's or pork knuckles * 10 oz. veal or lean pork *
* 3 oz. mixed vegetables without cabbage * allspice * pepper * bay leaf *
* salt * 3 cloves garlic*

Clean, chop and scald knuckles and cook slowly with vegetables, salt, seasoning and meat. When meat and knuckles are tender drain off stock. Separate meat carefully from bones and cut into small pieces. Combine meat with stock and ground garlic. Pour into mold large enough to hold aspic (the liquid should cover the meat) and chill.

Skim off fat before serving. Unmold aspic into round plate and cut. Serve with vinegar or lemon or horse-radish in vinegar.

Poultry in Aspic in Molds

*14 oz. poultry meat left-overs baked or cooked * 3 cups chicken stock *
* 1/2 medium onion * 3 egg whites to clear aspic * 2 tbs. gelatine*

Place onion on hot stove to brown. Place onion in chicken stock. If desired add seasoning. Add cooked left-overs to stock and cook for a while. Take out all meat and skim off fat.

Drain off stock, season and mix with gelatine. If necessary clear with egg whites and cool.

Separate meat from skin and cut into pieces.

Cover bottom of small molds or cups with a thin layer of cooling aspic, chill. Arrange garnish (vegetables in season) on chilled aspic. Divide meat into equal portions and place in separate molds. Add a few spoons of aspic and chill so that garnish becomes fixed in the aspic. Pour cooling aspic over meat so that the meat is completely covered and chill. Unmold, arrange on platter and garnish with vegetables in season.

Serve with cold sauces.

Ham or Pâté in Aspic

*10 oz. canned Polish ham or 10 oz. pâté (game or poultry) * 15 tbs. cooling aspic * 2 eggs*

Slice ham (or pâté) into 10 slices of equal thickness. Cut off fat from ham, leaving only edge of 1/3 inch. Arrange pieces, two to a serving, on a rectangular plate.

Cook hard-boiled eggs, cool in cold water and peel. Cut into slices or pieces.

Prepare garnish of vegetables in season in two colors. Cut them into equal rounds or 1/2 rounds. (Carrots and raw leeks should be cut in even slices). Garnish each serving with a piece of egg and vegetable slices, arranging the same design on each serving.

Pour one tablespoon of mushy aspic on each portion and let set. Cover with remainder of aspic and chill.

Serve with tartare sauce or mayonnaise.

Chicken in Aspic

*S t o c k: 8 cups water * 1 lean chicken * 5 oz. mixed vegetables without cabbage * 1 medium onion * salt * bay leaf * allspice * A s p i c: 3 cups stock * 3 egg whites to clear aspic * 2 tbs. gelatine * G a r n i s h: fruit stewed or bottled (plums, cherries, halves of greengage plums, cornel, etc.) or vegetables in season and lettuce*

Cook chicken with vegetables, onion, salt and seasoning. Cool in stock. Remove cold meat and drain off stock. Mix gelatine with 3 cups of stock and clear with egg whites. Drain slowly and chill aspic.

Separate from skin and cut the chicken into parts. Cut off wings and legs. Cut legs at joints and score on inner side along the length of the bone. Holding meat, remove bones carefully so as not to tear meat. Cut legs lengthwise into two parts. Cut 3 to 4 thin fillets from each half of breast. Cover bottom of plate with cooling aspic and chill.

Arrange portions of meat on the aspic: one piece of dark meat and one piece of white meat on top. Garnish each portion with drained fruit from compote or cooked vegetables in season. Pour cooling aspic twice over chicken. Chill each time. The aspic should not be in too thick a layer above the chicken.

Chop the remaining aspic and garnish plate.

Before serving garnish plate with a few small lettuce leaves cut in half lengthwise.

Serve with cold sauces.

Veal Galantine

S t o c k: *8 cups water ∗ 2 calf's knuckles ∗ 5 oz. mixed vegetables without cabbage ∗ salt ∗* M e a t   m i x t u r e: *1 lb. veal ∗ 1 lb. pork ∗ 3 oz. fat back ∗ 3 eggs ∗ salt ∗ pepper ∗ small clove garlic ∗ nutmeg ∗ 7 oz. ham or marinated tongue ∗* A s p i c: *3 cups stock ∗ 3 egg whites to clear aspic ∗ 2 tbs. gelatine ∗* G a r n i s h: *tomatoes or carrots ∗ green peas ∗ lettuce leaves ∗ cucumber*

Clean knuckles, cut lengthwise and place in small amount of boiling water. Bring to a boil once and drain.

Clean vegetables and cover with hot water. Add knuckles and salt to taste and cook.

Prepare meat mixture. Rinse veal and pork and separate from bone. Grind three times together with fat back. Add eggs, salt and seasoning and mix together.

Grease napkin with butter; place meat mixture on napkin and spread. Cut ham or tongue in cubes or strips and arrange along the longer side of meat. Form into a big roll.

Roll the meat in the buttered napkin and tie both ends. Tie roll with string every inch.

Place roll in boiling stock and cook 1 1/2 hours. Bring to a boil on large flame and cook on medium fire.

When meat is done, cool in stock.

Place cooled meat on plate and cover top with a slightly weighted board so that the top part of the roll is flattened.

Mix 3 cups of stock with gelatine, clear and chill. Remove the roll from the napkin on the following day and cut into 1/2 inch slices.

Arrange slices evenly on a plate and garnish with aspic cut into cubes and sliced vegetables in season.

Chicken or Turkey Galantine

S t o c k: *8 cups water ∗ 7 oz. mixed vegetables without cabbage ∗ poultry wings, legs and bones ∗ bay leaf ∗ pepper ∗ allspice ∗ onion ∗ salt ∗* M e a t m i x t u r e: *large chicken or small turkey hen (not too fat) ∗ 2 oz. stale roll ∗ 1/2 cup stock ∗ 4 oz. veal ∗ 3 oz. fat back ∗ 4 oz. pork ∗ 1 small onion ∗ 1 1/2 tbs. fat ∗ 3 oz. smoked boiled tongue ∗ 2 eggs ∗ salt ∗ ∗ nutmeg ∗ pepper ∗* A s p i c: *3 cups chicken stock ∗ 3 egg whites to clear aspic ∗ 2 tbs. gelatine ∗* G a r n i s h: *tomatoes or carrots ∗ 2 hard--boiled eggs ∗ cucumber ∗ green peas ∗ lettuce leaves*

Clean and rinse chicken. Cut off wings at the second joint. Score the meat and remove the bone of the remaining part of the wing. Break off bone at the shoulder joint. Set bone aside.

40

Score the meat on legs and break off bone at the knee joint. Put bone aside. Turn chicken onto breasts and cut skin along the spine, from the bottom to the neck with a small, sharp knife.

Pry the skin and meat, separating the bones first on one half and then on the other half of the back. Cut the meat away from the bone, being careful not to tear the skin.

Pull meat from the shoulder bones and collar bone and in the same manner separate meat from the remaining leg bones.

Prying with fingers, pull away breast meat from the bone and cut off breast bone from the tendons holding it to the skin.

Cut away skin with meat at the anus.

Put aside meat and skin and scrape off remaining meat from bones.

Cut tendons of meat at the wing tips and legs.

Cook the stock with bones, cleaned legs, wing tips, seasoning and vegetables.

Rinse the pork meat and stew with onion in fat.

Soak roll in stock and squeeze out.

Grind three times raw veal together with fat back, roll and stewed pork. Add salt, pepper, nutmeg, 2 eggs to meat mixture and knead well.

Sew up all cuts in chicken or turkey skin. Lay out chicken or turkey meat and salt.

Cut off slices of chicken or turkey meat from thicker parts and arrange them evenly in places where there is no meat (as for instance on the back). Spread stuffing on the meat so that the whole of the meat is spread with an even layer. Arrange tongue, cut into cubes or strips, on the top of stuffing and roll. Sew up skin, roll in a napkin and wind the string around the roll in spirals.

Place the roll in strained and boiling stock and cook slowly for 2 hours. When meat is cooked, skim fat off stock and cool the meat in the stock. Press it down lightly with a weighted board.

On the following day remove the meat and steam off the stock to 3 cups. Add gelatine to the stock, clear and chill.

Cut the galantine into thick slices. Arrange in the order in which they have been sliced on plate. Garnish with slices of hard-boiled eggs and vegetables in season. Pour setting aspic and chill as usual. Garnish plate with aspic cut into cubes.

Serve with tartare sauce.

41

APPETIZERS IN MAYONNAISE

Fish in Mayonnaise

*5 oz. mixed vegetables without cabbage * salt * bay leaf * allspice *
* 1 medium onion * 6 cups water * 2 tbs. vinegar * 2 1/2 lb. fish * 1 1/2
cups mayonnaise*

Clean vegetables, and cook stock adding seasoning. Drain off, add salt
and vinegar and pour stock into long pan for boiling fish.
Clean fish. Place 2 carrots inside fish and arrange fish on rack with
its back turned on the rack and fasten with string.
Place rack with fish into boiling stock and cook on very slow fire. Remove
from fire and cool in stock. Remove fish with rack and let all moisture
drip off. Place fish on a long plate.
Prepare 2 egg yolks mayonnaise according to recipe on page 314.
Season mayonnaise with vinegar and sugar. If desired sauce may be thinned
with stock. Sauce should, however, be thick.
Surround fish with sauce. Dilute part of the sauce with stock and pour
over the fish so that sauce flows smoothly to the plate.
Garnish with sliced, cooked vegetables. Place allspice in eyesockets and
a sprig of parsley in the mouth.
Garnish plate with green peas, tomato slices and lettuce leaves cut in half
lengthwise.

Cups of Fish in Mayonnaise

*2 lb. raw fish or 1 lb. cooked fish left-overs * 1 cup mayonnaise*

Clean fish and cook with vegetables, salt and seasoning or use left-overs
from cooked fish as well as the edible organs out of the fish and the meat
scraped from the head especially of a carp or perch. Cut fish into small
pieces.
Prepare thick mayonnaise (see page 314).
Mix 1/3 of mayonnaise with the fish and season to taste.
Form small oval portions with a spoon and place on plate.
Arrange mayonnaise around each portion. Dilute the remainder of the
mayonnaise and pour over each portion so that part of the mayonnaise
will flow onto the plate.
Garnish the portions of fish and mayonnaise with colorful vegetables in
season.

Fish Vinaigrette

F i s h   m i x t u r e: *3 cups cooked fish meat * 2 cups cooked potatoes ** *4 tbs. mushrooms in vinegar * 2 tbs. gherkins * 1/2 cup green peas ** *3 eggs * S a u c e: 2 egg yolks * 4 tbs. oil * 1 tsp. mustard * salt * sugar*

Remove bones and skin from cooked fish and cut into small pieces.
Cook potatoes and cut into small cubes.
Cut gherkins and mushrooms into small cubes.
Cook peas (if not canned) in small amount of water with salt and sugar. Drain.
Cook hard-boiled eggs, cool, shell. Cut into small cubes.
Prepare sauce. Cream egg yolks, adding oil gradually. Add mustard, salt and sugar to taste at the end.
Mix all ingredients with sauce, season and arrange on salad dish. Garnish with vegetables in season.

Veal in Mayonnaise

S t o c k: *5 oz. mixed vegetables without cabbage * veal bones * 8 cups water * salt * M e a t   r o l l: * 3 lb. veal (round or shoulder) * salt ** *garlic * S a u c e: 1 1/2 cups mayonnaise * G a r n i s h: carrots from stock * radishes or tomatoes * cucumber or pickle * lettuce leaves*

Rinse vegetables and bones, clean, add salt and cook stock in fish pan.
Rinse meat and separate from bones (add bones to stock).
Beat meat into thin slice, salt and rub with garlic.
Roll the meat, place on napkin and roll. Tie with string every inch. Tie both ends of napkin with string.
Place meat into boiling stock and cook slowly for 1 1/2 hours. Leave in stock until cool. Remove from stock and unroll napkin.
Prepare mayonnaise according to recipe on page 314.
Cut cold meat into thick slices and arrange on plate.
Surround meat with mayonnaise and garnish with sliced vegetables and lettuce.

Veal in Mayonnaise with Sardines

*4 lb. veal round * salt * S t o c k: 4 cups water * 7 oz. mixed vegetables without cabbage * 1 large onion * allspice * bay leaf * about 4 tbs. vinegar * salt * S a u c e: 4 egg yolks * 1 cup oil * lemon juice * 1 tbs. sugar * salt * pepper * 8 sardines * G a r n i s h: lettuce leaves * tomatoes or carrots * cucumber or leek*

43

Rinse veal, remove bones with a sharp knife. Beat meat into a rectangular slice of even thickness. Salt.

Roll the meat tightly and tie string around the roll in a spiral.

Place roll in fish pan and cover with boiling water. Add cleaned vegetables, onion, bones that have been chopped fine, salt, seasoning and vinegar to taste. The water should not be too sour. Bring meat to a boil quickly, lower flame and cook slowly on an even fire for 2 hours. The meat must be covered with stock the whole time.

Remove meat from fire when cooked, remove vegetables and bones and let meat stand in stock in cool place over night.

Remove meat, unwind string and cut meat with a sharp knife into 1/2 inch slices.

Arrange slices on long plate in order as cut.

Press three cooked egg yolks through sieve. Place in bowl and add one raw egg yolk.

Press sardines through sieve.

Cream egg yolks in bowl, adding sardine oil and some oil. Creaming egg yolks add lemon juice to taste. Be careful not to add too much juice. When all oil is used for the mayonnaise, add the sardine paste, salt, pepper and sugar to taste.

Complete by pouring the thick sauce over the meat.

Garnish plate with lettuce leaves cut lengthwise and sliced vegetables in season.

Mayonnaise Salad

*3 oz. dried white beans * about 1 cup water * 10 oz. cauliflower or savoy cabbage * 7 oz. celery root * 3 oz. parsley * 5 oz. carrots * 3 medium apples * 1 medium pickle * 1/2 medium onion or chives * 1 cup mayonnaise * salt * sugar * lemon juice*

Rinse beans and soak in cold, boiled water. Cook in the same water.

Clean vegetables, rinse and cook. Cut into strips or cubes.

Rinse apples and cut into cubes.

Peel pickles and slice thin.

Chop onion.

Prepare 1/2 recipe of mayonnaise dressing according to recipe on page 314.

Mix with vegetables, add salt, sugar and lemon juice to taste.

Arrange the salad on a porcelain dish and garnish with vegetables in season.

Let stand in cool place.

Serve as an appetizer, with canapés, hard-boiled eggs, fish or meat appetizers or other cold dishes.

Mayonnaise Salad with Meat

*1 3/4 lb. potatoes * 2 medium apples * 1 medium cucumber or pickle *
* 1/2 lb. cooked or roasted meat or poultry * 1 cup mayonnaise * salt *
* sugar * lemon juice * 2 tbs. mustard*

Select waxy potatoes. Cook, cool and cut into small cubes.
Cut cucumber and apples into cubes or strips.
Cut meat into cubes.
Prepare mayonnaise dressing according to recipe on page 314 (1/2 portion).
Mix all ingredients with dressing, season with salt, sugar and lemon juice
to taste (mustard may be added).
Place salad on rectangular plate, garnish and let stand in cool place.
Salad may be arranged in separate servings on lettuce leaves.
Serve as an appetizer.

Mayonnaise Salad with Fish or Crayfish

*7 oz. cooked vegetables * 1 medium cucumber or pickle * 1 hard-boiled
egg * 7 oz. boiled fish (left-overs, internal edible parts and head meat) *
* 10 crayfish tails (boiled) * 1 lb. cooked potatoes * 1 large apple *
* 3 tbs. cooked green peas * salt * lemon juice * sugar * 3/4 cup mayonnaise * 1 tbs. mustard*

Prepare as meat salad.

Smoked-Fish Salad with Potatoes

*2 lb. potatoes * 10 oz. smoked fish (cod, kipper) * 1 medium onion or
chives * salt * vinegar * sugar * 2 tbs. oil*

Cook potatoes, peel and cut into cubes.
Remove skin from fish, remove bones and cut fish into pieces together
with roe.
Chop onion or chives.
Mix all ingredients. Add oil, salt, vinegar and sugar to taste.
Finish as meat salad.

Smoked-Fish Salad with Vegetables

*5 tbs. cooked white beans * 1 medium onion * 10 oz. smoked fish (cod) *
* 1 medium pickle * 1 1/2 lb. potatoes * sugar * vinegar * salt * pepper *
* 3/4 cup mayonnaise*

Prepare as above.

Herring Salad with Beans

*1/2 cup dried white beans * 1 large apple * 1 medium cucumber or pickle * 1 medium onion * 1 lb. potatoes * 1 1/2 salted herrings * 1 tbs. mustard * 3 tbs. oil * vinegar * sugar * salt*

Rinse herrings, soak, clean and skin.
Rinse beans, soak and cook. Drain.
Cook potatoes, peel and cut into cubes.
Cut apple, cucumber and herrings into cubes.
Cut onion into thin slices.
Combine all ingredients. Season and add mustard or vinegar to taste.
Finish like meat salad.

Herring Salad with Vegetables

*1/4 cup dried white beans * 1 medium cucumber or pickle * 1 1/2 cups cooked vegetables * 1 lb. potatoes * 1 large apple * 1 medium onion * * 1 1/2 salted herrings * salt * vinegar * sugar * 1 cup mayonnaise*

Prepare as above.

Herring Salad in Mold

*2 salted herrings * 1 1/2 lb. potatoes * 2 small pickles * 2 eggs * 3 oz. carrots * 1 1/2 cups mayonnaise * salt * vinegar * sugar * chives*

Rinse herrings and soak for several hours, changing the water. Peel potatoes, cook in salted water, cool and cut into fine cubes.
Cook hard-boiled eggs, cool, peel and chop fairly coarsely.
Grate pickles coarsely.
Clean raw carrots, rinse and grate finely.
Prepare 1 1/2 cups mayonnaise dressing (see page 314). Season well and divide into two equal parts.
Clean herrings and cut into cubes.
Arrange in round mold: 2 layers of potatoes, sprinkling each layer with pickles, eggs, carrots, herring. Press each layer with a spoon and spread with mayonnaise.
Chill salad and unmold.
Even out sides and spread with remaining half of mayonnaise. Sprinkle with fine chopped chives.
Serve on a round plate.

Celery-Root Salad with Mayonnaise and Walnuts

*1 lb. peeled celery root * salt * lemon juice * vinegar * 1 1/2 cups mayonnaise * 1/2 cup chopped walnuts * sugar*

Clean celery root, and cook in salted water with lemon juice on a high flame in enamel pot. Drain celery. Add sugar and vinegar to hot stock to taste. Cut celery into thick round slices and even rounds with cookie cutter. Cover warm celery with stock with addition of vinegar and sugar. Prepare mayonnaise.
Chop walnuts.
Drain celery in sieve and arrange on a glass salad dish in rows. Celery rounds are in semi-flat position. Cover with mayonnaise and sprinkle with walnuts.
Garnish sides of dish with equal cuts of lettuce leaves or savoy cabbage.

Asparagus in Mayonnaise

*2 lb. thick asparagus * 1 cup mayonnaise * salt * sugar*

Boil water with sugar and salt.
Remove outer hard parts of asparagus. Rinse and bind in two bunches. Place in boiling water and cook. Drain and cool.
Prepare thick mayonnaise dressing according to recipe on page 314.
Cut asparagus, leaving only soft, edible parts. Arrange on small plate with cut stems joining and with tips toward the edge of the plate. Cover with thick mayonnaise dressing, leaving tips uncovered to about 1 1/2 inches. Garnish sides of dish with cut lettuce leaves.
The asparagus left-overs may be cut into cubes and used in vegetable salad.

VEGETABLE APPETIZERS

Tomatoes Stuffed with Cucumbers

*10 large firm tomatoes * 5 medium cucumbers * 3/4 cup heavy sour cream * salt * vinegar * pepper * green dill*

Peel cucumbers, shred and salt. After a while pour off excess juice. Mix with sour cream and pepper. Add vinegar to taste.
Rinse tomatoes, cut around at about 1/3 the height and scoop out.
Drain off juice from scooped out tomatoes and fill generously with cucumber mixture just before serving. Cover with cut off tops so that cucumber mixture is seen on the sides. Sprinkle with green dill.

47

Arrange tomatoes on plate in two rows.
Tomatoes may be stuffed with shredded pickles without sour cream.
(The pulp scooped out of the tomatoes and the juice may be used for soups and sauces).

Tomatoes Stuffed with Salads

*10 uniform medium tomatoes * one half of the recipe for meat, fish or herring salad * lettuce leaves * 6 tbs. mayonnaise*

Prepare salad. Stuff tomatoes and finish as in recipe for tomatoes above. Cover with mayonnaise before serving.

Tomatoes Stuffed with Cheese and Chives

*5 uniform medium tomatoes * 3/4 cup cottage cheese * 4 tbs. sour cream * * 2 tbs. chives * salt*

Cut cottage cheese into small cubes. Rinse chives, shake off water and chop fine.
Mix cheese with sour cream and chives, add salt to taste.
Stuff and serve as in recipe for tomatoes stuffed with cucumbers.

Cucumbers Stuffed with Salads

*3 long and large cucumbers * a few tablespoons of meat or fish salad * * salt * 6 tbs. mayonnaise * lettuce leaves*

Prepare salad (see page 45 or page 46).
Rinse cucumbers, peel and scoop out with spoon. Rub with salt on the inside.
Stuff cucumbers with salad, pressing in stuffing with spoon.
Cut cucumbers with a sharp knife into slices of about one inch thick.
Garnish plate with lettuce leaves cut lengthwise and arrange slices flat.
Garnish plate with tomato slices.
Frost cucumbers with thick mayonnaise, pressing it through a tube.

Cucumbers Stuffed with Ham or Veal

*3 long and large cucumbers * 4 oz. ham left-overs or 7 oz. boiled or roasted veal * 4 tbs. cold béchamel sauce * salt * lettuce leaves * tomato * 6 tbs. mayonnaise*

48

Prepare cucumbers as in recipe above.

Grind meat and mix with thick béchamel sauce (see page 316). Stuff cucumbers with mixture.

Finish as cucumbers stuffed with salads.

Cover with mayonnaise before serving.

HOT APPETIZERS

Brains on Toast

*10 slices of long canapé bread * 2 1/2 tbs. butter for bread * 10 oz. brains * 3 tbs. butter * 1/2 small onion * 2 eggs * salt * pepper * 2 tbs. butter for bread crumbs * 2 tbs. bread crumbs.*

Rinse brains and remove membrane. Chop fine.

Chop onion fine and brown lightly in butter. Mix with brains, sauté. Add salt and pepper to taste, add raw eggs and fry stirring constantly.

Cut bread into 1/2 inch slices and butter on both sides. Brown bread crumbs in oven and mix with melted butter.

Place brain mixture on toast and spread out evenly. Place toast on baking sheet with buttered side down. Sprinkle with bread crumbs browned in butter. Place in oven and heat well. Before serving sprinkle with chopped green parsley.

Serve with barszcz or as an appetizer.

Mushrooms on Toast

*10 slices of long canapé bread * 2 1/2 tbs. butter for bread * 1 oz. stale roll * milk for soaking roll* 7 oz. mushrooms * 3 1/2 tbs. butter * salt * * pepper * 1 raw egg yolk*

Peel mushrooms and shred fine.

Add a little water to mushrooms; add butter and stew until tender. Season with salt and pepper. Before removing from fire brown lightly, stirring constantly. Add roll that had been soaked in milk and squeezed out. Add egg yolk. Mix.

Butter toast on both sides.

Place mushroom mixture on toast and spread evenly. Place on baking sheet with buttered side on the bottom and bake.

Serve garnished with green parsley as appetizer or with clear soups served in cups.

Sprats on Toast

*10 slices of long canapé bread * 2 1/2 tbs. butter for bread * 1 oz. stale roll * milk for soaking roll * 7 oz. sprats or 1 kipper * salt * pepper * 2 tbs. butter * 1 tbs. sour cream*

Prepare sprat or kipper stuffing. Cut off heads and tails, skin, clean, leaving bones and press through sieve with roll that had been soaked in milk and squeezed out. Cream butter and add mixture.
Add salt and pepper and enough sour cream so that the mixture will be easy to spread.
Butter toast on both sides.
Cover one side of toast with sprat mixture and place on baking sheet with spread on top. Heat in very hot oven.
Serve immediately with grated cheese, tomato or carrot slices and chopped greens.
Serve as appetizer or with clear soups in cups.

Baked Frankfurters on Toast

*10 slices of long canapé bread * 2 tbs. butter for bread * 5 pairs frank-furters * 4 tbs. flour * 2 1/2 tbs. butter * 2 tbs. tomato preserves * about 1/2 cup sour cream * salt * sugar * 1 raw egg*

Prepare thick tomato sauce. Melt butter, add flour and brown lightly. Combine with tomato preserves and sour cream and season with salt and sugar. When sauce cools mix with egg yolk.
Remove skin from frankfurters and cut in half across.
Butter toast on both sides.
Place fankfurter halves on toast and cover with tomato sauce which is so thick that it does not flow.
Place toast on baking sheet with buttered side down and place in very hot oven. Bake.
Serve immediately as an appetizer.

Raised Rolls with Cabbage

S t u f f i n g : *1 small cabbage * 3 1/2 tbs. butter * 1/2 medium onion * * salt * pepper * 1 tbs. sugar * L e a v e n : 2/3 oz. yeast * 1 tbs. sugar * * 3 tbs. milk * D o u g h : 2 1/4 cups flour * 6 tbs. butter * 2 egg yolks * * 3/4 cup sour cream * salt*

Prepare stuffing. Rinse cabbage, remove leaves and cook. Squeeze out cabbage thoroughly through towel and put through food chopper.

Cut heavy paper into small rectangular pieces of 3 by 4 inches and grease with fat.

Prepare dough. Make leaven and let it rise (see page 336). Cream egg yolks and add flour to yolks. Pour in leaven, add sour cream, salt and knead dough. When all the ingredients are well mixed, add butter gradually, knead well and let rise. Cut onion and brown in butter, add ground cabbage, salt, pepper, sugar to taste and sauté.

Divide dough into small pieces (about 2/3 oz. each) and pull out into rectangular shapes.

Place hot cabbage mixture on each piece, spread and roll tightly. Roll each piece in paper and arrange on sheet with the end of dough and paper downward. Let rise (16 rolls).

Bake raised rolls in hot oven (35 to 40 minutes).

Remove from oven, strip off paper and arrange on plate.

Serve hot as appetizer or with clear soups.

Frankfurters in Raised Dough

*9 pairs of frankfurters * L e a v e n: 2/3 oz. yeast * 1 tbs. sugar * 3 tbs. milk * D o u g h: 2 1/4 cups flour * 6 tbs. butter * 2 egg yolks * 3/4 cup sour cream * salt*

Prepare leaven with yeast and let rise (see page 336). Cut flour into butter, place in bowl and add egg yolks, leaven, salt and enough sour cream to make thick dough to be rolled out on the board. Knead dough well and let rise.

Roll out dough quite thick and divide into equal rectangles the length of a frankfurter.

Rinse frankfurters in warm water and remove skin. Divide in halves and roll in dough. Pinch dough together at both ends.

Divide the paper into pieces the length of the pasties, grease the paper and roll each pasty in paper. Place with part where paper is folded and let it rise.

When the dough rises bake in hot oven. Remove paper and arrange and serve as above.

Crispy Fingers with Potatoes

*10 tbs. lard * 5 oz. cooked potatoes * 1 egg * 2 cups flour * 2 tbs. caraway seeds * salt * baking powder * 1 egg to brush dough*

Cut flour into fat, mix with potatoes. Add caraway seeds, salt and baking powder and mix well.

Add egg and knead dough enough to combine egg. Form fingers the size of the small finger.

Place fingers on greased sheet and brush with egg. Bake.

Serve hot with clear soups or as appetizers with liquor or tea. Do not store.

Raised Fingers with Caraway Seed

L e a v e n : *2/3 oz. yeast * 1 tsp. sugar * 3 tbs. milk * * D o u g h : 2 1/4 cups flour * 6 tbs. butter * 2 egg yolks * 3/4 cup sour cream * 1 egg to brush dough * 1 tbs. caraway seeds * salt*

Prepare leaven and let rise.

Cut flour into butter on board and place into bowl.

Beat in egg yolks, add leaven, sour cream and salt.

Knead dough and let rise.

Divide dough into three parts. Place each part separately on well floured board and form long thin sticks, the size of a small finger.

Cut fingers (4 inches long) and place on greased sheet. Brush with beaten egg and sprinkle with salt and caraway seeds.

Let rise. Then bake in hot oven until a golden brown (20 minutes).

Arrange in a pyramid on a glass plate.

Serve with clear soups or liquor.

Kulebiak

Cabbage and Mushroom Pasty

S t u f f i n g : *2 lb. cabbage * 2 medium dried mushrooms * 1 medium onion * 3 1/2 tbs. fat * 1 tbs. sugar * salt * pepper * 3 eggs * * L e a v e n : 2/3 oz. yeast * 1 tbs. sugar * 3 tbs. milk * * D o u g h : 2 1/4 cups flour * * 6 tbs. butter * 2 egg yolks * 3/4 cup sour cream * salt * 1 egg to brush dough*

Rinse and cook mushrooms and cut into small cubes.

Prepare stuffing. Shred cabbage, add cubed mushrooms and onion, fat and a little mushroom stock and cook until tender on small flame. Steam off liquid at end.

Cook hard-boiled eggs, cool and remove shells. Chop coarsely and mix with cabbage. Add sugar, salt and pepper to taste.

Prepare dough. Make leaven. Let it rise.

Cut in flour with butter and place in bowl. Add egg yolks, the raised leaven, salt, sour cream and knead into dough firm enough to be rolled out. Let rise. When dough is double its size, place on board and roll out into a rectangular piece. Spread the cooled and dry cabbage mixture along one edge of dough and roll.

Grease a long baking pan, place dough in pan and let rise again.

When dough has risen, brush with egg, and pierce deep. Bake (3/4 of an hour).

Serve hot immediately on removal from the oven.

Raised Pasties with Meat

S t u f f i n g : *1 lb. pork meat * stale roll * milk for soaking * 2 1/2 tbs. fat * 1/2 medium onion * salt * pepper * (egg white)* L e a v e n : 1/3 oz. yeast * 1 tbs. sugar * 3 tbs. milk * D o u g h : 2 1/4 cups flour * 3 egg yolks * 3 tbs. butter * 1/2 cup milk * salt * lard for frying*

Prepare ground, cooked-meat mixture as for potato dumplings with meat (see page 306).

Prepare yeast dough. Make leaven and let rise.

Pour leaven into flour. Add egg yolks, salt. Combine with melted butter and milk and knead dough so that it is firm enough to roll out. Let rise. When dough is double its size, divide into 10 parts. Form each piece with fingers into a pancake. Place 1/10 of the stuffing into each pancake, fold and shape into an oval pasty.

Place the pasties on a floured board and let rise again (as for doughnuts).

When dough is double its size, dust off flour and place on heated fat (2 inches deep) with the raised side to the bottom. Cover and cook slowly until a golden yellow. Turn over and brown without cover on other side. Serve hot.

Pâté in Short Pastry

P â t é: *1 hare forepart and giblets * 1 lb. pork meat * bay leaf * 4 oz. raw fat back * 3 oz. stale roll * 2 eggs * pepper * nutmeg * ginger * salt * 1 small onion * 2 1/2 tbs. fat * D o u g h : 2 1/4 cups flour * 1/2 cup butter * 3 egg yolks * 3/4 cup sour cream * salt*

Rinse hare forepart, giblets, meat and fat back.

Melt fat in pot and place meat in pot. Cook on all sides over a large flame. Add chopped onion, bay leaf and baste with water. Cook under cover until tender.

Cut roll, add to meat and cook for a while.

Separate tender meat from bone and cut fat back. Grind all ingredients through fine sieve. Mix with eggs.

Prepare dough. Cut in butter with flour and make an indentation in center. Add pinch of salt, egg yolks and sour cream and knead dough until all ingredients are well mixed. Cover dough in bowl and let cool in a cold place.

Roll out dough and line bottom and sides of pâté mold. Prepare a piece of rolled-cut dough to cover top.

Fill in mold with pâté mixture and cover with rolled-out dough. Seal sides as for pie.

Brush top with beaten egg and garnish with strips of dough. Pierce pâté to the bottom at many points. Bake in hot oven until golden brown. Place napkin on plate and remove pâté from mold. Cut into one-inch slices and serve hot.

The pâté filling may be prepared with game meat or pork or poultry.

Pasties with Brains

D o u g h: *1 1/2 cups flour * 11 tbs. butter * 1/2 egg * 1 egg yolk * about 5 tbs. sour cream * salt ** S t u f f i n g: *10 oz. brains * 3 tbs. butter * 1/2 small onion * salt * pepper * 1 egg*

Prepare dough. Cut in flour with butter.

Add one egg yolk and one half of an egg. Add sour cream, salt and mix with knife. When all the ingredients are mixed, place dough on plate sprinkled with flour. Place dough in cool place. Let stand overnight.

Prepare stuffing. Rinse brains and remove membrane. Cut into cubes.

Brown onion in butter lightly and mix with brains, salt and pepper. Heat well and mix with egg.

Roll out dough 1/3 inch thick, forming it into a round.

Cut rounds 2 1/2 inches in diameter. Cut out center of every second round with a smaller cutter.

Brush rounds without holes with egg white and cover with rings. Press. Place on baking sheet quite far apart and bake in very hot oven.

When dough rings are browned and dry on top, remove from oven.

Fill with hot stuffing and heat in oven.

Serve hot as appetizer or with clear soups.

Meat Pasties

D o u g h: *1 1/2 cups flour * 11 tbs. butter * 1/2 egg * 1 egg yolk * about 5 tbs. sour cream * salt * S t u f f i n g: 10 oz. cooked meat * 2 oz. stale roll * 1/2 small onion * 2 1/2 tbs. fat * salt * pepper * (broth)*

Prepare stuffing. Soak roll and squeeze out. Brown onion lightly. Grind meat together with roll and onion and mash. If the stuffing is too dry add broth. Add salt and pepper and mix thoroughly.
Prepare dough and bake as in recipe for pasties with brains.

Cabbage and Mushroom Pasties

D o u g h: *1 1/2 cups flour * 11 tbs. butter * 1/2 egg * 1 egg yolk * about 5 tbs. sour cream * salt * S t u f f i n g: 1/2 large cabbage * 2 dried mushrooms * 3 tbs. fat * 1 small onion * salt * pepper*

Prepare dough the night before as in recipe for pasties with brains. Cover and let stand in cool place overnight.
Prepare stuffing. Wash mushrooms and cook in small amount of water. Cut into fine cubes.
Cut cabbage, chop onion and cover with mushroom stock. Add fat and cook. Let stock steam off.
Add mushrooms, salt and pepper to taste. Steam off cabbage so that there is no juice left.
Reserve a small piece of dough for decoration and then divide the remaining dough in half and roll into two rectangles 1/4 inch thick.
Divide the stuffing in half. Place one half of the stuffing, arranging it along the longer side of the rectangle and roll it up tightly in the dough. Paste the dough on the lower side.
Roll the second rectangle of dough with the second half of the stuffing. Place both rolls on baking sheet at some distance from each other and brush tops with egg white. Garnish with strips of dough and mark portions (6). Place rolls in very hot oven and bake. Cut into diagonal slices and serve while hot. (Or bake beforehand and before serving heat in very hot oven and cut).
Serve on a heated plate as appetizer or with clear soups.

Vol-au-Vent with Game Meat

D o u g h: *1 1/2 cups flour * 11 tbs. butter * 1 egg yolk * 1/2 egg * about 5 tbs. sour cream * salt * S t u f f i n g: roasted hare legs and left-overs from haunch * sauce from roasted hare * about 1 cup sour cream * 2 tbs. flour * salt * seasoning*

Prepare dough. Cut flour into butter. Add one egg yolk and one half of an egg. Add salt and knead dough with sour cream.

Place dough in bowl, cover and let stand in cool place overnight. The following day roll the dough to 1/4 inch and line the bottom of a cake pan with it.

Make two rings from the remainder of the dough with a diameter the size of the bottom of the pan. Brush with egg yolk, bake separately.

When baked, place the rings one on top of the other on the baked bottom. Prepare stuffing. Use the roasted hare legs or left-overs from roasted hare.

Separate the meat from the bones and heat together with sauce. Garnish with sour cream, salt and flour. Bring to the boil and season. Place the prepared hot meat on the hot crust. Fasten the crust rings and cut from the center toward the ridge.

Serve immediately on heated plate.

Prepared in the same manner: vol-au-vent with veal paprika or chicken paprika or with chicken in thick stew sauce garnished with egg yolks.

Vol-au-Vent with Mushrooms (Boletus Edulis)

D o u g h: *1 1/2 cups flour * 11 tbs. butter * 1 egg yolk * 1/2 egg * about 5 tbs. sour cream * salt * S t u f f i n g: 1 lb. fresh Boletus Edulis * 1/2 small onion * 2 1/2 tbs. butter * 1 tbs. flour * 1/2 cup sour cream * salt * pepper * green parsley * 1 egg yolk*

Clean mushrooms, rinse and shred fine. Add butter, onion and sprinkle with water. Cook and steam off liquid.

When mushrooms are tender garnish with sour cream and flour. Bring to the boil (the mixture must be thick). Add salt, pepper, green parsley and mix with raw egg yolk.

Prepare dough, bake and finish as for vol-au-vent with game meat.

Vol-au-Vent with Cauliflowers or Asparagus

D o u g h: *1 1/2 cups flour * 11 tbs. butter * 1 egg yolk * 1/2 egg * about 5 tbs. sour cream * salt * S t u f f i n g: 1 large cauliflower or 1 lb. asparagus * 1 tsp. sugar * salted water * 3 1/2 tbs. butter * 1/2 cup flour * 3/4 to 1 cup sour cream * salt * 2 egg yolks*

Prepare dough as for vol-au-vent with game meat.

Rinse cauliflower, clean, leaving the leaves that are wedged in. Cook in salted water (with 1 tsp. sugar) until tender, drain and separate into flowerets. Cut away core and branches. Prepare a white gravy with butter, flour and sour cream and bring to the boil. Add the cut cauliflower. Add salt and mix with egg yolks. If necessary mixture may be thinned with cauliflower stock. The stuffing should be thick.

Finish and serve as above.

Vol-au-vent with asparagus is prepared in the same manner.

Vegetable Bouquet on Crust

D o u g h: *1 1/2 cups flour * 11 tbs. butter * 1 egg yolk * 1/2 egg * about 5 tbs. sour cream * salt * S t u f f i n g: 1 medium cauliflower * 7 oz. carrots * * 5 oz. green peas * 9 oz. beans * 6 oz. kohlrabi * 5 1/2 tbs. butter * 1 tomato * green dill * 2 tbs. bread crumbs*

Prepare dough as for vol-au-vent with game meat.

Prepare young vegetables. Cook cauliflower and drain.

Prepare young kohlrabi as in recipe on page 125.

Prepare carrots and green peas as in recipe on page 149.

Cook beans and drain.

When all vegetables are about prepared, place dough into oven and bake one piece for bottom and one ring.

Arrange hot vegetables on hot crust according to variety along the radius of the crust. Sprinkle cauliflower and beans with butter mixed with browned bread crumbs. Sprinkle kohlrabi with dill. Garnish dish with tomato slices.

Serve hot.

Sausage Rounds in Dough

*10 thick slices of sausage (not fat) with garlic * 1 cup flour * 2 tbs. oil * * 1 egg yolk * 1 egg white * salt * 1/2 cup water * 5 1/2 tbs. fat for frying*

Prepare dough. Add water to flour. Add one egg yolk, salt and mix thoroughly. Add oil and beaten egg white. The dough must be so thick that it will not flow off the sausage.

Remove skin from the sausage rounds (cut thick and round). Take each round of sausage on fork and dip in dough and place in hot fat. Fry on both sides until golden brown like pancakes.

Serve on rectangular plate covered with a napkin and garnished with lettuce leaves and lemon or tomato quarters.

Frankfurters in dough may be prepared in the same way and served as appetizer or with barszcz.

Ham in Dough

See meat dishes page 237.

Ham Stuffed with Rice and Raisins

*8 slices of canned Polish ham * 1 tsp. mustard * 1/2 cup cooked rice *
* 1/2 cup chopped celery root * 1/2 cup chopped raisins * 1/4 tsp.
paprika * 1 egg * salt * milk*

Spread the mustard on the slices of ham. Mix rice with celery root, raisins,
paprika and egg. Salt. Place stuffing on ham slices, roll them up and
skewer securely. Place on greased sauté pan, brush the top of rolls with
milk, cook in a fairly hot oven (375°F) for a short time. Serve with
Cumberland sauce.

Brains à la Polonaise

*1 1/2 lb. calf's, beef or pork brains * 2 eggs * 3 tbs. butter * 1 medium
onion * salt * pepper * 2 tbs. bread crumbs * 2 1/2 tbs. butter for bread
crumbs * green parsley*

Rinse brains and remove membrane. Chop into large cubes.
Brown onion lightly with butter. Add brains and cook, stirring constantly.
Add salt and pepper to taste.
When brains no longer smell, add raw eggs and mix. Cook with brains
until eggs are firm. Sprinkle with butter mixed with browned bread
crumbs. Sprinkle with green parsley. Serve with fried eggs as appetizer
or use as stuffing for pasties, pancakes, etc.

Calf's Brains on Shells

*1 lb. brains * water * vinegar * salt * allspice * pepper * 1/2 bay leaf *
* B é c h a m e l   s a u c e: 3 1/2 tbs. butter * 1/2 cup flour * 1 1/2 cups
milk * salt * lemon juice * 2 egg yolks * G a r n i s h: 2 tbs. bread
crumbs * 2 1/2 tbs. butter * 2 egg whites * green parsley * tomato *
* 5 slices of lemon * lettuce leaves * 1 oz. Parmesan*

Boil water and add vinegar, salt and seasoning to taste.
Rinse brains, remove membrane, place in colander, dip in boiling water
and cook until brains turn white. Drain.
Prepare sauce. Melt butter, add flour and sauté. Set aside.
Add milk and cook stirring constantly. Add salt and lemon juice to taste.

Mix with egg yolks.

Remove from fire.

Brown bread crumbs in butter. Grate cheese.

Beat egg whites.

Cut brains in large cubes and mix with sauce.

Place in shells, sprinkle with cheese and browned bread crumbs. Garnish with egg whites on one side.

Arrange on sheet and place in very hot oven. Bake until golden brown.

Prepare tomatoes (lemon) and green parsley.

Garnish each shell with tomato slices (1/2 slice of lemon) and chopped green parsley.

Serve on rectangular plate covered with a napkin.

Asparagus or Cauliflower on Shells

*2 lb. asparagus or cauliflower * salt * sugar * B é c h a m e l   s a u c e:
5 1/2 tbs. butter * 1/2 cup flour * 1 cup sour cream * salt * 2 egg yolks *
* G a r n i s h: 2 tbs. bread crumbs * 2 1/2 tbs. butter*

Rinse asparagus and peel. Cook in boiling water with salt and sugar.

Drain and cut edible parts of asparagus into 3/4 inch pieces.

Prepare sauce. Melt butter, add flour and sauté. Remove from fire.

Add sour cream and bring to the boil, stirring constantly.

Add salt and mix with egg yolks and asparagus.

Place in shells and sprinkle with bread crumbs browned in butter. Bake in very hot oven until golden brown.

Serve shells on rectangular plate covered with a napkin.

Eggs Baked in Molds

*8 eggs * S a u c e: 4 1/2 tbs. butter * 1/2 cup flour * 1 cup sour cream
or milk * salt * 2 egg yolks * G a r n i s h: 3 tbs. Parmesan * 2 tbs. bread
crumbs * 2 1/2 tbs. butter * green parsley * tomato or radishes*

Cover eggs with cold water and cook hard-boiled eggs. Cool in cold water.

Prepare sauce. Melt butter and add flour. Remove from fire. Mix with sour cream and cook, stirring constantly. Add salt and raw egg yolks. Grate cheese.

Brown crumbs in butter.

Peel cooled eggs. Separate yolks and chop egg whites into thick pieces. Mix egg whites with béchamel sauce and add salt. Place in small molds greased with butter.

Press egg yolks through sieve over the shells.

Sprinkle with cheese and pour butter with crumbs over the molds. Place in oven and bake until golden brown.

Garnish with green parsley, tomato or radish slices.

Serve on rectangular plate covered with a napkin.

Eggs in Sour Cream

*10 eggs * 1 tbs. flour * 1 1/2 cups sour cream * salt * greens*

Mix heavy cream with flour. Add salt to taste and heat stirring constantly.

The cream must be rich and of a good quality so that it does not curdle.

Break eggs on hot cream, one near another and low over the surface. Heat on a medium flame.

Do not stir. Cook eggs in cream until firm. The egg yolks should be seen above the surface of the cream and should not be firm.

Before serving sprinkle with chopped green parsley.

Bigos

Hunters' Dish

*4 cups sauerkraut * 1/2 medium cabbage * 1 lb. pork meat without bone * 7 oz. sausage * 2 oz. smoked bacon * 1 medium onion * 3 tbs. fat * 2 tbs. flour * 2 cloves garlic * salt * pepper * bay leaf * allspice * 3 dried mushrooms * 5 tbs. thick tomato preserves*

Cut sauerkraut several times. Cover with water and parboil in uncovered pot.

Rince cabbage and shred. Cover with small amount of water, add mushrooms, garlic and cook in uncovered pot.

Rinse pork, cut into cubes, salt and sauté in fat until brown. Add to sauerkraut and add seasoning. Cook slowly.

Cut bacon into cubes, melt the cubes without browning. Add to sauerkraut.

Remove skin from sausage and cut into large cubes.

When sauerkraut and meat is cooked, add sausage and cooked cabbage. Cook sliced onion in fat, add flour and prepare roux. Garnish bigos with the roux and season to taste. Cook on slow fire. There should be very little sauce in the bigos.

Boiled Frankfurters

*5 pairs of frankfurters * water * mustard * horse-radish in vinegar*

Boil water.

Rinse frankfurters in warm water and place in pot with tight lid (it is best to use fire-resistant glass ware).

Cover frankfurters with boiling water, cover and keep on slow fire for 10 minutes. Do not boil.

Place pot on flat plate and serve frankfurters in water in which they were heated. Serve with mustard and horse-radish in vinegar.

Frankfurters in Tomato Sauce

*5 pairs of frankfurters * tomato sauce*

Prepare tomato sauce (see page 318).

Rinse frankfurters in warm water and place in simmering sauce a few minutes before serving. Heat and serve in fire resistant dish. Do not keep frankfurters in sauce for a long time.

Tripe à la Warsaw

*2 lb. beef tripe * 1 cup mixed vegetables without cabbage * 1/2 lb. beef bones (joints) * 1/2 lb. marrow bones with marrow * 3 1/2 tbs. butter * 3 tbs. flour * 3 3/4 cups strong beef broth * spices * ginger * * nutmeg * pepper * marjoram * salt * 3 tbs. Parmesan cheese * 2 tbs. bread crumbs * 2 tbs. butter for bread crumbs * green parsley*

Clean tripe thoroughly, scraping with knife. (Be particularly careful with the honeycomb type). Wash with hands and rinse several times in warm water. Bring water to the boil and place tripe in it. Parboil tripe, drain off and rinse again in warm water. Drain and squeeze out with hands.

Boil 2 quarts of water. Place in tripe and cook slowly until almost tender (about 4 hours).

Divide vegetables into 2 parts. Place bones and one half of vegetables in separate pot. Prepare rich broth. Pour this broth into tripe, when water has boiled out and when tripe is almost ready. Cook until tripe is tender. Rinse second part of vegetables and clean. Shred and cover with a small amount of rich broth and cook until soft. Remove from fire.

Drain off tender tripe and cut into thin strips (1 1/2 inches long). Steam off stock from tripe if necessary. There should be 3 to 4 cups left. Remove marrow from bones, chop fine and add to tripe.

Prepare roux. Melt butter, add flour and brown until golden brown, stirring constantly. Add tripe stock and bring to the boil, stirring constantly.

Add cooked vegetables to the tripe and marrow. Add roux and all seasoning to taste. Mix everything and bring to the boil. If necessary add tripe stock. There should be enough sauce to be visible. Place on low flame and cook a little.

Grate cheese.

Brown crumbs with butter.

Chop green parsley fine.

Place tripe into round fire-resistant plate, sprinkle with cheese, pour butter and crumbs on top and place in oven to bake for 15 minutes.

Before serving sprinkle with green parsley.

Serve with suet balls (see page 104) with marrow or suet or with potatoes garnished with browned butter.

SOUPS AND ADDITIONS TO SOUPS

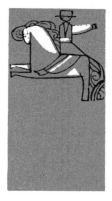

SOUPS

The custom of serving soups is very popular in Poland. Polish soups consist of many nutritious and satisfying products, thickened with fat under various guises, and most commonly with sour cream. They may be varied, since they are prepared of all kinds of products. Soups are composed of: soup stock and the main ingredient from which the soup takes its name and garnish. Soup stock is made of vegetables cooked in water with bones, meat or dried mushrooms, or fruit, depending on the type of soup prepared. Since the stock in which the potatoes, beans, peas and other vegetables have been cooked, constitutes the base of the soup, no ingredients that pass from the products to the stock are wasted. The main ingredient of vegetable soups are vegetables. Generally they are simmered separately with an addition of water and fat, and then combined with the soup after the products in the stock have been cooked and drained. Properly balanced and prepared soups may contain, in addition to the caloric value, a good supplement of protein by combining a small amount of animal protein to a large amount of vegetable and flour protein.

The final step is thickening soups. Soups may be garnished with roux, cream or sour cream, milk, egg yolks or potato starch and water. There is a small amount of flour in each garnish which should be brought to the boil in the soup. Then the flour swells and dissolves and thickens the soup. The dissolved flour serves to combine the ingredients of the soup with the stock. In addition to the flour each garnish contains fat: bacon, lard, margarine, butter, etc.

When all the ingredients have been combined, the soup should be garnished with flour, seasoned with salt, sugar, sour ingredient and aromatic herbs. A properly seasoned soup stimulates appetite and satisfies. Some products are added to soups uncooked, just before serving it in plates. These are mostly aromatic ingredients like dill or green parsley, more rarely chives, lemon slices, raw egg yolk or whipped sour cream. They enhance the taste, aroma and nutritious value and the appearance of the soup.

Aside from the garnished soups, thick with vegetables and nutritious, there are also the clear, condensed ungarnished soups, such as broth, Julienne soup, tomato, beet barszcz or cucumber on broth, etc. But these soups have their special use. They are served hot in cups, in small amounts for luncheon to stimulate appetite. They are served usually with a more substantial side dish like: hot pasties made of pancake batter, yeast, French or flaky crust. The filling is made of meat, brains or vegetables (cabbage). Toast spread with stuffing may also be served. Almost every vegetable soup or fruit soup is served with products containing carbohydrates that are cooked separately. These are principally noodles, fluffy cereal, potatoes, white toast.

All the soup recipes in this book are intended for five portions, that is to say 5—6 cups of prepared soup.

Potato-Starch Thickening for Fruit Soups

*5 cups stock and fruit pressed through a sieve * 2 tbs. potato starch*

Prepare fruit stock, press fruit through sieve and bring to the boil.
Combine potato starch in a small amount of water, add to hot fruit stock and bring to the boil, stirring constantly.

Cream Garnish for Soups

Sweet or sour cream, when added to soups, should not be brought to the boil. It should be heated when added to the soup. If, however, in order to thicken the soup, we add flou. to the cream then the thickening should be brought to the boil in the soup. Sour cream may be used as a garnish for almost all soups (except for those made of sauerkraut). This is the most popular soup garnish in Poland.

*5 cups soup * 1/2 to 1 cup sour cream * 3 tbs. flour*

Bring prepared soup to the boil.
Mix flour and cream together with rotary beater until smooth.
Add a few tablespoons of simmering soup and stir.
Pour cream mixture to the soup and bring to the boil.
Flour may also be added directly to the soup; then mix the flour with water, add to the soup and bring to the boil; serve cream directly in each plate and the thickened soup poured over it at the table.

Varieties and Uses of Roux

1. White Roux

*3 tbs. fat * 4 tbs. flour * 1 cup cold milk or water * hot soup stock*
Melt fat, combine flour and heat until the flour loses its raw smell. Remove from fire and dilute with milk or water, mix until smooth. Bring to the boil, adding hot stock and stirring constantly. The roux is not browned at all.
This roux is rarely used in thickening soups. It is most commonly used to garnish vegetables (spinach, kale) or with béchamel sauce.

2. Light Yellow Roux

*3 tbs. fat * 4 tbs. flour * 1 cup cold water * hot soup stock*
Melt fat, add flour and stirring constantly sauté to a light yellow. Remove from fire, dilute with cold water. Bring to the boil, adding hot stock and stirring constantly.
This roux is most often used to thicken soups (vegetable, potato, tomato, celery, etc.), vegetables and sauces. Before adding liquid, the flour and fat should be browned lightly to the color of browned bread.

3. Dark Brown Roux

*3 tbs. fat * 4 tbs. flour * 1 cup cold water * hot soup stock*
Melt fat, add flour and stirring sauté to a dark golden color. Remove from fire and dilute with cold water. Bring to the boil, adding hot stock and stirring constantly.

Dark golden roux is used rarely as a garnish.

It is used to thicken a few soups, most often potato soup with dried mushrooms and sauerkraut soup "Kapuśniak".

4. Roux with Onion

*3 tbs. fat * 1 small onion * 4 tbs. flour * 1 cup cold water * hot soup stock*

Mince onion and sauté in fat. Add flour and stirring constantly brown to a golden color. Remove from fire and dilute with cold water. Bring to the boil, adding hot stock and stirring constantly.

Onion roux is widely used in thickening soups as well as sauces and vegetables.

It is used to thicken all soups made with cabbage, mushrooms, various types of potato soups as well as pea and bean soups and others.

Soup Stocks

8 oz. mixed vegetables for soup stock = 3 oz. carrots * 2 oz. savoy cabbage * 1 oz. parsley * 1 oz. celery root (celeriac) * 1 oz. leek

1. Vegetable Stock as a Basis for the Soup

*8 cups water * 8 oz. mixed vegetables * 1 tbs. salt*

Clean vegetables with a brush under running water, scrape, rinse quickly, cover with boiling water, salt and cook 20 or 30 minutes.

When vegetables are soft, drain the stock and garnish.

The vegetables may be added to the soup or discarded.

2. Mushroom Stock as a Basis for the Soup

*8 cups water * 1 oz. dried mushrooms * 8 oz. mixed vegetables without cabbage * 1 small onion * allspice * pepper * 1 tbs. salt*

Wash mushrooms in lukewarm water, rinse, cover with cold water, add cleaned vegetables, onion and seasoning and cook in covered pot on a medium flame.

When the mushrooms are soft, drain liquid and garnish. The mushrooms may be added to the prepared soup or to macaroni or pasties.

3. Bone Stock as a Basis for the Soup

*8 cups water * 1/2 lb. to 1 lb. soft soup bones (joints) * 8 oz. mixed vegetables * 1 tbs. salt*

Rinse beef or veal soup bones, chop in fine pieces and cover with water, boil (1 hour).

Clean vegetables with a brush under running water, scrape, rinse, cut larger vegetables and add to parboiled bones; salt and boil.

When the meat on the soup bones is soft, drain liquid and garnish soup. Cut the meat into pieces and add to soup. If there is more meat it may be used as filling for pasties, pies, etc. The cooked vegetables may be used in a salad.

4. Fruit Stock as a Basis for the Soup

*5 cups water * 1 1/2 lb. fruit * 2 cloves * cinnamon * lemon peel*

Rinse fruit carefully under running water, cut large fruit into several pieces without removing skin.

Cover with boiling water, add seasoning, cook on large flame in covered pot.

When fruit is soft, drain and press fruit through sieve.

The stock with fruit pressed through sieve may be garnished with flour and sour cream or potato starch.

CLEAR SOUPS

Broth and Boiled Beef

*8 cups water * 1/2 lb. soup bones (joints) * 2 lb. beef (rump) * 1 dried mushroom * pepper * bay leaf * allspice * 8 oz. mixed vegetables * * 1 medium onion * salt * green parsley*

Chop bones into fine pieces, cover with water and parboil.

When the bones are parboiled, rinse the meat and place in stock together with seasoning. Cook slowly.

Cut onion in half and brown by placing it (flat surface downward) on hot stove or flame.

Before meat is tender, add cleaned vegetables, onion, salt. Cook until meat is tender and drain.

When tender, the meat should be cut across the fiber and placed on platter, garnished with cut vegetables and sprinkled with broth.

The meat should be served with potatoes, dill pickles, fresh cucumber salad, beet salad. sauces like: horse-radish, dill, tomato, mushroom, onion, mustard. Broth should be served with farina, rice, macaroni, łazanki (see page 100), cereal cubes, dropped noodles, marrow balls, soup puffs, meat pasties. Before serving sprinkle broth with chopped green parsley.

Chicken Broth and Boiled Chicken

*8 cups water * 1 chicken * allspice * pepper * 8 oz. mixed vegetables * * 1 medium onion * salt * green parsley*

Cover whole chicken with boiling water, add seasoning and cook over slow fire.

When chicken is parboiled, add cleaned vegetables, browned onion, salt and cook until tender.

When tender, remove chicken and carve, place parts on serving dish, garnish with cut vegetables taken from vegetable stock.

The chicken may be served with green peas, tomato sauté or stewed tomatoes, boiled vegetables, bilberry or apple compote. The broth may be served with French dumplings, soup puffs, rice, macaroni or pasties. Before serving sprinkle broth with chopped green parsley.

Rosolnik

*8 cups water * 1/2 lb. beef (plate, shank) * 10 oz. mixed vegetables * * 1/2 of a small cauliflower * 3 oz. string beans * 5 oz. veal or beef kidney * 1 1/2 tbs. fat * 3 dill pickles * salt * allspice * bay leaf * green parsley*

Rinse meat and bones, cover with water, add salt, allspice and bay leaf, cook over slow fire.

Clean vegetables, cut in thin strips. Take one half for soup stock and the other half for stewing in a separate pot. Cut the beans into small pieces and remove strings, cut the cauliflower into flowerets, add to stewed vegetables.

Pare the dill pickles, cut into thin rounds and cook.

Cut the kidney into thin rounds and simmer in fat until tender. Add soup stock from time to time.

When the meat is tender pour off the broth and add to broth portions of vegetables, kidneys and dill pickles. Add salt to taste and chopped green parsley.

Clear Tomato Soup

Easter Soup

*7 cups water * 1 lb. beef (plate, shank, brisket) * 1 small onion * 8 oz. mixed vegetables * 6 medium tomatoes (or 6 tbs. tomato paste) * 1 1/2 tbs. butter * salt*

Rinse meat and bones, cover with water and cook on slow fire. Cut onion in half, brown on hot ring.
Clean vegetables.
When meat is parboiled, add onion and vegetables; cook until meat is tender, skim fat off soup if necessary, add salt to taste.
Wash tomatoes, cut into segments, cook with butter in small amount of water, press through sieve.
Drain stock and add to tomato purée.
Serve with poached eggs, soup puffs, diablotins, French dumplings, etc. The meat may be used to make stuffing for pasties, dumplings and rolled pancakes.

Clear Tomato Soup on Ham Broth

See above for ingredients. Instead of beef and vegetable stock use broth of smoked ham.

Clear Dill-Pickle Soup

Prepare as tomato soup substituting dill-pickle juice for tomatoes.

Clear Mushroom Soup

Prepare stock as for tomato soup. Instead of tomatoes prepare stock made of 5 medium mushrooms, 1/2 small onion and pepper.
Serve with poached eggs.

Clear Beet Barszcz on Broth

*7 cups water * 5 medium beets * 1 lb. beef (plate, shank, brisket) * 8 oz. mixed vegetables * 1 dried mushroom * allspice * pepper * bay leaf * * 1 medium onion * 1 cup sour beet juice (see page 471) * salt * sugar * * 1 to 2 cloves of garlic*

Wash beets under running water, remove skin, cut finely, cover with boiling water, cook until tender, drain. Set liquid apart.

Rinse meat and bones, cover with water; before meat is tender add vegetables, browned onion, seasoning; cook soup stock until ready, drain. Add meat stock to beet liquid; add sour beet juice, salt and sugar to taste. Add minced garlic, bring to a boil.

Skim fat off soup.

Serve in soup plates or cups.

If soup is served on plates, accompany with uszka (see page 101) containing various stuffings, soup puffs, navy beans, potatoes cooked separately.

If soup is served in cups, accompany with rolled pancakes, flaky or French pasties filled with meat, brains, cabbage or mushrooms or with diablotins.

Clear Beet Barszcz on Ham Broth

Easter Soup

Follow recipe given above. Substitute broth of smoked ham for beef and vegetable stock.

Clear Beet Barszcz on Fish Stock

Christmas Eve Soup

Follow recipe for clear beet barszcz. Use stock made with fish heads and fish left-overs. Prepare as above.

Royal Broth

*8 cups water * 1 lb. beef (round) * 1/4 chicken * 8 oz. mixed vegetables * * 1 medium onion * allspice * bay leaf * salt*

Rinse meat and bones, rinse chicken, cover with boiling water, add salt and cook on medium flame.

Before broth is cooked add vegetables, browned onion, seasoning; cook until ready, drain.

Skim fat off soup before serving.

Serve with soup puffs, pasties, crispy fingers, diablotins, tomato cream.

THICK SOUPS WITHOUT GARNISH

Introduction to Gruels and Barley Soups

Detailed recipes for preparing a variety of cereal dishes, which are very popular in Poland, are given below.

Attention must be drawn, however, to several points which may make the preparation of gruels and barley soups more difficult.

Cereals have a property of increasing their bulk when cooked in liquid. This swelling is dependent on many factors, like the variety of grain and the properties of starch contained in the grain, the degree of the dryness of the grain, the time of cooking, etc. For this reason the amount of water necessary to cook cereal in gruels and barley soups is not given in exact but in approximate proportions.

Cereal for barley soups is always cooked separately on a very low flame, for then the cereal distends properly, does not boil over or burn. If despite the amount of water given in the recipe the cereal begins to thicken, then add boiling vegetable and bone stock intended for the soup. Do not add water. This prevents the preparation of too much soup, which would have less body and lose flavor. The recipe should yield not more than 1 1/2 quarts of soup to serve 5 persons in a two or three course dinner. If liquid is not added at the proper moment to the thickening cereal it will not be cooked properly. It is difficult to mix a thick cereal with the stock. Moreover, the cereal may cling to the sides and bottom of the pan, and may also scorch, making the dish uneatable.

Farina Gruel

*3 oz. farina * 4 to 6 parts of water to one part of cereal * 2 tbs. butter * * salt*

Bring water to the boil.

Mix cereal with small amount of cold water.

Combine mixture with boiling water; cook stirring constantly until soft and gruelly (about 10 minutes). Add salt to taste and pour into tureen. Add fresh butter.

Oatmeal Gruel

*12 tbs. oatmeal * 4 to 6 parts of water to one part of cereal * 2 tbs. butter * 4 cups milk * salt*

73

Mix oatmeal with cold water.

Cook until thickened (about 25 minutes) on small flame. Salt. (Mixture may be pressed through sieve).

Pour into tureen and stir in warm milk, or serve on plates undiluted with milk. Add fresh butter.

Rice Gruel

*1 cup rice * 4 to 6 cups water * 2 egg yolks, raw * 2 tbs. butter * salt*

Rinse rice, drain. Add drained rice to cold water, cook on small flame until it thickens (about 30 minutes).

Add salt. (Cooked rice may be pressed through sieve.)

Pour into tureen and stir in egg yolks and unmelted butter.

Barley Gruel

Prepare as rice gruel. Use pearl barley.

Krupnik

Barley Soup

*6 cups water * 8 oz. mixed vegetables without cabbage * 1/2 lb. soup bones * 2 dried mushrooms * 1/2 cup pearl barley * 3 to 4 parts of water to one part of cereal * 3 tbs. butter * 3 potatoes * salt * green parsley * green dill*

Clean vegetables, bones and mushrooms, prepare stock.

Wash cereal, mix with water, add part of the butter and cook until it thickens.

Drain stock, cut vegetables and mushrooms.

Cook cubed potatoes in the stock.

Add stock to cereal, vegetables and mushrooms, add salt and bring to the boil.

Pour into tureen, add remaining, unmelted butter and finely chopped green parsley and dill.

May be served with sour cream or raw egg yolks, stirred in.

Rumford Soup

*8 cups water * 8 oz. mixed vegetables * 1/2 cup dried peas * 1 medium potato * 1/2 cup rice (or pearl barley) * 2 parts of water to one part of rice * salt * 1 tbs. fat * 1 1/2 tbs. unmelted butter * green parsley*

Pick over peas.

Soak peas for several hours in cold boiled water.

Cook peas in the water in which they have been soaked.

Measure rice, rinse and drain.

Boil two parts of water to one part of rice, add salt, fat and rice. Cook. When water is absorbed, place in hot oven and bake until dry. Remove from oven and place in tureen.

Clean vegetables, grate and cook stock in covered pot on very high flame. When vegetables are cooked, cook peeled and cut potatoes separately in vegetable stock.

Press peas and potatoes throughout sieve, mix all ingredients and add salt to taste. Add chopped green parsley and unmelted butter to soup tureen and stir.

Masury Cabbage Soup

*8 cups water * 1/2 lb. smoked meat bones (spare ribs) * 2 1/2 cups sauerkraut * caraway seeds * 1 small onion * 2 tbs. fat * 3 medium potatoes * salt * pepper*

Rinse meat bones, cover with water, cook stock.

Cut sauerkraut, add caraway seeds, cook in uncovered pot on high flame until tender.

Chop onion and brown lightly in fat.

Peel potatoes, cut.

Drain stock, cook potatoes in stock, then press throughout sieve, add sauerkraut, browned onion, meat scraped off bones, salt, pepper and pour into tureen. Serve with bread or yellow peas.

Zarzucajka

*6 cups water * 1 large onion * 3 medium potatoes * bay leaf * allspice * * 1 cup sauerkraut * 3 tbs. cut smoked bacon fat * salt * pepper*

Peel onion and chop finely.

Peel potatoes, cut into parts.

Bring 6 cups water to a boil, add potatoes, onion, bay leaf and allspice. Cook. When potatoes are cooked, add finely cut sauerkraut together with juice, bring to the boil once, add salt and pepper to taste.

Cut bacon fat into small pieces, melt and brown. Add to soup before serving.

Serve with whole rye bread.

Zalewajka

3 cups water ∗ 1 large onion ∗ 4 medium potatoes ∗ about 2 cups sour rye or oat juice (see page 472) ∗ 3 1/2 tbs. cut smoked bacon fat ∗ salt ∗ ∗ pepper

Chop onion fine and cook in water.
Add pared and cut potatoes and cook until tender.
Add sour juice to taste, bring soup to the boil, add salt and pepper; before serving add browned bacon fat. Serve with bread.

Polish Żur

Sour Rye or Oat Soup

6 cups water ∗ 1/2 lb. soup bones ∗ 7 oz. mixed vegetables ∗ 1 dried mushroom ∗ 2 cups sour juice (see page 472) ∗ salt ∗ bay leaf ∗ allspice ∗ ∗ 1 cup sour cream or 3 1/2 tbs. cut smoked bacon fat

Clean vegetables, mushroom and soup bones, add bay leaf and allspice, prepare stock, drain stock, bring to the boil.
Pour juice into boiling stock, bring to the boil and add salt.
Place sour cream in tureen, add soup stirring constantly. Or cut and melt bacon fat, add to soup and pour into tureen. Serve with potatoes.

Polish Żur with Sausage

3 cups water drained from cooked potatoes ∗ 1/2 lb. sausage ∗ 2 cups sour juice (see page 472) ∗ salt ∗ 2 cloves garlic ∗ 2 tbs. cut bacon fat

Water drained from cooked potatoes should be brought to the boil. Add sausage cut in slices. Add sour juice, bring to the boil, add salt to taste and grated garlic. Before serving add browned bacon fat.
Serve with potatoes or bread.

Bean Soup with Zacierki

8 cups water ∗ 3/4 cup dried white beans ∗ 8 oz. mixed vegetables without cabbage ∗ 3 tbs. cut bacon fat ∗ 1/2 small onion ∗ pepper ∗ ∗ salt ∗ green parsley

Soak beans in cold boiled water for several hours; cook in the water in which they have been soaked.
Wash vegetables, scrape and prepare stock.
Prepare zacierki (see page 100).

When vegetables are cooked, drain stock and cook noodles in stock; cut vegetables. Melt bacon fat.

Brown onion in fat.

Mix all ingredients, add salt and pepper to taste and chopped green parsley.

Czarnina

Black Soup

*Fresh blood (from 2 ducks, or 1 goose or 1 pig) * 1 tbs. 6⁰/₀ vinegar * 7 cups water * fowl giblets * 1 lb. soup bones * 2 dried mushrooms * 8 oz. mixed vegetables * 2 oz. honey cake * 1 oz. fat back * 1 cup dried prunes or 1 cup dried cherries * sugar * salt * vinegar*

To blood drained from freshly-killed animal add 1 tbs. vinegar and stir thoroughly; place in cold place under cover.

Cook stock with duck or goose giblets (gizzard, liver, heart, wings and legs which have been cleaned), soup bones and mushrooms.

Before meat is tender add cleaned vegetables and a piece of fat back, cook until tender, drain stock.

Soak a piece of honey cake in the stock, crush with spoon until smooth as paste, add to soup.

Cook prunes in small amount of water, remove pits and cut prunes; add with prune water to soup.

Cut giblets into thin strips and add to soup.

Add blood mixed with vinegar to soup, stirring constantly. Bring to the boil.

Add sugar and salt as well as vinegar to taste. Serve immediately.

Serve with łazanki prepared separately.

SOUPS GARNISHED WITH SOUR CREAM, ROUX OR EGG YOLK

Creamed Barszcz

*7 cups water * 4 medium beets * 1/2 lb. soup bones * 8 oz. mixed vegetables * salt * allspice * pepper * bay leaf * 1 medium onion * 1/2 to 1 cup sour cream * 3 tbs. flour * 1 cup sour beet juice (see page 471) * * sugar * 1 clove garlic * 3 eggs*

Clean vegetables and soup bones, wash beets, take off skin, cut into pieces, add salt, seasoning and onion, cook together and drain.

Thicken stock with sour cream and flour, bring to the boil, add sour beet juice, sugar and garlic to taste. If necessary add salt. Cook hard--boiled eggs, remove shells, cut each egg into four parts and place in soup tureen.

If the color of the barszcz is not strong enough a small beet should be added: take small beet, remove skin, grate, place in colander, place in soup so that the colander is on surface of soup. Press beet with spoon. Serve barszcz with potatoes or small beans.

Ukrainian Barszcz

*8 cups water * 8 oz. mixed vegetables * 5 oz. beets * 3/4 cup dried white beans or 1 1/2 cups string-beans * 3 medium potatoes * 1 cup tomato purée or 5 medium tomatoes * 1/2 to 1 cup sour cream * 3 tbs. flour * * salt * sugar * 2 tbs. chopped green dill * chives*

Soak beans in boiled and cooled water for a few hours, cook in the same water.

Grate vegetables and beets, cover with boiling water, prepare stock (if using string-beans, cook with vegetables).

When vegetables are tender, add potatoes cut in cubes and cook together. Rinse tomatoes, cook in separate pot, press through sieve.

To soup stock with vegetables and potatoes add beans with water in which they have been cooked, add the tomato purée, bring to the boil, add sour cream and flour; add salt and sugar to taste, bring to the boil. Before serving add chopped greens.

Serve with buckwheat groats or potatoes.

Vegetarian Beet Barszcz

*6 cups water * 1 lb. beets * 1 tbs. 6⁰/₀ vinegar * 10 oz. mixed vege-tables * allspice * bay leaf * 2 cups sour beet juice or dill-pickle juice * * 1 cup sour cream * 3 tbs. flour * salt * sugar * 2 cloves garlic * * green dill*

Wash beets, remove skin, grate coarsely, cover with 3 cups of hot water, add one tablespoon of vinegar, bring to the boil on small flame and set apart.

Clean vegetables, grate coarsely. Season and cook on large flame, drain. Drain water from beets and set apart.

Add beet water to vegetable stock, bring to the boil, thicken with sour cream and flour, add sour beet juice to taste and bring to the boil once;

add salt, sugar and garlic to taste. Before serving, add dill chopped fine.

Serve with potatoes or white small beans cooked separately.

Wołyń Barszcz

*8 cups water * 6 oz. beets * 1/2 lb. lean pork meat * 8 oz. mixed vegetables * 10 oz. cabbage * caraway seeds * 3 medium tomatoes * salt * * 1 1/2 tbs. sugar * 1/2 cup sour cream * green dill * 1 clove garlic*

Choose medium beets; wash, cook in skin, remove skin and cut into strips.

Clean vegetables and cook with meat. Cut meat into small pieces.

Wash cabbage and cut into large cubes, add caraway seeds and cook in uncovered pot.

Wash tomatoes, cover with small amount of meat stock, stew tomatoes and press through sieve.

Add meat mixture to cabbage, as well as the tomato purée, and beets; mix thoroughly, bring to the boil, season with salt and sugar.

Before serving add sour cream, grated garlic and chopped dill.

Cold Barszcz with Beet Greens

*8 cups water * 1 lb. veal and veal bones * salt * 5 oz. mixed vegetables * * (6 crayfish) * 2 cloves garlic * 1 small onion * bay leaf * 1/2 lb. young beets with greens * 1 tbs. chopped green dill * 1 small dill pickle or 1 fresh cucumber * 3 eggs * 1 cup sour cream * 3 tbs. flour * 1 cup sour beet juice or dill-pickle juice * sugar*

Wash bones, clean off meat, add salt, prepare stock; before stock is ready add meat, vegetables, garlic, onion, bay leaf. Cook.

(Wash crayfish with a brush under running water, cook in soup stock. Remove meat from crayfish tails and place in tureen).

Wash young beets with greens, cut in wide strips, cook in water with small amount of sour juice, place in tureen with liquid.

Wash eggs, boil until hard, remove shells, cut lengthwise into four parts, place in tureen.

Rinse dill, chop fine and place in tureen.

Remove skin from dill pickle or cucumber and cut in thin rounds; place in tureen. Drain stock from bones and vegetables, skim fat, add flour and sour cream, bring to the boil.

Pour soup into tureen, add sour beet or dill-pickle juice; add sugar and if necessary salt to taste. Cool.

Instead of crayfish, veal cooked in soup stock cut in fine pieces may be served.

Cold Żur with Beet Greens (Chard Greens)

*2 cups water * 8 oz. beet greens * 4 cups sour rye or oat juice * 1 1/2 cups sour cream * salt * 1 1/2 tbs. sugar * 2 to 3 eggs * 2 tbs. chopped chives * * 2 tbs. chopped green dill*

Cool hard-boiled eggs in water, remove shells and cut in cubes.
Wash beet greens, chop leaves and stalks, cover with small amount of water, cook quickly; add sour juice, bring to the boil, add sour cream and season with salt and sugar to taste.
Before serving mix with eggs and fine chopped chives and dill. Heat. In summer the soup may be served chilled.
Serve with potatoes.
If there are no young beet greens use soft and tender leaves of full grown beets. Cook young beets in skin separately, peel, cut in strips or grate on side with large round perforations. Mix with cooked leaves, add sour juice and finish soup as above.

Lamb Soup

*8 cups water * 1/2 lb. to 1 lb. lamb scraps and bones * 3 oz. mixed vegetables * salt * 1 small onion * 5 medium potatoes * 3 tbs. fat * 3 tbs. flour * 1 clove garlic * pepper * green parsley * green dill*

Rinse meat and bones, prepare stock; when meat is parboiled add cleaned vegetables, salt and browned onion, cook until tender.
Peel potatoes and cut into cubes.
Drain stock and cook potatoes in it.
Melt fat, add grated garlic and flour, brown until yellow and set apart.
Add some cold stock to flour mixture to form thin soup; add to remainder of stock, bring to the boil.
Cut the meat and vegetables cooked in the stock and add to the soup; add pepper, green parsley and dill.

Veal-Tripe Soup

*8 cups water * 2 lb. veal tripe * 8 oz. mixed vegetables without cabbage * * salt * 3 tbs. fat (butter) * 4 tbs. flour * marjoram * pepper*

Wash tripe carefully in several waters and squeeze out water with hands. Clean vegetables, cover with boiling water, add salt, parboil; add tripe and cook.

When tripe and vegetables are tender, cut into fine pieces, thicken soup with roux, bring to the boil, season to taste with salt, marjoram and pepper. Serve with suet balls (see page 104) or with sliced bread.

Bean Soup

*8 cups water (or stock made with smoked meat) * 1 1/2 cups dried white beans * 1/2 lb. soup bones * 8 oz. mixed vegetables without cabbage * * 3 tbs. cut fat back or smoked bacon fat * 1/2 small onion * 3 tbs. flour * salt * marjoram*

Pick over beans. Wash and soak in boiled water that has been cooled; cook beans in the same water until tender.

Clean vegetables and bones, rinse and prepare stock.

Press cooked beans through sieve, add to stock.

Cut fat back or smoked bacon fat, melt.

Cut onion into slices and brown in fat (until yellow).

Add flour to onion and fat, brown and set apart.

Dilute flour garnish with cold stock; bring to the boil stirring constantly, add to soup; add salt to soup and bring to the boil. Sprinkle with marjoram.

The soup may be served with white toast, bread or macaroni.

Pea Soup

*8 cups water (or stock made with smoked meat) * 1 1/2 cups dried peas * * 1/2 lb. pork soup bones or knee or knuckle * 8 oz. mixed vegetables without cabbage * 3 tbs. cut fat back or smoked bacon fat * 3 tbs. flour * salt * marjoram * garlic*

Prepare like bean soup.

Mushroom Soup with Cream

*8 cups water * 1 oz. dried mushrooms * 8 oz. mixed vegetables without cabbage * 6 pepper-corns * 1 medium onion * 1/2 to 1 cup sour cream * * 3 tbs. flour * salt*

Wash mushrooms thoroughly in warm water, rubbing with fingers.
Prepare stock with mushrooms, vegetables and pepper.

When mushrooms are tender, drain, cut into thin strips and place in tureen.

Mix flour with sour cream.

Pour into boiling stock, bring to a boil; add salt to taste.

Serve with large pearl barley, macaroni, dropped noodles, rolled pancakes cut into strips, toast.

Mushroom Soup with Roux

*8 cups water * 1 oz. dried mushrooms * 8 oz. mixed vegetables without cabbage * 6 pepper-corns * 1 medium onion * 3 tbs. fat * 3 tbs. flour * * salt * pepper*

Wash mushrooms thoroughly in warm water, rubbing with fingers. Cover with cold water and cook stock with vegetables, onion and pepper.

Melt fat, mix with flour, brown until yellow, set aside. Mix with cold water into thin paste.

When mushrooms are tender, drain off stock. Cut mushrooms into thin strips and place in tureen; mix soup stock with flour garnish, bring to the boil; add salt and pour soup into tureen, mixing well.

Serve with pearl barley, macaroni, dropped noodles or rolled pancakes cut into strips.

Farina Soup

*6 cups water * 3 bouillon cubes * 3 tbs. butter * 5 tbs. farina * 3 tbs. flour * salt * green parsley * chives*

Dissolve bouillon cubes in boiling water.

Brown farina lightly in butter, add flour, brown again.

Set aside; mix thoroughly with cold water, making thin paste; add to bouillon, bring to a boil, salt.

Add chopped green parsley and chives.

Serve with white toast.

Vegetable Soup (Julienne)

*8 cups water * 1 lb. veal or beef with bones * 4 oz. mixed vegetables * * 4 oz. spring carrots * spring kohlrabi * 3 tbs. green peas * 5 oz. string beans * 1 small cauliflower or 7 oz. savoy cabbage * 3 tbs. butter * 4 tbs. flour * salt * green parsley * green dill*

Clean mixed vegetables and meat, prepare stock, drain off.

Clean spring vegetables, washing carefully, cut carrots in halves, cut kohl-rabi into thick strips, remove green peas from pods, divide cauliflower into flowerets, remove string from beans and cut into diagonal pieces.

Cook vegetables in small amount of soup stock on high flame.

Melt butter, mix with flour, brown until yellow, set apart.

Dilute flour mixture with cold water into thin paste, add to soup stock, add cooked spring vegetables, bring to the boil, season with salt.

Chop green parsley and dill and place in tureen.

Serve with toast, dropped noodles, soup puffs or French dumplings.

Vegetable Soup with Roux

*8 cups water * 1 lb. soup bones * 8 oz. mixed vegetables * 5 oz. savoy cabbage * 4 oz. spring carrots * 1 small cauliflower * 3 tbs. green peas or 7 oz. string beans * 2 medium potatoes * 3 tbs. butter * 4 tbs. flour * salt * * green parsley * green dill*

Clean mixed vegetables and bones, prepare soup stock.

When mixed vegetables are tender, drain off stock, cut cooked vegetables and place in tureen.

Clean spring vegetables, cut spring carrots and savoy cabbage into strips, wash cauliflower and separate flowerets, cut string beans; cover all vegetables with small amount of boiling stock and cook.

Rinse potatoes, peel and cut in small cubes; cook in soup stock.

Melt butter, mix with flour, brown lightly, set apart.

Dilute flour garnish with cold water until the consistency of thin paste; mix with soup stock and cooked vegetables, bring to the boil; add salt.

Pour into tureen, add green parsley and dill.

Serve with toast.

Vegetable Soup with Cream

*8 cups water * 1/2 lb. soup bones * 5 oz. mixed vegetables * 7 oz. savoy cabbage * 4 oz. carrots * 1 small cauliflower * 3 tbs. green peas * 3 tbs. pea beans or 7 oz. string beans * 2 medium potatoes * 1 cup sour cream * * flour * salt * green parsley * green dill*

Clean bones and mixed vegetables, prepare stock, drain off.

Rinse, clean and shred vegetables, cook in small amount of water on high flame in covered pot. Cook pea beans separately.

Peel potatoes, cut in cubes, cook in soup stock. Mix with vegetables.

Mix flour with cream and add to soup; bring to the boil, add salt to taste and mix with chopped green parsley and dill.
Serve with toast, dropped noodles, rice.

Vegetable Soup Purée

*8 cups water * 1/2 lb. soup bones * 10 oz. mixed vegetables * 2 tbs. flour *
* salt * 1 cup sweet cream * 1 to 2 egg yolks * green dill*

Clean bones and mixed vegetables and prepare stock. Drain off.
Press vegetables through sieve, add to stock, bring to the boil.
Mix flour in cold stock, add to soup, bring to the boil; add salt.
Pour cream into tureen, mix well with raw egg yolks and soup. Add chopped dill.
Serve with toast or soup puffs.

Cauliflower Soup

*8 cups water * 1 lb. soup bones * 8 oz. mixed vegetables * 1 medium
cauliflower * 3 tbs. butter * 3 tbs. flour * 1 cup sour cream * salt*

Clean bones and mixed vegetables, prepare stock.
Rinse cauliflower, remove leaves, separate into flowerets, cut the core into strips.
When vegetables are tender, drain off stock and cook cauliflower in it.
Melt butter, mix with flour, brown lightly and set apart.
Add cold water to flour garnish and mix until it becomes the consistency of thin paste, add to the stock. Add sour cream, season with salt, bring to the boil and pour into tureen.
Garnish with farina or dropped noodles. May also be served with toast or soup puffs.

Cauliflower Soup with Sweet Cream and Egg Yolks

*8 cups water * 1 lb. soup bones * 8 oz. mixed vegetables * 1 medium
cauliflower * 3 tbs. flour * salt * 1 cup sweet cream * 1 to 2 egg yolks*

Clean bones and mixed vegetables, prepare stock, drain off, bring stock to the boil.
Rinse cauliflower and separate into small flowerets, cut core into thin strips; place cauliflower in boiling stock liquid and cook until tender.

84

Mix flour with some cold stock, add to soup and bring to the boil; add salt.

Place sweet cream in tureen, add raw egg yolks and mix thoroughly; add soup and mix.

Serve with soup puffs or toast.

Kohlrabi Soup with Sweet Cream and Egg Yolks

*8 cups water * 1 lb. soup bones * 8 oz. mixed vegetables * 10 oz. kohlrabi * * 3 tbs. flour * 1 cup sweet cream * 1 to 2 egg yolks * salt*

Clean mixed vegetables and soup bones, prepare stock.

Rinse kohlrabi, peel, cut into segments, cook on hot flame in water in an uncovered pot; press kohlrabi through sieve and place into drained off stock.

Mix flour in some cold stock, add to soup and stirring constantly bring to the boil. Add salt.

Place sweet cream into tureen, mix with raw egg yolks and soup.

Serve with toast or soup puffs.

Kapuśniak

Sauerkraut Soup

*8 cups water * 1/2 lb. pork soup bones * 2 dried mushrooms * 8 oz. mixed vegetables * 2 1/2 cups sauerkraut * 1 medium onion * caraway seeds * 3 tbs. fat (fat back or smoked bacon) * 1/2 small onion * 4 tbs. flour * * salt * pepper*

Clean mixed vegetables and soup bones, wash mushrooms rubbing with fingers, prepare stock, drain off.

Cut sauerkraut, if too sour, drain off juice; add chopped onion, caraway seeds and a small amount of water; cook until tender on high flame in uncovered pot.

Cut up mushrooms previously cooked in stock.

Cut small onion and brown lightly in fat.

Add flour to browned onion, brown and set apart.

Dilute flour garnish with some cold stock, bring to the boil stirring constantly, add to soup stock, add mushrooms and cabbage; season with salt and pepper and bring to the boil. Pour into tureen (add uncooked sauerkraut juice to taste).

Serve with bread, potatoes, peas.

Cabbage Soup

*8 cups water * 1/2 lb. soup bones * 8 oz. mixed vegetables * 10 oz. cabbage * 1 medium onion * caraway seeds * 1/2 to 1 cup sour cream * 3 tbs. flour * salt*

Clean mixed vegetables and soup bones, and prepare stock. Drain off stock and bring to the boil.

Cook shredded cabbage with onion and caraway seeds in a small amount of water, in an uncovered pot.

Mix flour with sour cream, add to stock and bring to the boil.

Add cabbage and season with salt.

Serve with whole potatoes or bread.

Soup from Kaszuby

*8 cups water * 1/2 lb. soup bones * 8 oz. mixed vegetables * 1 medium onion * caraway seeds * 10 oz. cabbage * 3 tbs. tomato preserves * 1/2 to 1 cup sour cream * 3 tbs. flour * salt*

Rinse vegetables and soup bones, prepare stock and drain off.

Cook shredded cabbage with onion and caraway seeds in a small amount of water, in an uncovered pot. Place in stock, add tomatoes and bring to the boil.

Mix flour with sour cream, add to soup and salt to taste.

Serve with potatoes.

Savoy-Cabbage Soup

*8 cups water * 1/2 lb. soup bones * 8 oz. mixed vegetables * 10 oz. savoy cabbage * 2 medium potatoes * 2 1/2 tbs. butter * 3 tbs. flour * 1 cup sour cream * salt * pepper * garlic*

Rinse vegetables and soup bones, clean, prepare stock.

Shred cabbage and cook in a small amount of water, in uncovered pot on high flame.

Rinse potatoes, peel and cut into small cubes.

Drain off soup stock and place potatoes in it. Cook.

Melt fat and brown with flour, dilute with cold soup stock; add to soup and bring to the boil. Add cabbage, season with salt, garlic and pepper to taste.

Serve with bread.

Caraway-Seed Soup

*8 cups water * 1/2 lb. soup bones * 5 1/2 tbs. fat * 2 tbs. caraway seeds *
* 7 tbs. flour * salt*

Rinse bones, clean and prepare stock. Drain off.
Brown caraway seeds in butter. When they begin to pop, add flour and brown until yellow.
Dilute with cooled stock into thin paste, bring to the boil, drain and add remaining stock and salt to taste.
Serve with bread or toast.

Dill Soup

*8 cups water * 1/2 lb. soup bones (veal) * 8 oz. mixed vegetables * 1/2 to 1 cup sour cream * 4 tbs. flour * salt * 5 tbs. chopped green dill * (1—2 egg yolks)*

Rinse vegetables and soup bones, clean, prepare stock and drain it off.
Mix flour with sour cream, add to stock, bring to the boil and add salt.
Rinse dill, chop and place in tureen. Raw egg yolks may be added as garnish.
Serve with potatoes, dropped noodles, French dumplings.

Macaroni Soup

*8 cups water * 1/2 lb. veal soup bones * 8 oz. mixed vegetables * 1 1/2 cup cooked macaroni or spaghetti * 1 cup sour cream * 3 tbs. flour *
* 4 tbs. yellow cheese * green parsley * salt*

Rinse vegetables and soup bones, clean, prepare stock and drain it off.
Prepare macaroni, cut in thin stripes and cook in stock, or cook spaghetti.
Mix flour with sour cream, add to soup and bring to the boil.
Grate cheese, add to boiling soup, add salt to taste and chopped parsley.

Cucumber Soup

*8 cups water * 1 lb. beef and beef bones * 8 oz. mixed vegetables * 2 1/2 cups shredded young cucumbers * 3 tbs. flour * salt * 3 tbs. butter * 2 egg yolks * 1 cup sweet cream*

Rinse vegetables, meat and bones, clean, cover with boiling water, cook until tender and drain off stock.

Rinse cucumbers, peel, shred; add a small amount of water, cook until tender, press through a sieve and mix with stock.

Garnish soup with flour and water mixture, bring to the boil and season with salt.

Before serving, cream butter with egg yolks, add a little hot soup, mix well and pour into soup; add sweet cream and serve immediately.

Serve with toast.

Dill-Pickle Soup

*7 cups water * 1/2 lb. soup bones * 8 oz. mixed vegetables * 1 cup shredded dill pickles (see page 473) * 1/2 to 1 cup sour cream * 4 tbs. flour * * 1 cup dill-pickle juice * salt*

Rinse vegetables and soup bone, clean, prepare stock and drain off. Shred dill pickles into fine strips.

Garnish soup with flour and cream, bring to the boil; add uncooked dill pickles and pickle juice, salt to taste. Heat.

The shredded pickles may also be added when cooked.

Serve with potatoes, dropped noodles or cooked farina cooled and cut into cubes.

Tomato Soup with Sour Cream

*8 cups water * 1/2 lb. soup bones * 8 oz. mixed vegetables * 5 medium tomatoes * 1 1/2 tbs. butter * 1 medium onion * 1/2 to 1 cup sour cream * * 3 tbs. flour * salt * sugar*

Rinse vegetables and soup bones, clean, prepare stock and drain off.

Rinse tomatoes, cut into segments, add a few spoons of boiling water, onion and butter and cook on high flame in covered pot. Press tomatoes through sieve, add to stock and bring to the boil.

Mix flour with cream and garnish soup; bring to the boil stirring constantly; season with salt and sugar to taste. Pour soup into tureen. Serve with fluffy rice, macaroni, dropped noodles, potatoes. The tomatoes may also be pressed through sieve when raw and added to the soup. The soup must then be heated.

Tomato Soup with Roux

*8 cups water * 1/2 lb. soup bones * 8 oz. mixed vegetables * 5 medium tomatoes * 1 1/2 tbs. butter * 1 medium onion * 3 tbs. fat (butter) * 3 tbs. flour * salt * sugar*

Rinse vegetables and bones, clean and prepare stock. Drain off stock.
Rinse tomatoes, cut into segments and cook with butter and onion over a large flame. Press through sieve.
Melt butter, mix with flour, brown lightly and set apart.
Mix roux with cold water into thin paste, add to stock and tomatoes, bring to the boil; add salt and sugar to taste.
Serve with soup puffs, rice, macaroni, dropped noodles, potatoes.

Giblet Soup

*8 cups water * 8 oz. mixed vegetables * chicken giblets, (gizzard, liver, heart, wings, legs) * 1/2 cup fine pearl barley or rice * 1 1/2 tbs. butter * * 3 parts of water to 1 part of cereal * salt * 1 cup sour cream * 2 egg yolks * green parsley*

Rinse vegetables, clean and prepare stock with giblets.
Rinse cereal, cover with 3 parts of water and cook until thick with butter, adding stock. Cut vegetables and meat taken from stock.
Drain off stock, add to cereal; add meat and vegetables cooked in stock and season with salt.
Pour cream into tureen, mix with soup, stir in egg yolks and add green parsley.

Leek Soup

*8 cups water * 8 oz. leeks * 1/2 lb. soup bones * 8 oz. mixed vegetables * * 3 medium potatoes * 2 1/2 tbs. butter * 3 tbs. flour * 1/2 to 1 cup sour cream * salt * pepper*

Rinse leeks, remove wilted leaves, cut off roots and cut into small pieces; cover with small amount of boiling water and cook until tender in uncovered pot.
Rinse soup bones and vegetables, clean and prepare stock; drain off.
Peel potatoes, cut into small cubes and add to stock. Cook until tender.
Add cooked leeks with stock to soup.
Melt butter and brown with flour. Mix roux with cream and stock and add to soup. Bring to the boil and add salt and pepper to taste.

Polish Crayfish Soup

*8 cups water * 1/2 lb. veal and veal bones * 8 oz. mixed vegetables * 30 medium crayfishes * dill * salt * 5 tbs. butter * 1 cup sour cream * 2 tbs. flour * salt*

Rinse vegetables, clean and prepare stock with meat.

Brush crayfishes under running water and place in boiling water to which dill and salt have been added; cover and cook 10 minutes on medium flame.

Remove meat from trunk and claws, place in tureen. Set apart meat from tails.

Grind the red shells or dry and pound into powder, adding butter.

Cover powdered shells with a small amount of stock and cook on low flame. Skim off butter and place in cup with cold water. Place the powdered shells in stock and bring slowly to the boil. Drain off through fine sieve. Mix flour with cream and garnish stock that has been drained.

Bring soup to the boil and add salt.

Remove congealed butter off water in cup and add to soup. Mix soup with crayfish meat in tureen.

Serve with fluffy rice and crayfish tail meat.

Fish Soup with Sour Cream

*8 cups water * 8 oz. mixed vegetables * 2 fish heads and edible internal parts, fish bones or 1 lb. fish * bay leaf * allspice * 1/2 to 1 cup sour cream * 2 tbs. flour * salt * pepper * (green parsley)*

Prepare stock with vegetables, fish internal parts, fish heads (carp is recommended), bay leaf and allspice. Drain off stock.

Separate edible parts from head and together with internal parts press through sieve and add to stock.

Bring soup to the boil, garnish with flour and cream and season with salt and pepper.

Serve with łazanki, toast or soup puffs.

Rice Soup

*8 cups water * 1/2 lb. soup bones * 8 oz. mixed vegetables * 1/2 cup rice * * 3 tbs. butter * 3 tbs. flour * salt * 2 egg yolks*

Rinse vegetables and soup bones, clean and prepare stock.

Cook rice separately in stock.

Melt butter and mix with flour; brown lightly, set apart. Add enough water to make thin paste and bring to the boil stirring constantly.

When vegetables are tender, drain off stock.

Cut vegetables and place in tureen.

Add roux to stock and other ingredients and bring to the boil. Add salt.
Cream yolks in tureen and add soup.
Serve with toast.

Celery-Root Soup with Cream and Egg Yolks

*8 cups water * 1/2 lb. soup bones * 8 oz. mixed vegetables * 2 medium onions * 8 oz. celery root * salt * 1 cup sweet or sour cream * 1 to 2 egg yolks*

Prepare stock with vegetables and bones, drain off.
Rinse celery root thoroughly, clean, grate and cook in a small amount of water on a high flame; press through sieve washing down with soup stock.
Add celery root to stock, season with salt to taste and mix with cream and egg yolks just before serving.
Serve with toast, soup puffs, French dumplings.

Celery-Root Soup with Roux

*8 cups water * 1/2 lb. soup bones * 8 oz. mixed vegetables * 10 oz. celery root * 3 tbs. butter * 3 tbs. flour * salt*

Rinse vegetables and soup bones, clean and prepare stock. Drain off stock.
Rinse thoroughly celery root, clean grate and cook in a small amount of water on a high flame. Press root through sieve washing down with stock.
Melt butter and mix with flour, brown lightly.
Dilute mixture with cold water to make thin paste. Add to stock; add celery purée, salt to taste and bring to a boil.
Serve with toast, French dumplings, soup puffs.

Asparagus Soup with Sour Cream

*8 cups water * 1/2 lb. veal bones * 8 oz. mixed vegetables * 1 lb. asparagus * 1 cup sour cream * 3 tbs. flour * salt * pinch of sugar * 1 to 2 egg yolks*

Rinse vegetables and bones, clean and prepare stock. Drain off stock.
Rinse asparagus, scrape, cut off tips, cut remaining stalks into small parts; cook in stock and press through sieve.
Cook asparagus tips in drained stock.
Mix flour with sour cream and garnish soup. Bring to the boil stirring constantly. Add salt and sugar to taste.
Cream egg yolks in tureen, pour soup stirring constantly.
Serve with toast or soup puffs.

Asparagus Soup with Sweet Cream and Egg Yolks

*8 cups water * 1/2 lb. veal bones * 8 oz. mixed vegetables * 1 lb. aspa-ragus * 2 1/2 tbs. flour * salt * (sugar) * 1 cup sweet cream * 1 to 2 egg yolks * 1/2 cup cold stock*

Prepare as asparagus soup with sour cream. Garnish soup with cold stock mixed with flour. Instead of sour cream use sweet cream and egg yolks as garnish.

Sorrel Soup

*8 cups water * 1/2 lb. soup bones * 8 oz. mixed vegetables * 7 oz. sorrel * * 1 cup sour cream * 3 tbs. flour * salt * 1/2 cup milk*

Rinse bones and vegetables, clean and prepare stock; drain off stock.
Rinse sorrel, remove stalks, put through food chopper. Place one half in tureen; cook remaining sorrel in small amount of water.
Add cooked sorrel to stock and garnish with flour and sour cream; bring to the boil, season with salt to taste.
Pour soup and milk into tureen and mix with uncooked sorrel.
Serve with hard-boiled eggs, fluffy rice.

Potato Soup with Sour Cream

*8 cups water * 1/2 lb. soup bones * 8 oz. mixed vegetables without cab-bage * 2 dried mushrooms * 4 medium potatoes * 1/2 to 1 cup sour cream * 2 tbs. flour * salt * green parsley * green dill*

Rinse vegetables, mushrooms and bones clean and prepare stock.
Rinse potatoes, peel, cut into cubes.
Drain off stock; cook potatoes in stock.
Mix flour with cream, garnish soup; bring to the boil, stirring constantly.
Season with salt, add chopped green parsley and dill.

Potato Purée with Sour Cream

*8 cups water * 1/2 lb. soup bones * 8 oz. mixed vegetables without cab-bage * 3 medium potatoes * 1/2 to 1 cup sour cream * 2 tbs. flour * salt * * green dill * green parsley*

Rinse vegetables, clean and prepare stock.
When vegetables are tender, rinse potatoes, peel, add to stock and cook.

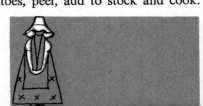

Take the potatoes and half of the vegetables and press through sieve, washing down with stock.

Mix flour with cream, add to boiling stock and bring to the boil. Season with salt, add chopped green dill and green parsley.

Potato Soup with Roux

*8 cups water * 8 oz. mixed vegetables * 2 dried mushrooms * 4 medium potatoes * 3 tbs. fat * 1 small onion * 3 tbs. flour * salt * green parsley * * green dill*

Rinse vegetables and mushrooms and clean; prepare stock.

Peel potatoes and cut into cubes.

When vegetables are tender, drain off stock. Place potatoes in stock and cook.

Melt fat, cut onion and sauté lightly; add flour and mix; brown until yellow and set aside.

Add cold water to roux to make thin paste. Add to stock. Add cut vegetables, bring to the boil. Season with salt, add chopped green parsley and dill.

Solferino Soup

*8 cups water * 1/2 lb. bones * 5 oz. mixed vegetables * 2 medium potatoes * 3 1/2 tbs. fat * 1 small onion * 4 medium tomatoes or 3 tbs. tomato paste * 2 1/2 tbs. flour * salt * paprika*

Rinse vegetables and bones, clean and prepare stock. Drain off stock.

Rinse potatoes, peel and cut into pieces; cook in stock.

Press potatoes and half of vegetables through sieve, washing down with stock; mix with tomato purée.

Cut onion and sauté lightly in fat.

Add flour to onion, brown and set aside.

Add cold stock to roux to make thin paste; add mixture to stock, season with salt and paprika to taste and bring to the boil.

Serve with toast or bread.

Potato Soup à la Poznań

*8 cups water * 8 oz. mixed vegetables * 2 dried mushrooms * allspice * bay leaf * 4 medium potatoes * 3 tbs. fat * 1 small onion * 3 tbs. flour * salt * * vinegar (6%)*

Rinse vegetables and mushrooms, clean and cook with seasoning.
Peel potatoes and cut into cubes.
When vegetables are tender, drain off stock and cook potatoes in it.
Cut onion and brown lightly in fat.
Add flour to onion and brown. Set aside.
Add cold stock to flour garnish to form thin paste. Mix with stock, add salt and bring to the boil. Add vinegar to taste.
Cut up mushrooms and place in tureen.

MILK SOUPS

Milk Soups with Cereal

Milk soups may be prepared with cereal cooked in milk or cooked separately until dry and fluffy. Hot milk is poured over the latter just before serving.

A quick cooking cereal is generally prepared directly in milk, so that milk is not cooked too long. The quick cooking cereals are farina and oatmeal. Other cereal, like corn groats and the Cracow cereal are cooked in water and diluted with milk when the cereal is almost cooked. Farina and oatmeal should be first mixed with a small amount of cold water and poured into boiling milk. Stirring constantly bring to the boil and cook slowly (about 10 minutes).

The cereal cooked dry and fluffy as an addition to milk, is prepared in salted water (see page 140) without fat. The cereals prepared in this manner and added to milk are: groats, roasted and not roasted, millet, oat, corn cereal and rice. Cereal cooked in water should be salted regardless of whether it is to be served with sugar or without. Sugar is often added to millet and rice.

Almost all cereal soups are served hot, the only exception being the Nothing soup, which is prepared with egg yolks, creamed with sugar and vanilla, and garnished with steamed meringue.

Milk Soups with Noodles

Noodles served with some milk soups are cooked in milk. Other varieties of noodles are cooked in water and when cooked and drained are covered with boiling milk.

Pinch noodles, dropped noodles, French and biscuit noodles are cooked in milk. These noodles are small or made of light batter which cooks quickly. Thus milk does not lose its value. Home made macaroni, łazanki and ready made varieties are first cooked in salted water, drained and added to lightly salted, hot milk. Milk soups with noodles are served with salt in Poland.

Nothing Soup

*3/4 cup rice * 3 parts of milk with water (1 part of milk with 2 parts of water to 1 part of rice) * 3 egg yolks * 4 1/2 tbs. sugar * vanilla * 5 cups milk * 3 egg whites * powdered sugar (to taste)*

Rinse rice. Mix one part of milk with two parts of water and bring to the boil. Pour in rice and cook.
Cream egg yolks with sugar, add vanilla.
Boil milk.
Beat egg whites until stiff, fold in powdered sugar gradually and beat until stiff. Place beaten egg whites by the tablespoonful into boiling milk, cook and turn over.
Remove dumplings and place in plates.
Pour hot milk into tureen and mix with creamed egg yolks and rice.
This soup may be served hot or cold.

Pumpkin Soup

*1 lb. pumpkin * 5 cups milk * 3 bitter almonds * salt * sugar*

Rinse pumpkin, peel, cut into small cubes. Add small amount of water, cook and press through sieve.
Make zacierki (see page 100).
Cook zacierki in milk.
Crush almonds into powder.
Add pumpkin to zacierki in milk stirring constantly so that soup does not curdle. Add almonds, salt and sugar to taste.

Carrot Soup

*7 oz. mixed vegetables * 2 medium carrots * 2 cups water * 4 cups milk * * 4 tbs. flour * salt * sugar*

Rinse mixed vegetables and carrots, scrape. Grate carrots and cover with small amount of water. Add mixed vegetables uncut and cook.
Remove vegetables when tender (may be used for salad).
Press carrots through sieve.
Garnish soup with flour, bring to the boil and set apart.
Add full milk to soup, season with salt and sugar to taste.
Serve with potatoes garnished with crisp bacon fat or with dumplings.

Kohlrabi Soup

Follow recipe for carrot soup.

Whey Barszcz

*4 cups whey (not too sour) * 2 tbs. flour * 2 cups buttermilk or sour milk * 1 cup sour cream * sour beet or dill-pickle juice * salt * green dill*

Bring whey to the boil.
Garnish boiling whey with flour, and bring to the boil. Set aside and cool.
Mix with buttermilk and sour cream.
Add beet or dill-pickle juice to soup to taste. Add salt and rinsed and chopped green dill.
Serve with potatoes garnished with crisp bacon fat or with bread.
This soup may be served hot or cold.

Sorrel Soup on Whey

Prepare like whey barszcz. Rinse sorrel and grind. Cook in its own juice. Add to the garnished soup.

Chłodnik

Sour-Milk Soup with Beet Greens

*8 oz. beet greens (young leaves with stalks of red beets) * 1 cup water * * lemon juice or vinegar * 1 cucumber or dill pickle * 3 eggs * 4 cups sour milk * 1 cup sour cream * 3 tbs. chopped green dill and chives * salt*

Rinse beet greens, cut and cook in water adding small quantity of lemon juice or vinegar. Cool.

Peel cucumber or dill pickle and slice into thin rounds.
Shell and chop the hard-boiled eggs.
Stir sour milk thoroughly and mix with beet greens and stock. Add cucumber or pickle, eggs and sour cream. Add salt. Add chopped green dill and chives.
Serve with bread or potatoes.

FRUIT SOUPS

Fruit Chłodnik

Sour-Milk Soup with Fruit

*2 cups strawberries or raspberries * 4 cups sour milk * 1 cup sour cream * sugar*

Rinse fruit in colander. Drain well. Mash fruit. If using raspberries, bring to the boil and then press through sieve.
Stir milk thoroughly with a hand beater and mix with fruit purée and cream.
Add sugar to taste and cool.
Serve with toast or white bread cut into thin slices.

Prune-Jam Soup

*1 cup prune jam * 5 cups water * cloves * cinnamon * 2 tbs. potato starch or corn starch * 1/2 cup water * sugar*

Bring to the boil water with jam and seasoning.
Stir starch into cold water (1/2 cup). Add to hot mixture and bring to the boil. Add sugar to taste and pour into tureen. May be served with an addition of sour cream.
Serve with crisp toast, bread, potatoes.

Clear Fruit Soup

*4 cups cut fruit (apples, pears etc.) * 5 cups water * cloves * cinnamon * * 1/2 cup water * 2 tbs. potato starch or corn starch * about 1/2 cup sugar*

Rinse fruit and cut into segments. Cook in skin with seasoning.
Press through sieve and bring to the boil.

Dissolve starch in cold water (1/2 cup). Pour into simmering stock stirring constantly and bring to the boil. Add sugar to taste.
Fruit soups with starch garnish may be served cold with toasted roll slices or cubes (made of sweet roll), or with dumplings.

Clear Apple Soup

Prepare as above.

Rhubarb and Prune Soup

Prepare as above.

Cherry Soup

Prepare as above. Increase amount of sugar to 1 cup.

Fruit Soup with Sour Cream

*4 cups cut fruit (apples, pears, plums, cherries or sweet cherries) * 4 cups water * cloves * cinnamon * 1 cup sour cream * 3 tbs. flour * about 1/2 cup sugar*

Rinse fruit and cut into segments. Cook in skin with seasoning.
Press fruit through sieve, washing down with stock (remove pits from plums first). Bring to the boil.
Mix flour in sour cream and stirring pour into hot stock. Bring to the boil.
Add sugar to taste.
Serve with toasted roll slices or cubes (made of sweet roll), or with dumplings.

Sweet-Cherry Soup

Prepare as above.

Plum Soup

Prepare as above.

98

Blueberry Soup

Prepare as above.

Raspberry Soup

Prepare as above.

Blackberry Soup

Prepare as above.

ADDITIONS TO SOUPS

Farina or Cracow-Groats (Fine-Buckwheat) Cubes

*3/4 cup water * salt * 1/2 cup farina or Cracow groats * 5 tbs. water *
* green parsley*

Salt water and boil.
Mix farina with 5 tbs. cold water and stir.
Pour on boiling water. Cook, stirring constantly. Add chopped parsley.
Dampen flour board with water, pour out cereal and spread 1/2 inch
thick with knife dipped in water, shaping cereal in square.
When cool cut in cubes.
Serve with broth, milk, cucumber, mushroom soups and others.

Fluffy Rice for Soups

*3/4 to 1 cup rice * 2 times as much water as rice * 1 1/2 tbs. fat * salt*
Follow recipe on page 143.

Fluffy Millet or Barley Cereal for Soups

*1 cup barley (fine or pearl) or millet cereal * 2 times as much water
as cereal * 1 1/2 tbs. fat * salt*
Follow recipe on page 141.

Fluffy Cracow Groats (Fine Buckwheat) for Soups

*1/2 cup Cracow groats * 1 1/4 times as much water as cereal * 1 1/2
tbs. fat * salt*
Follow recipe on page 142.

Zacierki

Pinched, Cut or Grated Noodles

*1 cup flour * 1 egg * salt * 2 tbs. water * 3 tbs. flour to sprinkle dough*

Sift flour, add egg, salt and water, mix and knead well.
Pinch off between fingers or cut with knife into somewhat larger pieces.
Dough may also be grated coarsely. Sprinkle with flour when pinching,
cutting or grating.
Cook in milk or soup.

Łazanki

Square Noodles

*1 cup flour * 1 egg * 2 tbs. water * salt*

Sift flour, add egg, salt and water, mix and knead well.
Roll out dough very thin (the board should be seen through), leave to
dry. Cut the dried dough into long strips (width of 3 fingers). Arrange
long strips one at the top of the other. Move to the edge of the board.
Cut crosswise into small strips 1/3 inch wide, cut these strips into squares.
Throw squares lightly on the board after cutting. If the łazanki are to be
served with garnished soup then cook them in the soup before garnish
has been added. Cook łazanki for broth in boiling, salted water. When
łazanki rise to the top, drain and rinse with cold water. Place in tureen and
cover with part of soup so that they do not stick together.

Home-Made Macaroni for Soups

*1 cup flour * 1 egg * 1 tbs. water * salt*

Sift flour, combine with egg, salt and water and knead well.
Roll out thin so that the board shows through. Leave to dry.
Boil water with salt.
Cut the dried dough in half and roll up each half separately. Move roll
to the edge of the board and cut into very thin strips with a sharp knife.
Throw lightly on the board.
If the macaroni is to be served with garnished soup, cook macaroni in
soup before it is garnished.
Macaroni for broth throw on boiling water and drain when it rises to top.

Rinse with cold water and place in tureen covering immediately with part of the broth.

Uszka (Dumplings) with Mushroom Stuffing

S t u f f i n g: *5 dried mushrooms * 1 oz. stale bread * milk for soaking * * 1/2 small onion * 2 1/2 tbs. fat * salt * pepper * 1 tbs. bread crumbs * * 1 egg white * D o u g h: 2 cups flour * 2 eggs * 2 tbs. water * salt*

Wash mushrooms thoroughly in lukewarm water. Cook in small amount of water and drain. Grind mushrooms. Use stock for soup or sauce.
Soak white bread in milk, squeeze out milk and grind. Combine with mushrooms, cream well.
Cut up onion, fry in fat until golden.
Mix onion with mushrooms and bread. Add salt and pepper.
Sauté adding bread crumbs. Cool. Mix stuffing with egg white.
Prepare salted, boiling water for cooking the uszka.
Sift flour, mix with eggs and water and knead well.
Roll out dough thin and cut into squares (1 1/2×1 1/2 inches).
Place stuffing into square, fold into triangles and seal sides. Fold in bottom flaps to shape the uszka.
Cook in boiling, salted water. Serve with clear barszcz, cabbage soup, fish or pea soup.

Uszka with Meat Stuffing

Use meat left-overs. Grind.
Prepare as above.

Uszka with Fish Stuffing

Use fish left-overs. Grind.
Follow recipe for mushroom uszka.

Dropped Noodles

*1 egg * 3 tbs. flour * salt * water*

Mix egg with flour and water until smooth. Add salt and stir thoroughly. Pour batter in a thin stream on boiling liquid, stirring constantly. Bring to the boil.

Spoon-Dropped Dumplings

*1 egg * 2 1/2 cups flour * salt * water*

Place the measured flour in bowl and indent the center. Add egg, some salt and warm water and using a wooden spoon mix and beat dough.
Beat until bubbles appear on the surface. Boil water in a low pot and add salt to taste.
Dip metal spoon in boiling water until hot. Take small amounts of dough with spoon to form small dumplings. Put dumplings quickly into boiling water, shake off dumplings by striking spoon against the edge of the pot. When all dumplings are dropped, stir.
Cook under cover, drain and rinse with warm water. When water drips off, place in tureen and pour in soup just before serving.

French Dumplings with Flour

*2 1/2 tbs. butter * 2 egg yolks * salt * green parsley * 2 egg whites *
* 4 tbs. flour*

Cream butter and add yolks. Add salt and chopped parsley.
Beat egg whites until stiff.
Add egg whites to creamed mixture, sprinkle with flour and fold in. Test dough for thickness by dropping on hot soup. If the dough dissolves, add flour.
Dip metal spoon in boiling soup and heat. Take small amounts of dough on heated spoon and place in boiling soup. Shake dough off spoon by striking against the edge of the pot.
Cook dumplings under cover on medium flame.
If dumplings are to constitute an addition to broth, cook in boiling salted water. When cooked, drain carefully with a draining spoon and put in tureen. French dumplings should be prepared just before serving.
They are usually served with soups.

French Dumplings with Farina

*2 1/2 tbs. butter * 2 egg yolks * salt * 3 egg whites * 2 tbs. farina *
* 2 tbs. flour*

Cream butter and egg yolks, season with salt.
Beat egg whites until stiff.
Add egg whites to creamed mixture and sprinkle with farina and flour.

Fold in. Test dough for thickness. If it dissolves in boiling soup add flour.

Dip metal spoon in boiling soup and heat. Take small amounts of dough on spoon and place in boiling soup, shake dough off spoon by striking against the edge of the pot.

Cook dumplings in covered pot on medium flame. Drain carefully, put into tureen.

If dumplings are to be served with broth, cook in boiling salted water and when ready mix in tureen with broth. Dumplings must be prepared just before serving.

They are usually served with soups.

French Dumplings with Liver

*2 1/2 tbs. butter * 2 egg yolks * green parsley * 2 egg whites * 2 oz. liver * 3 tbs. flour * salt * pepper*

Grind liver and press through sieve.

Cream butter and egg yolks, add chopped green parsley.

Beat egg whites until stiff and mix with liver and flour. Add pepper and salt and test dough for thickness. If it dissolves in boiling soup, add flour.

Dip metal spoon in boiling soup and heat. Take small amount of dough on spoon and place in boiling soup, shake off dough by striking spoon against the edge of the pot.

Cook dumplings in soup in covered pot on medium flame.

Prepare dumplings just before serving.

Serve with broth.

French Dumplings with Mushrooms

*2 1/2 tbs. butter * 2 egg yolks * 3 tbs. chopped cooked mushrooms * * salt * pepper * 2 egg whites * 3 tbs. flour*

Grind mushrooms taken from soup stock.

Cream butter and egg yolks. Mix with mushrooms, salt and pepper.

Beat egg whites stiff and sprinkle with flour. Combine with mushroom mixture. Test dough for thickness. If it dissolves in boiling soup, add flour.

Dip metal spoon in boiling soup and heat. Take small amount of dough on spoon and place in boiling soup, shake off dough by striking spoon against the edge of the pot.

Cook dumplings in covered pot on medium flame.

Prepare and cook dumplings just before serving.
Serve with mushroom soup and barszcz.

Fluffy French Dumplings

*2 egg whites * 2 egg yolks * salt * 2 or 3 tbs. flour*

Beat egg whites.
Add yolks to egg whites one at a time, beating constantly. Combine with salt and flour. Test dough for thickness. If it dissolves in boiling soup, add flour.
Dip metal spoon in boiling soup and heat. Take small amounts of dough on spoon and place in boiling soup, shake off dough by striking spoon against the edge of the pot.
Cook dumplings in covered pot on medium flame.
If dumplings are to be used as an addition to broth, cook in boiling salted water, drain and mix with broth in tureen.
Fluffy French dumplings are served with broth or milk.

Pulpety

Suet Balls

*5 oz. beef kidney suet * 4 eggs * 1 1/2 cups bread crumbs * salt *
* marjoram * pepper*

Remove membrane carefully from suet, grind or chop finely, cream in bowl into smooth mass.
Add eggs one at a time to suet, stirring continuously into a fluffy consistency.
When the eggs combine with suet, add fine sifted bread crumbs gradually. Add salt and spices to taste.
Place mixture on heavily floured board, shape into thin roll, cut into small pieces.
Shape into balls with hand (about the size of a walnut).
Heat the tripe broth (or salted water), add suet balls so that they float freely and cook slowly. Cut to test for doneness, remove carefully with draining spoon, and while piping hot, place beside the tripe.

Bone-Marrow Balls

*8 tbs. cut beef bone marrow * 2 egg yolks * salt * green parsley *
* marjoram * 3 egg whites * 9 tbs. bread crumbs*

Remove marrow from bone, cut into pieces and mash thoroughly.

Cream marrow, adding one egg yolk at a time. Add salt, green parsley and marjoram.

Beat egg whites and combine with marrow mixture and bread crumbs.

Test dough for thickness. If it dissolves in boiling water, add bread crumbs.

Flour board thickly. Place dough on board and shape into roll.

Cut into even pieces and knead in flour, shaping small balls.

Place in boiling salted water and cook on low heat. Drain and place around tripe. Add generous amount of butter with bread crumbs.

Serve with broth or tripe soup.

Meat-Suet Balls

*4 oz. beef kidney suet * 1 small onion * 1 lb. and 2 oz. cooked meat * * 3 eggs * 3/4 cup bread crumbs * salt * pepper * nutmeg * 4 tbs. flour*

Remove membrane from suet.

Bake onion.

Grind meat together with suet and onion, cream in a bowl adding eggs one at a time.

When the mixture is blended, add sifted bread crumbs, salt and spices.

Place the thoroughly creamed mixture on floured board, shape into roll, cut into pieces.

Shape pieces into balls (not too large). Meat balls for soups should be smaller.

Boil salted water, add balls, cook slowly, covered.

Test for doneness by cutting one of balls.

Remove with draining spoon.

Serve piping hot with tomato or mushroom sauce or with soups.

Pancake Pasties with Meat or Brains

S t u f f i n g: *1/2 small onion * 1 1/2 tbs. fat * 4 tbs. stale bread * 1/2 lb. cooked meat * 1 egg white * salt * pepper * broth (water)* B a t t e r: *1/2 cup milk * 1 egg * 1 cup flour * 1/2 cup water * salt * a piece of fat back (skin) to grease pan* B r e a d i n g: *1 1/2 eggs * 3 tbs. bread crumbs * 2 1/2 tbs. fat for frying*

Prepare stuffing. Chop onion, sauté in fat until yellow.

Soak bread in water and squeeze out moisture.

Grind cooked meat and bread. Combine with egg white and onion. Add salt and pepper. If necessary dilute with broth.

Prepare batter. Combine milk, egg and flour and mix thoroughly with hand beater. Add water and salt.

Heat pan and rub with bacon fat until the whole surface gleams.

Pour batter on hot pan. Pour excess batter back into mixing bowl.

Cook pancake on an even flame.

When the batter is firm, turn over helping with fingers or a spatula.

Cook on other side and place on upturned plate.

Spread stuffing on pancakes. Turn up sides of pancakes. Form into rolls of even length. Mix 1 1/2 eggs with a fork.

Roll pasties in egg, drain, roll in bread crumbs and fry in fat. Fry on all sides. May be also fried without egg or crumbs.

Serve hot with clear soup.

Meat Spiral (Snails)

S t u f f i n g: *4 tbs. stale bread * 1 1/2 tbs. fat * 1/2 small onion * * 1/2 lb. cooked meat (pork) * 1 egg white * salt * pepper * B a t t e r: 1/2 cup milk * 1 egg * 1 cup flour * salt * 1/2 cup water * bacon fat (skin) to rub pan * B r e a d i n g: 1 1/2 eggs * 3 tbs. bread crumbs * * 2 1/2 tbs. fat for frying*

Prepare stuffing. Soak bread in water and squeeze out.

Chop onion and brown in fat until golden.

Grind bread and cooked meat.

Combine with onion, egg white, salt, pepper and if necessary dilute with broth.

Prepare batter. Mix milk, egg and flour thoroughly with hand beater.

Add salt and water.

Rub heated pan with bacon fat until surface gleams.

Pour batter on pan and pour excess batter back into mixing bowl.

Cook on an even flame.

When the pancake is firm, turn onto other side.

Cook on other side and place on upturned plate.

Cut pancakes in half, spread stuffing on halves and form into rolls without folding sides.

Form roll into spiral and paste end with egg white. Place with pasted end to board. Dry.

Mix 1 1/2 eggs with a fork.

Roll spirals in egg, drain and roll in bread crumbs.

Fry on both sides in heated fat, on high flame.

Serve with clear soups.

Toasted Roll Slices

5 oz. stale rolls

Cut stale rolls into thin slices, place flat on baking sheet and brown in oven.
Serve with fruit soups.

Toasted Roll Cubes

*3 oz. stale rolls * 1 tbs. fat (butter)*

Cut rolls into cubes.
Melt butter. Mix with roll cubes.
Place in oven and brown until golden.
Serve in soup plate as an addition to soups.

Crisp Toast

*1 cup flour * 1 egg * salt * lard or frying fat*

Sift flour and knead well with egg and salt.
Roll out dough thickly. Do not sprinkle with flour.
Cut into small rounds with thimble or small cooky forms.
Heat fat and try for temperature. Place toast tidbits on hot fat. Brown.
Turn over and brown on other side. Remove from pan with draining spoon and drain on paper.
Place toast tidbits on plate, sprinkle with sugar.

Diablotins

*2 tbs. grated yellow cheese * 1/2 cup flour * 3 tbs. butter * 1 egg yolk * * salt * 1 egg white * paprika*

Grate cheese on fine grater.
Cut in flour with butter, combine with egg yolk. Knead crisp dough, adding salt and one half of the cheese.
Roll out dough and cut out rounds with cooky cutter.
Brush with egg white and sprinkle with cheese and paprika.
Bake until lightly browned.
Serve with clear soups or for buffet meals.

107

French Pasties with Brains or Meat

Follow recipe on page 54 or 55, using half of the proportions given.

Crayfish Tails

*4 tbs. butter * 1 cup fresh bread crumbs * 1 1/2 tbs. chopped green dill * salt*

Cream butter, combine with bread crumbs. Add chopped green dill and salt to taste.
Fill crayfish shells with mixture.

Crisp Cubes for Broth

*2 1/2 tbs. butter * 3 egg yolks * salt * 1 cup flour * 3 egg whites * butter to grease skillet*

Cream butter, adding one egg yolk at a time. Add salt. (If desired add chopped ham).
Beat egg whites and mix with creamed mixture and flour.
Melt and heat butter on skillet. Place dough in skillet and bake in hot oven.
Cool. Cut into small cubes. Serve with clear soups.

Tomato Cream

*1 cup broth * 2 eggs * salt * thick tomato paste to taste*

Break eggs into cold broth and stir thoroughly. Add salt and paste to taste.
Place broth into small cups 3/4 full. Place cups into pan filled with water and steam under cover for about 3/4 of an hour.
Remove cups and cool cream. Unmold and cut into even strips.
Place strips in deep soup plates and pour over hot soup.
Serve with broth, clear tomato soup or mushroom soup.

Soup Puffs

*1/2 cup water * 2 1/2 tbs. fat * salt * 1/2 cup flour * 1 1/2 eggs * * butter to grease baking sheet*

Boil water with fat and salt in a quart-sized pot.
Add flour and set aside. Stir with spoon until flour is smooth. Using flat spoon stir on low heat.
When the dough is clear and thick remove to bowl.
Combine eggs with hot dough. Beat for 20 minutes.
Set dough aside to cool.
Grease sheet.
Remove dough from bowl and shape into roll on board. The roll should be no thicker than the small finger. Cut off small pieces and place on sheet that is placed under board. Place pieces at equal distances on sheet. When part of the sheet is covered, draw the sheet out from under the board. The puffs may be also pressed through a tube.
Bake in a very hot oven until lightly browned and remove onto flat plate.

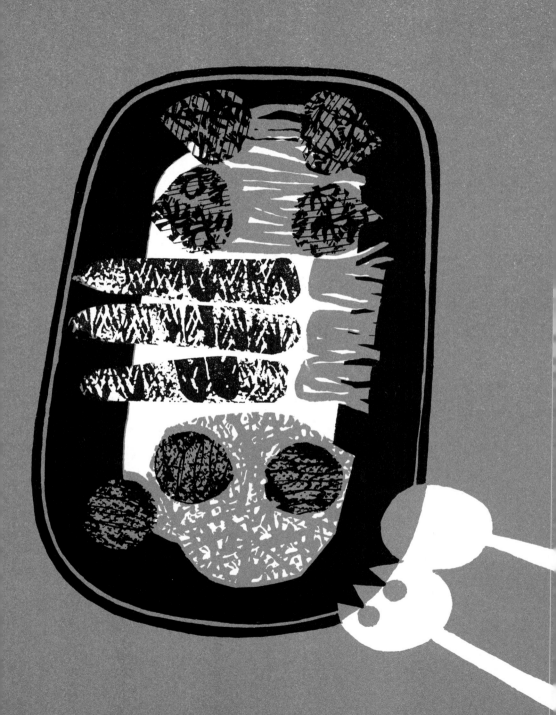

VEGETARIAN DISHES

SALADS AND RELISHES

The following are used in preparing relishes and raw salads:

1. Almost all leafy vegetables, all types of lettuce (summer and winter varieties), all types of cabbage and sauerkraut, endive, leek, chives and onion greens.
2. Tomatoes, sweet peppers (both red and green, especially pickled), cucumbers and dill pickles.
3. Radishes, black radish and turnip.
4. Carrots.
5. Celery root (celeriac).
6. Beets, very seldom.

Lettuce is served uncut. Tomatoes and cucumbers are sliced thickly or in sections (like oranges). Other, firmer vegetables like cabbage and leek are shredded finely, and carrots and black radish are grated. We usually season chopped vegetables with lemon juice and oil or with a prepared dressing. This prevents changes of color, flavor and the nutritive value of the chopped vegetables when they are exposed to the air. That is why the dressing is an important ingredient of raw salads. Dressings are prepared in various ways: it may be French dressing with oil and lemon juice, mayonnaise with egg yolk and oil or fresh, thick sour cream, an indispensable ingredient of many Polish dishes. All Polish relishes and raw salads have a delicate, tart-sweet flavor. We use grated, unpeeled tart apples, dill pickles and their juice, fresh tomato juice or thick preserved tomato sauce, lemon or currant juice. The tartness tempered with small amounts of sugar brings out the natural sweetness of the vegetables. Salt and sugar are added at the end in order not to cause the premature formation of juices. Many aromatic spices are also used: onions and chives, fresh dill and parsley, horse-radish, mustard and coriander.

Raw salads are served with fresh garnishes: lettuce and cabbage leaves, slices of leek, carrots, unpeeled cucumber, tomatoes and finely chopped greens.

Relishes and raw vegetable salads are served with salted herring, hors d'oeuvres, hot meat, fish and vegetable dishes — both fried and baked.

Onion Relish

*3 large onions * salt * vinegar * pepper * 2 tbs. oil * greens for garnish*

Peel onions, slice in rings, sprinkle with salt, vinegar, pepper and oil, garnish with greens.

Onion Relish with Sour Cream

*2 large onions * 1 medium apple * 1 medium dill pickle * 5 tbs. sour cream * salt * sugar*

Peel onions, rinse, shred finely with pickle and washed, unpeeled apple. Combine ingredients with sour cream, salt and sugar to taste.

Endive with Sour Cream or Oil

*10 stalks of French endive * salt * green parsley or dill * wine vinegar or lemon juice * 1 tbs. sugar * 2 tbs. oil or 3/4 cup sour cream*

Rinse the stalks of endive thoroughly, drain, cut in 1 inch pieces, place in bowl, salt.
Rinse and chop finely green parsley and dill.

Mix all ingredients with endive, add vinegar and sugar to taste and sprinkle with oil or prepare sour cream dressing and mix with the cut endive. Place on salad dish.

Endives can be prepared French style by sprinkling them with lemon juice and olive oil.

Endive in Mayonnaise

*10 stalks endive * salt * vinegar * sugar*

Rinse endive thoroughly, drain, cut into pieces 1 inch long, sprinkle with salt.

Prepare mayonnaise with 1 egg yolk (see page 314).

Add endive to mayonnaise, mix, season with vinegar and sugar to taste.

Black Radish with Carrots

*8 oz. black radish * salt * 1 medium carrot * 3/4 cup cottage cheese * * 1 cup sour cream * chives or onion*

Scrub radish, pare, grate coarsely, salt, press with plate, drain.

Finely grate cleaned, scraped carrot.

Combine carrot with radish, add crumbled cottage cheese, sour cream and chopped chives.

Serve with bread.

Red Radishes

2 bunches of young red radishes

Rinse radishes with leaves thoroughly.

Remove large leaves, leave smaller ones, cut off root end.

Place unpared radishes on small plate.

Serve with bread, salt and butter.

Apples with Horse-Radish and Sour Cream

*2 tbs. grated horse-radish * 5 medium apples * 3/4 cup sour cream * * salt * sugar*

Rinse horse-radish, scrub, grate finely.

Wash apples and grate coarsely, unpared.

Add sour cream, horse-radish, salt and sugar to taste, mix.
Arrange on rectangular salad plate, garnish with leaves of savoy cabbage or lettuce.

Vegetable Salad

*2 tbs. mustard * 1 egg yolk * 5 tbs. olive oil * 3 cups grated, mixed vegetables * 2 apples * salt * sugar * chives, green parsley or dill*

Prepare dressing: add olive oil gradually while creaming egg yolk, add mustard to taste.
Rinse vegetables, clean, grate finely. Rinse apples, pare, grate.
Combine with vegetables.
Mix immediately with dressing, season with salt and sugar.
Arrange salad in rectangular salad bowl, garnish with finely chopped greens.

Shredded Cabbage

*4 cups shredded white cabbage * 1/2 cup grated black radish * 2 tbs. grated horse-radish * 1/2 medium onion or chives * 3/4 cup sour cream * salt * sugar*

Shred cabbage finely, salt lightly.
Pare radish, grate finely.
Clean horse-radish, grate, chop onion.
Mix cabbage with cream and other ingredients, add salt and sugar to taste; if necessary add a few drops of vinegar or lemon juice.

Red Cabbage and Apples

*4 cups shredded red cabbage * salt * 2 apples * 1/2 onion * 2 1/2 tbs. oil * sugar * pepper*

Shred cabbage, remove core and thick leaves. Salt and set aside to soften.
Wash apples thoroughly, grate coarsely.
Chop onion.
When the cabbage softens, mix with oil, apples and onion, add sugar and pepper to taste.

Sauerkraut and Onion

*3 cups sauerkraut * 1 medium onion * 2 1/2 tbs. oil * sugar * pepper *
* caraway seeds*

Cut up sauerkraut several times and mix with finely-chopped onion.
Sprinkle with salad oil and seasonings.

Sauerkraut and Grated Carrots

*1 medium carrot * 2 1/2 cups sauerkraut * 1 medium onion * sugar *
* pepper * 2 1/2 tbs. salad oil*

Scrub carot under running water, grate finely.
Cut sauerkraut several times and mix with carrot, diced onion, season
with sugar and pepper, sprinkle with salad oil.

Sauerkraut with Tomato Juice

*4 cups sauerkraut * 1/2 cup thick tomato juice * 1 medium onion *
* sugar * 2 1/2 tbs. salad oil*

Cut up sauerkraut several times, mix with tomato juice, diced onion and
sugar. Sprinkle with salad oil.

Savoy Cabbage and Cucumber

*4 cups chopped savoy cabbage * salt * 1 large cucumber * 3/4 cup sour
cream * sugar * green dill * vinegar or lemon juice*

Chop cabbage finely, salt and set aside to soften.
Rinse cucumber, pare, slice in rings.
Mix cabbage with cucumber, sour cream, add sugar, sprinkle with chopped
green dill, add lemon juice or vinegar to taste.

Savoy Cabbage with Tomato Juice

*3 1/2 cups chopped cabbage * salt * 1 medium dill pickle * 1 medium
apple * 1/2 cup thick tomato juice * 3/4 cup sour cream or 2 tbs. salad
oil * green dill * sugar*

Chop cabbage finely, salt and set aside to soften.
Wash apple and grate coarsely together with dill pickle.
Mix the cabbage with apple, dill pickle, sour cream (or oil) and tomato
juice, garnish with green dill, add a pinch of sugar if necessary.

Carrots, Beets and Horse-Radish

*2 1/2 cups grated carrots * 1 1/2 cups grated beets * 2 tbs. grated horse--radish * 5 tbs. sour cream * vinegar * salt * sugar*

Rinse vegetables, clean, pare, grate finely.
Combine all ingredients with sour cream, season with vinegar, salt and sugar.

Carrots, Apples and Horse-Radish

*2 1/2 cups grated carrots * 2 medium apples * 1 tbs. grated horse-radish *
* 3/4 cup thick sour cream * salt * sugar*

Rinse carrot, scrub, grate finely.
Wash apple thoroughly, grate coarsely, unpeeled.
Peel horse-radish, grate.
Mix all ingredients with sour cream, season with salt and sugar.

Carrots, Parsley and Celery Root

*1 1/2 cups grated carrots * 1 cup grated celery root * 1 cup grated parsley root * 1 medium onion or 2 tbs. chopped chives * 3/4 cup sour cream * salt * sugar * vinegar or lemon juice*

Rinse vegetables, clean, peel, grate finely, chop onion finely.
Add onion, sour cream, salt and sugar to taste to grated vegetables; add lemon juice or vinegar if necessary.

Mizeria

Cucumbers in Sour Cream

*5 medium cucumbers * a pinch of salt * vinegar * 3/4 cup sour cream *
* 2 tbs. chopped green dill * (pepper)*

Rinse cucumbers, pare slice in thin rings or shred.
Add salt to cucumbers, mix, cover with plate, press with light weight.
When moist, drain off a little of the juice.
Place on salad platter.
Add vinegar to taste, mix, pour over with sour cream; garnish with chopped dill (or pepper).

Dill Pickles with Onion

*4 medium dill pickles * 1 medium onion*

Shred dill pickles, chop onion and combine.

Tomatoes and Onions

*8—10 medium tomatoes * 1 large onion * pepper * green parsley or dill *
* 2 tbs. salad oil * salt*

Rinse tomatoes, slice in rings with sharp knife, place in rows on salad plate.
Chop onion, sprinkle onion over tomatoes, garnish with pepper and greens, sprinkle with salad oil, salt.

Tomatoes and Dill Pickles .

*3 medium tomatoes * 2 medium dill pickles * 1 small onion * green dill *
* juice from dill pickles * (2 tbs. salad oil)*

Wash tomatoes, slice in rings with sharp knife.
Slice dill pickles in rings.
Chop onion.
Place tomato rings on platter alternating with dill pickles. Top with onion and chopped green dill, sprinkle with dill-pickle juice and salad oil.

Leek in Mayonnaise

*6—8 medium leeks * salt * mayonnaise*

Cut off green part of leaves, clean the rest and rinse thoroughly, slice in thin rings, salt lightly (use the dark green, hard leaves in soups).
Prepare one-egg mayonnaise dressing, season highly.
Place sliced leek in rectangular salad platter, pour over with dressing, garnish with carrot rings and leek.

Radishes with Chives and Dill

*30 radishes * 3 tbs. chopped chives and green dill * salt * 3/4 cup sour cream*

119

Rinse radishes, slice in rings together with the smaller leaves.
Rinse chives and green dill, drain off water, chop finely. Mix all ingredients.
Immediately before serving salt to taste, mix with sour cream; if necessary add vinegar or lemon juice to taste.

Lettuce with Vinegar

*3 large heads of lettuce * wine vinegar * (3 tbs. olive oil)*

Rinse lettuce thoroughly under running water, clean, divide in parts, drain.
Prepare wine vinegar diluted with water.
Place lettuce on salad plate, pour over vinegar (to taste), mix.
Before serving sprinkle with olive oil if desired.
Lemon juice may be used instead of vinegar.

Lettuce, Polish Style

*3 large heads of lettuce * lemon juice or wine vinegar * 2 tbs. sugar *
* 1/2 to 1 cup sour cream * 1 1/2 tbs. chopped green dill * 2 eggs*

Rinse lettuce thoroughly under running water, clean, divide in parts, drain.
Dilute vinegar with water, add sugar.
Pour dressing over lettuce, mix.
Pour sour cream over lettuce before serving, garnish with chopped green dill.
Garnish with hard-boiled eggs cut into segments.

Lettuce and Radishes

*2 heads of early lettuce * 10 radishes * 1 tbs. chopped chives * 2 tbs.
chopped green dill * 1 egg * 1/2 cup sour cream * salt*

Rinse lettuce several times under running water; allow to drain in colander, cut up.
Rinse radishes, cut up with young leaves.
Rinse chives and green dill, drain off water, chop finely.
Chop hard-boiled egg.
Mix all ingredients, add sour cream and salt to taste.
Prepare immediately before serving.

120

Green Winter Salad

*3 stalks of endive or 5 cups of rampion or Romaine lettuce * salt * 3 tbs. salad oil * vinegar*

Clean vegetables, rinse, shake off water, separate leaves, place on salad plate.
Sprinkle with salt, salad oil and vinegar.

COOKED VEGETABLES

Cooked vegetables are prepared in several ways in Poland:
1) vegetables cooked in a small amount of water and seasoned with butter or with bread crumbs browned in butter (polonaise topping).
2) vegetables cooked in a small amount of water and seasoned with a roux or sour cream.
3) a few vegetables are cooked in a large amount of water.
4) vegetables which after cooking are prepared into cutlets, casserole dishes, puddings, etc.
Vegetables may be served as a main course or used as side dishes with meats and vegetarian dinners.
The most popular dishes are: spinach with eggs and potatoes, beans in tomato sauce with sausage, omelet with green peas or spinach, cabbage with tomatoes and potato dumplings, sauerkraut with mushrooms and potatoes, cauliflower or string beans with polonaise topping, etc.
A typical summer vegetable dish is the vegetable bouquet which is made up of cooked vegetables garnished with butter. It includes string beans, new carrots, cauliflower, new potatoes with green dill, all cooked separately with a few slices of tomato and a fried egg.
Other vegetarian dishes such as puddings, soufflés, casseroles, cutlets consist of more complicated ingredients and require more skill and time to make. Although they contain a variety of products, they are not as nutritious as the simpler dishes, since the processes which they undergo during preparation lower their nutritious value; that is why they are not used extensively.
Vegetables may also be served as side-dishes. These dishes should be skilfully and tastefully combined. Thus, for vegetarian dinners, we select usually vegetables with a tart and pronounced flavor since they supplement the mild and bland flavor of flour dishes. We use carrots, string beans, cauliflower, tomatoes, and potatoes but not cabbage with veal.

We usually combine all forms of cabbage with pork. Tomatoes, string and navy beans, raw and braised onions make a good side dish for lamb. We serve beets, carrots, cauliflower, string beans in sour cream with beef. In addition to cooked vegetables a raw salad is a "must" as a second side dish. Relishes and raw salads, made up as a rule of raw vegetables or fruits, are extensively used in Poland.

Beets in Sour Cream

*8 medium beets * 1 cup sour cream * 2—3 tbs. flour * salt * wine vinegar or lemon juice*

Clean beets with a brush under running water, cook covered in large amount of water.
Drain cooked beets, cool, peel, grate.
Combine flour with sour cream, pour over beets, add a little boiling water, mix, heat, add salt and vinegar to taste, serve in salad bowl.

Young Beets in Sour Cream

*10 medium young beets * 1 cup sour cream * 1 tbs. flour * salt * wine vinegar or lemon juice * 2 tbs. chopped green dill*

Clean young beets with a brush under running water, rinse, peel, grate.
Cook grated beets in small amount of water over high heat, covered.
Combine flour with sour cream, pour over beets, stir while cooking, add salt and vinegar, chopped green dill to taste, serve in salad platter.

Beets in Brown Gravy

*8 medium beets * 3 tbs. fat * 1/2 small onion * 2 tbs. flour * salt * sugar * * wine vinegar or lemon juice * (green dill)*

Rinse beets, clean with brush under running water, cook covered in large amount of water.
Drain cooked beets, cool, peel, grate.
Chop onion, fry in fat to light brown, add flour, brown lightly, set aside.
Dilute with cold water to thin consistency, stir while cooking, combine with beets, heat, add salt, sugar and vinegar to taste.
Serve on platter.

Beets in Brown Gravy with Apples

*5 medium beets * 2 large cooking apples * 3 tbs. fat * 1 small onion *
* 2 1/2 tbs. flour * salt * sugar*

Rinse beets, clean with brush under running water, pare, grate and cook covered in small amount of water on hot flame, use the liquid for gravy.
Rinse apple, pare, grate.
Slice onion, brown lightly in fat, add flour, brown lightly, set aside.
Dilute gravy with cold liquid (or cold water) to thin consistency, stir while cooking, mix with beets, heat, mix with apples, add salt and sugar to taste, serve on platter.

Boiled Turnip Balls

*4 cups turnip balls * salt * sugar * 3 tbs. butter*

Rinse turnips, pare, hollow with French ball cutter.
Cook water with salt and sugar, add balls when water is boiling, and cook until tender, uncovered (about 3/4 hour).
Drain when tender, pour over with browned butter.
Serve as a side-dish with lamb.

Brussels Sprouts

*6—7 cups Brussels sprouts * salt * sugar * 3 tbs. bread crumbs * 3 tbs. butter*

Cook water with salt and sugar.
Clean wilted leaves from sprouts, rinse several times, drop into boiling water, cook uncovered until tender, drain.
Place on platter, add unmelted butter, mix, or pour over with bread crumbs browned in butter (polonaise topping).

Stewed Onions

*20 medium onions (of uniform size) * 3 tbs. fat * 2 tbs. flour * salt * sugar *
* wine vinegar*

Peel onions, rinse, drop in boiling water, parboil and drain. Cover with boiling water again and cook covered until tender.
Prepare yellow roux with fat and flour, dilute with the cooking liquid, heat, combine sauce with onion. Add salt, sugar and vinegar to taste.
Serve with fried or roast meats.

Boiled Beans

*2 1/2 cups beans (seed) * salt * 2 tbs. chopped fat back * 1 small onion*

Pick over beans, rinse, soak in cooled, boiled water for a few hours. Cook beans in water in which they were soaked until tender. If the liquid evaporates add small amounts of boiling water.
Salt beans when almost ready, drain before serving.
Chop onion finely, brown in fat.
Place beans on platter, pour over with fat back and onion or serve dotted with butter.

Boiled String Beans

*2 lb. string beans * sugar * salt * 3 tbs. bread crumbs * 3—4 tbs. butter*

Boil a little water, add salt and sugar.
Rinse beans, remove strings pulling lengthwise along the pod.
Drop cleaned beans in boiling water, cook over high flame, covered, turn to ensure even cooking.
Brown bread crumbs in butter and pour over drained beans on platter or serve dotted with unmelted butter.

String Beans in Sour Cream

*2 lb. string beans * 1 small onion * 2 tbs. flour * 1 1/2 tbs. butter * 1 cup sour cream * salt * wine vinegar*

Rinse beans, remove strings, cut obliquely.
Chop onion.
Cook beans with onion in small amount of water over high flame, covered. Prepare a light golden roux, add to beans, stir while heating. Add sour cream, salt, add vinegar to taste, mix, serve in salad bowl.
Serve with potatoes and fried eggs.

Dried Peas

*2 1/2 cups dry round peas (whole) * salt * 4 1/2 tbs. fat back * 1 small onion*

Pick over peas, rinse, soak in cooled, boiled water for a few hours.
Cook until tender in water in which peas were soaked (allow water to evaporate), add salt.

Render the fat back, remove cracklings, brown onion lightly in fat, combine with cracklings.
Drain peas, place in salad bowl, pour over with fat back.

Green Peas

*2 cups husked peas * 1 tsp. flour * sugar * salt * 2 tbs. butter*

Rinse peas, husk.
Remove the internal membranes from part of the pods.
Cut up pods into small macaroni-like pieces.
Cook peas (and pods) covered in a small amount of water over high flame.
When tender, reduce liquid, sprinkle with flour, add salt and sugar to taste, heat.
Add butter to peas, heat.
Serve in salad bowl.

Cauliflower

*1 large cauliflower * salt * sugar * 2 tbs. bread crumbs * 3 tbs. butter*

Boil water with salt and sugar.
Clean cauliflower, leaving the leaves near the flowerets, rinse, place in the boiling water (flowerets down), cook over high heat without covering.
Brown bread crumbs in butter and pour over cauliflower.
The cauliflower may be served dotted with unmelted butter.

Kohlrabi

*1 1/2 lb. young kohlrabi * 1 tbs. flour * salt * sugar * 2 tbs. butter * green dill*

Rinse kohlrabi, remove large leaves, do not cut off center ones.
Cut off tops together with small leaves, peel the rest, cut into cubes, coarsely chop tops with small leaves.
Cook kohlrabi uncovered in a small amount of water on high flame.
Drain off liquid, sprinkle kohlrabi with flour, add salt and sugar to taste, combine with the liquid, heat, add butter, place in salad bowl, garnish with chopped green dill.

Boiled Savoy Cabbage

*1 large head of savoy cabbage * salt * sugar * 2 tbs. bread crumbs * 3 tbs. butter*

125

Boil water with salt and sugar.

Clean cabbage, rinse, divide into four parts, place in boiling water, cook until tender, uncovered, drain well on colander.

Brown bread crumbs in butter.

Place cabbage on heated platter, dot with browned bread crumbs.

Boiled Cabbage in Sour Cream

*1 small head of cabbage * 1/2 small onion * caraway seeds * 1 cup sour cream * 2 tbs. flour * salt*

Rinse cabbage, remove withered leaves, shred.

Chop onion.

Pour a small amount of boiling water over cabbage, add onion and caraway seeds, cook.

Combine flour with sour cream, add to cabbage, stir while cooking, salt, serve in salad bowl.

Boiled Cabbage in Sour Cream with Tomatoes

The same proportions as above plus five medium tomatoes or 3 tbs. tomato paste.

Prepare cabbage as above.

Rinse tomatoes, simmer, strain and add to cabbage.

Boiled Cabbage in Sour Cream with Dill Pickles

The same proportions as above plus 3 medium dill pickles.

Prepare cabbage as above.

Slice pickles into rings, add to cabbage, season with pickle juice, heat well.

Boiled Cabbage in Brown Gravy

*1 head of cabbage (2 1/2 lb.) * 1/2 small onion * caraway seeds * 3 tbs. fat * 1/2 small onion * 3 tbs. flour * salt * wine vinegar * sugar * pepper*

Remove withered leaves from cabbage, rinse, shred fine, pour boiling water over cabbage, add onion and caraway seeds and cook on high flame uncovered.

Chop onion, brown lightly in fat, add flour, brown lightly, set aside.
Dilute gravy with cold water and liquid from the cabbage to a thin consistency, heat, combine with cabbage, salt, add vinegar, sugar and pepper to taste, serve in salad bowl.

Boiled Cabbage with Apples

*1 head of cabbage (2 lb.) * 1/2 small onion * caraway seeds * 2 large tart apples * 3 tbs. fat * 1/2 small onion * 2 tbs. flour * sugar * salt*

Remove withered leaves from cabbage, rinse, shred finely, pour boiling water over cabbage, add onion and caraway seeds, cook on high flame uncovered.
Pare apples, grate.
Dice onion, brown lightly in fat, add flour to fat. brown lightly, set aside.
Dilute gravy with cold water and liquid from the cabbage to a thin consistency, stir while cooking, combine with cabbage, cook, mix with apples, add salt and sugar to taste; serve in salad bowl.

Red Cabbage with Roux

*1 1/2 heads of red cabbage (2 1/2 lb.) * 3 tbs. fat * 3 tbs. flour * sugar * * salt * wine vinegar*

Clean cabbage, shred, pour over with boiling water and cook on high flame, covered.
Melt fat, add flour, brown to light golden color, set aside.
Dilute gravy with cold water and liquid from the cabbage, stir while cooking, mix with cabbage, heat, add salt, vinegar and sugar to taste, serve in salad bowl.
Serve red cabbage with frankfurters, fried fish, partridge, duck and goose.

Sauerkraut with Roux

*4—5 cups sauerkraut * caraway seeds * bay leaf * allspice * 3—4 tbs. fat * * 1 small onion * 3 tbs. flour * salt * pepper*

Cut up sauerkraut several times, if too tart, rinse, add a little water and cook uncovered, with spices, on high flame.
Chop onion, brown lightly in fat, add flour, brown lightly, set aside.
Dilute gravy with cold water and cooking liquid, stir while cooking, mix with cabbage, add salt and pepper, heat, serve in salad bowl.

Fat left over from frying doughnuts and cracklings from rendered fat may be used for added flavor.

Sauerkraut with Mushrooms

*4—5 cups sauerkraut * 3 medium, dried mushrooms * caraway seeds * bay leaf * 3—4 tbs. fat * 1/2 small onion * 3 tbs. flour * salt * pepper*

Wash mushrooms and rinse in warm water.
Cut up sauerkraut several times, if too tart, rinse, add a little boiling water, then the mushrooms and cook with spices, uncovered, over a high flame.
Dice onion, brown lightly in fat, add flour, brown lightly, set aside.
Dilute the roux with cold water and cooking liquid, stir while heating.
Remove the mushrooms from the cabbage, chop fine.
Combine the roux with the cabbage, add mushrooms, salt, pepper, heat, serve on platter.

Steamed Cabbage in Light Roux

*1 small head of cabbage (2 1/2 lb.) * salt * liquid from boiled potatoes * * caraway seeds * 1 small onion * 3—4 tbs. fat * 2 tbs. flour * salt * pepper*

Remove withered leaves from cabbage, shred, salt lightly, squeeze with hands to soften, press under small weight.
When the cabbage begins to be juicy, pour over with boiling water or liquid from boiled potatoes, place in a warm place so that it sours quickly: prepare 3 days before cooking.
When sour, add a small amount of boiling water to cabbage and cook with caraway seeds, uncovered, over a high flame.
Chop onion, brown lightly in fat.
Add flour to the onion and fat, brown lightly.
Dilute the roux with cold water and liquid from the cabbage to a thin consistency, stir while heating, combine with the cabbage, add salt and pepper to taste, serve on platter.

Carrots and Turnips

*3 cups diced carrots * 2 cups diced turnip * 4 tbs. fat back * 2 tbs. flour * * salt * sugar * marjoram*

Clean vegetables, cut in small cubes, pour over with hot water and cook uncovered until tender.

Make a yellow roux from the flour and fat back, dilute with vegetable liquid. Stir while cooking, mix with cooked vegetables, add salt, sugar and marjoram to taste, heat, serve on platter. Serve with potatoes.

Carrots

*3 1/2 cups grated carrots * 1 tbs. flour * salt * sugar * 2 tbs. butter*

Scrape carrots under running water, grate, add a small amount of water and cook covered on a high flame.

Pour off liquid, sprinkle the carrots with flour, add salt and sugar to taste, combine with the liquid, heat, add unmelted butter, mix, place on platter.

Young Carrots

*20 young carrots * salt * sugar * 2 tbs. butter*

Scrape carrots under running water, cut the larger carrots in half, add a small amount of water and cook covered on a high flame.

Steam off water, add salt and sugar to taste, mix, add unmelted butter, heat, serve on platter.

Carrots and Peas

See Vegetable Plates.

Carrots and String Beans

See Vegetable Plates.

Carrots and Kohlrabi

See Vegetable Plates.

Tomatoes Sautéed

*10 medium tomatoes * 5 tbs. butter * salt * pepper * green parsley*

Select ripe, firm tomatoes (with little juice), rinse, cut into 1/4 inch slices. Heat butter well on hot skillet, add the tomatoes, not too many at a time and sauté quickly on both sides on high heat.

Serve directly from the skillet with the sauce formed during sautéing.
Before serving, sprinkle with salt, pepper and chopped parsley.
Serve with fried and roasted meats, vegetables and vegetarian dishes.

Leeks in Roux

*10 medium leeks * 3 tbs. fat * 2 tbs. flour * salt * pepper * wine vinegar*

Wash and trim leeks (use the large leaves for soups) very carefully. Cut
leeks into one-inch pieces, pour over with boiling water and cook covered
over high heat.
Melt fat, add flour, stir while browning lightly, set aside.
Dilute the roux with broth (or water) into a thin consistency, mix while
heating, combine with leeks, salt, add a little pepper and vinegar to taste,
serve on platter.

Pea Purée with Smoked Fat Back

*2 1/2 cups dried peas * 2 tbs. fat * 1 clove garlic * 2 tbs. flour * salt * 2 tbs.
smoked fat back*

Wash and sort whole peas, soak for a few hours before cooking (in cooled
boiled water).
Cook peas in water in which they were soaked, drain.
Strain tender peas through sieve.
Melt fat, add crushed garlic, mix with flour, brown lightly.
Dilute the roux with the cooled cooking liquid to thin consistency, stir
while heating.
Combine the strained peas with the roux, salt, heat.
Render the tickly sliced, smoked fat back or brown onions in fat back
to a light gold color.
Place the pea purée on platter, pour over with fat.
Serve with smoked meat, knuckles or hot ham.

Pea Purée with Fried Onions

*2 1/2 cups dried peas * 2 1/2 tbs. rendered fat back * 1/2 small onion *
* salt*

Cook peas as above, grind in food chopper or strain through a sieve.
Render the fat back, remove cracklings, brown the finely chopped onions
in fat, combine with cracklings. Salt.

Serve the pea purée on platter, poured over with fat, onions and cracklings.

Boiled Asparagus

*15 medium-thick sticks of asparagus * salt * sugar * 2 tbs. bread crumbs * * 3 tbs. butter*

Boil water with salt and sugar.
Wash and clean asparagus, scrape the thick ends. Tie in a bundle and cook in water, drain, arrange in two rows on rectangular platter, with tips towards center.
Brown bread crumbs in butter, pour over asparagus.

Spinach with Roux

*4 cups cooked spinach * 3 tbs. fat * 4 tbs. flour * 3/4 cup milk * salt * * (garlic)*

Cook water with salt.
Wash spinach, remove roots, rinse in parts under running water in a colander.
Place in boiling, salted water, cook uncovered on high heat until spinach is crushed easily between fingers.
Drain spinach thoroughly, grind in food chopper.
Melt fat, add flour, sauté lightly.
Dilute the roux with milk, stir while heating.
Combine spinach with the roux, add salt and garlic to taste, heat, arrange on platter. Serve with fried or boiled eggs, with potatoes, groats or as a side-dish to meats, omelets, filled pancakes.

Kale with Roux

Prepare as above.

Boiled Young Potatoes

*3 lb. young potatoes * salt * 3 tbs. butter * green parsley * green dill*
Salt water, boil.
Clean potatoes, add to boiling water, cook covered on high heat, drain.

Chop green parsley and dill.
Top potatoes with unmelted butter and chopped parsley and dill, cover saucepan, shake potatoes a few times so that the butter spreads evenly, arrange on platter.

Boiled Potatoes

*10 medium potatoes * salt * 2 1/2 tbs. butter * (green parsley) * (green dill)*

Clean and pare potatoes.
Place in pot, add boiling water to cover 3/4 from top, salt and cook covered on high heat so that all the liquid evaporates. Add butter to potatoes when cooked, combine and place on platter, garnish with chopped parsley and dill.

Boiled Potatoes in Skins

*10 medium potatoes * water*

Select potatoes uniform in size and variety. Pour cold water over potatoes, cook.
Serve on platter, serve butter and salt on the side.

Potato Purée

*10 medium potatoes * salt * 3 tbs. butter * 5 tbs. milk * green parsley * * green dill*

Boil potatoes in salted water, mash.
Add butter and hot milk, combine and beat over heat.
Arrange on round platter, pour over with butter, garnish with chopped parsley and dill.

Home-Fried Potatoes

*10 medium potatoes * 1 medium onion * 4 tbs. fat * salt * green parsley * * green dill*

Wash potatoes, cook in skins, peel, cut in medium slices.
Melt fat, brown onion lightly and then remove.
Fry potatoes slowly in the fat so that the bottoms are crispy, sprinkle with salt.
Before serving, garnish with greens and fried onion (or chives in season)

French-Fried Potatoes

*10 medium potatoes * beef suet (or other fat for frying) * salt*

Clean and pare potatoes.

Slice each potato into 8 parts, or slice in rings, or in thick strips, pour over cold water, dry on towel.

Prepare frying pot with rendered and strained fat.

Have fat the same temperature as for doughnuts (see page 348). When fat has the correct temperature, place a small amount of potatoes in it, fry not too quickly until lightly golden.

With a draining spoon remove the light golden potatoes into the other empty pot, cover and set aside for a while. Then place again in very hot fat and fry quickly to golden brown.

Drain potatoes on absorbent paper.

Arrange on platter, salt and serve immediately.

Serve with meats, fish and poultry.

The potatoes may be fried earlier to a golden color, placed in an empty pot and kept covered. Before serving, place in hot fat, brown, drain and salt. The same fat may be used several times for frying. Two pounds of potatoes absorb about 3 1/2 to 5 oz. of fat during frying but they must float in deep fat during frying.

Baked Potatoes

*10 medium potatoes * salt*

Clean potatoes, do not peel.

Spread a thick layer of salt in the baking pan, place potatoes and put in oven, turn a few times during baking.

When the potatoes are soft, remove, arrange on round platter on a folded napkin, and serve hot from the oven.

Serve with salt and butter.

VEGETABLE SALADS

Polish Ćwikła

Grated Beets with Horse-Radish

*8 medium beets * wine vinegar * 2 tsp. caraway seeds * 3 tbs. grated horse-radish * salt * sugar*

Wash beets, cut off thin root, boil in a large amount of water, drain, cool. Dilute vinegar with water so that it is not too tart.

Rinse caraway seeds, clean horse-radish, grate.

Peel the beets, grate. Combine all ingredients, add salt and sugar if necessary, place in jar; the beets should be covered with the diluted vinegar so that they do not mold.

Wrap the jar in waxed paper, keep in cold place.

Prepare a few days before using.

Serve with boiled beef, ground patties and other meat or vegetable dishes.

Bean Salad in Mustard Sauce

*2 1/2 cups dried beans * 1 1/2 tbs. mustard * 2 tbs. salad oil * 1 medium onion * salt * (wine vinegar) * sugar*

Pick over beans, rinse, soak in a large amount of cooled boiled water.

Cook beans until tender in water in which they were soaked, drain.

Cream mustard, while adding oil.

Chop onion finely.

Combine mustard sauce with beans, add salt, onion (vinegar), sugar, mix.

Thin with cooking liquid from the beans.

Red Cabbage Salad

*1/2 medium head of red cabbage * salt * wine vinegar * 1 medium onion * * 2 large apples * sugar * (2 tbs. salad oil)*

Boil water, add vinegar and salt.

Clean cabbage, shred, cook in water covered on high heat, drain when half done (crispy).

Chop onion, wash apples, grate coarsely.

Mix cabbage with onion, apples, sugar and vinegar (sprinkle with oil).

Cooked navy beans may be added to this salad.

Cabbage in Mustard Sauce

*1/2 small head of white cabbage (2 lb.) * salt * 1 1/2 tbs. mustard * 2 tbs. salad oil * 1 medium onion * sugar * pepper*

Shred cabbage finely, immerse in boiling, salted water, bring to the boil a few times in an uncovered pot, drain, cool; use the cooking broth for soups. Add mustard, oil, onion, sugar and pepper to the cabbage, thin with cooking broth if necessary, mix.

Sweet Pepper Salad

*5 sweet peppers * 1 medium onion * 3 tbs. oil * a few allspice berries ** 1 bay leaf * 1 tbs. wine vinegar * salt * sugar*

Clean red or green fresh peppers, cut off stems, remove seeds cut into wide strips.
Wash onion, peel, cube, add to peppers, pour in a little boiling water, add olive oil and spices and simmer until tender, evaporate water. Season the peppers with salt, vinegar and sugar to taste.

Cooked Vegetable Salad
(from mixed vegetables used in soup)

*2 1/2 cups diced cooked mixed vegetables (without onion) * 1 apple ** 1 dill pickle * 1/2 onion or chives, or leek * (green dill) * şalt * sugar ** wine vinegar * 2 tbs. salad oil*

Cube mixed vegetables finely.
Wash apple, and grate coarsely together with dill pickle.
Chop onion and greens.
Combine all the ingredients, add salt, sugar and vinegar to taste, sprinkle with oil

Cooked Vegetables in Mustard Sauce

*1/2 cup dried beans * 3 medium potatoes * 8 oz. carrots * 4 oz. kohlrabi ** 8 oz. savoy cabbage or cabbage * 2 oz. celery root * 1 apple * 1 dill pickle * 1 small onion or chives * 3 tbs. oil * 2 tbs. mustard * salt * sugar ** (green parsley, green dill)*

Pick over beans, rinse, soak for a few hours, cook in soaking water.
Clean potatoes under running water, cook.
Clean and cook vegetables or use vegetables from soup broth.
Cut cooked vegetables in strips, potatoes in slices.
Grate dill pickle and unpeeled apple.
Chop onion or chives finely.
Cream mustard in deep bowl adding oil gradually. Combine the sauce with the vegetables, add salt and sugar to taste. Sprinkle with chopped green parsley and dill.
The vegetable salad may be prepared with oil and vinegar instead of mustard sauce. This salad is a good way of using left-over vegetables from soups.

Leek Salad

*10 medium leeks * sugar * salt * wine vinegar * 2 tbs. salad oil*

Clean leeks, cut off green, tough leaves.
Boil water with salt and sugar, immerse leeks and cook uncovered. Pour off some of the water and add vinegar to taste. It should have a tart-sweet flavour. Allow the leek to cool in this broth.
Place on platter, slice each leek lengthwise and horizontally, dot with oil. Serve with fried meats and fish.

Potato Salad with Onions

*8 medium potatoes * (2 tbs. chopped green dill) * 2 tbs. chopped chives or onion * wine vinegar * salt * sugar * 3 tbs. salad oil * (6 radishes)*

Clean and peel potatoes, cook.
Clean and chop finely green dill, chives or onion.
Cube potatoes, combine with green dill, onion (or chives), add vinegar, salt and sugar to taste, dot with salad oil.
Arrange in salad bowl, garnish with radishes (cut into thin rings) and chopped greens.

DUMPLINGS, NOODLES, MACARONI AND CEREALS

Cooked-Potato Dough

Clean potatoes, cook, peel, grind in food chopper.
Measure potatoes with a cup, well pressed down, then place on board.
Add flour, half the amount of the potatoes. Flour must be measured without pressing. Mix the dough with eggs, add a pinch of salt, knead for only a short time until the ingredients combine.
Boil water with salt in a flat, covered pot.
Divide dough into several parts, shape into rolls. Divide each roll into small pieces with a knife, shape into dumplings (sticks, balls, cushions).
Prepare fat for pouring (butter or melted fat back).
Immerse dumplings in portions in sufficient amount of boiling water, so that they can float, mix, cover and cook on medium heat.
When the dough loses its raw flavour and when cut is of a uniform color place on colander, pour over with hot water, drain, arrange on heated platter, pour over with fat.

Kopytka

Cooked-Potato Dumplings

*2 cups flour * 4 cups cooked potatoes * (1 egg) * salt * 2 1/2 tbs. butter *
* 2 tbs. bread crumbs*

Clean potatoes, cook in skins, peel, grind, cool, measure.
Mix with measured sifted flour, add a pinch of salt, knead with egg (or
without egg). Roll out on a floured board, cut and shape into small balls,
small cushions or cut into small finger-shaped dumplings. Flattened balls
with a well in the middle are called kopytka.
Drop the dumplings into the boiling salted water. Cook and drain. Pour
over with hot water, arrange on a heated platter and serve immediately.
Serve with braised meats, sauerkraut in roux, with sauces or dotted with
fat or bread crumbs browned in butter.

Raw-Potato Dumplings

*10 medium potatoes * 5 medium potatoes cooked on the previous day *
* salt * 3 tbs. fat back for garnishing * 1 medium onion*

Peel potatoes, grate finely into a bowl.
Press out juice, set aside; after standing pour off juice.
Mix the raw potato pulp with the potato starch which has remained on the
bottom of the bowl, add mashed cooked potatoes. Salt.
Shape into small balls.
Cook one for trial, if the dough falls apart, add a little potato starch.
Cook in salted water on a medium flame quite long, taste, and when
cooked remove with draining spoon.
Serve poured over with fat back and cracklings or chopped onion browned
lightly in fat.

Rolled Dough

1. Kneading Dough

Sift flour, set aside part for sprinkling.
Make a well in the flour.
Beat egg, pour into flour, add a pinch of salt and water, mix with knife;
when the flour and egg combine, clean the dough off the knife and
knead with the palm until all ingredients blend. The dough should form
a uniform and satiny mixture on being cut. The more the dough is

kneaded the more air will it contain and the fluffier will it become during cooking.

2. Rolling Dough

Divide the kneaded dough into portions.
Roll out each portion from the center in all directions, pressing evenly with the rolling pin and giving the dough a round shape; cover the remaining portions with a plate so that they do not dry out.
Flour the board before rolling so that the dough does not stick to the board or the rolling pin.
Rolled dough should be dried and sprinkled lightly with flour.

3. Cutting Dough

Noodles: Cut the rolled-out and dried dough into even strips (1 1/2 inch wide). Arrange strips one on top of the other. Move to the edge of the board. Cut arranged strips crosswise into 1/8 inch-wide noodles (1 1/2 inches by 1/8 inch). After cutting the noodles separate them, toss on board and allow to dry thoroughly.
Macaroni: Cut the rolled-out and dried dough in half. Wind each half separately into rolls about the width of 3 fingers, place the roll on the edge of the board and cut crosswise into very thin strips. After cutting toss on board.
Łazanki (Square Noodles): Cut the rolled-out and dried dough into long strips (width of three fingers). Arrange long strips one on top of the other, move to the edge of the board and cut crosswise into small strips 1/3 inch wide, then arrange small strips one on top of the other and cut across into squares 1/3 inch wide.

4. Cooking the Noodles

When the dough is ready, pour water into a flat saucepan with a cover, salt and boil.
Prepare fat for dotting the noodles and all equipment necessary for cooking, draining and arranging the noodles on platter.
Roll out the dough and cut (see rolling and cutting the dough).
Drop the noodles into the boiling, salted water, dropping in only enough to cover the bottom of the saucepan and so that they float in the water. Mix, cover, cook.
Test: a) piercing dough with a fork (dough should be uniform) or b) according to smell — when the dough loses its raw smell, it is ready.

Place the cooked dough in a colander with a draining spoon, pour over with hot water, drain, drop the rest of the dough in the water.

Place the cooked dough from the colander on a heated platter, pour over with fat, mix, cover, heat on top of double boiler.

Serve immediately in a bowl.

Cut Noodles

*4 1/2 cups flour * 1 egg * 1/2 cup water * salt * 2 1/2 tbs. butter or fat back with cracklings*

Sift flour, add a pinch of salt, knead with egg and water, roll out rather thick, set aside to dry.

Put on salted water for boiling the noodles.

Brown onion in butter or render fat back and brown cracklings.

Sprinkle the dried dough with flour, cut into long strips of the same width, place one on top of the other, shift to the edge of the board, cut noodles with a sharp knife.

Cook in boiling water, drain, pour over with hot water, drain, place on heated platter, combine with fat.

Home-Made Macaroni

*4 1/2 cups flour * 2—3 tbs. water * 4—5 eggs * salt * 2 1/2 tbs. fat*

Sift flour, make a well, beat eggs, pour into flour, add a little cold water and salt, knead very thoroughly.

Divide dough into portions and roll out thin so that the grain of the board is visible. Set aside for drying.

Cut the dried dough in half, roll up each half separately, move to the edge of the board and cut with a sharp knife into very thin strips.

Toss the macaroni over floured board immediately after cutting. Boil a large amount of salted water, add macaroni, cook. When it rises to the surface, drain, pour over with hot water, drain, add fat, serve on heated platter.

Łazanki

Square Noodles

See page 100.

Spoon-Dropped Dumplings

See page 102.

French Dumplings

See page 102.

Economy French Dumplings

*2 1/2 tbs. butter * 1 egg * 2 cups flour * salt * water * pinch of baking powder * 1 1/2 tbs. fat*

Cream butter and egg yolk.

Blend with flour, beaten egg white, salt, water and baking powder, work in thoroughly with spoon.

Heat metal spoon in boiling water, take dough on spoon, place in boiling salted water, shake dough off spoon by tapping at the edge of the pot.

When all dumplings are dropped, stir, cover.

When cooked, drain dumplings, pour over with warm water, drain. Cook dumplings in portions, when made in large quantities.

Place on heated platter, combine with fat.

Serve immediately after cooking.

Fluffy and Medium-Fluffy Cereals

Measure cereal and water as specified in recipe. Bring water to the boil with added salt and fat. Rinse cereal, combine with boiling water and cook slowly on a medium flame. When the water is absorbed, stir the cereal with a fork and complete cooking by placing over boiling water or in oven. Remove cereal after 30 minutes and turn out into plate, separating the grains with a fork.

Medium-fluffy cereal is prepared in the same manner. Its consistency depends on the ratio of water to the cereal, that is why the amount of water specified in the recipe must be followed. When the cereal is dryer then usual the amount of water may be insufficient. A few spoons of water should then be added. The method of preparing cereal gruel is given in the section entitled "Milk Soups", page 94.

Unparched Fluffy Buckwheat Groats

*2 1/2 cups unparched coarse buckwheat groats * 1 1/4 times as much water as groats * 2 tbs. fat * salt*

Measure the groats, measure 1 1/4 times more water than groats, bring to the boil, add salt and fat to water.

Add groats to boiling water and cook on slow flame until the water is absorbed.

Then mix groats, cover and place in oven to bake through.

When the groats are soft, remove, separate with a fork.

Serve with milk, meat with gravy or with sauces and eggs.

Groats may also be prepared in double boiler as well as in oven. Water in bottom pot should be kept boiling until the groats are tender.

Parched Fluffy Buckwheat Groats

*2 1/2 cups parched coarse buckwheat groats * 1 1/2 times as much water as groats * 2 tbs. fat * salt*

Cook 1 1/2 times as much water as groats, add salt and fat to water, add the groats to boiling water, cook slowly until the water is completely absorbed.

Stir the groats, cover, place in oven, bake.

When the groats are fluffy, remove, separate the groats with a fork, and arrange in a round platter.

Serve with milk, with sauces and as a side-dish for braised meats.

Fluffy Millet Grits

*2 1/2 cups millet grits * 2 times as much water as millet grits * 2 tbs. fat * * salt*

Measure the grits, boil twice as much water, add salt and fat to water. Sift or rinse grits on colander, drain, place into boiling water and cook on low flame.

When all the water is absorbed, mix, cover and place in oven to roast through. Remove when tender, separate with a fork, place on round platter.

Serve with meats in gravies, green dill or tomato sauces or with milk.

If the grits are stale and bitter, they should be parboiled by dropping into boiling water and drained. Proceed according to recipe.

Fluffy Barley Cereal

Use fine or pearl barley cereal.
Prepare the same as millet grits.

Medium-Fluffy Barley Cereal

*2 1/2 cups barley (fine or pearl) cereal * 3 times as much water as barley * 2 tbs fat * salt*

Measure the barley, boil three times as much water as barley, add salt and fat.

Rinse barley in colander, drain, place in boiling water, and cook covered on very low flame.

When the barley is soft, arrange portions with spoon.

Serve with milk, sauces, fat back or with meat in gravies.

Fluffy Cracow Groats (Fine Buckwheat)

*2 1/2 cups Cracow groats * 1 1/4 times as much water as meal * * 3 1/2 tbs. fat * salt*

Prepare the same as unparched fluffy buckwheat groats.

Buckwheat Meal for Meats

*2 1/2 cups buckwheat meal (Cracow meal) * 1 1/4 times as much water as meal * salt*

Measure and pick over buckwheat meal.

Cook 1 1/4 times as much water as meal, add salt.

Add meal to boiling water, cook over low flame.

When all the water is absorbed, cover, place in oven.

When done, put through food chopper (with blade for grinding nuts) or strain through a sieve directly onto platter, cover, heat over boiling water.

Serve with braised or stewed meats.

Corn Meal

*2 1/2 cups corn meal * 2 times as much water as meal * 3 1/2 tbs. fat * salt*

Measure corn meal.

Cook twice as much water as meal, add fat and salt.

Drop meal into boiling water and stir while cooking over low heat.

When the water is absorbed, mix, cover, place in oven.

Separate with a fork when done, place in small mounds in platter.

Serve with milk, braised round steak, goulash, tomato sauce or plum jam.

142

Oatmeal

*4 cups oatmeal * salt * 5 times as much water as oatmeal*

Measure oatmeal, pour over with boiling salted water and cook over low flame, stirring from time to time until completely gruelly.
Serve poured over with milk.

Fluffy Rice

*2 1/2 cups rice * 2 times as much water as rice * 3 tbs. fat * salt*

Measure rice, pick over, rinse (if musty, pour over with boiling water a few times, drain and rinse under cold water, drain).
Boil twice as much water as rice, add fat and salt.
Add rice to boiling water, cook over low heat.
When the water is absorbed, mix, cover, place in oven.
When the grains are separate and fluffy, remove, and separate grains with fork, place on heated platter.

Fluffy Rice with Onion

*2 1/2 cups rice * 2 tbs. fat * 1/2 small onion * salt * 2 times as much water as rice*

Measure rice, pick over, rinse.
Chop onion finely, brown lightly in fat.
Boil twice as much water as rice, add salt and fat with onion.
Drop rice into boiling water, cook over low heat.
When the water is absorbed, mix, cover and place in oven.
When the rice is fluffy, remove, and separate grains with fork, arrange on heated platter.
Serve with meats in sauce.

Medium-Fluffy Rice

Prepare the same as medium-fluffy barley.

VEGETARIAN DINNERS

The most important meatless dishes are those made with dough, cereals and vegetables. To supplement their protein value it is necessary to combine them with eggs, milk and cheese. Since they usually have a very mild flavor (especially dishes with dough, cereals or potatoes) they should be seasoned with garnishes having a distinctly strong aroma and taste. Such products as dried mushrooms, tomatoes, onions, green dill, horse-radish serve this purpose whether cooked or in the form of sauces. Sauces help in making dishes such as noodles and fluffy cereals more palatable.

Products made of flour may be prepared salty or sweet with the addition of fruits and fruit products.

VEGETABLE PLATES

Vegetable Bouquet

*7 oz. carrots * 1/2 cup green peas * 1 lb. string beans * 1 medium cauliflower * 10 medium young potatoes * salt * sugar * 5 tbs. butter * * 2 tbs. bread crumbs * green dill * tomatoes * lettuce*

Wash all vegetables.
Cut carrots in a few parts, mix with peas, add a little water and cook until tender — add salt, sugar and a pat of butter, heat.
Cook string beans by pouring over with boiling water with salt and sugar. Cook cauliflower the same way.
Wash potatoes, clean, pour over with boiling water, add salt, cook, drain. Brown bread crumbs in butter.
Arrange vegetables on heated platter, dot beans, cauliflower, and potatoes with browned bread crumbs, garnish potatoes with green dill and garnish the whole with sliced tomatoes and lettuce.

Jerusalem Artichoke (Topinambour) in Béchamel Sauce

Prepare the same as cauliflower in béchamel sauce (see page 146).

Fresh Lima Beans with Butter

*2 lbs. fresh lima beans * salt * butter*

Boil water.

Husk the beans, add to boiling water, when parboiled, salt, cook through, drain.

Serve on round platter; serve butter on the side.

Beans in Tomato Sauce

*2 cups dried white beans * cooled boiled water * 5 medium tomatoes or 3 tbs. tomato paste * 3 1/2 tbs. fat (bacon or smoked fat back) * 1 small onion * 2 1/2 tbs. flour * cooking liquid from beans * salt * vinegar * * pepper * (sugar)*

Pick over beans, rinse, soak in a large amount of cooled boiled water.

Cook beans in soaking water, drain.

Rinse tomatoes, cut into segments, cook in small amount of water, strain.

Chop onion, fry in fat, add flour, brown lightly, set aside.

Dilute the roux with the cooking liquid and the strained tomatoes, stir while cooking.

Add beans to the sauce, add salt, vinegar, pepper, (sugar), mix, heat over low flame.

Serve with eggs, sausage, frankfurters.

Beans in Caramel Gravy

*2 cups dried white beans * cooled boiled water * 3 1/2 tbs. fat (bacon or fat back) * 1 small onion * 2 1/2 tbs. flour * bay leaf * allspice * cooking liquid from beans * salt * pepper * (wine vinegar) * 1 1/2 tbs. caramelized sugar*

Pick over beans, rinse, soak in a large amount of cooled boiled water.

Cook beans in soaking water, drain.

Brown sugar to golden color, prepare the caramel.

Chop onion, brown lightly in fat, add flour, brown lightly, add bay leaf and allspice, set aside.

Dilute the roux with the cooking liquid of the beans and caramel, stir while cooking, combine beans with sauce, add salt, pepper, vinegar to taste, heat over a very low flame.

Serve with frankfurters, eggs.

Dried Bean or Pea Cutlets

*2 cups dried white beans * cooled boiled water * 3 1/2 tbs. fat * 1/2 small onion * 1 egg * salt * pepper * B r e a d i n g: 5 tbs. flour * 1 egg * 7 tbs. bread crumbs * 5 tbs. fat for frying*

Pick over beans, rinse, soak in cooled boiled water.

Cook beans in soaking water, drain.

Chop onion, brown lightly in fat.

Put half the beans through the food chopper.

Mix the ground and unground beans with the browned onion, egg, salt and pepper.

Sprinkle the board with flour, shape the cutlet mixture into a thick roll, divide with a knife into 1 inch-thick parts.

Shape into high round cutlets, dip into beaten egg, then bread crumbs, score top of cutlets.

Heat fat, fry cutlets over high heat to a light-gold color; arrange on a long platter.

Serve with sharp sauces or salad.

Fried Summer Squash with Tomatoes

*3 lb. summer squash * 5 tbs. fat * 1 lb. tomatoes * 1 small onion * salt * * sugar * pepper*

Clean squash, peel, cube or slice thickly, fry on both sides.

Clean tomatoes, cut into pieces, chop onion finely, dot with boiling water, cook together, strain.

Add fried squash with fat to tomatoes, and braise over low heat reducing the liquid.

Before finishing, season with salt, sugar and pepper.

Squash is braised over very low heat as it overcooks quickly and easily.

Cauliflower in Béchamel Sauce

*1 medium cauliflower * salt * 2 tbs. sugar * B é c h a m e l   s a u c e: 3 tbs. butter * 5 tbs. flour * 1 cup milk * salt * lemon juice * 2 egg yolks * * T o p p i n g: 2 tbs. grated Parmesan or Swiss cheese * 2 tbs. bread crumbs * 2 tbs. butter for bread crumbs*

Clean cauliflower, slit deeply.

Heat water with salt and sugar, add cauliflower head down, cook until tender.

Prepare sauce. Melt butter, combine with flour, set aside, dilute with milk, stir while cooking, add salt and a drop of lemon juice. Before finishing add raw egg yolks.

Grate cheese.

Brown bread crumbs in butter.

Drain cooked cauliflower, place in casserole, pour over with béchamel sauce, sprinkle with cheese, add butter with bread crumbs, place in oven. Serve in casserole.

Cabbage Boiled in Milk

*1 small head of cabbage * 1 cup milk * salt * 2 1/2 tbs. sugar * 3 1/2 tbs. butter * 2 tbs. bread crumbs*

Clean cabbage, shred coarsely, remove core.

Boil a little water, place cabbage in water, parboil, pour in milk, add sugar and salt to taste, cook quickly uncovered, drain.

Arrange on platter, dot with bread crumbs browned in butter.

Parzybroda

Boiled Cabbage and Potatoes

*1 small head of cabbage * 5 medium potatoes * 4 1/2 tbs. fat * 4 tbs. flour * salt * pepper*

Cut cabbage into thick cubes.

Clean potatoes, slice, place with cabbage, pour over with a small amount of boiling water, cook uncovered.

Prepare a light-golden roux with fat and flour, dilute with cooking liquid from cabbage, combine with cabbage, cook, season with salt and pepper. Serve with black bread.

Cabbage Cutlets

*1 small head of cabbage * stale roll (3 oz.) * 1/2 cup milk for soaking * * 3 tbs. fat * 1/2 small onion * 1 egg * salt * pepper * nutmeg * B r e a d - i n g: 4 tbs. flour * 1 egg * 6 tbs. bread crumbs * 5 tbs. fat for frying*

Clean cabbage, cut into pieces, boil in water, squeeze out in towel.

Soak roll, drain off milk.

Slice onion, brown lightly in fat.

Put cabbage and soaked roll through food chopper.

Mix with onion, egg, salt and spices.

Sprinkle flour on board, shape the mixture into a thick roll, divide into 1 inch pieces.

Shape into small, round, high cutlets, dip in egg and bread crumbs, score top of cutlets.

Heat fat, fry cutlets over high heat to a light-gold color on both sides. Arrange on long platter.

Serve with tart sauces, especially horse-radish or tomato sauce and with lettuce.

Baked Cabbage

*1 small head of cabbage * stale roll (3 oz.) * 1/2 cup milk for soaking * * 3 1/2 tbs. fat * 1 small onion * 1 egg * salt * pepper * nutmeg * 1 tbs. potato starch * 1 tbs. butter for greasing baking pan * 2 tbs. bread crumbs for pan * 1/2 cup sour cream for dotting*

Prepare mixture as for cabbage cutlets (see above). Add 1 tbs. potato starch. Mix. Grease a long baking pan, sprinkle with bread crumbs, spread mixture in pan, even, smear the surface with sour cream. Bake until brown in a hot oven.

Serve with potatoes and horse-radish or tomato sauce.

Corn

*10 ears of sugar corn * salt * sugar * butter*

Select young juicy corn.

Boil water with salt and sugar.

Remove husks and silk from corn, rinse, place in boiling water, cook over high flame, drain.

Serve wrapped in a napkin on rectangular platter, serve butter on the side.

Masurian Carrots

*2 lb. carrots * 3/4 cup milk * 5 medium potatoes * salt * sugar * 5 tbs. fat (fat back, butter)*

Clean and wash carrots and potatoes, cut in cubes, pour over with a small amount of boiling water and cook.

When parboiled add milk, salt and sugar to taste, cook over low heat until tender.

Before serving dot with fat back and cracklings or butter.

148

Carrots and Peas with Toast

*2 1/2 cups grated carrots * 1 cup green peas * 3 tbs. butter * 2 tbs. flour *
* salt * sugar * T o a s t: 10 slices of white bread * milk for soaking *
* 2 eggs * 8 tbs. bread crumbs * 1/2 cup fat for frying*

Clean carrots, rinse and grate; young carrots may be sliced or diced;
cook covered in a small amount of water over high flame.
Shell peas, add to carrots, when parboiled, reduce water. Add butter,
flour, salt and sugar to taste to the carrots mixed with peas, heat, if
necessary add water so they are not too dry.
Place sliced bread on platter, sprinkle generously with milk.
When the bread absorbs milk, dip in egg, bread crumbs, fry in hot fat
to golden color.
Arrange carrots and peas on round platter with the toast all around.

Carrots and String Beans with Toast

*2 1/2 cups cut carrots * 1 1/2 cups cut string beans * 3 tbs. fat * 2 tbs.
flour * salt * sugar * T o a s t: 10 slices of white bread * milk for soaking *
* 2 eggs * 8 tbs. bread crumbs * 1/2 cup fat for frying*

Clean and slice young carrots.
Clean beans, remove strings, slice, add to carrots, pour over a small
amount of boiling water and cook.
Prepare a light gold roux, dilute with cooking liquid, combine with vege-
tables, add salt and sugar to taste, heat.
Serve with fried toast or potatoes (see above).

Carrots and Kohlrabi with Toast

*2 1/2 cups cut carrots * 1 1/2 cups cut kohlrabi * 3 tbs. fat. * 2 tbs. flour *
* salt * sugar * T o a s t: 10 slices of white bread * milk for soaking *
* 2 eggs * 8 tbs. bread crumbs * 1/2 cup fat for frying*

Prepare the same as carrots and string beans.
Serve with fried toast or potatoes (see above).

Vegetable Cutlets

*4 cups mixed cooked vegetables * 2 medium cooked potatoes * 3 tbs. fat *
* 1 small onion * 1 egg * salt * (pepper) * 3 tbs. mixed greens * 6 tbs.
bread crumbs * 5 tbs. fat for frying*

149

Put cooked vegetables through food chopper. Peel onion, slice, brown lightly in fat. Combine vegetables with onion, egg, salt, mixed greens (and pepper); if the cutlet is too thin, add bread crumbs.

Mix thoroughly, divide into 10 parts.

Bread each part, shape into small, high, round cutlets and fry to a golden color on both sides.

Serve with tart sauces or cucumbers, potatoes, lettuce, sauerkraut.

Stewed Cucumbers

*10 medium young cucumbers * 4 tbs. butter * 3 tbs. flour * salt * lemon juice * green dill*

Peel cucumber, cube, pour over with a small amount of boiling water, and simmer.

Prepare a white roux from butter and flour, dilute with cooking liquid, combine with cucumbers, heat, season with salt and lemon juice and garnish with chopped green dill. Serve with French fried potatoes.

Stewed Tomatoes

*10 medium tomatoes * 4 1/2 tbs. butter * salt * 4 tbs. sugar*

Wash tomatoes, add butter, dot with boiling water and simmer until tender over low heat.

Season with salt and sugar.

Serve with fried and roast meat (especially rare), with eggs and potatoes, with fried or baked vegetarian dishes.

Tomatoes Stuffed with Rice

*4 dried mushrooms * 1 small onion * 3 tbs. butter * 3/4 cup rice (groats, pearl barley) * 10 medium firm tomatoes * 3/4 cup sour cream * 4 tbs. grated Parmesan cheese * 1 1/2 tbs. butter for dotting * green dill * salt*

Prepare stuffing. Wash mushrooms, rinse, cook covered. Drain. Chop.

Dice onion finely, brown lightly in fat.

Measure rice, groats or barley. Add water to mushroom liquid to obtain twice as much as cereal, add salt to taste, onion in fat and chopped mushrooms. Boil.

Add the cereal to boiling mixture and cook over low heat.

When the water is completely absorbed, stir, cover and bake in oven. Rinse tomatoes, scoop out centers (use centers for sauce). Stuff the tomatoes with cereal quite compactly, cover the top, place in casserole. Pour sour cream over each tomato, sprinkle with grated cheese, dot with butter and place in hot oven.

When the tomatoes soften, garnish with green dill.

Serve in casserole.

Fried Celery Root

*10 thick pieces of cleaned celery root * salt * lemon juice * 3 tbs. butter * * 6 tbs. flour * 1/2 cup milk * 7 tbs. bread crumbs * 1 egg * 5 tbs. fat for frying*

Select medium-sized celery root, clean and scrub under running water (cut the fine root and use for soups); pare, slice in rings about 1/2 inch thick, select rings of uniform size (use rest for soups).

Pour boiling water over celery root, add salt and lemon juice, cook slowly, do not overcook.

Remove slices carefully with ladle, drain, cool.

Prepare a very thick sauce: melt butter, combine with flour, sauté lightly, dilute roux with cold milk and stir while cooking, add salt to taste.

Dip the celery root slice into sauce (use a fork), then bread crumbs, dip in beaten egg, and then again in bread crumbs.

beaten egg, and then again in bread crumbs.

Place the breaded celery into heated fat and brown quickly on both sides. Serve immediately after frying with tomato sauce.

Asparagus in Béchamel Sauce in Shells

*10 thick stalks of asparagus * salt * sugar * B é c h a m e l s a u c e: 4 tbs. butter * 6 tbs. flour * 1 cup sour cream * salt * lemon juice * 1 egg yolk * * T o p p i n g: 2 tbs. bread crumbs * 2 tbs. butter * 3 tbs. grated Parmesan cheese*

. Clean asparagus, cut off soft parts and cook in boiling water with salt and sugar, drain and cut asparagus into 1/4 inch pieces.

Grate cheese. Brown bread crumbs in butter.

Prepare sauce. Melt butter, add flour, blend, set aside.

Dilute roux with sour cream, stir while cooking.

Add salt, lemon juice and egg yolk, combine with cut asparagus. Place asparagus in shells, even out, dot with butter and bread crumbs, sprinkle with cheese, bake.

151

Young Spinach

*3 cups cooked young spinach and radish leaves * 3 tbs. butter * 5 tbs. flour * 1 cup milk * salt * pinch of sugar * (garlic)*

Clean spinach and radish leaves and rinse several times in a large amount of water, cut off roots from spinach, cut up leaves together with stems.

Prepare a white roux, with butter and flour. Dilute with milk, stir while cooking, add diced spinach and radish leaves, combine, add salt and sugar to taste.

Cook a while. Crushed garlic may be added.

Serve with eggs and potato purée or fluffy groats, fluffy buckwheat meal, toast, etc.

Spinach with White Roux and Eggs

*4 cups cooked spinach * 3 tbs. butter * 5 tbs. flour * 3/4 cup milk * * salt * pinch of sugar * garlic*

Boil salted water. Clean spinach. Wash. Cut off stems.

Place in boiling salted water, cook, uncovered, over high flame until spinach comes apart when pressed between the fingers. Drain thoroughly, put through food chopper.

Melt butter, add flour, combine, heat, set aside.

Dilute roux with milk, stir while cooking, combine with spinach, add salt, sugar and crushed garlic to taste, cook.

Serve with fried or poached eggs, with potatoes, fried toast, etc.

Potato Baskets

*5 medium potatoes * salt * 1 1/2 tbs. butter * 1/2 cup milk * thick tomato paste * 2 egg yolks * 2 tbs. butter for dotting*

Clean and peel potatoes, cook in salted water, drain, mash, combine with butter, add a little milk to make a purée of average consistency, shape over heat.

Divide potato mixture into three parts, add raw egg yolks to one, combine, add tomato paste to another, combine to a brightly colored mass, the third one should remain white.

Put each part through a pastry bag, squeeze a small round ring as basket base and then three layers, one on top of the other.

Press directly on a heated platter, arrange in alternate colors, and fill with cooked vegetables: the white baskets with carrots, the red ones with cauliflower, the yellow with Brussels sprouts; dot the top with butter. Place in hot oven, remove immediately before serving.

Potato Cutlets

*10 medium potatoes * 3 tbs. fat * 1/2 small onion * 1 egg * 1/2 tbs. potato starch * salt * pepper * nutmeg * B r e a d i n g: 5 tbs. flour * * 1 egg * 5 tbs. bread crumbs * 5 tbs. fat for frying*

Clean and pare potatoes, cook, drain, put through food chopper.
Chop onion, brown lightly in fat.
Combine potatoes with onion, egg, potato starch, salt and spices.
Place potato mixture on floured board, shape into a thick roll, divide into parts (1 inch thick).
Shape in flour into high, small round cutlets, dip in egg and bread crumbs, score.
Heat fat, fry to light gold on both sides over high heat.
Serve on long platter.
Serve with tart sauces, salad or as a side-dish with vegetables.

Potato Pancakes with Onions

*10 medium potatoes * 1 medium onion * salt * 5 tbs. fat for frying*

Clean and pare potatoes, grate, squeeze out. Pour out liquid.
Combine grated potatoes with starch settled on the bottom, with grated onion and salt. Shape into uniform balls.
Heat part of fat in skillet, place balls on hot fat, flatten with a spoon, shape.
Fry to golden color on both sides over high flame, add fat when necessary.
Serve immediately after frying while they are crispy.
Serve with mustard, horse-radish, salads.

Steamed Potato Pancakes

*10 medium potatoes * 3/4 cup milk * salt * 1/2 cup fat for frying*

Clean and peel potatoes, grate, add boiling milk, combine quickly, add salt to taste.

Heat fat on skillet. Drop potato mixture from spoon, flatten and brown on both sides.

Serve immediately after frying.

They can be served piquantly or with sugar, cranberries, etc.

Potatoes Braised with Fat Back and Onion

*15 medium potatoes * 5 tbs. fat back (smoked) * 2 medium onions * * salt * pepper * 1/2 cup water * 2 tbs. fat*

Cut fat back in strips.

Chop onion finely.

Peel potatoes, slice, place part on bottom of saucepan.

Place half the fat back on top of the potatoes, sprinkle with part of onion, salt, pepper.

Place another layer of potatoes, top as above, cover with potatoes.

Dot the whole with fat, add water, cover saucepan, place in hot oven.

Bake until all the water evaporates. When tender serve in platter. Serve with dill pickles, cabbage salad, horse-radish and beets, etc.

Tart Potatoes

*8 medium potatoes * 3 1/2 tbs. fat * 1 small onion * 5 tbs. flour * * allspice * bay leaf * pepper * salt * vinegar*

Clean and peel potatoes, cut in thick cubes, pour over with boiling salted water, cook, drain.

Chop onion, brown lightly in fat, add flour, brown, stir while diluting with water or cooking liquid from vegetables, add spices, salt and vinegar to taste, heat. Add potatoes to sauce, braise for a short time over low heat, stirring from time to time.

Serve when potatoes are tender.

Potato and Mushroom Casserole

*1/2 lb. fresh mushrooms (champignons) * 1 medium onion * 2 tbs. butter * 1 cup sour cream * salt * pepper * 8 medium potatoes * 2 tbs. butter for dotting*

Clean and dice mushrooms.

Chop onion finely, brown lightly in butter, add the diced mushrooms, a little water and braise slowly, covered.

When mushrooms are tender, combine with sour cream, add salt and pepper to taste.

Clean potatoes, peel, slice, place in boiling salted water, cook and drain; use the liquid for soup.

Combine potatoes with mushrooms, place in casserole, dot with unmelted butter.

Bake until potatoes are tender.

Serve in casserole with raw salads.

Potatoes Baked in Sour Cream

*8 medium potatoes * salt * 2 small onions * 3 tbs. butter * 2—3 tbs. chopped green dill * 1 cup sour cream*

Clean and peel potatoes, slice and cook by adding to boiling salted water, drain.

Chop onion finely, brown lightly in butter, place in casserole, mix with green dill and sour cream.

Add cooked potatoes to this sauce, salt to taste, cover, place in oven, bake until tender, being careful to prevent burning or too thick a sauce. If the sauce is too thick, add a little water.

Serve in casserole with raw salad.

Potatoes au Gratin in Béchamel Sauce

*10 medium potatoes * salt * B é c h a m e l   s a u c e: 3 1/2 tbs. butter * * 5 tbs. flour * 1 cup sour cream * salt * 2 egg yolks * lemon juice * * T o p p i n g: 1/3 béchamel sauce * 2—3 tbs. milk * 1 egg * 1 1/2 tbs. butter * 4 tbs. grated Parmesan*

Clean, pare and slice potatoes, parboil by dropping in boiling salted water, drain.

Prepare sauce. Melt butter, add flour, mix, brown lightly.

Dilute the roux with sour cream, stir while heating, if necessary add a little milk (the sauce should be thick).

Add salt and lemon juice to sauce, combine with egg yolks and half the grated cheese.

Add 2/3 of the sauce to the potatoes, mix, place in casserole, level. Dilute the rest of the sauce with a little milk, mix with egg, pour over top of potatoes, sprinkle with grated cheese, dot with butter and bake. Serve with raw vegetable salads.

Potatoes Baked with Eggs

*10 medium potatoes * 4 eggs * 3 tbs. fat * 1 medium onion * salt * * pepper * 1 cup sour cream * 1 1/2 tbs. fat for greasing casserole*

Wash and cook potatoes, slice.
Hard-boil the eggs, cool, slice.
Chop onion, brown lightly in fat.
Grease bottom and sides of casserole.
Divide potatoes in 3 parts, place 1/3 on the bottom of the casserole, pour over fat with onion, add salt and pepper.
Cover the layer of potatoes with half the eggs, add a layer of potatoes and onion, add salt and pepper, cover with eggs and potatoes, pour over with sour cream, place in hot oven.
Serve with raw vegetable salad.

Potatoes à la Nelson

*4 dried mushrooms * 1 medium onion * 3 tbs. fat * 4 tbs. flour * 1 cup sour cream * salt * pepper * 10 medium potatoes*

Prepare sauce. Wash mushrooms, rinse, pour over with a small amount of water and cook, reduce liquid, squeeze liquid from mushrooms, put through food chopper.
Dice onion finely, brown lightly in fat. Add flour, heat. Dilute roux with the mushroom liquid and sour cream, add salt and pepper to taste, cook.
Cook potatoes in skins, drain, cool, peel, slice, sprinkle with salt. Grease casserole, place potatoes in layers. Dot every layer with fat, chopped mushrooms and sauce, pour the rest of the sauce over the surface, bake in hot oven.
Serve in casserole with raw vegetable salad.

PREPARATION AND SERVING OF PUDDINGS

Grease sides and center of pudding mold with butter and sprinkle with sifted bread crumbs or flour.
Put on water for cooking pudding in a pot with a tight-fitting cover, in which the pudding mold fits without difficulty.
Prepare the pudding mixture, place in form, even out, close the mold with tight fitting cover and set in pot with boiling water. The water should cover about 3/4 of the mold, so that it stands upright.

During cooking it is necessary to add small amounts of boiling water, so that the evaporating of the water does not cause the pudding to burn.

The pot in which the pudding is steaming should be covered. Pudding should be steamed over medium heat for 3/4 hour. When the pudding begins to shrink from sides, remove from water, uncover, place on board, cut pudding from mold. Unmold by inverting on a hot platter. Mark portions with a hot knife, dot the top with browned butter or with a part of the sauce, serve the rest of the sauce in gravy boat.

Cauliflower or Broccoli Pudding

*1/2 medium cauliflower * salt * sugar * 1 cup milk * 5 tbs. butter * * 1 cup flour * 6 eggs * 1 tbs. butter for mold * 2 tbs. bread crumbs for mold * 3 tbs. butter for dotting * 2 tbs. bread crumbs for browning*

Prepare the pudding mold, put up water for steaming the core. Wash and clean cauliflower, cut into strips, cook all in boiling water with salt and sugar to taste, drain, divide cauliflower into small flowerets.

Heat milk with a little butter, add flour, mix quickly so that the sauce is not lumpy, place over low heat and cook, stirring until thick and shiny.

Place sauce in bowl, add egg yolks one at time to hot dough, mix 20 minutes with wooden spoon.

Beat egg whites, fold into dough, blend with dough and cauliflower, add salt to taste, and place in mold. Cover form and place in pot with boiling water. Steam over medium heat for 3/4 hour.

Unmold, place in round platter, mark portions with knife, dot with browned butter or butter with bread crumbs. Serve immediately after cooking.

Asparagus Pudding

*15 medium stalks of asparagus * salt * sugar * 1 cup milk * 5 tbs. butter * * 1 cup flour * 6 eggs * 1 tbs. butter for mold * 2 tbs. bread crumbs for mold * 3 tbs. butter for dotting * 2 tbs. bread crumbs for browning*

Clean asparagus, drop in boiling water and cook with salt and sugar, drain. Cut up the tender parts of the asparagus into pieces 3/4 inch long, discard rest. Proceed as above.

Cabbage Pudding

*1 small head of cabbage * 2 tbs. fat * 1 small onion * stale roll (3 oz.) *
* milk for soaking * 3 tbs. butter * 4 eggs * 2 tbs. bread crumbs * salt *
* pepper * sugar * nutmeg * 1 tbs. butter for mold * 2 tbs. bread crumbs
for mold * 3 tbs. butter for dotting * 2 tbs. bread crumbs for browning*

Clean cabbage, cut into large pieces, place in boiling salted water, cook.
Prepare pudding mold, put on water for steaming.
Brown onion lightly in fat. Soak roll in milk, drain off milk.
Drain cooked cabbage, cool, squeeze out water through towel, put cabbage,
onion and roll through food chopper.
Cream butter, add egg yolks one at a time.
Combine cabbage, onion and roll with creamed yolks, add 2 tbs. bread
crumbs, add salt, pepper, sugar and nutmeg to taste, mix thoroughly.
Beat egg whites, mix pudding mixture with beaten egg whites, place in
mold, cover, place in pot with boiling water.
Steam for 1/4 hour. When ready, remove from mold, place on round
platter, mark portions with a knife, dot with butter or butter with bread
crumbs. Serve immediately after unmolding.

Spinach or Kale Pudding

*2 cups cooked spinach * stale roll (3 oz.) * milk for soaking * 3 tbs.
butter * 4 egg yolks * salt * garlic * nutmeg * 5 egg whites * 1 tbs. butter
for mold * 2 tbs. bread crumbs for mold * 3 tbs. butter for dotting *
* 2 tbs. bread crumbs for browning*

Put up water with salt for cooking spinach. Clean and wash spinach,
drain.
Place spinach in boiling water, cook uncovered over high heat until the
spinach comes apart when pressed between the fingers, drain on colander,
squeeze out water with spoon.
Prepare pudding mold, put on water for steaming.
Soak roll in milk, drain off milk, grind together with spinach.
Cream butter, add egg yolks one at a time.
Combine spinach and creamed egg yolks, add salt, garlic, nutmeg to taste,
blend thoroughly.
Beat egg whites, combine with pudding mixture.
Place pudding mixture into mold, cover and set for steaming. Steam
for 3/4 hour.
Unmold on round platter, mark each portion with a knife, dot with butter,
or butter with bread crumbs, or serve with sour cream or tomato sauce.
Serve immediately after unmolding.

DISHES MADE WITH FLOUR

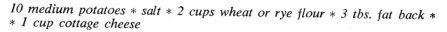

Lemieszka

Potato and Flour Porridge with Cheese

*10 medium potatoes * salt * 2 cups wheat or rye flour * 3 tbs. fat back *
* 1 cup cottage cheese*

Pour boiling water to cover peeled potatoes, salt, cook.
Mash potatoes without draining and add flour while hot.
Mix thoroughly and heat simultaneously.
When flour has all been blended, cover pot, place over very low heat until the mixture thickens.
When the dish loses its raw aroma, arrange on a platter, forming half-moons with a spoon, dot with fat back, sprinkle with crumbled cheese.
Serve with sour milk.

Prażucha

Gruel

*4 cups wheat or buckwheat flour * 2 cups water * salt * 3 1/2 tbs.
butter or smoked fat back * 1 cup cottage cheese*

Place flour in oven, brown to golden color, mix frequently.
Cook water with salt.
Pour boiling water into flour, beat briskly with a flat spoon in order to avoid lumps while heating; place porridge over very low heat until it thickens and has no raw aroma.
Melt butter.
Dip a tablespoon into the butter, place small dumplings of the gruel on a platter, dot with butter, sprinkle with cheese.
Serve with fresh or sour milk.

Knedle Filled with Onion

*F i l l i n g: 4 1/2 tbs. fat * 2 small onions * 5 tbs. bread crumbs * salt *
* pepper * D o u g h: 2 cups flour * 10 medium potatoes * (1 egg) *
* salt * 3 tbs. butter or fat back for dotting*

Prepare filling. Chop onion finely, place in hot fat, stew slowly. Add bread crumbs, salt and pepper to taste, mix, fry, cool.

Prepare dough. Wash potatoes, cook, peel, put through food chopper. Combine grated potatoes with sifted flour, add egg and salt, knead. Shape into a roll.

Cut roll into little cakes, spread with filling, seal and shape into balls.

Cook the balls in boiling salted water, remove with draining spoon, pour over with warm water, place on heated platter, dot with browned butter or fat back, and serve immediately.

Knedle Filled with Mushrooms

F i l l i n g: *5 dried mushrooms * 3 tbs. bread crumbs * 2 tbs. fat * * 1 small onion * salt * pepper ** D o u g h: *10 medium potatoes * 2 cups flour * (1 egg) * salt * 3 tbs. butter or fat back for dotting*

Prepare filling. Wash, clean and rinse mushrooms, add water, cook, drain, put through food chopper (use the cooking liquid for sauces or soups).

Chop onion, brown lightly in fat, add bread crumbs, heat, mix with mushrooms, add salt and pepper to taste.

Prepare dough and knedle as in previous recipe.

Knedle Filled with Sauerkraut

F i l l i n g: *1 1/2 cups sauerkraut * 1 1/2 tbs. fat * 1/2 small onion * * pepper * salt ** D o u g h: *10 medium potatoes * 2 cups flour * (1 egg) * * salt * 3 tbs. butter or fat back for dotting*

Prepare filling. Cut up sauerkraut, cook in small amount of water, drain, chop.

Brown onion lightly in fat, combine with cabbage, add salt and pepper to taste, heat.

Prepare dough and knedle as given above.

Leniwe Pierogi

Cheese Dumplings

*2 1/2 cups drained cottage cheese * salt * 3 tbs. butter * 4 egg yolks * * 5 egg whites * 1 1/4 cups flour * 2 tbs. bread crumbs * 3 tbs. butter*

Strain cheese through sieve.

Cream butter, add egg yolks, one at a time, salt, add cheese, cream.

Beat egg whites, fold into mixture, sprinkle with flour and mix dough lightly.

160

Place dough on floured board, form into a rather thick roll, flatten with knife, score, cut into small pierogi (pierogi expand during cooking). Drop pierogi in portions into boiling salted water, cook, remove with draining spoon onto round platter, dot with browned butter and bread crumbs (polonaise topping) and serve immediately to avoid their becoming flat.

Leniwe Pierogi Made with Potatoes

*4 cups cooked potatoes * 2 cups flour * 1 cup drained cottage cheese * * 1 egg * salt * 3 tbs. butter or fat back * (sugar)*

Clean potatoes, peel, cook, put through food chopper, cool. Combine with sifted flour and cheese, knead with egg, add a pinch of salt.
Shape on floured board into roll (not thicker than 1 inch), flatten, cut into diagonal strips (1/2 inch wide). Drop pierogi into boiling salted water, drain, place on heated platter, dot with browned fat. Powdered sugar may be used to garnish pierogi.

Leniwe Pierogi Made with Potato Starch

*3 cups cottage cheese * 3 medium cooked potatoes * 1 egg * 2 cups flour * 2 tbs. potato starch * salt * 3 1/2 tbs. fat back or butter * 2 tbs. bread crumbs*

Clean and pare potatoes, cook, put through food chopper together with cheese.
Add egg, flour and potato starch to the mixture, salt to taste, work into dough.
Divide dough into parts, shape into roll (not thicker than 1 inch), cut into diagonal strips (about 1/2 inch wide) of uniform size.
Drop into boiling salted water in parts, cook, remove with draining spoon, drain. Place on platter dot with butter and bread crumbs. Serve immediately.

Dropped Dumplings with Cheese

*5 cups flour * salt * 3 eggs * water * 3 1/2 tbs. butter or fat back * * 1 cup cottage cheese*

Sift flour, place in bowl, add salt, eggs and water, work thoroughly with spoon into a thick batter, easy to be picked up with spoon (precaution should be taken not to add too much water).
Cook water with salt, heat metal spoon in boiling water, take dough on

spoon, place in boiling water and drop dumplings by tapping at the edge of the pot.

Stir dumplings in water, cook covered, and when they lose raw aroma, drain, place on platter, dot with fat back and serve with crumbled cottage cheese.

Oatmeal Dumplings

*5 cups oatmeal * 1 cup milk * water * 1 1/2 cups flour * 3 eggs * salt * * 2 tbs. fat back*

Boil milk, pour over oatmeal, add a little water, stir and cook until it thickens.

Add wheat flour, eggs, salt to oatmeal, and work thoroughly with spoon. Drop dumplings into boiling salted water with a spoon (see above), mix, cover, cook slowly, drain, place on heated platter, dot with fat.

Serve with fat back, with tomato or fruit sauces or without fat and with milk.

Buckwheat Dumplings with Cheese

*2 cups buckwheat flour * 1/2 cup boiling water * 3 cups wheat flour * * salt * 1 cup cottage cheese * 3 tbs. fat back*

Pour boiling water into buckwheat flour, mix with a spoon, add wheat flour and a pinch of salt, work thoroughly.

Put up water with salt, drop small dumplings into boiling water (see above), stir, cover and cook.

Render fat back, brown cracklings.

Drain dumplings, pour over with warm water, drain, place on platter, mix with fat, sprinkle with cheese, cover, heat over boiling water and serve immediately.

Steamed Dumplings au Gratin

*1 cup water * salt * 1/2 cup butter * 1 cup flour * 4 eggs * 1 tbs. butter for greasing casserole * 1 tbs. butter for garnish * 4 tbs. Parmesan or Swiss cheese*

Cook water with salt and butter.

Place flour on a sheet of paper and add gradually to boiling water, stirring quickly to avoid lumps.

162

Stir constantly while cooking until the water evaporates and the dough no longer sticks to the bottom of the pot.

Remove from heat, place in bowl and while hot, add eggs, one at a time, mixing constantly.

Cook water with salt. Boil.

Drop dumplings with a spoon, shaping them uniformly small.

Cover and bring to a boil once over medium heat.

Test by piercing one dumpling. When the dumplings are cooked through, remove carefully with a draining spoon, place in three layers in a caserrole. Dot each layer with butter and grated cheese. Place in very hot oven so that it bakes quickly and brown. Bake about 10—15 minutes. Serve immediately.

Pyzy

Silesian Yeast Dumplings

L e a v e n: *1 oz. yeast * 1 cup milk * 2 cups flour * 1 tbs. sugar *
* D o u g h: 2 cups flour * 3 eggs * 3 tbs. butter * salt * 1 tbs. butter
for greasing * 2 tbs. butter for garnish*

Dilute yeast with milk, add flour and sugar. Mix with a spoon, set in warm place to rise. Let rise by 50%, then add rest of flour, add the eggs, melted butter and salt and blend thoroughly with spoon, if necessary add a few spoons of milk but dough should be rather thick.

Smooth and set in warm place to rise again.

Prepare a shallow wide saucepan for cooking the pyzy, one in which a strainer will fit with cover.

Place a piece of white thick percale, greased with butter, on the bottom of the strainer.

When dough doubles its bulk, shape with hands, smeared with melted butter, into large balls (1 1/2 inch in diameter).

Place them at intervals on the bottom of the strainer, cover and set aside to rise again.

Cook water in pot. When the pyzy double in size, place the strainer with pyzy on top of pot with boiling water and steam covered for 3/4 hour without removing cover. The water should boil not too strongly. After 3/4 hour, uncover and test with a toothpick. If the toothpick comes out dry, remove from the steam helping with a knife and arrange on platter dotted with melted butter and a sweet or sour sauce (or serve with roast loin of pork or braised roast beef).

Noodles with Cheese

*4 1/2 cups flour * salt * 1 egg * 1/2 cup water * 3 tbs. butter or fat back with cracklings * 1 cup cottage cheese*

Sift flour, add a pinch of salt, knead with egg and water, roll out quite thick, set aside to dry (see page 137—138).

Put up salted water for cooking noodles.

Sprinkle dough with flour, cut into even wide strips, place one on top of the other, shift to the edge of board, cut with sharp knife, when cut, throw over floured board.

Drop noodles in boiling salted water, drain, pour over with hot water, drain, place on heated platter, mix with fat, cover, heat over boiling water. Serve with crumbled cottage cheese.

Łazanki with Cabbage or Sauerkraut

*1 medium head of cabbage or 2 lbs. sauerkraut * 4 1/2 tbs. fat * 1 medium onion * salt * pepper * sugar * D o u g h: 4 1/2 cups flour * 1 egg * * 1/2 cup water * 3 tbs. fat back or butter * salt*

Clean cabbage of withered leaves, rinse, cut into pieces, cook in salted water, drain, squeeze out in towel, put through food chopper (cook sauerkraut uncovered in a small amount of water).

Chop onion, brown lightly in fat.

Mix cabbage with browned onion, add salt, pepper and sugar to taste, heat (if sauerkraut is used, do not add sugar).

Prepare dough. Sift flour, add a pinch of salt, knead with egg and water, roll out fine, set aside to dry.

Cut the dried dough (see page 138).

Toss lightly on floured board after cutting.

Cook łazanki in boiling salted water, drain, pour over with hot water, drain.

Mix the cooked łazanki with hot cabbage, place on heated platter, dot with fat, cover and heat over boiling water.

They may be placed in greased casserole, dotted with fat back and baked in oven.

Baked łazanki may be served with mushroom or tomato sauce.

Baked Łazanki with Cheese

*4 1/2 cups flour * 1 egg * 1/2 cup water * salt * 1 1/2 cups cottage cheese * 1 egg * 3 1/2 tbs. butter*

Prepare dough, divide in parts, roll out finely, set aside to dry. Cut the dried dough (see page 138).

Mash cheese, combine with egg and salt (or sugar if the łazanki are to be served sweet).

Brown butter.

Place łazanki in boiling salted water, cook, drain, pour over with hot water, drain, mix with butter and cheese, salt to taste (sugar may be added if dish is to be served sweet).

Place in greased casserole, dot with butter, and bake.

Serve in casserole.

Macaroni with Vegetables and Tomatoes

*1 cup grated carrots * 1/2 cup grated parsley root * 1/2 cup grated celery root * 2 medium onions * 3 tbs. fat * paprika * 1 lb. macaroni * * 4 tbs. diced bacon * 4 tbs. tomato paste * salt*

Wash and clean vegetables, grate, add fat, paprika and brown lightly in skillet, stirring constantly so they brown evenly. Place browned vegetables in saucepan, add a little stock and braise until tender, reducing the liquid, add salt to taste.

Cook macaroni.

Combine the cooked macaroni with the hot vegetables, bacon, tomato paste, if necessary add salt, heat.

The dish may be served immediately after heating, or baked in oven.

Baked Macaroni with Eggs

*1 lb. macaroni * 5 eggs * salt * 3 tbs. grated Parmesan cheese * 2 tbs. butter * tomato sauce (see page 318)*

Prepare tomato sauce with sour cream.

Cook macaroni.

Mix macaroni with 3/4 tomato sauce and half the grated cheese, place in casserole and even top, pour over with rest of tomato sauce.

Make five wells with a spoon on the surface of the macaroni, place an egg in each well, salt, sprinkle with grated cheese and dot with butter.

Bake in hot oven, until the eggs set. When ready garnish each egg with greens.

Baked Macaroni in Mushroom Sauce

*1 lb. macaroni * 5 eggs * salt * 3 tbs. grated Parmesan cheese * 3 1/2 tbs. butter * mushroom sauce (see page 317)*

Prepare as above.

Baked Macaroni with Mushrooms

*1 1/2 lb. fresh champignons * 3 1/2 tbs. fat * 1 medium onion * 1 lb. macaroni * salt * pepper * green parsley*

Clean mushrooms, chop, add a little fat, a piece of onion, pour over a small amount of water, and braise until tender, reducing the liquid.
Brown the rest of the fat and onion lightly.
Cook macaroni.
Combine cooked macaroni with mushrooms and browned onion, add salt and pepper to taste.
Place in greased casserole, dot with fat, bake in oven. Serve sprinkled with chopped parsley.

Pierogi

Filled Dumplings

Prepare filling.
Prepare dough. Knead dough somewhat thinner than for macaroni, knead throughly.
Divide dough into parts, place in bowl, cover. Roll in parts into circular shapes about 1/8 inch thick, sprinkle with flour so that it does not stick to board.
Put up salted water for cooking the pierogi.
Cut dough with round cutter.
Place filling with a teaspoon on each round.
Fold in half, seal by pinching with fingers, being careful that the filling does not stick out of edges (pierogi would unseal during cooking). If the dough is too dry, smear the edges with egg white.
Place the pierogi on a sieve.
Gather together all the remaining scraps of dough, knead, roll again, cut rounds, fill and seal pierogi.
Dice fat back, render, brown cracklings or melt butter.
Place pierogi in portions in boiling, salted water, cook, remove with

a draining spoon onto colander, pour over with hot water, drain, arrange on heated round platter, dot with fat, combine, cover and heat over boiling water. The pierogi may be sealed in another way with special utensils made for this purpose: roll dough into rectangular shape, brush off flour; place filling on half of dough at uniform spaces apart; cover with another layer of dough and cut with special cutter for pierogi; this cutter also seals the edges.

Pierogi with Cabbage

Filling: *1 small head of cabbage * salt * 4 1/2 tbs. fat * 1 small onion * * pepper * (1 cup cottage cheese) * D o u g h: 4 1/2 cups flour * salt * * 1 egg * 3/4 cup water * 3 tbs. butter or fat back*

Remove withered leaves from cabbage, divide in parts, cook in salted water, drain, cool, squeeze out in towel.
Chop onion, brown lightly in fat.
Combine cabbage with onion and fat, fry, add salt and pepper (cheese).
Put on salted water for cooking pierogi.
Prepare dough. Sift flour, add a pinch of salt, knead dough with egg and water, somewhat thinner than for noodles, work thoroughly. Divide in parts, roll out into 1/8 inch thickness. Cut out medium-sized rounds.
Place filling on rounds, fold in half.
Seal edges, place on floured board or in sieve.
Drop in portions into boiling salted water, drain, pour over with hot water, place on heated round platter, pour over with fat, cover, heat on top of boiling water.

Pierogi with Sauerkraut and Mushrooms

Filling: *2 lb. sauerkraut * 8—10 dried mushrooms * 3 1/2 tbs. fat * * 1 small onion * salt * pepper * D o u g h: 4 1/2 cups flour * salt * * 1 egg * 3/4 cup water * 3 tbs. fat back*

Squeeze out sauerkraut (if too tart), add mushrooms, cook uncovered in a small amount of water over high heat.
Chop onion, brown lightly in fat.
Squeeze out water from sauerkraut in towel, put through food chopper, combine with fat and onion, heat, add salt and pepper to taste.
Put up boiling water for cooking pierogi.
Prepare dough. Sift flour, add a pinch of salt, knead with egg and water, somewhat thinner than for macaroni, divide into portions.

Roll out into 1/8 inch thickness, cut out into medium-sized rounds.
Place filling on each round, fold in half.
Seal edges, place on board or in sieve.
Drop in portions into boiling salted water, cook, remove with draining spoon onto colander, pour over with hot water, drain, place on heated round platter, pour over with fat, cover, heat over boiling water.

Russian Pierogi

Filling: *10 medium potatoes * 1 cup cottage cheese * 1 medium onion * * 3 tbs. fat * salt * pepper * * D o u g h: 4 1/2 cups flour * salt * 1 egg * 3/4 cup water * 2 tbs. butter or rendered fat back * 1 cup sour cream*

Prepare filling. Peel potatoes, cook (or cook in jackets), put through food chopper with cheese.
Slice onion, brown lightly in fat.
Combine potatoes, cheese with onion, salt and pepper (if necessary thin with water).
Prepare dough. Sift flour, add a pinch of salt, knead with egg and water, somewhat thinner than for macaroni, divide into portions.
Put up salted water for cooking pierogi.
Roll dough out into 1/8 inch thickness.
Cut out into medium-sized rounds.
Place filling on each round, fold in half. Seal edges.
Place on board or sieve.
Drop in portions into boiling salted water, cook, remove with draining spoon onto colander.
Pour over with hot water, place on heated round platter, pour over with fat, cover, heat over boiling water.
Russian pierogi may be served with sour cream.

Pierogi with Buckwheat Flour and Cheese

Filling: *1 cup cottage cheese * 1 egg yolk * salt * 3 tbs. sour cream * * D o u g h: 1 1/2 cups buckwheat flour * 1/2 cup boiling water * 2 cups wheat flour * 3 tbs. butter*

Cream cheese with egg yolk and salt, if too thick, dilute with a little sour cream.
Put up water for cooking pierogi.
Sift buckwheat flour, knead, adding boiling water, add wheat flour, salt, knead.

168

Roll out into 1/5 inch thickness, cut out rather large rounds (2—3 inches in diameter). Place filling on each round, fold in half.

Seal edges, place on board or in sieve.

Brown butter to be used for dotting.

Drop pierogi in boiling salted water, cook slowly (test by cutting one pieróg); when cooked, drain, pour over with hot water, drain, place on heated round platter, pour over with butter, cover, heat over boiling water. Serve with sour cream.

Naleśniki

Pancakes

Add egg to milk and mix well. Add flour and beat until smooth.

Add water and salt to batter and stir until smooth. Heat griddle with a long handle over a uniformly-heated pad (not on an open flame). Grease the whole surface of griddle with fat back held on a fork. Pour batter on greased pan. Move griddle so that the batter spreads evenly. Pour off the batter that does not cling to the griddle. The pancakes should be thin. Bake batter over a hot pad. When it has steamed off somewhat, grasp pancake with fingers of both hands and turn. Bake until done. Slide the baked pancake onto a plate. Heat griddle and grease with fatback and bake the following pancake. It is best to bake pancakes on two pans of equal size.

Naleśniki (Pancakes) Made without Egg Whites

*1 egg * 1/2 cup milk * 1 cup flour * 1/2 cup water * salt * fat back for greasing skillet*

Combine egg, milk and flour thoroughly until lumps disappear.

Add water, salt, mix.

Grease bottom of skillet with fat back so that surface is glossy.

Pour batter into hot skillet, and when the batter covers entire bottom and adheres, pour off excess batter.

Cook over medium heat. When the batter sets, turn on other side. Cook on other side. Slip onto upturned plate.

Use for preparing filled pasties or for cutting into noodles for soups.

Naleśniki (Pancakes) Made with Egg Whites

*4 egg yolks * 1 cup milk * 1 1/2 cups flour * 1/2 cup water * salt * 4 egg whites * fat back for greasing skillet*

Blend egg yolks, milk and flour, add water, salt.

Beat egg whites, add blended mixture into beaten egg whites, combine.

Fry in two skillets simultaneously, grease bottom of skillets with fat back so that surface is glossy.

Pour batter quite thickly on heated skillet.

When the batter stops steaming, turn, cook on other side, place on overturned plate.

Use with mushroom sauce, or eat with jam or sweetened cottage cheese.

Naleśniki (Pancakes) Filled with Cabbage

F i l l i n g: *1 small head of cabbage * 3 1/2 tbs. fat * 1 small onion * salt * * pepper * sugar * * B a t t e r: 1/2 cup milk * 1 egg * 1 cup flour * salt * * 1/2 cup water * fat back for greasing skillet * * B r e a d i n g: 1 1/2 eggs * * 5 tbs. bread crumbs * 3 tbs. fat for frying*

Prepare filling. Rinse and clean cabbage, cut into pieces, cook in salted water, squeeze out in towel, put through food chopper. Chop onion finely, sauté in fat, mix with cabbage, add salt, pepper and sugar to taste, cook.

Prepare dough. Mix egg, milk and flour thoroughly, add water, salt, mix,

Heat skillet, grease with fat back until glossy.

Pour batter on hot skillet, and when part of the batter adheres to bottom of skillet, pour off excess batter. Fry on even heat.

When the batter ceases to steam, turn, cook on other side, place on overturned plate.

Place filling on cooked pancakes, fold in the sides of the pancake toward the middle, shape into rolls of uniform length. Dip rolls into egg then in bread crumbs and brown on all sides (or brown without breading).

Arrange on rectangular platter or a round one with mushroom or tomato sauce or serve as a garnish to clear soups.

Naleśniki (Pancakes) Filled with Groats and Mushrooms

F i l l i n g: *2 dried mushrooms * 3/4 cup groats (coarse buckwheat) * * twice as much cooking mushroom stock as groats * salt * pepper * 2 tbs. fat * 1 small onion * * B a t t e r: 1/2 cup milk * 1 egg * 1 cup flour * salt * * 1/2 cup water * fat back for greasing skillet * * B r e a d i n g: 1 1/2 eggs * 5 tbs. bread crumbs * 3 tbs. fat for frying*

Prepare filling. Wash mushrooms, rinse, cook, drain off liquid, chop mushrooms. Cook the groats in mushroom stock.

Chop onion, brown lightly in fat.

Mix groats with onion, chopped mushrooms, salt and pepper.
Prepare, cook and fill pancakes as above.
Serve with mushroom or tomato sauce or with raw vegetable salad.

Naleśniki (Pancakes) Filled with Mushrooms

F i l l i n g: *1 lb. fresh mushrooms (champignons) * 1 medium onion *
* 2 tbs. fat * 1/2 cup sour cream * 1 tbs. flour * salt * pepper * B a t t e r:
1/2 cup milk * 1 egg * 1 cup flour * 1/2 cup water * salt * fat back for
greasing skillet * B r e a d i n g: 1 1/2 eggs * 5 tbs. bread crumbs * 3 tbs.
fat for frying*

Prepare filling. Wash and clean mushrooms thoroughly, drain, chop finely,
add diced onion and fat and simmer covered.
Add sour cream with flour to mushrooms when tender, add salt and
pepper to taste, boil, the mushrooms should be thick and not float in
sauce.
Prepare, cook and fill pancakes as above.

Naleśniki (Pancakes) Filled with Spinach

F i l l i n g: *2 cups cooked spinach * 1 1/4 tbs. butter * 3 tbs. flour * 1/4
cup milk * 1/2 clove garlic * salt * B a t t e r: 4 egg yolks * 1 cup milk *
* 1 1/2 cups flour * salt * 1/2 cup water * 4 beaten egg whites * fat back
for greasing skillet * 4 1/2 tbs. butter for frying*

Prepare filling. Clean and wash spinach, cook by placing in boiling salted
water, drain off water, put through food chopper.
Melt butter, add flour, cook, set aside.
Dilute the roux with cold milk, stir while cooking, add spinach, ground
garlic and salt. Heat.
Prepare and cook pancakes with beaten egg whites (page 169).
Cover pancakes with filling, fold in four, fry.
Arrange on round or rectangular heated platter.

Bliny

Buckwheat Pancakes

*2 oz. yeast * about 3 cups warm milk * 4 cups wheat flour * 2 cups buck-
wheat flour * 1/2 cup butter * 5 egg yolks * salt * 5 egg whites * 5 tbs.
butter for frying*

Dissolve yeast in milk, add flour and buckwheat flour and mix. When all the ingredients are combined, place batter in a warm place for 3 hours, mixing every time the dough rises.

After three hours, add melted butter, egg yolks and a pinch of salt to the batter, beat thoroughly, mix with beaten egg whites and set aside to rise for 10 minutes. Melt butter for frying.

Heat 2—3 small skillets. Pour in a teaspoon of butter and then add a little of the foamy batter skimmed from the surface with a small ladle. Bliny should be just as thin as Polish pancakes. They should be cooked on medium heat and not over an open flame (on asbestos plate). When bliny are lightly browned on one side, raise with a knife, pour 1/2 teaspoon of butter underneath, turn and cook on other side.

Place ready bliny on plate, put over boiling water and keep covered so they do not dry or fall.

It is best to serve bliny right from the skillet, a few at a time.

Serve with browned butter and caviar, with chopped herring, or with sour cream on the side.

The proper side-dish for bliny is chopped herring or black caviar.

EGG DISHES

Eggs in the Viennese Manner

*10 eggs * 3 1/2 tbs. butter * salt*

Place eggs in boiling water. Cook in covered pan 3 to 4 minutes.
Take eggs out of water with spoon, remove part of shells and drop 2 eggs into each high glass. Add raw butter and salt.
Serve with bread or rolls and butter.

Poached Eggs (Mollet)

*3—4 tbs. vinegar (6%) * salt * 10 eggs*

Bring water with salt and vinegar to a boil.
Break eggs directly over the surface of the boiling water. Cook for a while until egg white films over.
When ready, remove each egg separately with a draining spoon. Place on small platter and pour over with sauce.

Serve with sauces and potatoes or Cracow groats (fine buckwheat), or with vegetables (like spinach, string beans), or with sour cream, tomato sauté, etc.

Fried Eggs

*4 tbs. butter (or fat back) * 10 eggs * salt * green parsley*

Melt and heat butter in egg skillet.

Break eggs into browned butter and fry until whites are done on the bottom.

Sprinkle with parsley and add salt. Place eggs on round platter (or cook in small skillet and serve in same).

May be served with vegetables or cereal, with potatoes, macaroni, aromatic sauces or breads.

Scrambled Eggs

*3 1/2 tbs. butter (or fat back) * 10 eggs * 5 tbs. water * salt*

Brown butter.

Break eggs into cup, add water, beat and add salt.

Pour into browned butter and cook stirring slowly. When firm but still the consistency of jelly, remove from fire.

Serve in skillet in which eggs were cooked, with bread.

May be cooked with ham cut into large cubes, grated cheese (Ementhaler, Edam's), chives, smoked bacon sliced thick and browned before adding eggs.

Scrambled Eggs with Sausage

*10 eggs * 5 tbs. water * salt * 1 oz. bacon * 5 to 7 oz. sausage*

Mix eggs in cup; add water and salt and mix thoroughly.

Melt bacon fat. Remove skin from sausage and cut into cubes. Brown slightly in bacon fat.

Pour eggs into partly cooked sausage and cook stirring constantly. When eggs are firm serve immediately.

Scrambled Eggs with Tomatoes

*2 medium tomatoes * 3 1/2 tbs. butter * 10 eggs * 3 tbs. water * salt * * pepper * green parsley*

Rinse tomatoes and cut into thick slices.
Heat butter well in two-eared skillet. Place in tomato slices and fry quickly on both sides.
Beat eggs in cup; add water and salt to taste and mix.
Pour eggs on tomatoes and cook until eggs become firm. Stir carefully not to crush tomatoes. Before serving sprinkle with green parsley and pepper. Serve in skillet.

Peasant Scrambled Eggs

*3 1/2 tbs. flour * 3/4 cup milk * 7 eggs * salt * 2 1/2 tbs. fat back*

Combine flour with a small amount of milk and mix until smooth. Add remainder of milk, eggs and salt and beat thoroughly.
Heat fat in skillet. Pour in eggs. Stir constantly until eggs are done medium. Chives may be mixed in before serving.
Serve in skillet.
Peasent scrambled eggs may be served with fried potatoes.

Peasant Scrambled Eggs with Tomatoes

*2 medium tomatoes * 2 1/2 tbs. butter * 3/4 cup milk * 5 tbs. flour *
* 7 eggs * salt * pepper*

Cut tomatoes into slices.
Heat fat in skillet and arrange tomato slices. Fry quickly on both sides.
Combine flour with a small amount of milk. Add remainder of milk, eggs and salt and mix thoroughly. Pour over tomatoes and cook until firm, stirring carefully in order not to crush tomatoes.
Sprinkle with green parsley and pepper before serving.
Serve in skillet.

Eggs Fried in Shells

*10 eggs * 10 oz. stale rolls * milk for soaking * 1/2 small onion * 1 1/2 tbs. fat * green parsley * 1 raw egg * salt * pepper * 3 tbs. bread crumbs *
* 3 1/2 tbs. fat for frying*

Cover eggs with cold water and cook until hard. Drain and cool in cold water.
Cut eggs in shells lengthwise with a sharp thin knife. Remove eggs carefully and put aside.

Soak rolls and squeeze out. Brown onion in fat. Chop green parsley or chives.

Grind eggs and all ingredients.

Add raw egg and mix with salt and pepper. Place stuffing in shell halves. Sprinkle with bread crumbs. Fry in hot fat on high flame.

Serve with spinach, potatoes or with sorrel soup or barszcz.

French Omelet

*5 eggs * 2 tbs. water * salt * green parsley * 3 tbs. butter * tomato slices or green cucumber slices, lettuce leaves, etc.*

Break eggs into cup and mix. Add water, salt, green parsley.

Heat butter in skillet, pour in eggs and heat on medium fire.

When mixture sets (it must be liquid on top), lift edges with knife so that uncooked mixture flows under cooked mixture.

When mixture is set like jelly, roll two sides to center or fold omelet in half.

Slide omelet off skillet with knife onto heated plate. Spread it out and dress with vegetables in season (chopped green parsley, lettuce, radishes, tomato or cucumber slices, etc.).

Spring Omelet

Follow recipe for french omelet. Add to eggs one spoon of chopped chives, green dill and green parsley.

Dress with radishes and green lettuce.

French Omelet with Cauliflower, String Beans or Asparagus

F i l l i n g: *2 medium cauliflowers or 1 1/2 cups string beans or 10 sticks of asparagus * salt * sugar * 2 tbs. butter * O m e l e t: 5 eggs * 2 tbs. water * salt * green parsley * 2 1/2 tbs. butter*

Prepare vegetables. Rinse cauliflowers, remove large leaves and remove core. Rinse beans and remove strings. Rinse asparagus and clean.

Place vegetables in boiling water. Add salt and sugar and cook until tender. Divide into two parts.

Brown 2 tbs. of butter lightly.

Break eggs into cup, add water, salt and green parsley and mix well with fork.

Heat 2 1/2 tbs. of butter in skillet and pour in eggs. Cook omelet.

175

When eggs set on bottom, place cauliflower (or string beans or asparagus) in middle of the omelet and pour over with part of the browned butter. Fold two sides to center or fold in half.

Slide omelet with knife onto serving dish, spread it out.

Dress with cauliflower flowerets, asparagus tips, green lettuce. Pour over with remainder of browned butter.

French Omelet with Green Peas

Filling: *1 cup shelled peas (or canned peas) * salt * sugar * 2 1/2 tbs. butter * Omelet: 5 eggs * 2 tbs. water * salt * green parsley * 2 1/2 tbs. butter*

Rinse peas and cook in small amount of water (or use canned peas, drained).

Steam off water. Add butter, salt and sugar to taste, sauté.

Prepare omelet and serve as above.

The peas may also be cooked and sautéed in butter and added to the egg mixture before omelet is cooked.

When ready, fold in half. Serve on platter with melted butter on top.

French Omelet with Spinach

Filling: *1 1/2 cups cooked spinach * 1 1/2 tbs. butter * 2 tbs. flour * * 1/2 cup milk * salt * garlic * Omelet: 5 eggs * 2 tbs. water * salt * * green parsley * 2 1/2 tbs. butter*

Boil salted water.

Remove spinach stems, rinse carefully in bowl under running water.

Cook in boiling water. Drain and squeeze out water.

Melt butter and combine with flour. Brown and set apart.

Combine garnish with milk. Bring to the boil stirring constantly. Combine with spinach. Add salt and garlic and bring to the boil.

Prepare omelet and serve as in recipes above.

French Omelet with Mushrooms

Filling: *2 cups mushrooms (champignons) * 2 1/2 tbs. butter * 1/2 small onion * salt * pepper * Omelet: 5 eggs * 2 tbs. water * salt * * green parsley * 2 1/2 tbs. butter*

Clean mushrooms. Remove skin from mushroom tops and rinse.

Cut mushrooms into thin rounds. Cut larger mushrooms into strips.

Sprinkle mushrooms with water and add butter and onion. Add salt and pepper and cook stirring constantly.
Prepare omelet according to recipe given above.

French Omelet with Ham

Filling: *7 oz. ham * 2 1/2 tbs. butter * Omelet: 5 eggs * 2 tbs. water * salt * 2 1/2 tbs. butter*

Grind ham and heat in hot butter.
Prepare omelet and serve as in recipe above.

Eggs in Hot Sauces

*10 eggs * tomato sauce with sour cream or flour garnish, horse-radish, Béchamel, dill sauce*

Prepare chosen sauce.
Poach eggs (see page 172) or cook until hard and when still hot remove shells.
Place poached eggs in platter.
Pour sauce over them.
Serve with macaroni, rice, Cracow groats, potatoes.

Eggs in Cold Sauces

See Cold Appetizers, page 22.

MUSHROOM DISHES

Many varieties of wild mushrooms are known and eaten in Poland, particularly in regions with many forests. There are many savory dishes prepared with fresh mushrooms. These recipes have not been included in this book because it is difficult to identify the wild mushrooms that grow on two such distant continents, and there is a danger of mistaking them with the poisonous varieties. Recipes have been given using Polish exported, dried mushrooms of the valuable Boletus edulis variety, which cannot be cultivated, and the champignon which is cultivated in Poland as in other countries.

Stewed Champignons

*5 cups mushrooms (champignons) * 1/2 small onion * 3 tbs. butter * salt *
* pepper * (1 raw egg yolk)*

Clean mushrooms, rinse and remove skin. Cut into slices (discard stems).
Slice onion and add to mushrooms. Add a small amount of water, butter,
salt and pepper. Cook on medium flame in covered pot.
When mushrooms are tender, brown lightly stirring constantly.

Champignons Sautéed

*14 oz. young champignons * about 1 cup fat (butter) * salt * pepper*

Clean mushrooms, rinse and remove skin. Cut off stems. Drain off mush-
rooms.
Heat part of the butter in skillet and fry mushrooms on medium flame.
Before serving, sprinkle with salt and pepper.
Serve covered with butter in which they were fried.

Stuffed Champignons

*14 oz. champignons * 2 1/2 tbs. butter * green parsley * 1 egg yolk * 2 tbs.
bread crumbs * salt * pepper * 3 tbs. butter to sprinkle mushrooms*

Select uniform, medium-sized mushrooms with closed caps.
Remove stems and peel caps.
Cream butter, add egg yolk, chopped green parsley and mix with sifted
crumbs. Add salt and pepper to taste.
Stuff the mushroom caps with this stuffing, place in baking pan, sprinkle
with butter and bake.

Dried-Mushroom Patties

*10 dried mushrooms * 1 small onion * allspice * 2 1/2 tbs. fat * 1/2 small
onion * 3 oz. stale roll * milk for soaking * 1 egg * salt * pepper * 3 tbs.
bread crumbs * 6 tbs. fat for frying*

Wash mushrooms in warm water, rinse and cook with onion and allspice.
Drain mushrooms.
Chop onion and brown in fat until golden yellow.
Soak roll and squeeze out milk.
Grind mushrooms with roll. Mix with fried onion, egg, salt and pepper.

Form small, high patties from mushroom mixture and dredge in crumbs. Fry on high flame.

Serve with mushroom sauce or with vegetables (sauerkraut).

Breaded, Dried Mushrooms

*10 large, dried mushrooms * salt * 1 1/2 egg * 5 tbs. bread crumbs with flour * 4 1/2 tbs. fat for frying*

Use large mushroom caps that have been cooked in soup broth. Salt. Dredge in egg, flour and crumbs.

Fry in heated fat and serve hot with sauerkraut.

Dried-Mushroom Pudding

*4 dried mushrooms * 1/2 small onion * 1 1/2 tbs. fat * 3 oz. stale roll * * milk for soaking * 3 tbs. butter * 4 egg yolks * salt * pepper * 5 egg whites (beaten) * fat and bread crumbs for mold*

Wash mushrooms in warm water. Rinse and cook. Drain and grind.

Prepare a pudding mold. Cook water for pudding.

Sauté onion in fat.

Soak roll and squeeze out milk. Grind.

Cream butter, adding one egg yolk at a time and the ground mushrooms gradually. Add salt and pepper to taste.

Beat egg whites and mix with the mushrooms mixture. Place in pudding mold. Close mold and place in pot with boiling water. Steam for an hour.

Place pudding on round plate, cut portions and pour sauce over pudding.

Serve with mushroom sauce prepared on the mushroom stock.

MEAT

HOME METHODS OF TENDERIZING AND CONSERVING MEAT

Vegetable Marinade for 2 lb. of Meat
(beef, lamb, venison)

*1 medium onion * 1 small carrot * 1 small parsley * 2 oz. celery root (celeriac) * 3 tbs. salad or olive oil * 1 tbs. sugar * 1/2 bay leaf * 6 allspice berries * add a few juniper berries for game or lamb * add garlic for potted meats*

Rinse meat, drain, remove membrane and fat, leaving a "collar" of fat about one-third of an inch on lamb. Place meat in bowl of suitable size (not too large).

Rinse vegetables, clean, rinse again, slice in rings, sprinkle with oil, add sugar and crushed spices; crush until vegetables begin to secrete juices. Rub vegetables over the entire surface of the meat, place on meat and keep in a cool, dark place for 1—2 days.

Storing Meats in Sour Milk
(veal, beef)

Rinse meat, drain, place tightly in a glazed earthenware crock or non-chipped pot, cover with the uncooked milk and place in the cold without moving the meat. The milk should cover the surface of the meat completely. The milk, while souring, not only preserves the meat for a short time, but also helps tenderize it. Meat kept in sour milk is very crisp after roasting. Whey or buttermilk may be substituted for fresh milk.

Vinegar Marinade for 2 lb. of Meat
(game, especially hare, lamb and beef, duck, goose)

*2 cups water * 1 medium onion * 5 bay leaves * 6 allspice berries * 4 tbs. vinegar*

Rinse meat, drain, remove surface membrane and unnecessary fat.
Cook water with onion rings and spices; when onion softens, add vinegar; set aside and cool.
Place meat in earthenware bowl of suitable size, pour the cooled mixture over meat, cover with bay leaves and onion, place in a cool, dark place for about 2—3 days in summer and 5 days in winter.

Marinade for Pickling 10 lb. of Meat
(pork, beef, veal)

*5 bay leaves * 10 allspice berries * 4 whole cloves * 1 tsp. coriander * * 1 tsp. rosemary * 3 oz. salt * 1 1/4 tsp. saltpeter * 1 tbs. sugar * 1 quart water*

Rinse meat, drain, dry, bone.
Crush spices, mix with salt, sugar and saltpeter; divide in half.
Rub half of the mixture all over meat, place meat tightly in bowl of correct size (a small wooden tub is best, or earthenware crock, or an unchipped enamel bowl). Press with wooden cover, use stone weight (up to 11 lb.) and set in room temperature for 2 days.
Mix the rest of the spice mixture with water and after 2 days pour over the meat and place in cool spot (46°F).
Pickle the meat for 2—3 weeks, turning every other day; keep meat covered continually with wooden lid and weight. A smaller cut of meat, such as tongue, should be pickled for 10 days.

184

If there is no cool place, the meat should not be pickled, for it cannot be kept fresh for 2—3 weeks at room temperature.

PRINCIPAL METHODS OF PREPARING MEAT

Boiled Meat

Wash and crack loose bones, cover with cold water, add salt, simmer.
Rinse meat, do not bone, add to boiling liquid, simmer.
Clean, rinse mixed vegetables (see soups), add to meat when half cooked, then cook with meat.
Rinse onion, do not pare, slice, brown on open flame.
Add cabbage, onion, bay leaf, ground allspice, salt and pepper when meat is parcooked (about 1 1/2—2 hours), simmer.
When meat is completely tender, remove from stock and drain, cut in slices about 1/2 inch thick.
Arrange slices on warmed serving platter, sprinkle with broth.

Meat in Sauce Poulett

Prepare soup stock with bones.
Rinse meat, add to boiling stock, simmer, salt when parcooked, add cleaned mixed vegetables. After cooking there should be 1/2 cup of stock for each serving.
When meat is tender remove and drain, if necessary steam off the broth, slice meat and vegetables.
Cream butter, add flour, cream, add part of the hot broth, cream the entire mixture, add to pot with remaining boiling broth, cook while stirring.
Add salt and spices according to the recipe, mix with vegetables (or use vegetables to garnish meat).
Place meat on platter. Pour sauce over it, surround with barley, rice or serve with dumplings.

Ground Cutlets

Soak roll, drain water, put through food chopper.
Brown onion lightly in fat.
Rinse meat, cut in small cubes, put through food chopper, mix with roll, egg, onion, salt and pepper.

Combine and season.

Sift bread crumbs on plate.

Shape meat into oval cutlets, meat balls, a long roll for steaks or meat loaf.

I. Method of Shaping Cutlets:

Divide meat into equal parts, roll into smooth balls with hands after dipping hands in water.

Roll meat in bread crumbs.

Place each ball on a dry board.

When all parts are breaded, flatten all with a knife into oval or round shape about 2/3 inch thick.

Score with a sharp knife.

II. Method of Shaping Cutlets:

Place meat mixture on board sprinkled with bread crumbs.

Shape meat into thick roll, cut into even parts.

Form each part separately: transfer with a knife, place cut side on bread crumbs and shape on both sides, giving cutlet round or oval shape about 2/3 inch thick.

Score with a sharp knife.

Heat fat, fry cutlets over medium heat, browning both sides. Fry until juice is golden (not turbid), when pressed with the flat side of the knife.

Place on warmed platter, sprinkle with frying fat.

Ground meat should be served immediately after frying so that it does not dry out.

Breaded Meat

Prepare flour, beaten egg, fine bread crumbs, each on a separate flat plate.

Rinse meat, shape.

Immediately before frying, salt meat on both sides; meats such as veal, and fish, should be dried on a clean cloth after salting and then breaded.

Dip salted meat first in the flour then in the egg.

Remove meat from egg, drain, dip in bread crumbs on both sides, pat bread crumbs into the meat, shake off unnecessary bread crumbs; place breaded meat on a dry board.

Heat fat, fry meat immediately after breading to a golden brown, lower flame to complete frying (the thicker the piece, the longer it takes to fry).

Arrange cutlets, placing bones in one direction on a platter.

Meat in Dough

Place pork chops, veal cutlets or pieces of fish in boiling salted water. When cooked, remove on a colandar, drain and cool.
Prepare dough in a wide bowl.
Dip meat into dough with a fork, shake so that meat is not covered with too much dough.
Immediately after dipping in dough fry each piece of meat on both sides.
Arrange on a platter, each piece propped against the other.

Meat Fried English Style (Rare)

Rinse meat and, depending on the recipe, marinate in vegetables or fry without marinating.
Remove meat from marinade, clean off vegetables, slice across the grain in thickness given for each dish.
Flatten each piece lightly, pounding or pressing lightly with the fist (steak or filet); salt and pepper meat just before frying.
Heat a small amount of fat on a high flame, place meat on fat (3 portions on a medium-sized skillet) and brown quickly on both sides on a high flame; while turning meat, add butter, brown with the meat; the meat should be rare inside (light pink or red, according to taste); when using fresh butter do not brown, but after frying dot each piece of meat with butter.
Serve meat on a warmed platter immediately after frying and sprinkle with the frying fat.

Braised Pounded Meat in Natural Sauce

Rinse meat, cut into parts, pound larger pieces, salt, sprinkle with flour.
Heat fat on high flame, add meat, brown quickly, place in stewing pan.
Add onion, water, the frying fat and spices, braise slowly in covered pan.
When meat is tender, strain and thicken the sauce, cook, serve on platter.
With braised meats the size of pot is very important, i.e., the pot should be of suitable size (not too large) for the amount of meat and sauce.

Natural Roast ("From Oven")

Rinse meat and, depending on the recipe, marinate in vegetables or roast without marinating.

Remove meat from brine, clean off vegetables, pound, salt, and sometimes sprinkle with flour.

Heat fat in skillet on high flame, add meat, brown quickly on all sides, set in roaster of suitable size, pour over with frying fat, and place in medium oven (355°F). The correct size (not too large) of roaster is very important. Roast meat, basting with fat, add steamed sauce, sprinkle with water, so that the fat does not burn; roast about 1—1/2 hour depending on the kind of meat.

When meat is tender, finish sauce according to recipe.

Slice the meat quickly across the grain, set on a heated platter, cover with sauce and heat in the oven on the platter.

Serve remaining sauce in gravy boat.

Roasted Meat Rolls

Prepare stuffing according to recipe.

Rinse meat, bone, pound with meat hammer into thin slices, if some muscles are too thick — slit, beat; shape into an even, rectangular slice of meat. Salt meat, spread filling, roll tightly, tie, salt, sprinkle with flour.

Heat fat on skillet, brown the roll, transfer to a long, narrow tin of suitable size (not too large), add the frying fat, onion, a little water, place in heated oven.

Bake, basting with sauce, adding water to the sauce.

When meat is tender, cut and remove cord, cut in 2/3 inch slices, place the entire roll on platter.

Scrape the sauce from the sides of the baking tin, mix with the sauce in tin, heat, pour part of sauce over meat, serve remainder in gravy boat.

Roast Meat, English Style (Rare)

Rinse tender cut of meat, remove fat and membrane. Roast beef and leg of lamb should be marinated in vegetables for a few hours before roasting. Before frying, remove vegetables from meat.

Heat fat, salt meat, sprinkle with flour, add to the fat, fry on a high flame, remove to a roaster of suitable size (not too large), place in a very hot oven. After the meat is half-done baste with water and sauce; meat should be rare or medium-rare according to taste.

Slice finely, place the entire roast on a warmed platter.

Add butter to the sauce, cook, pour part of sauce over meat, serve rest in gravy boat.

VEAL

BOILED VEAL

Veal Tripe

*3 1/2 lb. veal tripe * 7 oz. mixed vegetables * 3 tbs. butter * 5 tbs. flour *
* salt * marjoram * pepper*

Carefully wash tripe, rinse, changing water several times, add boiling water,
cook and drain.

Make a stock with mixed vegetables, while stock is boiling, add tripe,
simmer (it cooks quickly), drain, cut in small strips.

Prepare a light-golden roux with butter and flour, add tripe (and sliced
vegetables from broth), add salt, marjoram and pepper to taste, mix, cook.
Serve with potatoes, potato dumplings, macaroni.

Boiled Veal Tongues

*1 1/2 lb. veal tongue * 5 oz. mixed vegetables * 1 medium onion * all-
spice * bay leaf * salt*

Scrub tongue under running water, remove salivary glands (from underside near root), rinse, add boiling water and boil until tender.

Wash mixed vegetables, clean, add together with spices to tongue, add salt, cook until very soft.

When meat is parboiled, remove and place in cold water, and when cooled, peel, place again in liquid and cook until tender. Drain.

Slice each veal tongue into 2—3 parts lengthwise (depending on size of the tongue) and serve covered with thick sauce. Serve with potatoes, and tomato, horse-radish, dill or mustard sauce using the cooking liquid as a base.

Pickled Veal Tongues

Scrub tongue under running water, remove salivary glands and pickle the same way as ham or veal, placing the tongues one beside the other. Pickle for 10 days.

Cook the same way as fresh tongue.

Boiled Veal in White Roux with Broth

*5 oz. mixed vegetables without cabbage * 2 1/2 lb. breast, shoulder or ribs of veal * S a u c e: 3 cups of cooled stock * 3 tbs. butter * 5 tbs. flour * * salt * green parsley or dill * (1—2 egg yolks)*

Wash vegetables, clean, bring to the boil.

Rinse meat and cook unboned over medium heat in the stock.

When meat is tender, drain liquid and steam to a quantity of about 3/4 of a quart.

Bone meat, slice thickly; serve each portion of meat with some bone (breast, shoulder).

Slice vegetables from stock with serrated knife.

Cream butter with flour in a deep plate, add a little stock, mix, pour into boiling stock, stir while cooking.

Add the meat to the sauce, salt, cook.

Place on round serving platter, surround with rice, garnish with vegetables. green parsley or dill. Raw egg yolks can be mixed into the sauce before serving.

Serve with rice, barley, noodles and boiled vegetables.

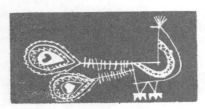

Pickled Round of Veal

*1 round of veal (about 11 lb.) * 6 tbs. salt * 3 tbs. saltpeter * 1 tbs. sugar *
* 1 tsp. coriander * 1 tsp. juniper * 4 cloves of garlic * 1 tsp. rosemary *
* 2 bay leaves * 10 allspice berries * 10 whole cloves * 4 cups water*

Crush all spices, mix with salt, saltpeter and sugar, set aside half.
Rinse meat, bone and rub half of the spice mixture into the meat, fit tightly
into porcelain or earthenware bowl, cover with wooden disk, press down
with a weight (about 10 pounds) and keep at room temperature for
2 days.
Boil 4 cups of water, mix the rest of the spice mixture with water, cool,
pour over meat and pickle for 2—3 weeks, storing it in a cool place (see
page 184). Meat should be turned every other day. Remove the meat from
the brine after 3 weeks, clean off spices, drain and hang until dry.
Pickled round of veal can either be boiled or roasted; if the entire round
is to be used it should be beaten and formed into a piece of uniform
thickness. Tie tightly, rolling all shreds into the inside, skewer tightly
an inch apart. Cook slowly in boiling water. After it is parcooked taste
water, if necessary salt to taste. Cool the round after cooking, remove,
place on platter, cover with board and weight and let stand until the next
day.
The round of veal can also be pickled with the bone. The leg bone
should then be cut off, and only about 1 1/2 inches of bone not attached
to the meat should be left. With a sharp, thin knife, pierce the meat along
the bone as close to the bone as possible (up to the knee joint). Slit and
press spice mixture into slits as near to the bone as possible, for this is
where the meat most easily spoils.

FRIED VEAL

Ground Veal Cutlets

*Stale roll (2 oz.) * milk for soaking * 2 tbs. fat * 2 egg yolks * 2 lb. shoulder
of veal * 2 egg whites * salt * 1/4 cup bread crumbs * 3 tbs. fat for frying*

Soak roll, drain off milk, chop.
Cream fat with yolks.
Clean meat, bone, chop and shape, sprinkling with milk.
Mix the creamed fat with the meat, add beaten egg whites, salt, shape.
Form meat mixture into balls (dampen hands in water).
Dry hands, bread balls by rolling in bread crumbs, flatten with knife into
oval shape.

Fry in hot fat (first on high flame, then medium) on both sides to golden color.

Arrange in row on long platter.

Serve with potatoes and carrots with peas, spinach or salad in season.

Pożarski Cutlets

Breaded Veal and Pork Patties

*2 lb. shoulder of veal * 9 oz. pork * 3 tbs. milk * 5 oz. stale roll * milk for soaking * 2 tbs. butter * 2 egg yolks * salt * B r e a d i n g: 5 tbs. flour * 1 1/2 eggs * 1/4 cup fine bread crumbs * 3 tbs. lard for frying * * 2 tbs. butter for frying*

Rinse meat, bone, grind, shape, sprinkle with milk.

Knead like dough.

Soak roll in milk, drain, grind.

Cream butter, adding egg yolks, mix with meat, soaked roll, add salt to taste, combine thoroughly, divide into 10 parts.

Form into balls, dip in flour, then in beaten egg and finally in fine bread crumbs.

Heat fat, add meat balls and fry till browned on both sides; when done, add butter and complete browning together with butter.

Serve immediately on a long, heated platter, sprinkled with fat.

Serve with potatoes and carrots with peas, spinach, boiled vegetables or raw salad in season (except for sauerkraut).

Ministers' Cutlets

Breaded Veal and Pork Patties

*2 lb. shoulder of veal * 9 oz. pork * 2 oz. stale roll * milk for soaking * * 3 tbs. butter * 1 egg * salt * pepper * B r e a d i n g: 5 tbs. flour * * 2 eggs * 2 tbs. fine bread crumbs * 1 stale roll * 3 tbs. lard for frying * * 3 tbs. butter for frying*

Rinse meat, bone, grind.

Soak roll in milk, drain, grind.

Knead meat carefully, mixing with roll and adding melted butter and egg gradually, add salt and pepper to taste, divide mixture into even parts.

Form into balls (with wet hands).

Dice finely small, hard roll and mix with sifted bread crumbs.

Dip meat in flour, then in beaten egg and then in bread crumbs and roll mixture, flatten balls into oval cutlets about 3/4 inches thick.

Heat fat on skillet and add the cutlets browning them on a medium heat; while turning cutlets add butter and brown together with meat. Serve with potatoes in various forms, raw salad in season, spinach, carrots, peas or boiled vegetables.

Veal Balls in Sauce

*2 oz. stale roll * milk for soaking * 2 lb. shoulder of veal * 4 tbs. of milk * * 3 tbs. fat * salt * 5 tbs. flour * 3 tbs. fat for frying * tomato sauce*

Soak roll in milk, drain, grind.

Rinse meat, bone, grind and mix well, knead like dough sprinkling with milk.

Mix the meat mixture with roll, melted fat and salt, divide into 10 portions. With wet hands form meat into balls, turn them over in flour.

Heat fat in skillet over high heat, brown meat quickly, transfer to pot. Prepare tomato or mushroom sauce according to choice (see page 317, 318), add meat balls, cook slowly, cover and braise on a low heat for about 10 minutes.

Serve with potatoes, pearl barley, macaroni and boiled vegetables.

Fried Veal Steaks with Sauce

*2 1/2 lb. round of veal * salt * 3 tbs. flour * 3 tbs. fat for frying*

Rinse meat, drain water, remove membrane and cut across the grain into steaks about 3/4 inch thick, reckoning about 2 small steaks per portion. Pound steaks carefully with meat hammer, shape ovally, score meat, place on plate, cover, set aside.

Before frying, sprinkle with salt and flour and brown on both sides, brown quickly, fry through on medium fire.

Prepare sauce according to taste (mushroom or tomato).

Serve steaks on platter, covered with hot sauce. Serve remaining sauce in gravy boat.

Veal-Brain Patties

*2 lb. veal brains * salt * vinegar * pepper * 5 tbs. flour * 1 1/2 eggs * * 1/2 cup fine bread crumbs * 4 tbs. fat for frying*

Boil water with salt, add vinegar.

Select undamaged brains, rinse, remove membrane, add to boiling water, boil several times, drain, cool.

Divide cooled brains in two, sprinkle with pepper and dip each part in flour, egg and bread crumbs.

Heat fat, add breaded brains and brown on both sides on a medium heat.

Serve with potatoes, raw salad in season, carrots and peas, spinach.

Veal Cutlets (Sauté)

*3 lb. veal-rib chops * salt * 3 tbs. flour * 2 tbs. fat for frying * 3 tbs. butter for frying*

Rinse chops, drain water, remove membrane.

Pound meat carefully with meat hammer into rather thin pieces, slit at several places around the edge so that the meat does not curl or become deformed during frying, form into round cutlets about 2/3 inch thick.

Immediately before frying, sprinkle with salt and flour.

Heat fat on skillet and fry cutlets quickly on a high flame until brown on both sides; when the cutlets are browned, add butter and fry through on a medium flame until butter browns.

Before cutlets are fried sprinkle water on the fat, mix well and heat, boil rapidly to reduce liquid.

Place cutlets on long, heated platter, placing bones all facing in one direction. Pour over with sauce.

Serve with fried egg, French-fried potatoes and boiled vegetables, spinach, carrots and peas, tomato sauté, raw vegetable salad in season (except for sauerkraut).

Breaded Veal Chops

*2 1/2 lb. veal-rib chops * salt * 5 tbs. flour * 1 1/2 eggs * 1/2 cup fine bread crumbs * 3 tbs. fat for frying * 3 tbs. butter for frying*

Prepare the cutlets as in the previous recipe, pound with meat hammer and slit on the edges so that the chops are not deformed during frying. Immediately before frying, sprinkle with salt, dip both sides of chop first in flour, then in beaten egg, and when drained — in fine bread crumbs; place the breaded chops on a dry board and press the surface of the chop with the hand so that the breading adheres to the meat.

Heat fat and fry cutlets on medium heat until brown on both sides.

While turning cutlets add butter and finish frying in butter. Serve the same side-dishes as for veal cutlets.

Veal Steaks (Sauté)

*2 1/2 lb. round of veal * salt * 3 tbs. flour * 3 tbs. fat for frying * 3 tbs. butter for frying*

Rinse meat, bone, cut and shape as for veal cutlets, Viennese style.
Immediately before frying, sprinkle with salt and flour.
Heat fat, add meat and fry on both sides until brown, first on a high heat. Finish frying with butter on lower flame.
Serve immediately after frying while the meat is still juicy, sprinkled with fat; when cutlets stand too long while hot, they dry up and lose their flavor. Serve with fried egg, lemon rings, potatoes (all forms) and raw salad, especially lettuce, with tomatoes, cucumbers with sour cream, dill pickle, tomato sauté and boiled vegetables (cauliflower, asparagus, green beans, carrots), spinach.

Veal Medalion

*2 1/2 lb. round of veal * salt * 4 tbs. flour * 3 tbs. fat for frying * 3 tbs. butter for frying*

Rinse meat, bone, remove membrane, cut into small steaks, cutting across the grain.
Beat meat with a meat hammer into flat square pieces, gash at corners, shape medalions with a knife into a round shape about 3/4 inch thick, even the sides and the surface, set aside.
Immediately before frying, sprinkle with salt and flour.
Heat fat on a skillet, brown meat on both sides.
Serve immediately after frying while the medalions are fresh and juicy; dot each medalion with butter. Serve with French-fried potatoes and lettuce with tomatoes, boiled vegetables, champignons.

Veal Cutlets, Viennese Style

*2 1/2 lb. round of veal * salt * 5 tbs. flour * 1 1/2 eggs * 1/2 cup fine bread crumbs * 3 tbs. fat for frying * 2 tbs. butter for frying*

Rinse meat, drain off water, bone, remove membrane and cut cutlets with a sharp knife against the grain, somewhat obliquely from top to bottom. Pound each cutlet with a meat hammer into a flat piece. Shape into an oval about 2/3 inch thick, smooth surface, place on platter, cover.
Immediately before frying, sprinkle with salt and dip both sides of cutlet

13*
195

first in flour, then in egg, and then in bread crumbs, press in crumbs so that the breading adheres to the meat.

Heat fat and brown cutlets on both sides over medium heat; when the meat is fried on one side, turn, add butter and fry until done.

Serve immediately after frying. Do not store in heat, since the breading comes off due to steam.

Serve with fried egg, lemon ring and potatoes of all kinds, carrots and peas, spinach, boiled vegetables, tomato sauté, raw salad in season (except for sauerkraut).

Breast of Veal, Viennese Style

*2 lb. breast of veal * salt * 5 oz. mixed vegetables * 4 tbs. flour * 1 1/2 eggs * 1/4 cup fine bread crumbs * 3 tbs. fat for frying*

Boil water with salt.

Rinse meat, add to water, parboil.

Rinse vegetables, clean, add to meat and simmer.

When meat is tender, remove (use stock for soup).

When meat cools somewhat, remove bones, place meat on a damp, square tray, cover with wooden board, press with small weight, let stand till completely cooled.

When the meat congeals, slice into rectangular, even portions.

Prepare flour, beaten egg, sifted bread crumbs.

Dip the pieces of meat in flour, then in beaten egg, drain, coat with fine bread crumbs, press crumbs into meat.

Heat fat, place meat in hot fat, brown quickly on both sides. Serve on a long platter.

Serve with potatoes and salad in season, carrots, spinach, etc.

Calf's Tripe, Viennese Style

*2 lb. calf's tripe * 5 oz. mixed vegetables * 1 medium onion * pepper * * 1 bay leaf * allspice * salt * 1/2 cup flour * 1 1/2 eggs * 1/2 cup fine bread crumbs * 4 tbs. fat for frying*

Clean tripe thoroughly, rinse, place in boiling water, parboil, drain. Place into small amount of water, cook together with vegetables, onion and spices. Salt after cooking.

Drain the tripe. Cool on a board, arrange into a rectangular shape, press with a wooden board, weight a little until completely cooled.

Slice cooled tripe into rectangles (about 2 pieces per portion), sprinkle with pepper.

Dip in flour, beaten egg and bread crumbs; fry in hot fat until browned on both sides, fry on a high flame.
Serve with potatoes and relish or lettuce, spinach, tomato sauté.

Calf's Tripe in Dough

*2 lb. calf's tripe * 5 oz. mixed vegetables * 1 medium onion * 1 bay leaf * pepper * salt * allspise * D o u g h: 1 cup water * 2 egg yolks * 2 cups flour * 2 tbs. oil. * 2 egg whites * salt * 1/2 cup fat for frying*

Cook tripe, cool and cut into rectangles as above.
Beat water thoroughly with egg yolks, flour and oil. Beat egg whites and mix with dough, salt.
Using a fork, dip cold portions of tripe into the dough.
Fry in hot fat to golden brown on both sides on a high flame; serve on long platter. Serve with potatoes and a highly-seasoned salad or relish.

Calf's Knuckles in Dough

*2 1/2 calf's knuckles * salt * 5 oz. mixed vegetables * 1 bay leaf * allspice * * pepper * D o u g h: 1 cup water * 2 egg yolks * 2 cups flour * 2 tbs. oil * 2 egg whites * salt * 1/2 cup fat for frying*

Scald cleaned feet, crack lengthwise.
Place in large amount of boiling water, bring to the boil, drain.
Place in boiling salted water together with vegetables and spices, cook slowly.
Drain knuckles when tender, while meat is still hot, separate from bone, arrange on board into a rectangle, press with small board under a little weight, set aside until cool.
Prepare dough. Beat water thoroughly with egg yolks, flour and oil. Beat egg whites, mix with dough, salt.
Cut cooled meat into rectangular slices, sprinkle with pepper and dip into the dough with a fork.
Fry in hot fat until golden brown on both sides.
Serve on long platter.
Serve with highly-seasoned raw vegetable salad or lettuce.

Calf's Knuckles, Viennese Style

*2 1/2 calf's knuckles * salt * 5 oz. mixed vegetables * 1 bay leaf * allspice * * pepper * 5 tbs. flour * 1 1/2 eggs * 1/2 cup fine bread crumbs * 5 tbs. fat for frying*

Boil knuckles and cool as in recipe above.

Carve meat into rectangular pieces; sprinkle with pepper, then dip in flour, beaten egg and bread crumbs; press bread crumbs into meat so they do not come off during frying.

Heat fat and fry meat until brown on both sides.

Serve with potatoes, raw salad in season or lettuce.

Calf's Brains à la Polonaise

*1 1/2 lb. calf's brains * 3 tbs. butter * 1 medium onion * 2 eggs * salt ** * pepper * 1 1/2 tbs. butter for bread crumbs * 4 tbs. fine bread crumbs*

Rinse brains, remove membrane, chop brains.

Chop onion finely, brown lightly in butter, add brain and fry while stirring slowly.

When the brains set, add raw eggs, mix, and keep frying until eggs set, then mix brains with salt and pepper.

Garnish with chopped green parsley or dot with bread crumbs browned in butter.

Calf's Liver (Sauté)

*1 1/2 lb. calf's liver * 3 tbs. flour * pepper * 6 tbs. fat for frying * salt ** * 1 large onion*

Rinse liver, remove membrane, cut into flat slices, remove tubes.

Sprinkle with flour and pepper right before frying.

Heat half of the fat, add liver, brown on very hot skillet, salt after frying.

Cut onion in rings, brown in the rest of the fat.

Place liver on long platter, dot with fat and onion and serve immediately.

Serve with potatoes and raw vegetable salad, lettuce, boiled vegetables, tomato sauté, mushrooms.

Breaded Calf's Liver

*1 1/2 lb. calf's liver * 1/2 cup flour * 1 1/2 eggs * 1/2 cup fine bread crumbs * 3 tbs. fat for frying * salt*

Rinse liver, remove membrane, cut into flat slices, remove tubes.

Prepare flour, beaten egg, fine bread crumbs.

Dip slices successively in flour, egg, drain, then in bread crumbs, press crumbs into meat.

Heat fat. Fry quickly on high heat so that inside remains rare; salt after frying.

Arrange on long platter.

Serve immediately with potatoes, raw salad in season, lettuce, boiled vegetables, spinach, tomato sauté.

Calf's Liver à la Nelson

*4 oz. champignons * 1 medium onion * 3 tbs. butter * salt * pepper * 1 1/2 lb. potatoes * 2 lb. calf's liver * 3 tbs. fat * 1 tbs. flour * 1 cup sour cream*

Rinse mushrooms, peel caps, chop finely, slice onions, add to mushrooms, add part of butter, salt, pepper, dot with water and braise covered, when nearly done, brown while stirring.

Pare potatoes, slice in wedges, parcook.

Rinse liver, remove membrane, cut into flat steaks, remove tubes, sprinkle each slice with pepper.

Heat fat, add liver in slices and fry each piece quickly until brown on both sides.

Liver should be rare inside.

Place the potato wedges in bottom of saucepan, add liver, mushrooms, salt and pepper, arrange, so that 3 layers of potatoes are interspersed with 2 layers of liver, sprinkle with water, add butter, cover and simmer.

When potatoes become soft, add cream, mix with flour, cook and serve immediately.

Fried Veal Kidneys

*1 1/2 lb. veal kidneys * pepper * 2 tbs. fat * salt*

Select kidneys not too fat, or remove the excess layer of fat; cut kidneys along the middle, but do not sever, wash carefully in several waters, squeeze out water.

Place kidneys on cut surfaces on meat board, press with hand to lay flat, sprinkle with pepper.

Heat fat on high heat, add kidneys cut side down and brown quickly on both sides, keeping the side covered with fat somewhat longer on the heat; kidneys should be somewhat rare inside.

Before serving, sprinkle all sides with salt.

Serve with French-fried potatoes, boiled vegetables, leafy salad, tomatoes, tomato sauté.

BRAISED VEAL

Braised Veal Kidneys

*1 1/2 lb. veal kidneys * 2 tbs. fat * 1 medium onion * salt * pepper*

Rinse kidneys, prepare as above, drain water thoroughly, soak in fresh water, squeeze in water, drain, squeeze.

Heat fat on skillet, fry kidneys to brown on both sides quickly, remove to saucepan, add fat from skillet, add sliced onion, a little water, pepper and simmer covered until tender, add salt to taste before ready.

Slice the cooked kidneys lengthwise in half or in three parts, depending on the size, and serve immediately on a very hot platter.

Serve with potatoes and boiled vegetables, sautéed tomatoes.

Braised Loin of Veal

*3 lb. loin of veal with kidney * salt * 3 tbs. fat * pepper * 1 medium onion * 3 tbs. flour*

Scrub and rinse loin.

Crack away chine bones lengthwise, leaving only the backbone, crack the backbone in several places; if the kidney is too fat, remove part of the fat, leaving about 1 inch near the kidney.

Loosen and take away the long semi-circular rib, cover the kidney with a patch (supple flesh overgrown with membrane) and secure kidney by fastening with string tied crosswise.

Salt the meat.

Heat fat on skillet, add meat and fry quickly to brown on both sides, place in a stewing pan, add fat from skillet, a little water and pepper, simmer covered, turning meat from time to time.

During braising add small amounts of water as needed; when meat is half--cooked, add sliced onion.

When meat is tender, remove and carve quickly with a sharp knife, along the cracked parts of the backbone, cut through bone (strike knife with a meat hammer); meat should be carved so that each portion of meat can be served with a bone. Mix the sauce with flour and salt to taste.

Place meat in saucepan and heat through a few times with the sauce since the fat near the kidney curdles quickly; place the entire loin on a heated platter, serve immediately.

Serve with potatoes and boiled vegetables.

Veal Stew

*2 1/2 lb. shoulder or loin of veal * salt * 5 tbs. flour * 3 tbs. fat * paprika *
* 1 medium onion * 1 bouillon cube (1 oz.) * 1 clove of garlic * 1 cup sour
cream*

Rinse meat from shoulder or loin. Carve in pieces,• salt, dredge with
flour.

Heat fat, fry meat quickly to golden color, place in saucepan, add fat,
paprika, diced onion, a little water, a bouillon cube and garlic.

Simmer covered until tender, adding water if needed. Add sour cream
mixed with 2 tbs. of flour and boil well. Salt to taste.

Serve on round platter with rice, potatoes, macaroni, spoon dropped
dumplings and boiled vegetables.

Pound Veal Steaks in Natural Gravy

*2 lb. round of veal * salt * 4 tbs. flour * 3 tbs. fat * 1 medium onion *
* 1 bouillon cube (1 oz.) * pepper*

Rinse meat, remove membrane, cut with sharp knife against the grain
into small steaks — about 2 per serving.

Pound steaks with light, flat meat hammer dampened in water, forming
round, oval or square steaks; sprinkle meat with salt and flour.

Heat fat on skillet, add meat and fry to brown on both sides, remove to
saucepan.

Chop onion, brown lightly in the fat left in the skillet, add to the meat,
add water, bouillon cube and pepper, bring to the boil, reduce heat and
simmer covered. When meat is tender, add 1 tbs. of flour, salt to taste and
bring to the boil. Serve with potatoes, raw salad in season, boiled vegetables.

Pound Veal Steaks in Mushroom Sauce

*2 1/2 lb. round of veal * salt * 3 tbs. flour * 3 tbs. fat * mushroom sauce *
* 1/2 cup sour cream*

Prepare and fry steaks as above.

Prepare mushroom sauce (see page 317).

Add sauce to fried steaks, braise covered until tender, on low flame; before
serving thicken sauce; if too thick, add water; when done, add sour cream.
Serve with noodles or potatoes.

Veal Steaks Stuffed with Fat Back and Paprika

*2 lb. round of veal * salt * garlic * 1/4 lb. fat back * paprika * 3 tbs.*
*flour * 3 tbs. fat for frying * 1 small onion * 1 bouillon cube (1 oz.)*

Rinse meat, remove membrane, cut across the grain in flat, small steaks —
about 2 steaks per portion, pound with light, flat meat hammer dampened
in water.

Rub salt and garlic into each steak.

Place a piece of fat back on the meat, sprinkle with paprika and salt, roll
tightly, fasten with thread or toothpick.

Dredge each steak with flour.

Heat fat, brown steaks quickly on both sides.

Chop onion finely, brown lightly in fat left in skillet.

Place fried meat with onion and fat into saucepan, add bouillon cube,
paprika, water and simmer covered until tender. Salt to taste.

Remove thread from meat, place steaks on platter, pour over sauce. Serve
with coarse or fine groats, rice, noodles, macaroni or potatoes.

ROAST VEAL

Stuffed Breast of Veal à la Polonaise

*2 lb. breast of veal * 4 stale rolls (medium size) * milk for soaking * 2 tbs.*
*butter * 2 egg yolks * salt * pepper * nutmeg * 4 tbs. chopped green dill ***
** 2 egg whites * 2 tbs. bread crumbs * 2 tbs. fat * 2 tbs. butter for roasting*

Rinse meat, make a pocket between the membranes.

With a thin. sharp knife, loosen the meat from the ribs, being careful not
to cut the membrane.

Remove the meat from each bone, break bones at joints, remove, crack
backbone in several places in order to make serving easier. Sprinkle meat
with salt.

Prepare stuffing. Soak rolls in milk, drain.

Cream egg yolks with 2 tbs. of butter, add roll, mix, add salt, spices,
chopped green dill, mix.

Beat egg whites, blend with mixture, add bread crumbs.

Spoon stuffing into pocket, skewer or sew to keep stuffing in place.

Heat fat, add meat, pour fat over meat, place in oven, roast until tender,
basting with gravy, add water if necessary (about 1 hour). Before roasting
is finished dot with 2 tbs. of butter.

Scrape sides of roasting pan, add to gravy, heat gravy.

Cut against the grain in 1/2 inch slices, together with bone of the back-bone; place on long platter, cover with sauce.
Serve with potatoes, raw salad, or cranberry sauce.

Roast Loin of Veal

*3 lb. loin of veal with kidney * salt * 3 tbs. fat * 1 medium onion * pepper*

Prepare the loin roast as for braised loin of veal, brown on skillet in hot fat. Place meat in roasting pan.
Pour fat from skillet over meat, sprinkle with water, place in medium oven and roast, baste frequently adding water when necessary. When meat is half done, add sliced onion, pepper, and roast through.
Remove when tender, slice quickly as for braised loin of veal; after slicing heat thoroughly and place on warmed platter.
Cover meat with part of sauce; serve rest of sauce in gravy boat. Serve with potatoes or boiled vegetables.

Stuffed Loin of Veal, Polish Style

*2 1/2 lb. loin of veal without kidney * 4 stale rolls * milk for soaking *
* 2 tbs. butter * 2 eggs * 4 tbs. chopped green dill * salt * pepper *
* nutmeg * 1 tbs. bread crumbs * 3 tbs. fat * 2 tbs. butter for roasting*

Rinse meat, chop chine bone lengthwise then remove, crack backbone carefully in a number of places to facilitate carving. Remove ribs.
Prepare stuffing. Soak rolls, drain, grind.
Cream butter adding egg yolks one at a time, add ground rolls, green dill, salt, pepper, nutmeg, mix.
Beat egg whites, fold into mixture, sprinkle with fine bread crumbs, blend.
Make a pocket between the membrane and fleshy part of meat, cutting the membrane up to the backbone, stuff the pocket and sew up on three sides or place stuffing in place where kidney was removed, and secure with supple part of meat, sewed up on sides except for side which forms the backbone (if using the latter method, prepare only half the amount of stuffing).
Salt meat and brown quickly in hot fat on skillet, place in roasting pan, add fat from skillet and a little water and set in medium oven.
Baste while roasting, adding water when necessary; when meat is almost done, add butter.
When meat is tender, remove and carve with sharp knife, use meat hammer to cut through backbone and serve with bone.

Rolled Veal with Ham Stuffing

*3 lb. round of veal * garlic * salt * stale roll (about 1 1/2 oz) * 1 tbs. fat * 1 small onion * 1 oz. fat back * 9 oz. boiled ham * 1/2 egg * pepper * * 3 tbs. fat for roasting * 2 tbs. butter for roasting*

Prepare meat. Rinse meat, place on meat board, if meat is too thick, groove it in several places.
Pound meat with dampened meat hammer into thin, flat, square piece.
Smooth surface of meat, salt and smear lightly with crushed garlic.
Prepare stuffing. Soak roll in water, drain.
Chop onion, brown lightly in fat.
Grind roll, fat back and ham, mix with egg, pepper, onion, salt. Spread stuffing on meat. Roll meat tightly, tie up with string every inch, salt.
Heat fat in baking tin on top of stove, brown meat on all sides.
Place in oven, pour gravy over meat, add water when necessary; when meat is almost done, add butter; roast until tender, remove from oven. Scrape sides of roasting tin, add to gravy, heat gravy; remove string from meat, slice about 1/2 inch thick; place on platter, pour gravy over the roast.
Serve with French-fried potatoes, leafy salad, tomatoes, cucumbers in sour cream, tomato sauté and boiled vegetables.

Roast Calf's Liver

*2 lb. calf's liver * pepper * 2 tbs. fat * 3 tbs. butter * salt*

Rinse liver, remove membrane and tubes, sprinkle with pepper.
Heat fat in roasting pan, add liver, pour fat over liver, place in hot oven, roast so that meat is rare inside; baste with fat while roasting; before removing from oven, add butter. Cut into thin slices, salt, arrange on platter in one piece, pour pan gravy over meat.
Serve with French-fried potatoes, green salad in season, boiled vegetables.

Roast Veal

*2 lb. round of veal * garlic * salt * 3 tbs. fat * 1 small onion*

Rinse meat. Crush garlic and salt. Rub into meat. Melt fat in roasting pan and brown meat in hot fat. Place in medium oven and roast. Baste frequently, adding water when necessary. When meat is half done, add sliced onion and roast through. Remove when tender. Serve with potatoes and cauliflower (with polonaise topping), plums in vinegar or raw-vegetable relishes.

BEEF

BOILED BEEF

Beef in Broth

*1 lb. beef plate * 9 oz. mixed vegetables * 1 medium onion * bay leaf *
* allspice * pepper * salt * green parsley*

Rinse meat, crack bones across the rib, add boiling water, simmer covered.
When meat is parboiled add cleaned, mixed vegetables, onion browned on
open flame, spices, salt. Simmer until tender.
Cook fluffy rice or macaroni (1 oz. uncooked per person).
Carve meat together with rib bones, slice mixed vegetables from soup.
Place 1 cup of broth in every plate, a portion of meat with bone, some of
sliced vegetables, and rice or macaroni, garnish with parsley.

Boiled Beef

*1/2 lb. bones * 2 lb. rump of beef * pepper * bay leaf * allspice * 8 oz.
mixed vegetables * 1 medium onion * salt*

205

Wash bones, clean, add water, boil.

Rinse meat, place in boiling stock with bones, add spices.

Cut onion into halves, brown on open flame or put (cut side down) on a hot range.

When meat is parcooked, add the cleaned, mixed vegetables, onion and salt.

Drain the meat when cooked, slice across the grain (about 1/2 inch thick).

Place the entire meat on platter, sprinkle with broth, garnish with sliced vegetables from broth.

Serve with sharp sauce, dill pickle, horse-radish and beet relish, sour cream and cucumber relish, plus potatoes.

Pickled Brisket of Beef in Broth

*Marinade for pickling * 2 1/2 lb. brisket of beef with bones * bay leaf * * allspice * salt * 9 oz. mixed vegetables*

Prepare ingredients for marinade and boil water.

Rinse meat, drain off water, crack rib bones, season meat with spices and salt, place in a tightly fitting crock, cover crock and press down with weight and marinate for 2—3 weeks (see page 184).

Remove meat after pickling, remove spices, pour over a little boiling water and cook slowly (about 2 hours); if the water is too salty after half an hour, drain and add fresh boiling water; if not salty enough, add salt. When meat is parcooked, add vegetables.

Remove meat when tender, carve into portions with bone, cutting against the grain, place on heated platter, sprinkle with broth. Serve with potatoes, sharp sauces, dill pickles, horse-radish and beet relish and boiled vegetables.

Boiled Beef Tongue

*2 1/2 lb. beef tongue * 7 oz. mixed vegetables * salt * bay leaf * allspice*

Clean tongue with brush under running water, remove salivary glands at root of tongue.

Add water to tongue and simmer for 2 hours.

Remove tongue, place in cold water, remove skin, place into broth again, add cleaned, mixed vegetables, salt, spices and cook thoroughly.

Remove tongue, when very tender, slice thinly slantwise.
Serve with potatoes and horse-radish or sharp sauces.

Pickled Beef Tongue in Broth

*Marinade for pickling * 2 1/2 lb. beef tongue * bay leaf * allspice * salt * * 7 oz. mixed vegetables*

Prepare ingredients for marinade and boil water.
Scrub tongue with brush under running water, remove salivary glands, rinse, squeeze out water, rub tongue well with spices and salt, place in tightly fitting bowl, cover with small wooden board and press down with weight; marinate for 10 days (see page 184).
Remove tongue, clean off spices, pour over a little boiling water and cook slowly (about 2—3 hours); if the stock is not salty enough after half an hour's cooking, add salt to taste.
When tongue is parcooked, remove, place in cold water and remove tough thick skin; place tongue once again in broth, add mixed vegetables, cook until very tender, otherwise it is not tasty.
Remove tongue when tender, carve into thin large slices. Serve hot with potatoes and sharp sauces or bake with béchamel or horse-radish sauce. Serve cold (cool in broth) with tartar sauce or horse-radish.

Udder Ragoût

*2 lb. beef udder * 9 oz. mixed vegetables * salt * pepper * 1 medium onion * 3 tbs. fat * 4 tbs. flour * nutmeg * 1 bouillon cube * green parsley*

Rinse udder several times, drain well, place in boiling water and cook changing water several times, drain.
Add hot water and cook until completely tender (about 4 hours). When parcooked, add mixed vegetables, salt, pepper and onion.
When meat is completely tender, cut into cubes, evaporate stock.
Prepare sauce. Brown flour lightly with fat, dilute with broth, add nutmeg, salt and bouillon cube to taste.
Place meat in sauce, mix, heat. Add chopped green parsley.
Serve with potatoes, fine groats and vegetables.

Tripe à la Warsaw

Prepare the same way as given in section on hot appetizers (page 61).

207

Udder Tripe à la Warsaw

Prepare the same way as tripe à la Warsaw. Use the udder instead of tripe. This type of tripe is very tasty and delicate.

Rinse the udder before cooking, squeeze thoroughly, place in boiling water and cook changing water several times, drain off this water and then add water for cooking. Cook until very tender (about 4 hours).

FRIED BEEF

Rib-of-Beef Chops

*Vegetable marinade * 3 lb. rib of beef * salt * pepper * 3 tbs. flour * 3 tbs. fat for frying * 2 tbs. butter for frying*

Divide rib of beef into 5 chops (about 1/2 inch thick), but do not separate chops. Have butcher cut off backbone so that only a piece of the bone remains for each chop; rinse meat, marinate in vegetables for 1—2 days (see page 183).

Remove membrane from meat, divide into 5 chops, pound immediately before frying, salt, sprinkle with flour and pepper.

Heat fat on hot skillet, brown meat quickly on both sides, leaving meat rare inside. While turning chops add butter for frying.

Serve immediately after frying on long platter. Garnish each chop with horse-radish butter or chive butter (see page 16). Serve with any type of potatoes, leafy salad and boiled vegetables. Prepare only with choice quality and tenderized beef.

Beef Steak, English Style

*2 lb. loin of beef * salt * 3 tbs. fat for frying * 3 tbs. butter for frying*

Rinse meat, remove fat, membrane and tendons, slice meat perpendicular to the base about 3/4 inch thick, pound steaks lightly.

Salt meat immediately before frying.

Heat fat, fry meat quickly on high flame, brown on both sides, leaving inside rare; while turning meat, add butter and brown together with meat. Add two tablespoons of water to the gravy, heat until brown and until the sediment sticking to the pan dissolves.

Serve with egg, onion, garnish with chives, horse-radish, herring butter and potatoes, raw salad in season, boiled vegetables, peas, etc.

Beef Brizol

*1 1/2 lb. loin of beef * salt * 2 tbs. flour * 3 tbs. fat for frying * 3 tbs. butter for frying*

Rinse meat, remove fat, membrane, tendons and grizzle, divide into 5 portions, cutting meat somewhat diagonally.

Place meat on the cut side on meat board dampened with water, pound lightly into flat steaks, being careful not to tear the meat, shape into round, flat, large steaks.

Heat fat on high flame in skillet. Salt meat, sprinkle with flour, and fry to brown on both sides; while turning meat add butter to complete frying. Add a little water to gravy, heat, mix and sprinkle meat with this gravy, serve immediately.

Serve with French-fried potatoes, raw salad in season, boiled vegetables, green peas.

Rib-of-Beef Chops with Onions

*Vegetable marinade * 4 1/2 lb. rib of beef * salt * 3 tbs. fat for frying * * 2 tbs. butter for frying * 1 medium onion*

Have butcher prepare meat into chops (without severing) and loosen chine bone (chops should be about 8 oz. each); marinate in vegetables for 1—2 days (see page 183).

Separate chops, salt, place in hot fat and brown on both sides.

Remove meat, quickly braise or brown onion (according to taste) and add butter.

Serve immediately, dotting each chop with a piece of browned onion. Serve with French-fried potatoes, leafy salad, tomatoes, cucumbers, dill pickles, horse-radish, boiled vegetables.

Prepare only with choice quality meat, well hung.

Loin-of-Beef Fillet with Mushrooms on Toast

*5 oz. champignons * 2 tbs. butter * salt * pepper * 5 slices of toast * * 3 tbs. butter for frying toast * 1 1/2 lb. loin of beef, fillet only * 3 tbs. flour * 3 tbs. fat for frying * 3 oz. meat paté*

Prepare mushrooms. Wash mushrooms, peel caps, slice thick, add butter, sprinkle with water and braise. Salt to taste, add pepper, brown lightly, turning carefully. .

Prepare 5 slices of toast about 1/2 inch thick, cut ovally, even off crusts, and just before serving fry in butter so that toast is crispy.

Prepare meat. Rinse, remove fat, membrane and grizzle, cut across the grain into 5 small steaks; sprinkle with salt, pepper and flour.

Heat fat in skillet, add meat and brown quickly on both sides on hot skillet, leaving steaks rare inside.

Place steaks on hot toast, spread some meat paté on top of steak, then add hot mushrooms, place on heated platter, place in oven to heat and serve immediately, rare. Serve with Madeira sauce.

Loin-of-Beef Fillet in Sauces

Prepare in the same proportions as above (meat and toast), without mushrooms, after placing meat on toast cover with thick tomato, mushroom or Madeira sauce.

Breaded Beef Brains

*2 beef brains * vinegar * salt * pepper * 5 tbs. flour * 1 1/2 eggs * 1/2 cup fine bread crumbs * 7 tbs. fat for frying*

Select undamaged brains. Prepare brains. After cooking, cool brain and cut into thick slices. Continue as given for veal-brain patties (see page 193).

Dewlap, Viennese Style

*Cooked dewlap of beef tongue * 5 tbs. flour * 2 eggs * 1/2 cup fine bread crumbs * 4 tbs. fat for frying*

Place cooked dewlap (remaining after slicing tongue) on platter, shape while hot, cover with a wooden board placing weight on cover, and cool. Remove dewlap the next day and slice uniformly, then bread in flour, egg and bread crumbs.

Fry quickly on hot skillet with hot fat and serve immediately.

Serve with potatoes, tart relish or vegetable salad.

Breaded Beef Udder

*2 lb. beef udder * 9 oz. mixed vegetables * salt * pepper * 1 medium onion * 5 tbs. flour * 1 1/2 eggs * 1/2 cup fine bread crumbs * 4 tbs. fat for frying*

Cook udder as described above (see page 207).

When meat is tender, drain and cool (use stock for soups).

Cut in large uniform slices, sprinkle with pepper, dip in flour, egg and bread crumbs.

Heat fat in skillet, add meat and fry on high flame until brown. Serve with potatoes and relish.

Mixed-Meat Cutlets

*2 stale rolls (about 4 oz.) * 1 medium onion * 1 tbs. fat * 1 lb. chuck or round of beef * 4 oz. pork * 1 egg * salt * pepper * 1/2 cup fine bread crumbs * 3 tbs. fat for frying*

Soak roll, drain off water, grind.

Slice onion, brown lightly in fat.

Rinse meat, grind, knead.

Add roll, onion, egg, salt and pepper to meat, mix.

Divide meat into even parts, shape into balls (or make a roll and then divide).

Cover meat balls with bread crumbs and flatten with a knife into an oval shape about 1/2 inch thick; score cutlet.

Heat fat, add meat, brown to golden color on both sides on high heat, then turn heat to medium flame.

When meat ceases to secrete rare juice on being pressed with flat side of knife, set on platter, one cutlet after the other.

Serve with potatoes, all kinds of raw salads, lettuce and vegetable.

Beef Brains à la Polonaise

Prepare according to instructions for calf's brains à la Polonaise (see page 198).

BRAISED BEEF

Beef Stroganoff

*1 oz. dried mushrooms * 3 tbs. butter * 1 medium onion * 4 tbs. flour * * 2 oz. tomato paste * salt * sugar * paprika * 1 bouillon cube * 2 lb. loin of beef * salt * pepper * 3 tbs. fat*

Prepare sauce. Wash mushrooms and rinse, cook, drain, chop in thin strips.

Melt butter, brown lightly with onion, blend with flour, fry, dilute with stock from mushrooms and tomato paste, add bouillon cube, heat, stir, add salt, paprika and sugar to taste.

Prepare meat. Rinse loin, remove fat, membrane and grizzle, slice into thin steaks about 1/2 inch thick, 2 inches long and 1/2 inch wide; sprinkle meat with salt, pepper and flour.

Heat fat and brown meat quickly on very hot skillet, leaving it rare inside. Serve meat immediately on heated plates, pour over with sauce. Serve with French-fried potatoes and boiled vegetables.

Beef Goulash

*2 lb. shank, chuck or brisket of beef * salt * 4 tbs. flour * 3 tbs. fat *
* 1 large onion * pepper * bay leaf * allspice * coriander * 1 bouillon cube*

Rinse meat, cube, salt and dredge each piece.

Heat fat, brown meat on hot skillet, remove to saucepan.

Slice onion, brown lightly in fat from frying.

Add onion with frying fat to meat, a little water, spices, bouillon cube, simmer slowly, covered, until tender, adding water when necessary; add flour just before completing cooking.

Serve goulash in bowl.

Serve with potatoes, noodles, dropped dumplings, fine or coarse fluffy groats and all kinds of vegetables.

Hungarian Beef Goulash

*2 lb. shank, chuck or brisket of beef * 2 oz. fat back * skin of fat back *
* 1 large onion * salt * paprika * 4 tbs. flour*

Cube meat, melt fat back in small saucepan, heat, add meat and fat back skin, onion, salt and paprika, cover saucepan and braise, first on high flame, then reduce heat, cooking slowly.

Add hot water when necessary, but allow meat to brown.

When meat is tender, mix flour with water, add to the meat, cook, if necessary season the sauce.

After meat is cooked 5 tbs. of tomato paste can be added.

Serve with noodles, potatoes, groats and all types of vegetables.

Roast Beef Braised in Natural Sauce

*2 lb. top sirloin, round, rump or chuck of beef * salt * 3 tbs. fat *
* 1 medium onion * bay leaf * allspice * 1 bouillon cube * 1 tbs. flour*

Rinse meat, pound well, salt.

Heat fat on skillet, add meat and brown on all sides on high heat.

Remove meat to saucepan, add fat, onion, bay leaf, allspice, water and simmer covered (about 1 hour); add cold water when necessary and turn meat. Before cooking is finished, add bouillon cube.

When meat is tender, add flour to gravy, cook, stir.

Carve meat with sharp knife into thin slices cut across the grain, cut diagonally from top to bottom; place entire roast on platter, pour over hot gravy.

Serve with potatoes, noodles and all kinds of vegetables.

Roast Beef Braised with Mushrooms

*2 1/2 lb. top sirloin, round or chuck of beef * salt * 3 tbs. fat * 1 medium onion * bay leaf * allspice * 1 oz. dried mushrooms * 1 bouillon cube * * 1 cup sour cream * 1 tbs. flour*

Prepare in the same way as roast beef braised in natural sauce; when meat is half-cooked add cleaned, dried mushrooms and bouillon cube; when mushrooms and meat are tender, remove mushrooms. Garnish sauce with cream and flour, dice mushrooms, add to sauce, cook and complete as above.

Serve with potatoes, noodles, boiled vegetables.

Marinated Braised Roast Beef

*Vinegar marinade * 2 1/2 lb. rump, top sirloin or round of beef * salt * * 3 tbs. fat * 5 oz. mixed vegetables * 1 bouillon cube * 1 cup sour cream * 3 tbs. flour*

Prepare marinade with vinegar, cool (see page 184).

Rinse meat, place in bowl, cover with brine and pickle for 2—5 days.

Remove meat, drain, salt.

Heat fat on skillet, brown meat on all sides, remove to saucepan, add fat from frying, finely-sliced vegetables, onion and allspice from the marinade and simmer covered, turning meat; slightly brown the sauce and vegetables.

Add marinade when sauce evaporates, and if sauce is too tart, sprinkle with water; before completing, add bouillon cube.

When meat is tender, remove, add sour cream and flour to sauce, heat, stir (if necessary color with caramel).

Carve into large thin slices, place entire roast on platter, cover with part of sauce, serve rest of sauce in gravy boat.

Serve with potatoes, noodles, dropped dumplings and beets.

Sztufada

Braised Beef

*4 1/2 lb. rump, round or top sirloin of beef * vegetable marinade * 3 oz. fat back * salt * marjoram * 5 tbs. fat * 1 bouillon cube * paprika * * 2 oz. tomato paste * 1/2 cup dry, red wine * garlic*

Choose a thick, compact piece of meat.

Rinse meat, remove membrane, rub well with spices and cover with vegetable marinade; place in bowl in cold place for 1—2 days (see page 183).

Slice fat back into thick chunks (1 1/4 inches × 1/4 inch), sprinkle with salt and marjoram.

Remove meat from marinade, clean off vegetables and insert fat back deeply into meat every 1 1/4 inches in alternate rows.

Heat fat on skillet, add meat and brown on all sides; place meat in saucepan, add drippings from skillet, the vegetables from the marinade, 1 bouillon cube, salt, paprika, sprinkle with water, cover, and simmer until tender (about 2 hours).

Remove meat when tender, cut in slightly diagonal slices across the grain 1/2 inch thick and return them in the same order to pot.

Strain gravy, add salt, tomato paste, wine and crushed garlic, heat, add to meat and heat quickly.

Place entire meat on platter, pour over sauce.

Serve with potatoes, dropped dumplings, potato dumplings.

Rolled Beef Steaks

*2 lb. round, rib, top sirloin or chuck of beef * salt * mustard * 1/4 lb. fat back * 2 dill pickles * 1 onion * pepper * 3 tbs. flour * 1/2 cup sour cream*

Rinse meat, remove membrane, cut across the grain into flat steaks, pound with dampened meat hammer. Salt. Spread thinly with mustard. Cut fat back and dill pickles (lengthwise). Cut onion. Place a piece of fat back, dill pickle and onion on each steak, sprinkle with pepper, roll tightly, fasten with thread or toothpick. Dredge each steak with flour. Heat fat on skillet. Brown steaks on both sides. Place well-browned steaks with fat into saucepan, add a little water and stew covered until tender. Mix remaining flour with sour cream, add to meat, add salt to taste. Bring to the boil. Serve with fluffy buckwheat groat (parched) and raw-vegetable relishes.

Pound Steaks in Natural Gravy

*2 lb. round, top sirloin, rib or chuck of beef * salt * 4 tbs. flour * 3 tbs. fat * 1 large onion * pepper * 1 bouillon cube*

Rinse meat, slice into flat steaks and pound with dampened meat hammer into thin slices.

Salt each steak and dredge in flour.

Heat fat, fry steaks until well-browned on both sides in hot skillet.

Slice onion, brown lightly in fat from frying.

Place browned steaks in saucepan, add onion and fat, add water, pepper, bouillon cube, stew until tender, covered, add cold water if necessary.

Serve on long platter covered with sauce.

Serve with potatoes, fluffy groats and lettuce or raw vegetable relish.

Pound Steaks in Tomato Sauce

*2 lb. round, chuck, rib or top sirloin of beef * salt * 4 tbs. flour * 3 tbs. fat * 1 medium onion * 1 bouillon cube * 2 oz. tomato paste * 1/2 cup sour cream * paprika*

Rinse meat, divide into five steaks and pound into thin slices.

Salt each steak, sprinkle with flour and brown in fat on both sides.

Place steaks in saucepan, add sliced onion, a little water, bouillon cube, stew till tender.

Rinse tomatoes, cut into small parts, add a little water, cook over hot flame, strain.

When the steaks are almost ready pour in tomato sauce, cook.

Mix flour with sour cream, add to tender meat, add salt and paprika to taste.

Serve with macaroni, dropped dumplings, potatoes and cooked vegetables.

Pound Steaks with Mushroom Sauce

*2 lb. round, rib, top sirloin or chuck of beef * salt * 4 tbs. flour * 3 tbs. fat * 1 oz. dried mushrooms * pepper * 1 medium onion * 1 bouillon cube * 3/4 cup sour cream*

Rinse meat, cut into flat steaks, pound, salt, sprinkle with flour.

Heat fat on skillet, brown steaks on both sides, place in saucepan.

Wash mushrooms and rinse thoroughly, parboil.

Chop mushrooms, add to meat, add salt and pepper.

Fry onion in fat left in skillet, add to meat, add bouillon cube and stew meat, add stock in which mushrooms were cooked (if necessary). When meat is tender, add sour cream to sauce.

Serve with coarse or fine groats, barley cereal, macaroni, potatoes and boiled vegetables.

Steaks à la Nelson

*1 oz. dried mushrooms * 1 small onion * 2 tbs. butter * 4 tbs. flour * * 1 cup sour cream * salt * pepper * 1 lb. potatoes * 2 lb. loin of beef * * 3 tbs. fat*

Prepare sauce. Wash mushrooms, rinse, add a little water, add onion, cook covered, drain, chop mushrooms into thin strips.

Brown butter lightly with flour, dilute with mushroom broth and sour cream, stir while cooking, add salt and pepper to taste, mix with mushrooms.

Pare potatoes, rinse, cut potatoes into wedges, cook on slow heat, do not overcook.

Prepare meat (fry meat after serving soup). Rinse meat, remove membrane, fat and grizzle, slice about 1 inch thick, salt and brown quickly on both sides, leaving inside rare.

Remove steaks to saucepan, place flatly; place a portion of cooked potatoes on each steak, add sauce, heat and serve while inside remains rare and juicy.

Serve meat in saucepan in which sauce was cooked (best in casserole).

Chopped Steaks with Pan Gravy

Me a t   m i x t u r e: *1 stale roll (1 oz.) * 1 small onion * 1 tbs. fat * * 3/4 lb. top sirloin or chuck of beef * 4 oz. pork * 1 egg * salt * pepper * * 7 tbs. fine bread crumbs * 3 tbs. fat for frying ** G r a v y: *fat from frying steaks * 1/2 small onion * 5 tbs. flour * salt * 1 bouillon cube * * pepper * allspice * bay leaf*

Soak roll, drain water, grind.

Slice onion, brown lightly in fat.

Rinse meat, grind, mix.

Mix meat with roll, onion, egg, salt, pepper, knead.

Sprinkle meat board with bread crumbs, place meat on board, shape into thick roll, cut into 10 parts, shape them in bread crumbs into small rolls.

Heat fat, fry steaks in skillet, place in saucepan.

Prepare gravy. Brown onion in fat from frying. Add flour, brown, set aside, dilute with water, stir while cooking, add salt, bouillon cube, strain gravy.

Pour gravy on steaks, add spices and drippings, simmer covered for a short time.

Serve on long platter, with gravy poured over steaks. Serve with fine or coarse groats, barley and all kinds of vegetables.

Chopped Steaks with Tomato Sauce

M e a t   m i x t u r e: *1 stale roll (1 oz.) * 1 small onion * 1 tbs. fat * * 3/4 lb. top sirloin or chuck of beef * 4 oz. pork * 1 egg * salt * * pepper * 7 tbs. fine bread crumbs * 3 tbs. fat for frying * S a u c e: 2 tbs. fat (and fat from frying steaks) * 3 tbs. flour * 1 oz. tomato paste * salt * pinch of sugar*

Prepare meat mixture as above, shape into steaks, fry.

Prepare sauce. Melt fat, add flour and fat from frying, brown flour lightly, dilute with water, cook, add tomato paste, salt, sugar.

Place steaks in sauce, braise on very low heat.

Serve with macaroni, dropped dumplings, potatoes and boiled vegetables.

Chopped Steaks Stuffed with Horse-Radish

S t u f f i n g: *5 tbs. horse-radish * 2 tbs. sour cream * paprika * M e a t   m i x t u r e: 1 stale roll (1 oz.) * 1 small onion * 1 tbs. fat * 3/4 lb. top sirloin or chuck of beef * 1/4 lb. pork * 1 egg * salt * pepper * * 5 tbs. fine bread crumbs * 3 tbs. fat for frying * S a u c e: fat from frying steaks * 1 cup sour cream * 3 tbs. flour * salt * paprika * * allspice * bay leaf*

Prepare stuffing. Scrub fresh horse-radish, rinse, grate, mix with 2 table-spoons of sour cream and paprika.

Soak roll, drain, grind.

Chop onion, brown lightly in fat.

Rinse meat, grind, knead.

Mix meat with browned onion, roll, egg, salt, pepper.

Divide meat mixture into 10 parts, flatten each part, place horse-radish on top, roll.

When all steaks are stuffed, shape them in bread crumbs into rolls of even length (about 3 inches).

Fry in skillet on all sides, remove to saucepan.

Prepare sauce. Brown flour lightly in fat from frying, dilute with sour cream and water, add salt, paprika, allspice and bay leaf. Bring to the boil.

Add sauce to steaks, simmer on very low heat, so that steaks do not fall apart.

Serve with macaroni, potatoes and boiled vegetables.

217

ROAST BEEF

Meat Loaf Stuffed with Eggs

*1 stale roll (1 oz.) * 1 small onion * 1 tbs. fat * 3/4 lb. top sirloin or chuck of beef * 1/4 lb. pork * 1 egg * salt * pepper * 4 tbs. bread crumbs * 3 hard-boiled eggs * green parsley * 3 tbs. fat for roasting*

Soak roll in water, drain, grind.
Brown chopped onion lightly in fat.
Rinse meat, grind, form mixture.
Mix meat with roll, onion, raw egg, add salt, pepper, mix, place meat mixture on board sprinkled with bread crumbs.
Boil eggs until hard, cool in cold water, peel, cut in quarters.
Shape meat with knife into rectangle; place quartered eggs along length, sprinkle with chopped green parsley.
Roll meat into thick roll (roll from side with eggs, so that eggs are in center after rolling), shape.
Heat fat on long, narrow baking tin, add meat, pour fat on top of meat, place in very hot oven and baste while roasting.
Scrape gravy from sides of tin, heat.
Slice meat thickly when done, place entire loaf on long platter, pour sauce over loaf.
Serve with potatoes, raw salad and cooked vegetables. The loaf can also be served cold (without sauce).

Meat Loaf Stuffed with Sausage

*1 stale roll (1 oz.) * 1 small onion * 1 tbs. fat * 3/4 lb. top sirloin or chuck of beef * 1/4 lb. pork * 1 egg * salt * pepper * 4 tbs. fine bread crumbs * 8 oz. pork sausage (raw or smoked) * 3 tbs. fat for roasting*

Soak roll in water, drain, grind.
Brown chopped onion lightly in fat.
Rinse meat, grind, knead.
Mix meat with roll, onion, egg, add salt, pepper, mix and place on board sprinkled with bread crumbs.
Shape meat mixture into rectangle.
Remove raw sausage from skin, place along one of longer sides (or skin smoked sausage and place on meat).
Roll into thick roll (start rolling from side with sausage so that sausage remains in center after rolling).

Heat fat in long, narrow baking tin, place meat on hot fat, pour fat on top of meat.

Place meat in very hot oven, roast until tender.

Scrape gravy from sides of baking tin, mix with gravy, heat.

Slice thickly when done, place entire loaf on long serving platter covered with sauce. Serve with potatoes and all kinds of vegetables.

The loaf can be served cold without sauce.

Meat Loaf in Sour-Cream Sauce

Meat mixture: *1 stale roll (1 oz.) * 1 small onion * 1 tbs. fat * * 3/4 lb. top sirloin or chuck of beef * 1/4 lb. pork * 1 egg * salt * * pepper * 4 tbs. fine bread crumbs * 3 tbs. fat for roasting * S a u c e: fat from roasting * 1 cup sour cream * 2 tbs. flour * salt * 1 bouillon cube * paprika * allspice * bay leaf * (caramel for color)*

Soak roll, drain.

Brown chopped onion lightly in fat.

Rinse meat, grind together with drained roll.

Mix meat with onion, egg, salt, pepper. Form. Place on board sprinkled with bread crumbs, shape into fat roll.

Heat fat, place meat in long, narrow baking tin, dot with fat, place in oven, baste while roasting.

Prepare sauce. Add cream and flour to fat from roasting, add salt, 1 bouillon cube and spices, stir while cooking, if necessary color sauce with caramel, dilute with water, pour over meat and roast for a short time with the sauce.

Slice into 1/2 inch slices when done, place on long serving platter, pour over part of sauce, serve remainder in gravy boat.

Serve with potatoes, dropped dumplings, macaroni and beets.

Loin of Beef

*2 lb. loin of beef * salt * 2 tbs. flour * 3 tbs. fat for roasting * 2 tbs. butter for roasting*

Rinse meat, remove fat, leave grizzle, pound lightly, salt, dredge with flour.

Heat fat, place meat in fat, sprinkle fat on top of meat.

Place in very hot oven, roast but allow to remain rare inside.

When meat is almost done, add butter.

After roasting meat, slice across the grain thinly and place entire roast on long platter, pour over gravy.

Scrape gravy from sides of tin, add a little water, mix, heat. Serve with French-fried potatoes, vegetable salad in season and boiled vegetables, tomato sauce, mushrooms, etc.

Grilled Loin of Beef

*Vegetable marinade * 2 lb. loin of beef * salt * 3 tbs. butter*

Rinse meat, remove fat and grizzle, cover with vegetable marinade (see page 183); set aside in cold place for a few hours.
Three quarters of an hour before serving, salt, place on hot greased grill, smear with butter and place in hot oven.
Roast loin, basting often with drippings from meat.
When meat is browned on surface, but medium-rare inside, remove immediately before serving and slice thinly, place on heated platter already garnished and serve piping hot.

Roast Beef, English Style

*Vegetable marinade * 2 lb. rump or loin of beef * 3 tbs. fat for roasting * * 3 tbs. butter for roasting*

Rinse meat, drain, and place in marinade for a day (see page 183).
Remove meat the following day. Sprinkle with salt. Heat fat on skillet, add meat, brown quickly on hot skillet, remove to roasting pan, dot with fat and place in very hot oven.
Roast rare. Sprinkle with gravy while roasting. When meat is almost done, add butter.
Cut into thin diagonal slices across the grain and place entire roast on heated platter.
Scrape sauce from sides of roasting pan, sprinkle with water, mix, heat, pour over meat.
Serve with French-fried potatoes or small boiled potatoes, fresh salad in season, boiled vegetables, tomato sauté, etc. Prepare only with choice quality meat.

Beef Roll Stuffed with Veal and Herring

S t u f f i n g: *1 herring * 1 stale roll (1 oz.) * 2 oz. fat back * 2 oz. raw veal * 1 clove garlic * 1/2 egg * M e a t   r o l l: 2 lb. rump of beef * salt * * 3 tbs. flour * 4 tbs. fat for roasting*

Soak herring on previous day, changing water, clean herring and chop. Soak roll in water, drain.

Rinse veal, slice, grind together with fat back and roll.

Add herring to mixture, then garlic, egg, mix thoroughly.

Clean beef, place on board, remove fat and membrane.

Pound meat with dampened meat hammer into flat thin slice, rectangular in shape.

Smooth surface of meat with knife, spread stuffing on top, roll meat, tie, salt and dredge with flour.

Heat fat on skillet, brown meat quickly, place in long, narrow baking tin, sprinkle surface of meat with fat.

Place meat in hot oven and roast until tender, baste while roasting, adding water as necessary.

Scrape sauce from sides of baking tin, mix with gravy, heat.

When meat is tender, remove string, cut roll into thick slices, place entire roll on long platter, pour sauce over meat.

Serve with boiled potatoes, French-fried potatoes and raw salad.

Beef Tongue in Béchamel Sauce

*2 1/2 lb. beef tongue * 7 oz. mixed vegetables * salt * bay leaf * allspice * * S a u c e: 4 tbs. butter * 7 tbs. flour * 2 1/2 cups broth * salt * 2 tbs. lemon juice * 2 egg yolks * 1 oz. Parmesan cheese * 1 tbs. butter for dotting * 2 tbs. bread crumbs*

Scrub tongue in water, remove salivary gland and boil until very tender as described on page 206.

Prepare sauce. Prepare white roux with butter and flour, dilute with cooled broth, stir while cooking, add salt to taste, lemon juice and mix thoroughly with raw egg yolks and cheese.

Carve tongue into thin slices (like ham), place entire tongue in roaster. Pour thick sauce over meat, dot with butter and bread crumbs, rest of grated cheese, and roast in very hot oven (about 20 minutes).

Serve with potatoes, raw vegetable salad and boiled vegetables.

Boiled Beef Baked in Horse-Radish Sauce

*2 1/2 lb. rump of beef * 9 oz. mixed vegetables * 1 medium onion * allspice * bay leaf * salt * P o t a t o p u r é e: 2 lbs. potatoes * salt * 1 tbs. butter * milk * H o r s e - r a d i s h s a u c e: 1 1/2 cups broth * 2 tbs. butter * 4 tbs. flour * 1 cup sour cream * 3 tbs. grated horse-radish * * salt * vinegar * sugar * 1 tbs. butter for dotting*

Rinse meat, pound with bones, place in boiling water, cook slowly.

Clean mixed vegetables.

Brown onion on open flame or place with cut side down on hot range. When meat is almost cooked, add onion, mixed vegetables, spices, salt, cook meat until very tender. Carve into slices 1/2 inch thick.

Prepare potato purée: cook potatoes, mash, add milk and butter, beat until fluffy.

Rinse horse-radish, core, grate.

Prepare white roux with butter and flour, dilute with broth, add sour cream, stir while cooking. Add horse-radish, salt, vinegar and sugar to taste.

Divide potato purée into two parts. Line the bottom of long serving platter with one part (serving platter should be heat resistent).

Place slices of meat on potatoes; slice vegetables from broth with serrated knife, place on top of meat.

Cover meat with second part of potatoes, even on top and on sides.

Spread half of the thick sauce over meat. Dilute the rest of the sauce with the broth, pour over top of whole, dot with melted butter and place in very hot oven for 20 minutes.

Serve on platter from oven.

Serve with boiled vegetables (cauliflower, Brussel sprouts, string beans) and raw vegetable salad in season.

Boiled Beef, Flemish Style

*2 1/2 lb. rump of beef * 9 oz. mixed vegetables * 1 medium onion *
* allspice * pepper * bay leaf * salt * P o t a t o   p u r é e: 2 lb. potatoes *
* salt * milk * 1 tbs. butter * S a u c e: 3 tbs. butter * 1/2 cup flour * 2 cups
broth * vegetables from broth * 1 oz. grated Parmesan cheese * 3 tbs. fine
bread crumbs * 2 tbs. butter for dotting * green parsley*

Rinse meat, pound with bones, place in boiling water and cook slowly on medium flame, do not add water.

When almost cooked, add onion, mixed vegetables, spices and salt. Cook. When meat is very tender, strain broth and cook so that 3/4 quart of liquid remains.

Slice vegetables (except for parsley), slice meat thinly, but leave as one whole.

Prepare potatoes. Cut out potato balls with French ball cutter, or cut into cubes or wedges. Cook remainder of potatoes, mash and prepare purée adding milk and butter.

Prepare Flemish sauce. Melt butter, add flour, blend, set aside.
Dilute sauce with broth, stir while cooking. Mix half the sauce with the sliced vegetables. Cool.
Place a layer of potato purée on heat resistant platter.
Brown bread crumbs in oven.
Spread the thick sauce between every two slices of meat, festen the double slices, place them in a row (in a sloping position) on the layer of potatoes.
Pour the other half of the sauce over all the meat, sprinkle with bread crumbs and cheese, dot with 1 tbs. melted butter.
Place meat in hot oven, roast (about 20 minutes).
Set the potato balls around the meat, dot with 1 tbs. melted butter and garnish with parsley.
Serve on platter in which meat was roasted.
Serve with boiled vegetables, and leafy salad.

Boiled Beef Baked in Béchamel Sauce

*2 1/2 lb. rump of beef * 9 oz. mixed vegetables * 1 medium onion * * allspice * pepper * 1/2 bay leaf * salt * Potato purée: 1 lb. pared potatoes * salt * milk * 1 tbs. butter * Béchamel sauce: 3 tbs. butter * 1/2 cup flour * 1 1/2 cup sour cream * salt * lemon juice to taste * 2 egg yolks * 1 oz. Parmesan cheese * 2 tbs. bread crumbs * 2 tbs. butter for dotting * green parsley*

Rinse meat, pound, place in boiling water, cook.
Clean mixed vegetables.
Brown half onion on open flame or directly on hot range.
When meat is almost cooked, add onion, mixed vegetables, spices, salt, cook meat until very tender.
Prepare potato purée (see page 132).
Prepare Béchamel sauce (see page 316).
Place potato purée on heat resistant platter.
Place sliced meat on potatoes. Cover with sliced vegetables.
Pour the sauce over all, sprinkle with bread crumbs, dot with butter.
Roast in hot oven. Garnish with green parsley.

LAMB

BOILED LAMB

Boiled Lamb in Broth

*2 1/2 lb. shoulder, breast or rack of lamb * salt * 8 oz. mixed vegetables with cabbage * 1 medium onion * allspice * bay leaf*

Rinse tenderized meat, do not bone, pour over with hot water and cook slowly, salt.
Brown onion on open flame.
When meat is parboiled, add mixed vegetables, browned onion and spices, cook through; when nearly done, add steamed savoy cabbage.
When meat is tender, pour off broth, cook sliced potatoes in it.
Cut meat into thin slices and serve hot with potatoes and various sauces.

Boiled Lamb in Onion Sauce

*2 1/2 lb. breast, rack or shoulder of lamb * 3 tbs. vinegar * 1 large onion * * 2 bay leaves * 10 allspice berries * salt * garlic*

Rinse meat, add to 1 quart of boiling water, add vinegar, onion and spices and simmer until tender. When parboiled add salt to taste and garlic.
Drain meat, carve into portions (serve breast and rack with bones), place on heated platter.
Serve with potatoes and white onion sauce (see page 320).

FRIED LAMB

Lamb Steaks, English Style

*2 1/2—3 lb. rack, loin or leg of lamb * vegetable marinade * salt * pepper *
* 2 oz. fat back * 2 tbs. butter*

Rinse tenderized meat, remove excess fat and membrane, marinate meat for 1—2 days (see page 183).
Before preparing meat, clean off vegetables, cut off carefully from bone, carve meat perpendicularly to the base across the grain into chops about 1 inch thick (depending on the thickness of the loin or other part of meat; if the loin or rack is thinner, then the chops should be carved so that after pounding they are about 3/4 inch thick).
Beat chop lightly with meat hammer, shape with knife and sprinkle with salt and pepper immediately before frying.
Slice fat back into strips, render, and brown lightly; set aside, heat fat on hot skillet, fry meat quickly on both sides, but allow it to be rare inside. When almost done, add butter.
Serve immediately after frying with fat back placed on top of each steak.
Serve with French-fried potatoes and leafy salad or boiled vegetables (the same as for cutlets), Chive, horse-radish or garlic butter may be used to dot the steaks instead of fat back.

Lamb Chops with Bone, English Style

*3 lb. thick rack, chops with rib bone * vegetable marinade * pepper * salt *
* 4 tbs. flour * 2 oz. fat back * 3 tbs. butter*

Separate the thick-rib chop end of the rack, remove excess fat and membrane, leaving a collar of fat about 1/2 inch thick, marinate in vegetables for 1—2 days (see page 183).
Remove meat just before using, clean off vegetables and carve into chops (2 rib bones per chop), chop off from back bone and set aside chops.

15 Polish Cookbook   225

Remove one rib bone carefully from each chop, do not damage the meat, clean the other bone, separate from the meat, cut the rib leaving only 1 1/4 inches of bone on each chop.

Set aside those chops where the meat is uniform without loose bits.

Remove the loose bits from the other chops and grind, divide the ground meat into equal parts, one for each chop.

Pound meat carefully with meat hammer, place a bit of ground meat on each chop, smoothen, and shape into oval chop; sprinkle with pepper, salt and flour immediately before serving.

Render the fat back, remove the cracklings, heat fat on skillet and fry cutlets to brown on hot skillet, turning carefully with a knife so they do not fall apart; the chops should be browned very well and fast so that they remain rare inside (about 4 minutes); while turning the chops, add butter to the fat and brown together with the meat. Lamb chops, English style, when prepared correctly, should be juice and tender when fried, they should be rare inside and not over-fried.

Serve the chops immediately on a heated platter sprinkled with the fat from the skillet.

Serve with French-fried potatoes, boiled potatoes cut into balls, leafy salad as well as beans, cauliflower, asparagus. Other types of potatoes may be used as well as white onion sauce (see page 320).

A small square of chive, horse-radish or garlic butter may be placed on top of each chop when served with French-fried potatoes and salad.

Grilled Lamb Chops

*3 lb. thick rib chops * vegetable marinade * salt * pepper * 4 tbs. olive oil for grilling*

Prepare chops the same as for fried lamb chops, English style (see above). Sprinkle chops with salt and pepper, smear with oil and place on hot grill. Grill in very hot oven for about 5—10 minutes; when brown, turn on other side. The chops should be grilled very quickly so they do not dry up.

Serve with boiled potatoes (cut into balls), French-fried potatoes, brown onion sauce, sauce Soubise etc.

Ground Lamb Patties

*1 1/2 lb. boneless lamb shoulder * 1 stale roll (2 oz.) * 3 oz. boiled potatoes * 1 small onion * 2 tbs. lamb fat * 1 egg * salt * pepper * 3 tbs. bread crumbs * 3 tbs. fat for frying*

226

Rinse meat, carve.

Soak roll in water, drain, and grind together with meat and potatoes.

Render the lamb fat, remove cracklings and brown onion lightly in fat.

Add fried onion, egg, salt and pepper to taste to meat, knead.

Divide meat into equal parts, shape into balls, dip in bread crumbs.

Make heart-shaped patties with knife and fry on medium heat on both sides; if juice is clear when pierced with a knife, set aside and serve immediately after frying; this guarantees the juiciness of the patties.

Serve with hot side-dishes only: potatoes in all forms, savoy cabbage, beets, turnip (thickened with roux), tomato sauté or stewed tomatoes, string beans or beans in gravy.

Rumanian Sausage

*1 1/2 lb. boneless shoulder of lamb * 1 stale roll (2 oz.) * 3 oz. boiled potatoes * 1 small onion * 2 tbs. lamb fat * 2 cloves of garlic * 1 egg * * salt * pepper * 7 tbs. bread crumbs * 3 tbs. fat for frying*

Prepare meat mixture as above; knead the meat mixture, to the consistency of yeast-cake dough, add 4 tablespoons of cold water, mix later with ground roll and other additions.

Divide meat into two small rolls per person, dip into bread crumbs and fry on all sides.

Serve with same side-dishes as ground lamb patties.

Shashlick

*3 lb. loin, rack or leg of lamb * 3 oz. lamb fat * 1 medium onion * * 2 1/2 cups rice * salt * paprika * 4 tbs. tomato paste * 10 oz. fat back * * 2 oz. fat back for frying*

Rinse meat and, without boning, marinate in vegetables for 1—2 days (see page 183).

Before preparing, remove vegetables from meat, remove bones carefully so as not to tear off meat (especially from the loin and rack).

Pour over loosened bones with a little cold water, salt and cook the stock.

Render the lamb fat, remove cracklings and lightly brown onion in fat.

Rinse rice, measure out 1 1/2 times more stock as rice, add salt, paprika, fat with onion, bring to a boil and add rice, cook slowly.

When the liquid is absorbed by the rice, mix with tomato paste and place covered in the oven; remove the baked rice and keep covered, placing the saucepan with rice in boiling water.

Carve meat into small rectangular flat steaks (about 1 1/2 inches long and 1/3 thick), pound with meat hammer, sprinkle with paprika and salt.

Cut fat back into thin flat slices, the same size as the meat, sprinkle with salt and paprika.

Place alternately slices of lamb and fat back on skewers, about 10 cubes of meat and fat back to a skewer.

Render fat for frying, remove cracklings, heat fat well on skillet, place the skewers with meat propping the skewers on the skillet edges and fry quickly on all sides, allow the inside of the meat to remain rare.

Place hot rice on heated platter, place meat with skewers on rice, pour over with fat from skillet and serve immediately.

The plates should be well heated.

Lamb Risotto

*1 1/2 lb. leg of lamb * 1 tbs. butter * 1/2 lb. raw bacon or raw smoked ham * 1 cup lamb stock * 1 large onion * 1 tbs. butter * 1 lb. rice * * 4 cups lamb stock * 2 tbs. Parmesan cheese * tomato paste*

Rinse meat, cut into 1 1/2 inch squares, place in skillet in melted butter, heat well.

Slice ham into thin strips, add to lamb, pour in 1 cup stock and braise slowly until tender.

Grate onion, braise in butter without browning.

Rinse rice, parboil, drain well.

Add the braised onion and 1 tbs. of Parmesan cheese to the rice, pour over with 4 cups boiling stock, cover and place in oven or on top of double boiler, cook until dry and fluffy.

Prepare clear tomato sauce.

Place meat when tender into heated casserole, cover with rice, add gravy from pan, dot with 1 tbs. of Parmesan, pour tomato sauce over the whole and roast (15—20 minutes).

Serve in casserole.

BRAISED LAMB

Braised Lamb with Savoy Cabbage

See Economy-Meat Dishes, page 299.

Braised Lamb with Potatoes

See Economy-Meat Dishes, page 300.

Braised Lamb with Beans

See Economy-Meat Dishes, page 300.

Marinated Braised Lamb

*3 lb. leg or loin of lamb * vinegar marinade * 1 cup dry red wine *
* 5 tbs. fat back for larding * a few juniper berries * salt * 3 oz. fat back *
* 5 oz. mixed vegetables without cabbage * bay leaf * 1 cup sour
cream * 2 tbs. flour * pepper*

Rinse meat, remove membrane and excess fat, cut out thigh bone from
leg, and leave only leg bone of about 1 1/2 inches in length; place meat in
cold vinegar marinade (see page 184); add wine to the marinade and
keep in cold place for 5 days.

Before preparing meat remove and squeeze out marinade, wipe with dry
linen or absorbent paper, lard with strips of fat back and rub in salt and
crushed juniper berries.

Render fat back, remove cracklings, heat fat on hot skillet and brown
meat on all sides on high flame.

Clean vegetables, rinse, and slice finely.

Remove meat to saucepan. Add fat, chopped vegetables, bay leaf and the
drained onion from the marinade, add water and braise slowly, covered,
until tender.

Turn meat during braising so that each time another part of the meat is
braised in the sauce; reduce liquid several times so that the vegetables
and onion may brown lightly in the fat (be careful not to burn the
ingredients of the sauce).

Sprinkle marinade into sauce and when it is tart enough, sprinkle with
water.

When the meat is tender (about 2 hours) remove, strain sauce, add sour
cream and flour, mix. Add salt and pepper to taste. Boil. Sauce should
be dark brown (if not brown enough, add caramel coloring).

Cut meat into thin slices with a sharp knife across the grain somewhat
diagonally to the base; place the entire sliced roast on heated platter, pour
over with sauce.

Serve with dropped dumplings, macaroni, potatoes and beets.

Lamb Ragoût

*2 1/2 lb. breast or shoulder of lamb * salt * 2 oz. fat back * 1 medium onion * 1 cup sour cream * 2 tbs. flour*

Rinse meat, divide breast with bone into 10 uniform slices (2 slices per portion), salt.
Render fat back, remove cracklings, heat fat on hot skillet and brown meat on all sides in skillet.
Remove meat to saucepan; fry onion in fat lightly, add together with fat to meat, add water and braise covered.
When meat is tender, add sour cream and flour to sauce.
Serve with rice, potatoes, macaroni and boiled vegetables.

Turkish Pilaff

*2 1/2 lb. breast of lamb * salt * 3 oz. lamb fat * 1 large onion * 2 1/2 cups rice * 8 tbs. tomato paste * 8 cups lamb stock * 2 tbs. butter * * paprika*

Rinse lamb, add to small amount of boiling water, add salt and parboil; reduce liquid to 3/4 of its content.
Render lamb fat, do not brown cracklings.
Slice onion, pour over with boiling water, cook quickly and drain.
Rinse rice, drain in colander.
Fry tomato paste lightly in lamb fat, dilute with stock, add salt to taste.
Carve meat with bones into 10 uniform slices.
Grease saucepan with butter, place a layer of rice at bottom, cover with half the meat, add half the onion, sprinkle with paprika and dot with fat skimmed from the stock; cover the layer of meat with a layer of rice and top with another layer of meat and onion, cover the whole with rice, smoothen the top and pour over with clear tomato sauce so that it covers the entire surface of the rice.
Cover saucepan, place in hot oven for 2 hours; when necessary lower temperature of the oven so that the rice does not become dry, do not stir while roasting; if the meat is completely tender, remove from oven sooner.
Butter may substitute for lamb fat but real pilaff is made with the latter.
Serve straight from the oven, piping hot.

ROAST LAMB

Loin of Lamb, English Style

*4 lb. thick loin of lamb * vegetable marinade * salt * 1 clove of garlic *
* 2 oz. fat back for roasting * 3 tbs. butter for roasting*

Rinse meat, remove membrane from surface of loin and the excess layer
of fat, leaving a layer about 1/2 inch thick, cut off all fat from the bottom
of the loin, remove kidney.

Prepare vegetable marinade with oil (see page 183), rub the marinade
into meat, place in crock and remove to cold place for 1—2 days so that
the meat becomes tenderized and aromatic.

Render fat back, remove cracklings, heat fat on skillet.

Rub meat with salt and garlic, place in hot fat and fry quickly on hot
skillet.

Remove meat to roasting pan, spread butter thickly on top. place in hot
oven and roast until half done (about 40 minutes), basting with the fat.
If the juice of meat is pink (but not red), when pierced with a fork, carve
into thin slices with a sharp knife, across the grain, somewhat diagonally
to the base, or chop into serving pieces in the same way as hare is carved
by severing the meat muscle and chopping the bone with a meat cleaver
on this spot.

Carve meat very quickly, place on heated platter, pour over with hot sauce,
serve immediately.

Serve with French-fried potatoes, string beans, cauliflower, asparagus,
green peas, tomato sauté, boiled turnip cut in balls and leafy salad.

Leg of Lamb, English Style

*2 1/2—3 lb. leg of lamb * vegetable marinade * salt * 1 clove of garlic *
* 2 oz. fat back for roasting * 3 tbs. butter for roasting*

Prepare and serve choice, tender leg of lamb the same way as lamb loin.
Loosen bone from thigh up to knee bone, leave rest of bone.
Carve leg of lamb across the grain somewhat diagonally to the bone.

Roast Baby Lamb

*Leg of baby lamb * salt * garlic * 2 oz. fat back*

Rinse leg of baby lamb, place in boiling water, boil, remove, rub with salt
and garlic.

Heat fat in roasting pan, add meat, pour over with fat and place in medium oven.

Roast for about an hour, baste often; when meat is tender, brown top, remove and carve across the grain somewhat diagonally to the surface of the bone.

Serve with French-fried potatoes and raw vegetable salad and cooked string beans or dry beans.

The roast can be served hot or cold (removing sauce when served cold).

PORK

BOILED PORK

Pickled Ham (Smoked)

*Marinade for pickling * 11—15 lb. ham*

Select a smaller ham, not too fat. Clean and rinse. Ham may be marinated in its entirety with the bone, skin and fat or boned and marinated in one flat piece together with the skin and fat. After marinating the ham is rolled, cutting it according to need so that one or two rolls are formed. The ham should be rolled uniformly thick and as far as possible entirely covered with skin. Prepare the ingredients for the marinade — divide in half.

Rub half of the ingredients of the marinade into the meat; slit the meat lengthwise, close to the bone, to the knee joint (which is inside the ham) with a long thin knife; insert part of the salt and spices in the opening.

Set the meat tightly in a wooden bucket or bowl, cover and press with a weight (about 10 lbs.); the ham should be left at room temperature for 2 days.

Dissolve the remaining spices in 1 quart of cold water which has been boiled, pour over the meat and remove to a cool, dark place (protect from freezing); marinate the meat for 3 weeks (for information on marinating meat, see page 184).

Remove meat from marinade, remove the spices and dry in the air, then smoke, or cook without smoking.

Boiled Ham

Boil water in a small kettle.

Place the ham, skin-side down, in the kettle of water; the water should cover the surface of the meat during the entire cooking time; after the meat is parcooked, simmer slowly, covered, on a low flame for about two hours. If the broth is too salty, pour off part and refill with boiling water; as the water evaporates, add more when necessary; when the bone begins to loosen from the meat, or if the meat can be pierced with a fork without pressure, remove from heat and cool in the broth; do not overcook.

Serve hot ham immediately after cooking, slice into 1/2 inch slices sprinkled with broth and place on serving platter.

Ham may also be warmed after being sliced cold. Place the slices in a suitable saucepan, pour boiling broth over the ham (either ham or beef), cover and warm; serve together with the broth.

If the ham is not too fat, it can be sliced (especially unsmoked ham) together with the skin and fat. If the ham is too fat, the skin should be removed in parts and the unnecessary fat cut off, leaving a layer of about 2/3 inch. Use the skin for cooking barszcz, cabbage soup, sour rye soup; dice fat finely and render immediately. Use for flavoring savory dishes.

Pickled Pig's Knuckles

*5 pickled pig's knuckles (knees) * 7 oz. of mixed vegetables * 1 medium onion * salt * coriander * allspice * bay leaf*

Remove the salt and saltpeter from the marinated pig's knuckles with a knife, if too salty soak in water, drain, pour over with boiling water and simmer until very soft.

When the meat is parcooked, add cleaned, mixed vegetables, onion, salt and spices, cook.

Serve with pea purée and horse-radish with vinegar.

Boiled Pig's Knuckles

*5 pig's knuckles (feet) cracked short (above the heel) * 1 medium onion *
* 3 oz. mixed vegetables * salt * allspice * 1 bay leaf*

Clean pig's feet (with hooves removed) thoroughly; if necessary, sear and scrub carefully, wash in warm water and rinse.

Heat water, place knuckles in water and simmer.

When meat is parcooked add onion, cleaned, mixed vegetables, salt, spices and cook until very tender.

Drain tender meat and serve immediately while very hot.

Serve with pea purée and horse-radish with vinegar, or with sauerkraut with roux.

Pickled Pork Shoulder

*Marinade for pickling * 3 1/2 lb. pork shoulder*

Select meat, not too fat, rinse, drain off water, bone carefully and set aside.

Prepare ingredients for the marinade. Divide into two.

Rub half of the ingredients into the meat, place in a bowl, press down with a weight and place in room temperature for 1—2 days; when it begins to secrete juice, pour over with the marinade and place in cold place. Pickle for two weeks (see page 184).

Remove meat from marinade, clean off spices, place in suitable saucepan, add boiling water and simmer until tender, do not overcook; if the stock is too salty, pour off stock after first half hour, and replace with fresh boiling water. Remove meat from stock, slice thinly across the grain.

Prepare pea or pea purée, place on serving platter in mounds surrounded by the slices of meat.

Pickled Loin

*Marinade for pickling * 3 1/2 lb. loin of pork*

Prepare and serve loin of pork as pork shoulder (see above).

Boiled Pork Tongues

*2 lb. pork tongues * 5 oz. mixed vegetables * 1 small onion * allspice *
* bay leaf * salt*

Cook in the same way as veal tongue (see page 189).

Pickled Pork Tongues

*Marinade for pickling * 2 lb. pork tongues*

Marinate and cook in the same way as pickled veal tongue (see page
190).

Boiled Spareribs

*1 1/2 lb. spareribs * 4 oz. mixed vegetables * 1 medium onion * salt *
* allspice * bay leaf*

Rinse spareribs, slice in two, pour over with boiling water and cook slowly.
When meat is parcooked add cleaned mixed vegetables, onion, salt and
spices, cook through.

Spareribs are most often cooked in soup or with vegetables, e.g., cabbage.

FRIED PORK

Pork Brizol

Loin-of-Pork Steaks

*2 lb. loin roast center cut without ribs * salt * pepper * 2 tbs. flour *
* 3 tbs. fat for frying * 2 tbs. butter for frying*

Rinse loin, remove unnecessary fat from surface, filet carefully so as not
to damage meat tissue.

Slice loin into even diagonal slices and pound carefully into flat, large
slices, being careful not to tear the meat.

Sprinkle each steak with salt, pepper and flour and fry on a hot skillet
to golden brown color.

Add butter to the fat before frying is completed. After the meat has been
fried add a few drops of water to the skillet to dilute the brown gravy
and when the water evaporates, serve the brizol topped with the gravy.
The meat may be dotted with raw butter.

Serve with French-fried potatoes, raw salad in season, boiled vegetables.

Fried Pork Chops

*2 lb. pork chops * salt * pepper * 2 tbs. flour * 4 tbs. fat for frying*

Select lean chops.

Remove excess fat before frying.

Rinse meat, cut off chine bone, and divide into individual chops, leaving a piece of rib about 1 1/4 inches long on every chop.

Scrub the bone, slit chops in a few places around the edge, pound with meat hammer.

Sprinkle chops with pepper, salt and flour immediately before frying.

Heat fat on skillet, brown chops on high flame, lower heat and fry through.

Serve with potatoes, chive or horse-radish butter, leafy salad; may also be served with tomatoes, cucumbers in sour cream or boiled vegetables.

Breaded Pork Chops

*2 lb. pork-rib chops * salt * 4 tbs. flour * 1 1/2 eggs * 5 tbs. bread crumbs * 5 tbs. fat for frying*

Rinse loin of pork, cut off long rib bones, leaving a 1 1/2 inch rib bone, remove excess fat, leaving a collar about 1/2 inch thick.

Cut meat into chops with rib bone; if the loin is thick, cut one chop with rib bone and one without; chop back bone in places where meat is cut, set aside chops.

Cut each chop carefully off backbone.

Clean rib bone off each chop carefully so that they do not separate from meat.

Pound lightly with meat hammer on one side, forming a pear-shaped chop, slit in a few places on the edge so that the meat is not mis-shaped during frying.

Sprinkle with salt on both sides immediately before frying.

Prepare flour, beaten egg, sifted bread crumbs.

Dip successively in flour and egg, drain, dip in bread crumbs, pat crumbs into meat.

Fry immediately after breading in hot fat on a high flame to a light golden color on both sides, fry through on low flame; do not allow to stand long while hot, since the meat loses its succulence.

Arrange chops in rows on long serving platter, with bones facing in one direction.

Serve with potatoes and sauerkraut, red or white cabbage, leafy salad or horse-radish with beet (ćwikła).

Breaded Pork Cutlets

Pork Schnitzel

*2 lb. fresh ham * salt * 4 tbs. flour * 1 1/2 eggs * 5 tbs. bread crumbs *
* 3 1/2 tbs. fat for frying * 2 tbs. butter for frying*

Rinse meat, remove excess fat and membrane, slice across the grain into flat uniform steaks. Pound lightly with dampened meat hammer so as not to curl the meat, shape into oval cutlets, salt.
Prepare the same way as breaded pork chops above.

Pork Chops in Dough

*2 lb. pork chops * salt * D o u g h: 1 cup water * 2 egg yolks * 2 1/2
cups flour * 2 tbs. oil * 2 egg whites * salt * 6 tbs. fat for frying*

Prepare cutlets as described for breaded pork chops (see page 236), salt. Prepare dough. Mix thoroughly water, flour, egg yolks and oil, beat egg whites, mix, salt.
Dip chops in dough immediately before frying, allow excess dough to drip off.
Heat fat, fry chops on very hot fat, at the beginning over high flame; when brown, fry through on lowered heat.
Arrange on serving platter with bones in one direction.
Serve with raw salad in season or vegetable salad.

Ham or Sausage in Dough

*5 thick slices of boiled ham * D o u g h: 2 egg yolks * 1 cup flour *
* 1/2 cup water * 1 tbs. oil * salt * 2 egg whites * 6 tbs. fat for frying*

Mix egg yolks, flour, water, oil and salt lightly with a beater (to the thickness of sponge cake batter). Add beaten egg whites.
Dip thick uniform slices of ham into dough.
Heat fat, fry ham on hot skillet.
Arrange meat in semi-horizontal row.
Serve with raw vegetable salad or sharp sauces.

Pork Tongues in Dough

*1 lb. pork tongues * 4 tbs. vinegar (6%) * 1 small onion * allspice
berries * 1 bay leaf * salt * D o u g h: 1/2 cup water * 1 cup flour *
* 1 egg * 1 tbs. oil * salt * 3 1/2 tbs. fat for frying*

Scrub tongues, cut off salivary glands, rinse.

Cook water with vinegar, onion and spices, add tongue and cook until tender.

When tongue is parcooked, remove thick skin and replace in stock, salt to taste and cook until very tender.

Remove meat, cook and cut diagonally into 1/2 inch slices.

Prepare dough. Add egg and flour to water, blend, mix well, add salt and oil, mix.

Immediately before serving dip slices of tongue into dough; when dough drains off a little, place in hot fat and fry quickly to brown.

Serve immediately after frying. Serve with raw vegetable salad in season.

Pork Fillet on Toast

M u s h r o o m s a u c e: *1 small onion * 3 oz. champignons * 2 tbs. butter * pepper * 1 tbs. flour * 1 cup dry red wine * 1 cup strong broth * * salt * T o a s t: 5 slices of white toast * 4 tbs. butter * M e a t: 1 1/2 lb. pork fillet (loin) * 2 tbs. flour * salt * 3 tbs. fat for frying*

Rinse mushrooms, peel, slice finely; cut onion, pour boiling water over onion, drain, add to mushrooms; sprinkle with water, add butter, pepper and stew until tender, brown somewhat before done.

Sprinkle flour on mushrooms, mix, dilute with wine and broth, boil while stirring. Salt to taste.

Butter toast on both sides (toast should be about 1/2 inch thick), brown in hot oven, keep warm in oven.

Rinse meat, remove membrane and fat, slice, perpendicularly to base, into 5 uniform portions.

Place them on meat board cut side down, shape, pounding with the fist into oval, thick steaks. Salt.

Heat fat on skillet, place meat and fry on medium flame on both sides until brown, place steaks on hot toast.

Pour off excess fat from skillet, pour 2 spoons of water into skillet, dilute drippings, add to mushrooms, bring to the boil; arrange steaks on toast on serving platter and pour over with mushroom sauce.

Serve with French-fried potatoes or boiled potatoes (cut into balls) garnished with green parsley.

Pork-Brain Cutlets

Prepare the same as veal-brain patties (see page 193). Since pork brains are smaller than veal brains, figure one pork brain per portion.

Pork Brains à la Polonaise

Prepare the same as calf's brains à la Polonaise (see page 58).

Chopped Pork Cutlets

Prepare the same way as cutlets from mixed meat, using pork shoulder (see page 211).

Pork Medalion

Fried Loin of Pork

*2 lb. loin of pork * salt * pepper * 2 tbs. flour * 3 tbs. fat for frying * * 3 tbs. butter for frying*

Rinse meat, remove meat carefully from chine bone.

Cut loin carefully with sharp serrated knife, against the grain, perpendicular to the base, into 5 uniform steaks, beat lightly with meat hammer on cut sides.

Immediately before frying, sprinkle meat with salt, pepper and flour.

Heat fat on skillet, add meat and fry on medium skillet to brown on both sides; while turning meat add butter and brown together with meat; butter can also be used to dot meat before serving.

Add two tablespoons of water to gravy and cook.

Serve immediately on heated platter, dotted with gravy from skillet.

Serve with French-fried potatoes, boiled potatoes (cut into balls), boiled vegetables and leafy salad.

Breaded Pork Medalion in Croutons

*2 lb. loin of pork * 1 small stale roll (1 oz.) * 3 tbs. bread crumbs * salt * * 4 tbs. flour * 1 1/2 eggs * 4 tbs. fat for frying*

Rinse meat, remove carefully from chine bone, place bones aside.

Slice loin with a sharp knife, against the grain, perpendicular to the base, into 5 uniform steaks, beat lightly with meat hammer on cut side.

Slice roll in fine pieces, shape in rectangular croutons, mix with bread crumbs.

Sprinkle steaks with salt and flour immediately before frying, dip into beaten egg, then into croutons, press breading into meat so that it adheres.

239

Heat fat on skillet and fry meat on medium flame on both sides to golden color; arrange medalions in semi-horizontal rows on heated platter and serve immediately after frying, while they are still juicy with crisp coating.

Serve with French-fried potatoes, boiled potatoes and boiled vegetables, raw vegetable salad in season, especially a leafy one.

Pork Liver (Sauté)

Prepare the same as calf's liver (sauté).

Breaded Pork Liver

Prepare the same as breaded calf's liver.

BRAISED PORK

Pork Kidneys in Tart Sauce

*2 lb. pork kidneys * 3 tbs. fat * 1 small onion * 3 tbs. flour * stock from kidneys * salt * pepper * vinegar * allspice * bay leaf*

Boil the water.

Rinse kidneys, slice rather thickly (about 1 inch), place in boiling water, bring to boil, drain.

Heat fat, brown meat, place in saucepan, stew in juice of meat in a covered pan.

Prepare sauce. Dice onion, brown lightly in fat, add flour, brown, set aside, dilute with cooled stock from kidneys, add salt, pepper, vinegar, allsipce, bay leaf. Cook, strain.

Pour sauce into meat, stew.

Serve on platter covered with sauce.

Serve with mashed potatoes or fluffy cereals.

Pork Goulash

*2 lb. pork picnic shoulder * salt * 2 tbs. flour * 3 tbs. fat * 3 medium onions * pepper * bay leaf * allspice * coriander * 1 bouillon cube*
Prepare the same as beef goulash (see page 212).

Sausage in Onion Sauce

*1 1/2 lb. smoked sausage * onion sauce*

Prepare brown onion sauce (see page 319).

Rinse sausage in warm water, slice in diagonal, uniform slices, place in sauce and braise slightly.

Serve with potatoes.

Braised Pork Chops

*2 lb. pork chops * salt * pepper * 2 tbs. flour * 2 tbs. fat for frying * 1/2 cup broth * caraway seeds * 1/2 cup dry white wine * 2 tbs. butter*

Prepare chops the same way as fried pork chops (see page 236), brown on both sides in skillet.

Transfer meat to saucepan, add caraway seeds and braise slowly, covered, adding broth and wine.

When the chops are tender, add butter to the sauce and when the butter melts, blend with the sauce and chops; serve immediately.

Serve with French-fried potatoes or boiled potatoes, raw salad in season and cauliflower or Brussel sprouts.

Braised Pork Roast

*2 lb. fresh ham butt or picnic shoulder * salt * 2 tbs. flour * 3 1/2 tbs. fat for frying * 1 medium onion * pinch of caraway seeds*

Rinse meat, remove excess fat and membrane, pound with meat hammer dampened in water, salt, sprinkle with flour.

Heat fat on skillet, fry meat to golden brown, remove to saucepan.

Add the fat from the skillet, onion and caraway seeds to the meat, add a little water, cover and braise on low flame until tender, adding water when necessary; brown sauce slightly while braising, being careful not to burn the sauce.

Slice meat finely across the grain, place entire roast on platter, pour over with the sauce.

Serve with potatoes, sauerkraut, or red cabbage with pan gravy, beets, dill pickle.

Braised Spareribs

Prepare the same as beef goulash with 1 1/2 lb. of spareribs (see page 212).

Chopped Pork Steaks in Tomato Sauce

Prepare and serve the same as chopped steaks made with mixed meat, using fresh pork shoulder (see page 217).

ROAST PORK

Roast Unsalted Bacon

*1 1/2 lb. unsalted bacon * salt * 2 medium onions*

Rinse bacon thoroughly, scrub, place in boiling, salted water and parboil.

Remove from stock (use liquid for cooking barszcz or cabbage).

Score skin deeply to the layer of fat, to form a pattern, salt bacon lightly, place in roasting pan, and set in hot oven, roast to golden brown, basting with melted fat.

Before roast is done, add sliced onion rings to fat, brown to light golden brown.

If the melted fat in the roasting pan begins to smoke and burn, sprinkle with water.

Remove bacon, cut in 1/4 inch slices; place on platter garnished with browned onion.

Use the melted fat for cooking other dishes. Serve bacon hot with potatoes and cabbage, or cold as an hors-d'oeuvre.

Unsmoked Sausage with Onions

*1 1/2 lb. unsmoked pork sausage * 4 tbs. fat * 2 medium onions * salt*

Tie sausage at both ends, rinse, place in saucepan, add a little water and simmer uncovered.

When the sausage begins to swell, pierce in several places so that steam evaporates and simmer slowly until tender, turning the sausage from time to time. Allow as much of liquid to evaporate as possible.

Add fat to liquid and onion rings, place in oven and roast until sausage is brown; brown onion in the fat. Salt to taste.

Serve with potatoes and sauerkraut or red cabbage with pan gravy.

242

Pork Meat Loaf

Prepare the same way as mixed-meat loaf, using pork shoulder (see page 218).

Dishes made with chopped pork meat are very tasty and juicy but much fatter than when made with mixed meat.

Roast Pork

*2 3/4 lb. fresh ham butt or loin of shoulder * salt * 2 tbs. flour * 3 1/2 tbs. fat * pinch of caraway seeds * 1 medium onion*

Select lean pork for roasting.

Rinse meat, do not remove deeply placed bones from meat, sprinkle with salt and flour.

Heat fat on skillet, add meat, brown on all sides.

Place meat in roasting pan, dot with fat, sprinkle with caraway seeds and place in medium oven.

Roast for about an hour, basting and dotting with water; when meat is half done, add onion to gravy and brown lightly. Cut meat in fine slices across the grain, place on heated platter garnished with onion and dotted with gravy.

Serve with potatoes, sauerkraut or dill pickles.

Rolled Pork Shoulder

*2 lb. boned picnic shoulder * salt * 1 clove of garlic * 4 tbs. fat * caraway seeds * 1 medium onion*

Pound meat with meat hammer into uniform thick rectangle. Smoothen and sprinkle with salt. Rub garlic into meat and roll into uniform thickness.

Fasten roll spirally.

Heat fat in narrow pan, place roll in pan, pour over hot fat, sprinkle with caraway seeds and place in medium oven.

Add sliced onion after 1/2 hour.

Roast meat about 1 1/4 hours, basting with gravy and adding water to gravy when necessary. When meat is tender, remove from oven, cut into 1/2 inch slices; place entire roast on heated platter, pour over some of fat and dot with onion.

Serve with potatoes and sauerkraut (thickened with roux), or fresh cabbage cooked with apples or tomatoes.

16*

Roast Loin of Pork

*2 lb. loin of pork (center cut) * salt * caraway seeds * 3 1/2 tbs. fat *
* 1 medium onion*

Scrub loin with knife; if layer of fat is too thick, remove so that only 1/2
inch layer remains.

Remove outside part of chine bone and rib bones.

Rub salt into meat and sprinkle with caraway seeds.

Heat fat in roasting pan. Place meat in hot fat, fat-side up, pour fat over
meat and place in medium oven. Roast slowly, basting from time to time,
adding water to the gravy.

When meat is half done, add diced onion to the bottom of the roasting
pan and roast together with the meat. While basting, do not dot with the
onion.

When meat is tender and nicely browned to a golden color, and the juice
of the meat is somewhat turbid when pierced with a fork, remove from
oven.

Cut meat into thin slices and place the entire roast on the bones, transfer
to long serving platter.

A typical side-dish for roast loin of pork is sauerkraut and potatoes.
Roast loin of pork may also be served with turnips, red cabbage, string
beans or cauliflower and lettuce.

Roast Fresh Ham of Sucking Pig

*Fresh ham of sucking pig * salt * coriander * 3 1/2 tbs. fat * 2 medium
onions*

Clean ham thoroughly, leave only little bone, rub with salt and with
ground coriander, set aside for 2 hours.

Heat fat in roasting pan, add meat, pour over with fat and roast in medium
oven, baste with gravy; add water to gravy so that it does not burn.

When meat is half done, add chopped onion to the gravy and fry in fat
to golden color.

Cut meat when tender into thin slices together with the skin and fat.

Serve with all kinds of cabbage, potatoes or potato dumplings.

Stuffed Sucking Pig

*1 small sucking pig * salt * 1/2 cup fat for, roasting * 3 1/2 tbs. fat back
for larding meat while roasting * S t u f f i n g   w i t h   g r o a t s: 2 cups
parched groats * 1 egg * 2 onions * 1/2 cup fat * 4 cups water * salt *

* sucking pig liver, heart, lungs * coagulated blood * pepper * marjoram *
* Stuffing with bread crumbs: 2 medium onions * 3 1/2 tbs.
fat * 3 tbs. butter * 3 egg yolks * 1 cup bread crumbs * haslet * 3 egg
whites * salt * pepper * marjoram

Scald sucking pig after slaughtering, scrub, rinse, dress, remove hooves, place in cold for 2 days. One hour before roasting, salt the meat inside and out.

Stuff the suckling, truss, place in roasting pan in lower section of oven, roast in hot oven; add water to fat so that it does not burn. Baste frequently with fat and smear fat back over surface of meat with a fork so that the skin becomes crisp.

Groat stuffing. Combine groats with raw egg, dry in oven.

Dice onion, brown in fat.

Boil water, add groats and browned onion, add salt and cook until thick, then bake in oven until dry and fluffy (see page 140).

Chop haslet fine, together with coagulated blood from slaughter, mix with groats, add salt, pepper and marjoram to taste.

Bread stuffing. Braise onions in fat without browning.

Cream butter with egg yolks.

Chop haslet finely and add to creamed butter and egg mixture. Add bread crumbs. Beat egg whites, combine all ingredients, add salt, pepper and marjoram to taste.

RECIPES FOR SOME POLISH SPECIALITIES OF SAUSAGE

Blood sausage, pâté sausage and head cheese are made with jowls, kidneys, tongues, spleen, skinless abdomen, pork head, lungs and heart, pigs' knuckles and feet, fresh bacon rind with 1/3 inch of fat back and suet (this may be the cheaper entrails' suet). Raw blood is also necessary for preparing blood sausage.

Preparation of Haslet

Clean the head. Singe the head without the brains, eyes, teeth and tongue, scrub thoroughly with a very sharp knife. Chop head lengthwise in two. Rinse. Place the cleaned head in boiling water, bring to the boil several times and then drain.

Rinse heart under running water, pressing out the coagulated blood.

Remove the lateral salivary glands from tongue, scrub with brush under running water. Cut kidneys in half lengthwise, rinse in a large amount of water, changing the water as long as the blood keeps running. Rinse spleen and lungs. Singe the bacon rind, scrub with sharp knife and rinse in warm water. Scrub the cleaned knuckles with sharp knife, rinse, chop lengthwise and crosswise.

Boil water with salt, add head, tongue and knuckles, cook on medium flame for half an hour. Add the rest of the haslet and bacon rind and simmer for about 1 1/2 hours. When the tongue is parboiled, remove and place in cold water, after a while remove skin of tongue and place back in pot to cook through. Simultaneously add a bay leaf and allspice. Taste the liquid; if necessary, add salt. Cook all the meat until very tender. As various parts of the meat are ready, remove them. The tongue, head and knuckles take the longest time to cook.

It is necessary to remove the abdomen and jowls on time, so that they do not over-cook. The fat should be tender but not flabby and the tissue should remain whole. The knuckles, head and bacon rind should be cooked until very tender.

The abdomen fat should be soaked in water and the water changed several times. The suet should be chopped finely, ground and rendered, not browning the cracklings. Remove the cracklings, add onions to the fat and brown slowly. The latter should be used for the sausage and pâtés.

Carving Meat for Head Cheese and Blood Sausage

Chop finely half of the meat, of the kidney, heart, neck and knuckles for head cheese. Use also the rind of the bacon with fat back sliced along the entire width (the rind and fat back together) into rather thick strips about 2 inches long. The knuckles and head should be boned while the meat is still warm and cut in pieces.

The other half of the meat may be used for sausage. This meat should be ground. Spleen and lungs are added to blood sausage and to liver sausage.

Kiszka Kaszanka

Blood Sausage with Groats

*4 quarts parched coarse buckwheat groats * 6—8 quarts broth from cooked pork meat * salt * 4 medium onions * 1 1/2 cups suet (abdominal) * 1 lb. cooked ground meat made from haslet * 1 1/2 quarts strained blood * * allspice * marjoram * large intestines of hog*

246

Sift the groats, wash in warm water, drain.

Add boiling broth to groats, add salt to taste, cover and cook, until dry and fluffy, over an asbestos plate or in a slow oven.

When the groats are tender and dry, remove, set aside and cool.

Render the suet, brown onion in fat to golden color. Add the fat with onion to the groats and the ground meat from the cooked haslet. Add strained raw blood. (The blood may be substituted with the same amount of fatty stock from the haslet). Season the mixture to taste. It should have a thin but firm consistency. If necessary add a little warm broth. Stuff the warm mixture into the cleaned, soaked intestines (in pieces about 10 inches long) rather loosely, so that the sausage does not burst. Fasten both ends of the sausage with a toothpick or sew with heavy thread. Boil water, turn down to very low heat, add the sausage and steam in water slightly below boiling point for about 45 minutes. If the water begins to boil, add a little cold water (1/2 cup), never permitting it to reach boiling point. Pierce the sausage with a straw after 45 minutes. If the straw is dry when removed, and the mixture does not stick to it, remove the sausage, place on meat board, one link after the other, and put in cool place.

Pork Pâté Sausage

*1 raw pork liver * 1 lb. fat back * 1 lb. cooked meat from kettle (see preparations) * 2 dry rolls (about 5 oz.) * 5 tbs. fat (rendered suet) * * 2 medium onions * 3 oz. fine bread crumbs * salt * pepper * allspice * * a few cloves of garlic * small intestines of hog*

Grind fat back and raw liver and the cooked meat from the kettle.

Soak rolls in broth of the meat, grind.

Brown onion with fat very lightly to golden color.

Mix ground meat with the ground roll and bread crumbs, add onion, salt and spices to taste.

Stuff the mixture loosely into cleaned, soaked intestines. Sew the ends of the casing or fasten with little sticks twisted around the intestines.

Cook water with salt in wide saucepan, place on very low heat or on an asbestos plate. When the water barely boils, place pâté sausage carefully into water and cook slowly for 1/2 hour, uncovered. Do not permit the water to boil, since the intestines will burst. When the water begins to boil, add 1/2 cup of cold water each time.

Remove the steamed pâté sausage after 1/2 hour, place on meat board and cool. Serve the following day when completely cohesive.

Liver Sausage

*2 raw pork livers * 3 1/2 lb. abdomen and jowl fat without skin * 5 tbs. fat * 2 medium onions * nutmeg * pepper * allspice * ginger * a few cloves of garlic * salt * 2 1/2 quarts broth from cooked pork meat*

Place liver in boiling water and cook slowly for 15 minutes, remove, cool, grind.

Grind half of cooked (but not over-cooked) abdomen and jowl fat, chop the other half finely.

Chop onions finely and brown lightly in fat to golden color.

Grind spices finely, crush garlic into pulp.

Add ground and chopped fat to the liver, add the browned onion, pour in the broth, salt and season mixture to taste. Stuff the mixture loosely into casing, fasten ends.

Boil water in saucepan, lower heat and when the temperature of the water is just under boiling, place sausage carefully into water and steam for about 30 minutes, not permitting the water to boil. Lower the temperature of the water when necessary by adding 1/2 cup of cold water at a time.

Remove sausage after 30 minutes, place evenly on meat board and put in cold place.

Serve the following day, when firm and cohesive.

Polish Pork-Head Cheese

*2 quarts broth from cooked pork meat * 4 medium onions * bay leaf * * (pork blood) * sliced meat (see page 246) * sliced bacon ring and fat back * salt * pepper * allspice * nutmeg * a few cloves of garlic * pork abdomen*

Heat 2 quarts of meat broth with onions and bay leaf. When it evaporates to 1 quart, mash the onion, skim off from broth. Strain the raw blood, add to broth, mix with sliced meat, mashed onion and blood, salt and season to taste. Head cheese is tasty when it is aromatic.

Stuff the entire mixture into cleaned, soaked abdomen or into large beef intestines, stuffing it about 3/4 full.

Sew up the opening of the abdomen securely with strong thread. Boil water with salt, lower flame, add head cheese and cook very slowly for about 1 1/2 hours, uncovered.

The water must completely cover the head cheese during cooking. Do not allow the water to boil strongly during cooking.

Remove head cheese when done, place in cold water, and when it cools slightly, drain, wipe, tie up in a clean towel and place on meat board, press with another weighted board so that the head cheese flattens a little. Remove the weight after 12 hours.

The head cheese should be carved with a sharp knife into thin slices and the rind should be removed after slicing.

Serve with horse-radish with vinegar, with home-made tomato paste, mustard and bread.

Polish Sausage

*2 lb. pork shoulder together with fat * salt * allspice * pepper * garlic * * pinch of saltpeter * small intestines of hog*

Slice meat into very fine cubes, add salt, allspice, pepper and crushed garlic to taste, mix with saltpeter.

Blend entire mixture into a mass with the consistency of yeast cake dough, pouring in 3/4 cup of water gradually.

Pack meat mixture tightly into cleaned, soaked intestines. In order to remove the air, prick often so that the casing does not burst.

Sew up both ends or twist a few times, fasten securely with fine thread. Dry somewhat, hanging in an airy place. If it is to be eaten quickly, smoke only lightly in cold smoke. If the sausage is to be stored for a long period of time, smoke thoroughly.

Marinated Pork Meat

See page 183, 184.

POULTRY

Selection of Poultry

Small pullets	fried	— breaded raw
	roast	— with bread stuffing, Polish style (with fine groats) au gratin
Large pullets	boiled	— in white sauce, chicken in aspic
	fried	— boiled, then breaded and fried
	roast	— with stuffing, Polish style (with fat back)
	braised	— chicken paprika (Hungarian style), chicken in vegetables;
Young Hen	boiled	— chicken in broth, chicken in white roux, chicken in aspic, chicken galantine
	fried	— Pożarski cutlet
	roast	— stuffed, Polish style
	potted	— chicken paprika

Hen and rooster	boiled	— chicken in broth, chicken in white roux, chicken in mayonnaise, chicken galantine, chicken pâté
	potted	— risotto, braised chicken with fresh vegetables, chicken paprika
Turkey	boiled	— turkey galantine, turkey in aspic
	roasted	— with or without stuffing, cold turkey
Duck	roast	— duck with apples, barbecued duck
	potted	— with tomatoes, with red cabbage, with fresh mushrooms
Goose	cooked	— goose à la Polonaise
	roast	— with apples, liver or groats stuffing

Preparing Fowl for Roasting

Wrap fowl in paper, set aside to tenderize for 1—2 days in cold, dark place.

On day fowl is to be used, prepare the stuffing, fill, skewer.

Fasten neck skin to back, place fowl on back, press wings to the side, tuck wings, fasten with thin string. Tie string under the back, tuck in neck skin and tie both ends of string where skewer was pulled through the wing, do not cut.

Pull legs towards the top, insert skewer through leg near the joint, draw string through breast ends piercing through second leg. Skewer the trunk to tied wing. This keeps all parts together and prevents drying during roasting.

Carving Fowl

Drain whole unstuffed roast or boiled fowl, place on back on meat board.

Cut off drumsticks by piercing skin and meat and cutting off at hip joint, divide in two at knee joint, place in hot broth or gravy.

Cut off wings and together with them the piece of the breast adjoining them.

Cut the trunk horizontally, separate front part from back, cut the collar joint, place the front part in hot broth or gravy.

Cut the back crosswise in 3—5 serving pieces, cut through the meat first, then the backbone with poultry scissors, place the whole on heated platter.

Cut the breast crosswise into 3—5 serving pieces, first cut through meat with sharp knife, and then the bone with poultry scissors, place all the pieces on the back.

Set drumsticks crossed, and the wings in their proper place. Dot chicken with broth or sauce.
Garnish platter with leafy salad, tomato rings, etc.

Chicken Pâté

See Cold Appetizers page 25.

Chicken with Broth

*1 chicken, not too fat * salt * 1 cup mixed vegetables * allspice * bay leaf * 1 medium onion*

Soak tenderized chicken in cold water, remove after two hours, drain off water, rub in salt.
Boil water, add chicken and cook slowly.
Clean mixed vegetables; when the chicken is parboiled, add vegetables to broth, add salt and spices, browned onion and cook covered.
Cut up chicken, serve in plate together with broth. Add fluffy boiled rice or macaroni cooked separately, garnish with chopped greens.

Chicken Stew

*1 chicken (about 3 lb.), not too fat * 1 cup mixed vegetables without cabbage * 1 medium onion * bay leaf * allspice * salt * 4 tbs. fat from broth or 3 tbs. butter * 5 tbs. flour * 1—2 egg yolks * green parsley*

Soak tenderized chicken in cold water for two hours.
Pour boiling water over chicken and cook slowly together with giblets. When chicken is parboiled, clean mixed vegetables, brown onion, add to the broth together with spices and salt, cook through. Drain.
Skim off fat from broth, boil broth down to 3 cups. Cool part of it.
Combine skimmed chicken fat or butter with flour in deep bowl, dilute with the cold broth, pour into boiling part of broth, stirring constantly, bring to the boil.
Carve chicken, slice vegetables from the broth with serrated knife.
Mix gravy with egg yolks, place chicken in gravy, heat quickly, place on round platter, surround with groats, rice, garnish with vegetables. Sprinkle with green parsley.
Serve with fluffy rice, pearl barley or French dumplings.

Potted Chicken with Vegetables

*1 medium-sized chicken * salt * 9 tbs. smoked bacon * 1 tbs. butter *
* 1 cup broth * 2 medium carrots * 2 medium parsley * 1/2 medium
celery root * 4 tbs. green peas * 1 medium onion * 1/2 cup string beans *
* allspice * 1 cup red wine * 1 tbs. sugar * 1 tbs. flour * 1 tbs. cold
water * 2 tbs. tomato paste * 1 tbs. chopped green dill*

Rinse tenderized young chicken, rub in salt and set aside for two hours.
Cut bacon in cubes, render in saucepan in which the chicken is to be potted.
Add butter to the bacon, heat fat, add chicken, pour over with fat, add
broth and braise slowly, turning so that it cooks evenly in the sauce.
Braise for about 3/4 hour.
Clean all vegetables, pare, slice in medium-sized strips. Chop onion finely,
cut beans diagonally.
Add the vegetables, allspice, a pinch of salt and sugar to the sauce, pour
in wine, braise together with chicken until tender (about 1 1/2 hours).
Combine flour with a little cold water, add to vegetables, stir while cooking,
add tomato paste and green dill.

Chicken Paprika

*1 chicken * salt * 1 small onion * 3 tbs. fat * paprika * 1 cup sour
cream * 2 tbs. flour * (caramel coloring)*

Salt chicken day before using. Soak in water for two hours before
cooking.
Remove chicken, drain off water, carve into servings.
Slice onion.
Heat fat, fry chicken, place in saucepan, add onion, salt, paprika, a drop
of water, fat from the skillet and braise until tender, adding water from
time to time; allow sauce to brown while cooking, but do not allow it to
burn.
Remove when tender, add sour cream and flour to gravy, salt, bring to the
boil together with the chicken, color with caramel to golden color.
Serve on a round platter.
Serve with fluffy rice, macaroni, spaghetti, French dumplings.

Chicken Cutlets

*5 fillets from chicken breast * salt * F i l l i n g: 1/2 lb. veal * 3 oz. beef
marrow * 1 egg yolk * salt * nutmeg * pepper * B r e a d i n g: 3 tbs.
flour * 1 egg * 5 tbs. bread crumbs * 2 tbs. fat * 2 tbs. butter*

Necessary here are 5 serving pieces cut from the breast of a chicken which has been halved lengthwise.

Cut off a fillet from the breast bone together with part of the wing which should be cut off at the first joint after the shoulder joint.

Skin fillets carefully with a small, sharp knife.

Skin wing carefully and discard skin.

Pound fillet lightly into a flat slice, taking care not to tear the meat.

The cutlet with bone should be long and pear-shaped.

Salt fillets.

Prepare filling. Grind veal twice with beef marow, combine in bowl with egg yolk, salt and spices.

Spread filling on cutlets, fold in half, press and bread first in flour, then in egg, and finally in sifted bread crumbs.

Heat fat and fry cutlets, immediately after breading, on both sides on a medium flame. When almost done, add butter.

Serve with green peas, cauliflower, asparagus and lettuce or tomatoes.

Roast Stuffed Chicken

*1 fat chicken * salt * 2 stale rolls * milk for soaking * 3 1/2 tbs. butter * * 3 egg yolks * pepper * 3 tbs. green dill * 3 egg whites * 2—3 tbs. bread crumbs * 3 1/2 tbs. fat*

Rinse chicken, drain off water, soak for 2 hours in water, remove from water, drain, rub in salt.

Soak rolls, press out milk, grind.

Rinse green dill, chop.

Cream butter with egg yolks, add roll, mix, add dill, salt and pepper to taste.

Beat egg whites, mix with yolks, add bread crumbs, (stuffing should have consistency of sponge cake batter).

Fill chicken with stuffing, leaving room for expansion, truss with needle and thread, prepare chicken for roasting and fasten with string.

Heat fat, place chicken on hot fat on its back, pour fat over top of meat, place in hot oven, baste while roasting, add water to gravy so that it does not burn.

When the chicken begins to brown, cover, roast until tender not allowing gravy to burn, sprinkle often with water, roast about 1—1 1/2 hours.

Cut chicken into serving pieces, place the whole on platter, garnish.

Serve with potatoes, fresh salad in season, boiled vegetables or cranberry compote.

Roast Chicken Risotto

*1 chicken * salt * 1 cup mixed vegetables * 1 medium onion * bay leaf *
* allspice * 1 1/4 cup rice * 4 tbs. Parmesan cheese * green parsley * 1 tbs.
tomato paste * paprika * 1 tbs. butter*

An older fowl may be used for this dish.

Salt a well tenderized chicken and set aside for 2 days. Carve into serving
pieces (4—6 pieces depending on the size of the chicken). Place pieces
tightly in saucepan, placing the legs and back pieces on bottom with breast
and thighs on top.

Pour boiling water on chicken, salt, cover and cook slowly.

After one hour add sliced vegetables, bay leaf and allspice as well as the
onion browned on open flame, cover and cook until chicken is tender.
There should be about 2 1/2 cups of broth after cooking.

Parboil rice in water, drain, pour the 2 cups of broth over rice, and cook
slowly.

When the broth is absorbed by the half-cooked rice, place in bowl, add
grated Parmesan, green parsley and tomato paste, mix, add salt and
paprika to taste.

Butter baking dish and place in layers of rice and cooked chicken alternately. Pour over with the rest of the broth and roast.

Serve with green peas and leafy salad.

Stewed Pullets

*3 pullets * 1 cup mixed vegetables without cabbage * 1 medium onion *
* bay leaf * allspice * salt * 3 tbs. butter * 5 tbs. flour * 1—2 egg
yolks * green parsley*

Prepare the same as stewed chicken (see page 252).

Stewed Pullets with Young Vegetables

*3 pullets * salt * 2 medium carrots * 1 slice of celery root (celeriac) * 1 me-
dium parsley * 1/2 cup green peas * 1 cup string beans * 1 cup kohlrabi *
* 1 small cauliflower * 1 medium onion * 3 tbs. butter * 3 tbs. butter for
sauce * 2 tbs. flour*

Rinse and salt pullets a few hours before using.

Place pullets in saucepan, pour a small amount of water over them and
cook for 15 minutes, turning them over once.

Rinse vegetables, clean, slice carrot, celery root, parsley into rather thick
rings, dice kohlrabi, cut string beans into oblique slices, divide cauliflower
into small flowerets, cut off stem.

255

When pullets are half cooked add butter, then add kohlrabi and cauliflower, and after a few minutes the rest of the vegetables and salt to taste; cook until pullets and vegetables are tender, reduce liquid; when pullets are tender, cut into serving pieces.

Prepare sauce. Melt butter, add flour, brown lightly, dilute with liquid from the pot, add vegetables, stir while cooking. The sauce should be rather thin.

Serve garnished with chopped green dill.

Potted Pullets with Asparagus or Cauliflower

*1 cup mixed vegetables * 3 pullets * 1 medium onion * salt * allspice * * bay leaf * 2 lb. asparagus * 1 medium cauliflower * 3 tbs. butter * 2 tbs. flour * 1 cup sweet cream * 1 tbs. sugar*

Rinse mixed vegetables, clean, pour over with boiling water and parboil. Place rinsed pullets into broth, so that entire meat is covered with broth, add onion, salt and spices, cook slowly until soft, reduce liquid to about 3 cups.

When the pullets are tender, pour off broth, cut up larger pullets into 4 serving pieces, smaller ones in half.

Clean and rinse asparagus, place in salted boiling water and parboil, remove, cut up into 3/4 inch slices and discard unedible parts, cook the rest in broth.

If cauliflower is used instead of asparagus, clean and cook by dropping into salted boiling water, drain, divide into flowerets.

Combine flour and butter in bowl, dilute with broth, pour into broth and asparagus, stir while cooking, add the sliced pullets to the sauce, and then the sweet cream, blending the sauce to the desired thickness, cook, add salt and sugar to taste. The sauce should be rather thick.

Heat the pullets in the sauce on a very low flame and serve on platter.

Fried Pullets à la Polonaise

*5 small pullets * salt * 6 tbs. flour * 3 eggs * 1/2 cup bread crumbs * 1/2 cup fat for frying * 3 tbs butter * green parsley*

Select small but fattened pullets. Rinse thoroughl:
Salt for 1/2 hour before using, place in bowl.
Cut each pullet in half lengthwise, dry with a cloth.
Twist wing, fold back, pull drumsticks upward, slit the skin of the body, insert legs, pull down to normal position.

Dredge each half thoroughly with flour.

Dip in egg, drain, dip in bread crumbs, press crumbs into pullet so that they do not become separated during frying.

Heat fat in deep skillet, add pullet, fry on medium heat so that it fries evenly (the pullet may be placed in warm oven after frying, so that it does not dry out).

Place on long platter, dot with browned butter, garnish with green parsley. The pullet may also be deep-fried.

Serve with young potatoes, cucumbers in sour cream (mizeria), lettuce with sour cream or compote.

Pullets, Hungarian Style

*3 small pullets * salt * pepper * 3 tbs. fat back * 1 medium onion * 2 cups broth * 2 tbs. butter * 2 tbs. flour * 4 tbs. tomato paste * paprika*

Salt pullets for an hour before using.

Sprinkle halved pullets with pepper, brown in fat, remove to saucepan, add fat from frying, sliced onion and braise, adding broth during cooking. Prepare a roux with butter and flour, dilute with tomato paste and add to the sauce, stir while cooking; if necessary add salt and paprika to taste. Cook the pullets in this sauce over very low heat, strain sauce before serving.

Serve with dropped dumplings.

Roast Pullets with Liver Stuffing

*3 larger pullets * salt * stale roll (3 oz.) * milk for soaking * 3 chicken livers * 3 1/2 tbs. butter * 3 egg yolks * 4 tbs. green dill * pepper * 3 egg whites * 3 tbs. bread crumbs * 3 tbs. fat * 3 tbs. butter for roasting * green parsley*

Rinse pullets thoroughly.

Salt for a few hours before roasting, place in bowl and keep in cold place.

Soak roll in milk, drain.

Grind the roll and livers in meat grinder.

Cream butter, add egg yolks one at a time, add ground liver and roll, combine, add salt, pepper and green dill.

Beat egg whites frothy, mix with stuffing; if necessary, add bread crumbs (mixture should have consistency of sponge-cake batter).

Fill pullets with stuffing, sew up.

Twist wing, place on backbone, pull drumsticks upwards, make an incision in the skin of the body, insert legs, pull down to normal position.

Heat fat in baking pan, place pullets tightly one beside the other and pour over with fat, place in well-heated oven.

Roast 3/4 — 1 hour, basting with butter and dotting with water.

After roasting, cut pullets in half, place on a long platter, pour over with part of gravy, serve rest of gravy in gravy boat.

Garnish with green parsley.

Serve with potatoes and cucumbers in sour cream (mizeria), lettuce with sour cream, or compote.

Roast Pullets à la Polonaise

*5 small pullets * salt * 4—5 tbs. butter * 3 tbs. green dill * 6 tbs. bread crumbs * 2 tbs. fat for roasting * 3 1/2 tbs. butter for roasting*

Salt small pullets for 1/2 hour before using.

Prepare stuffing. Cream butter, add salt, chopped green dill and bread crumbs, combine all ingredients.

Stuff pullets, truss.

Turn wings.

Gash only the skin of the abdominal cavity on both sides, place drumsticks in both openings, so that they are kept near the trunk of the body.

Place the pullets tightly one next to the other in shallow pan of suitable size to keep pullets tight, pour over with hot fat and place in hot oven, so that the surface of the meat browns quickly.

Dot the surface of the meat with melted butter during roasting and add a few drops of water to the gravy, so that it does not burn.

Roast about 45—55 minutes.

Pullets in Casserole

*5 small pullets * salt * 3 tbs. butter * 3 tbs. Parmesan cheese * 1 cup light cream * 1/2 tbs. flour * 2 eggs * 2 egg yolks * 2 tbs. Parmesan cheese * * 1 tbs. bread crumbs * 1 tbs. butter * 1 tbs. green parsley*

Salt small pullets for 1—2 hours before using.

Melt butter in saucepan, add pullets, pour over with butter and braise until tender, turning while braising to cook evenly.

When tender, remove, cut each pullet in half lengthwise, place in casserole, sprinkle with Parmesan cheese.

Combine flour with 3—4 spoons of cream into a smooth paste.

Heat the rest of the cream, pour in flour and cream mixture, stir while cooking, set aside and cool.

Add eggs and egg yolks to the cream, a pinch of salt, combine with sauce and pour over the chicken.

Sprinkle the top again with cheese and bread crumbs, dot with butter and place in hot oven for 25 minutes. Sprinkle with green parsley.

Serve with French-fried or young potatoes, lettuce or tomato salad.

Braised Duck or Goose with Red Cabbage

*1 duck or 1/2 goose, meaty but not fat * 3 1/2 tbs. fat * 2 1/2 lb. red cabbage * 1 medium onion * 2 tbs. flour * 1 1/2 tbs. fat from duck * salt * * sugar * vinegar (or 4 medium apples)*

Salt the tenderized duck for two hours before cooking, cut into serving pieces, fry in fat, pour over with boiling water and braise covered.

When meat is half done, add thinly shredded scalded cabbage and onion, braise covered until tender.

Prepare roux with flour and fat.

Thicken gravy with roux, add salt and sugar to taste. Add vinegar or shredded apples. Cook. Pour over the duck.

Serve with all types of potatoes.

Braised Duck with Tomatoes

*1 duck (not too fat) * salt * 2 tbs. fat back * 1 medium onion * bay leaf * * allspice * 2 whole cloves * paprika * 1/2 cup broth * 1/2 cup dry wine * * 5 medium tomatoes*

Rinse duck and rub in salt two hours before using.

Place duck in roasting pan, melt fat back, pour fat over meat, place in hot oven and baste with fat while roasting, roast until brown.

When the duck begins to brown and is about half done, place in saucepan; add sliced onion and spices, pour over with broth and braise slowly, covered, until tender.

Add broth during braising, and before done, pour in the wine, add sliced tomatoes and braise together.

When the meat is tender, remove, carve into serving pieces, arrange on platter, place in oven so that it does not dry; strain the sauce, boil, pour over the duck.

Serve with potatoes and dropped dumplings.

Marinated Duck

*Vinegar marinade * 1 duck (not too fat) * salt * 3 1/2 tbs. fat back * 1 medium onion * bay leaf * allspice * 1 cup sour cream * 2 tbs. flour * * ginger * nutmeg*

Prepare and cook vinegar marinade (see page 184).

Rinse duck, place in bowl, pour over with marinade and marinate for 1—2 days.

Remove duck, drain, rub in salt; after an hour place duck in roaster.

Melt fat back, remove cracklings, cover the duck with the fat, place in oven and baste with fat while roasting, add water to sauce as necessary. When meat is half roasted and brown, add onion with allspice and bay leaf, and roast through until tender, browning the sauce and onion. Remove duck when tender, carve into serving pieces.

Strain sauce, heat, add sour cream and flour, add ground ginger and nutmeg.

Stir while cooking. The sauce should be brown and have a tart flavor.

Place the carved duck into the sauce, heat well, place on heated platter, pour over sauce.

Serve with noodles or potatoes.

Roast Duck or Goose with Apples

*1 fatty duck * salt * 3 medium cooking apples * 1/2 tsp. caraway seeds * * 5 tbs. fat back * sugar for sprinkling apples*

Salt duck for 2 hours before using.

Rinse apples, cut into sections.

Slice fat back into strips.

Rinse duck, drain off water, stuff with apples, sprinkle with caraway seeds, tie pieces of fat back round the bird with string, place in roaster.

Place in hot oven, roast for 1—1 1/2 hours, baste while roasting, sprinkle sauce with water.

When duck is tender, remove, remove apples, carve meat into serving pieces, place the entire brid on platter, surround with apples, sprinkle apples with sugar, serve sauce separately in gravy boat.

Serve with cabbage and apples or red cabbage in wine sauce.

Goose à la Polonaise

*1 small, lean goose * salt * 1 cup mixed vegetables * 1 medium onion * * 3 1/2 tbs. fat * 3 tbs. flour * marjoram * nutmeg * 1—2 egg yolks*

Soak tenderized goose in cold water for 2—3 hours, rub in salt, divide in half, pour boiling water over goose and cook slowly.

Clean mixed vegetables. When meat is half cooked, add vegetables, onion and cook slowly, reducing liquid to 3 cups.

Prepare roux with fat and flour, dilute with the stock from the goose, add salt, nutmeg and marjoram to taste. Stir while cooking.

Carve goose into serving pieces, place in sauce, heat, mix with egg yolks before serving, arrange on platter with fluffly, parched barley.

Goose with Liver Stuffing

*1 goose, not too fat * salt * stale roll (3 oz.) * milk for soaking * goose liver * 1/2 cup goose fat * 3 egg yolks * pepper * nutmeg * green parsley * * green dill * 3 egg whites * 3 tbs. bread crumbs * 1/2 tsp. caraway seeds * * 4 oz. fat back*

Keep goose in porcelain dish in a cold place for a few days; soak for 2—4 hours before roasting, then salt and set aside for another 2 hours.

Soak roll, drain off milk. Put roll and liver through meat grinder, render fat from goose. Rinse and chop green parsley and dill.

Combine egg yolk with fat, add roll and liver, mix, add spices, green parsley, dill and salt.

Beat egg whites frothy, combine with mixture (stuffing should have consistency of sponge-cake batter), add bread crumbs.

Stuff goose, sew and fasten as chicken; then sprinkle with caraway seeds (or marjoram).

Cut fat back into thin slices, place fat back on goose (breast and legs), fasten the fat back with string.

Place in hot oven and baste while roasting, adding water when the sauce evaporates. When the goose begins to brown, cover so that it does not burn, roast through. Roast about 2 hours.

When tender, carve into serving pieces, place on platter, pour over with some of sauce. Serve rest in gravy boat.

Serve with potatoes, cabbage and apples, red cabbage in wine sauce, cranberry compote.

Goose with Groats Stuffing

Prepare like stuffed sucking pig with the same dressing.

Large goose should be tenderized for a week in a cold place; soak in water for 2 hours before using, remove, salt and roast after 2 hours.

Roast Stuffed Turkey

1 turkey or turkey hen ∗ *salt* ∗ S t u f f i n g 1: *Liver* ∗ S t u f f i n g 2: *Polish Stuffing* ∗ S t u f f i n g 3: *Ham and Rice* ∗ S t u f f i n g 4: *Sweet with Raisins* ∗ S t u f f i n g 5: *Chestnut*

Keep turkey for a few days in the cold to tenderize.

Two hours before roasting, dip the entire turkey in water.

Prepare for roasting. Dry inside and out, find the tendon around the knee joint, pull and remove so that the drumstick is not tough. Salt the turkey and set aside, then fill the inside and jowls and sew up; the turkey can be roasted with or without stuffing.

Place slices of fat back on the breast and place in hot oven in roaster, pour a little fat on bottom of pan.

Roast turkey hen for about 2 hours, cook turkey for 3 hours; pour sauce over top and add water to the sauce.

An hour before finishing, remove melted fat back, so that the entire surface of the meat browns; if it browns too strongly, cover.

If the meat is still tough and is already properly browned, cover to avoid burning.

Carve turkey after removing from oven. Cut off legs the same way as when carving chicken; cut legs in half lengthwise, cut off thigh, slice into three parts.

Slice the stuffing from the jowl with a very sharp knife, arrange on plate and place in warm oven.

Slice breast, without changing order. Cut across the abdominal cavity with the stuffing, and chop back into 5—6 pieces. First slice the stuffing, then place cleaver here so as to crack backbone. Place the entire turkey on platter, place the sliced breast on breast bone. Arrange the sliced stuffing into a whole. Place drumsticks on the sides, the thighs in their place. Sprinkle the turkey with sauce, place with platter in oven so that it is heated. The turkey can also be arranged in slices without the skeleton bone, placing the slices of meat with the slices of stuffing alternately and some sauce poured over the whole.

Stuffing No. 1 with Liver

Stale roll (3 oz.) ∗ *milk for soaking* ∗ *turkey liver* ∗ *6 tbs. butter* ∗ *4 eggs* ∗ ∗ *salt* ∗ *pepper* ∗ *green parsley* ∗ *bread crumbs*

Soak roll in milk, drain, grind.

Rinse liver, remove membrane, grind.

Cream butter, add egg yolks, one at a time while stirring; when the yolks combine with the butter, add salt, pepper, parsley and liver, mix. Combine at the end with bread crumbs.

Beat egg whites frothy, blend with mixture and if too thin, add 1—2 spoons of bread crumbs.

Fill turkey with stuffing at jowl and abdominal cavity, carefully lifting the skin dividing the membrane from the meat at the former crop, stuff abdominal cavity too; truss.

Stuffing No. 2 Polish Stuffing (with Bread Crumbs)

*Turkey liver * 3 oz. raisins * 1 tbs. chopped green parsley * 1 tbs. butter * * 3 egg yolks * 1 tbs. sugar * pepper * nutmeg * ginger * cloves * 3 egg whites *2 tbs. bread crumbs * salt*

Grate or grind turkey liver.

Clean raisins, rinse, drain off water.

Chop green parsley finely.

Cream butter, adding one egg yolk at a time.

Add ground liver to this mixture, parsley, spices and sugar, combine to fluffy mass. Add raisins at the end.

Beat egg whites, combine with mixture, add bread crumbs and salt, mix. Use for stuffing turkey. See above.

Stuffing No. 3 with Ham and Rice

*1 1/4 cups rice * 6 tbs. butter * 3 oz. boiled ham * 2 eggs * 1/2 cup sour cream * pepper * 1 tbs. green parsley * salt*

Rinse rice, parboil, add two cups of water, add butter, cover and cook until tender.

Chop ham finely.

When rice is tender add ham, eggs, sour cream, pepper and chopped parsley, mix; if necessary, add salt.

Use for stuffing turkey. See above.

Stuffing No. 4 Sweet Dressing with Raisins

*Turkey liver * 1/4 cup raisins * 1/4 cup almonds * 2 whole cloves * * nutmeg * 5 tbs. butter * 1 tbs. sugar * 3 eggs * 4 oz. bread crumbs * * salt*

Rinse liver, remove membrane, grind.

Rinse raisins and almonds, chop almonds; grind cloves and nutmeg.

Cream butter with sugar, add egg yolks one at a time while stirring, when the yolks combine with butter, add liver and spices, mix.

Beat egg whites, blend with mixture, sprinkle with bread crumbs and blend lightly. Salt.

Use for stuffing turkey. See above.

Bread crumbs for turkey should be prepared at home from dried rolls.

Stuffing No. 5 Chestnut Stuffing

*75 shelled chestnuts * 3 tbs. butter * 3 egg yolks * 1 1/2 tbs. sugar * 3 tbs. bread crumbs * 4 tbs. heavy cream * 4 egg whites * salt*

Rinse chestnuts. Incise both shells lengthwise, add cold water and cook slowly.

When chestnuts are parboiled, drain, set aside covered, shell and strain through sieve.

Cream butter, add one egg yolk at a time and sugar.

Add chestnuts and bread crumbs to butter, mix adding cream gradually.

Beat egg whites frothy, add gradually to chestnut mixture.

Add a little salt at end.

Stuff turkey: place some stuffing in abdominal cavity, some under skin on the breast, at the neck base and at the formed crop, truss.

Stewed Duck or Goose Giblets

*Giblets from goose or duck (gizzard, liver, wings, neck without skin, steamed feet without scales) * 2 dried mushrooms * 3/4 cup mixed vegetables * 1 medium onion * salt * bay leaf * allspice * 2 tbs. butter * 3 tbs. flour * 1 cup sour cream * 1 cup pearl barley*

Clean giblets, pour over with 4 cups boiling water, add washed and rinsed dried mushrooms and cook slowly.

When meat is half cooked, add cleaned, mixed vegetables, onion, salt and spices, cook until very tender.

Drain off liquid, slice gizzard, liver and mushrooms into strips, chop wings into 3 pieces, discard feet.

Make a light golden roux with butter and flour, dilute with broth, cook, add the sliced meat to sauce, mix, if necessary salt, cook; before serving add sour cream to taste.

Pick over barley, rinse, boil twice the amount of water as barley, add salt and fat skimmed from the liquid, add barley to boiling water and cook slowly.

When all the water is absorbed, place barley in oven and bake; put up the barley, when the meat is half-done.

Arrange the fluffy barley around the heated platter, and place meat, poured over with sauce, in the center, serve immediately.

Fried Goose Liver

*Goose liver * milk for soaking * salt * pepper * 2 tbs. fat back * 1 medium onion * 1 1/2 tbs. butter*

Rinse liver, soak for an hour in milk, remove, drain and sprinkle with salt and pepper.

Render fat back on a small skillet, fry liver quickly on high flame.

Slice onion. When liver is brown on one side, turn, add onion, add butter and brown together with the liver, allowing the liver to be rare inside.

If the liver is a large one, slice into serving pieces and serve immediately, covered with sauce and onion.

Stuffed Goose Neck

*Goose neck skin with fat inside *. goose liver, or 4 oz. calf's or pork liver * 7 oz. veal * 3 1/3 tbs. fat back * stale roll (2 oz.) * milk for soaking * 3 tbs. butter * 2 egg yolks * salt * pepper * nutmeg * 2 egg whites * * 1 cup mixed vegetables * bay leaf * allspice*

Remove skin from goose's neck together with the fat inside, clean skin. Rinse. Rinse liver, meat and fat back, grind. Soak roll, drain, grind.

Cream butter, add one egg yolk at a time, and when it blends with the butter add the meat mixture, add roll, salt and spices; combine into a uniform mass. Beat egg whites frothy, combine with mixture.

Fill the skin, but not too tightly as it may burst during cooking; sew up skin on both sides.

Clean mixed vegetables, rinse, add 4 cups of boiling water, add bay leaf and allspice, cook; place the stuffed neck in the boiling liquid and cook slowly, covered, add water when necessary.

If the filling begins to swell, pierce the skin in many spots so that the steam can escape and the skin will not burst; cook for about one hour.

Stuffed neck may be served hot or cold. This stuffing may also be prepared with goose liver only, omitting calf's liver and fat back by adding another egg and more stale roll (2 oz.).

265

GAME

Dressing Hare

Cover a large meat board with several layers of thick paper, prepare a wide bowl and pail.

Slit skin around the ankle bones of the legs with a very sharp knife.

Slit along the hind edge of the leg from the ankle bone to the tail.

Cut off forelegs up to ankle bone and the head at the first vertebrae of the neck.

Slit muscles of hind legs, and make a ring of string and hang the hare on a strong hook, by the hind legs. The hook should be placed on a wall higher than normal-sized person.

Pull the skin from the hare from the cut along the leg, with the aid of a knife at the beginning (cut the membrane connecting the skin with the body).

When both legs are skinned, cut off the tail, grasp the skin in both hands and pull forcefully to the bottom, gathering the skin in the hands as it is freed.

Remove skinned hare from the hook, chop off hind and fore legs at the ankle, place on meat board.

Slit the abdominal cavity up to breast, remove the entrails, cut off intestines at the anal opening. Save the lungs, heart, liver and kidneys and place in bowl.

Cut the anal opening deeply together with the surrounding parts.

Place the discarded entrails and the first layer of paper into the pail.

Rinse the rest of internal parts under running water until the blood coagulates, place in bowl.

Rinse the hare under running water; when the water dripping from the hare is only slightly colored, press out the water, place on meat board.

Remove the flaccid meat of the abdominal cavity from the loin, chop up the loin part and legs and place in vinegar marinade or vegetable marinade. Use the front parts of the hare and haslet for pâté.

Carving Roast Hare

Remove hare from pan after roasting, clean off gravy.

Slit meat across the loin, cut through the back bone at these same spots with poultry scissors. This should be done carefully so as not to separate meat from the bone.

Cut off thigh at hip joint and cut up into 2 or 3 parts.

Place entire hare on platter, pour over with sauce, serve rest of sauce in gravy boat.

Game Pâté

See Cold Appetizers page 27.

Braised Hare

*Vinegar marinade (see page 184) * 1 loin and hind legs of hare * 3 1/2 tbs. fat back for larding * salt * 2 tbs. flour * 3 1/2 tbs. fat * onion from marinade * bay leaf * allspice * 3/4 cup mixed vegetables without cabbage * some red wine * S a u c e: 1—2 tbs. flour * 1 cup sour cream * * salt * pepper*

Cover loin and legs of hare with vinegar marinade for 3—4 days.

Remove from marinade, remove membrane carefully from loin and legs with small sharp knife.

Lard the loin with fat back in two rows perpendicular to the backbone, salt, dredge with flour.

Heat fat, fry meat to golden brown on hot skillet, remove to sauce pan, add some marinade, onion, spices and sliced vegetables, braise covered until tender, pouring over with marinade a few times (few spoons); when the gravy is satisfactorily tart, pour over with some red wine, lightly brown the sauce with the vegetables while braising.

Remove meat, strain sauce, add flour and sour cream, boil, salt if necessary (add caramel coloring if desired), add pepper, add meat, simmer on very low flame. Carve meat as above, serve on long platter covered with sauce.

Serve with beets, macaroni, dropped dumplings, mashed potatoes.

Roast Hare

*Vegetable marinade (see page 183) * 1 loin and hind legs of hare * * 6 tbs. fat back for larding * salt * 2 tbs. fat * 2 tbs. butter * 1/2 cup red wine * 1/2 cup sliced mixed vegetables without cabbage * 1 medium onion * pepper * bay leaf * allspice * 1—2 tbs. flour*

Cover loin and legs of hare with vegetable marinade and marinate for 1—2 days in a cold place.

Before cooking, remove membrane and tendons, gash with a small sharp knife, lard with fat back, rub in salt, place in roasting pan of suitable size. Render fat, pour over meat, smear with butter, place in hot oven, and roast, basting with sauce, add wine to sauce.

Rinse cleaned, mixed vegetables, slice vegetables and onion in rings, place in fat together with the spices and roast together with the hare, browning lightly.

When the hare is half roasted, sprinkle with flour and roast through, remove when meat is tender, divide into serving pieces (as above) and place entire roast on platter.

Strain gravy, dilute to desired thickness with strong broth, boil, if necessary salt and cover the meat with this sauce.

Serve with potatoes, beets, red cabbage, cranberry and apple jam.

Roast Hare, Polish Style

*Vinegar marinade (see page 184) * 1 loin and hind legs of hare * 6 tbs. fat back for larding * salt * 2 tbs. fat for roasting * 2 tbs. butter * * 1/2 cup red wine * 1/2 cup sliced mixed vegetables without cabbage * * pepper * bay leaf * allspice * S a u c e : 1—2 tbs. flour * 1 cup sour cream * salt * pepper*

268

Cover loin and legs of hare with vinegar marinade and marinate for 3—4 days in a cold place. Before cooking remove membrane and tendons, lard with fat back, rub in salt, place in roasting pan of suitable size. Render fat, pour over meat, smear with butter, place in hot oven and roast, basting with sauce. Add wine to sauce. Rinse cleaned mixed vegetables in rings, place in fat together with the spices and roast together with hare. Remove meat when tender, divide into serving pieces (as above) and place entire roast on platter.

Strain sauce, add flour and sour cream, add salt and pepper to taste, bring to the boil. Cover the meat with this sauce. Serve with mashed potatoes, beets, red cabbage, cranberry and apple jam.

Loin of Venison

*Vegetable marinade (see page 183) * 3 1/2 lb. loin of venison * 6 tbs. fat back for larding * salt * a few juniper berries * 2 tbs. fat * 3 tbs. butter * 1/2 cup red wine * 2 tbs. flour*

Marinate loin of venison in vegetable marinade in cold place for 1—2 days. When the meat is tenderized, remove, cut away tendons and membrane carefully, lard the meat with fat back in two rows criss-crossing the backbone, rub in salt and juniper berries.

Heat fat in roasting pan of suitable size, place meat in pan, spread with butter and roast in medium oven.

Baste while roasting, sprinkle wine into fat from time to time so that the fat does not dry up and does not burn.

Remove meat when tender, remove fillets from both sides of backbone, slice into thin diagonal slices, place meat again on both sides of bones of backbone, and place the whole on platter. Add flour to sauce, boil, if necessary salt and cover the meat with sauce. Serve with French-fried potatoes and red-bilberry with horse-radish.

Roast Leg of Venison, Polish Style

*Vinegar marinade (see page 184) * 3 1/2 lb. leg of venison * 6 tbs. fat back for larding * salt * 2 tbs. fat for roasting * 2 tbs. butter * 1/2 cup red wine * 1/2 cup cut mixed vegetables without cabbage * bay leaf * * allspice * S a u c e: 2 tbs. flour * 1 cup sour cream * salt * 3 juniper berries*

Rinse venison, marinate for a few days in vinegar marinade, keep in cold place (about 38°F.).

Remove meat from marinade, drain, cut away membrane and tendons, and proceed the same way as roast hare, Polish style (see page 268); do not carve into serving pieces before roasting, but roast entire leg.

Venison Steaks

*Vegetable marinade (see page 183) * 2 1/2 lb. loin of venison * salt * * 2 tbs. flour * 3 tbs. fat * 3 tbs. butter*

Marinate tenderized loin of venison in vegetable marinade for 1—2 days in a cold place (about 38°F).
Remove loin from marinade, cut away membrane, remove carefully from backbone with sharp knife.
Carve diagonal steaks, about 1/2 inch thick, from the loin.
Pound steaks carefully with meat hammer, sprinkle with salt and flour, place in hot fat and brown; before steaks are completely fried add butter and brown together, add a drop of water so that the gravy boils.
Serve with sauce poured over steaks, with French-fried potatoes, red-bilberry with horse-radish, boiled cauliflower, Jerusalem artichokes.

Wild Boar in Red Wine

*Vegetable marinade (see page 183) * 2 1/2 lb. haunch of wild boar * * 2 tsp. salt * 7 oz. carrots * 3 1/2 oz. parsnips * 2 oz. onions * 1 clove garlic * 1 cup red dry wine * 5 peppercorns * 5 juniper berries * 1 bay leaf*

Marinate tenderized haunch of wild boar in vegetable marinade for 2 days in a cold place (about 38°F).
Remove from marinade. Cook in salted water until half done. Add carrots cut into slices, parsnips, onions and garlic. Add red wine. Flavor with pepper, juniper berries and bay leaf. Cook until meat is tender.
Slice and serve with horse-radish sauce. May also be served cold with Cumberland sauce.

Braised Partridges with Red Cabbage

*3 partridges * salt * 5 tbs. fat * 1 medium head of red cabbage * * 1 medium onion * 2 tbs. flour * fat from roasted partridges * salt * * sugar * vinegar * 1/2 cup red dry wine*

Rub salt into tenderized partridges, place in casserole, roast in oven on fat, add water, and braise till half done.

Shred cabbage, place in boiling water, drain, add to partridges, add chopped onion and a little water, braise until tender, uncovered; when partridges are tender, remove, carve lengthwise in half.

Prepare roux with flour and fat from roasted partridges.

Add roux to cabbage, add salt, vinegar and sugar to taste, add wine, heat together with cabbage. Serve with potatoes.

Roast Partridges with Fat Back

*3 partridges * salt * juniper berries * 6 strips of fat back * 3 tbs. fat*

Rinse partridges, dry and rub in salt and ground juniper.

Roll strips of fat back around the entire partridge, secure fat back with string, tying partridge crosswise.

Heat fat in small roasting pan, place partridges closely one beside the other, and place in hot oven.

Roast 3/4 hour, basting with sauce and sprinkling with water.

Cut thread after roasting, carve partridges in half lengthwise and serve on long platter, poured over with part of the sauce. Serve rest of sauce in gravy boat.

Serve with French-fried potatoes and red-bilberry and pear jam.

FISH AND CRAYFISH

Defrosting Fish

Cover fish with cold water and defrost at room temperature. When defrosted, squeeze water out of fish and prepare like cleaned fish.

Soaking Salted Fish

Scrape off salt and wash fish thoroughly. Cover with cold water and soak for a few hours in cool place. Change water several times.

Soaking Dried Fish

Rinse fish in warm water, cut into smaller pieces, so that fish will fit easily in bowl, and cover with cold water. Soak for 1 or 2 days depending on how dry the fish is. Keep soaking fish in cool place.

Cleaning Fish

Hold the fish by the tail through the paper and either cut off scales with a sharp knife from tail to head, or scrape them off together with slime. Rinse.

Cut the fish belly from tail to head, loosen the entrails and remove onto paper. Also remove spleen, food tract and bladder and throw them away with the second paper. Rinse the remaining organs, salt and set aside on a plate. Use for soup stock for fish soup or barszcz. Remove gills from head. Rub salt over exterior of fish and inside cavity. Place on a plate, cover and keep in cold place for a few hours before using.

Fish Fillets

Place cleaned fish on board and cut off fins. Remove skin from one half and then from the other (or fillet with skin according to the recipe used). Slit the skin along the back and around the head and then remove skin, cutting it away with a knife. The skin of a codfish need not be cut but may be torn off after slitting the fish around the head. When doing this, the fish must be held firmly with one hand.

Using a sharp knife, cut the flesh along the back and separate it cutting near the bones. Turn the fish over and repeat the process.

Put a little salt on the fillets and place on plate.

This fish may be used for frying and sautéing.

The bones and head should be used for stock, for aspic, sauce or soups.

Boiled Codfish with Butter

*2 lb. cleaned codfish without head * vinegar * S t o c k: 6 cups water *
* 2 oz. parsley * 2 oz. carrot * 2 oz. celery root * 1 small onion * bay
leaf * allspice * salt * G a r n i s h: 3 eggs * greens * 4 tbs. butter*

Remove skin from codfish, and membranes from cavity. Sprinkle fish with vinegar.

Prepare stock, drain off liquid and add salt.

Add fish to boiling stock and cook on low fire for 20 min.

Boil eggs, remove shell and chop with greens.

Brown butter.

Remove cooked fish, drain and arrange on plate. Sprinkle with egg and greens and dot with butter.

Serve with potatoes.

Codfish Roll

Fish mixture: *2 lb. codfish * 2 oz. stale roll * 1/2 cup milk to soak roll * 1 tbs. potato starch * 3 tbs. butter * 1/2 medium onion * * 1 egg * salt * pepper * Stock: 7 oz. mixed vegetables without cabbage * 6 cups water * 1 medium onion * allspice * bay leaf * salt*

Soak roll in milk and squeeze out.

Cut onion and stew in butter, do not brown.

Clean and rinse fish, remove skin. Fillet.

Grind fish with roll and onion. Add egg, potato starch, salt and pepper to taste.

Mix well.

Cover waxpaper or a piece of white percale with a thick coating of fat. Place fish mixture along the long side of the paper and form into a roll about 10 inches long. Tie with string at both ends.

Place roll in pot with the salted vegetable stock, tucking ends under.

Cook on slow fire for 45 min. to one hour.

Remove roll carefully and place on board. Unroll, easing with knife so as not to tear the surface.

Place roll on plate and cut into even pieces as thick as a finger.

Cover with hot sauce.

Serve with potatoes and horse-radish, tomato or mustard sauce.

Codfish Balls with Horse-Radish

Fish mixture: *2 lb. codfish * 2 oz. stale roll * 1/2 cup milk to soak roll * 1 medium onion * 3 tbs. fat * 1 tsp. potato starch * 1 egg * * salt * pepper * Stock: 7 oz. mixed vegetables without cabbage * * 6 cups water * 1 medium onion * bay leaf * allspice * salt*

Soak roll in milk and squeeze out.

Cut onion and stew in fat. Do not brown.

Clean and rinse fish. Remove skin. Fillet.

Grind fish with roll and onion.

Combine mixture with potato starch, egg, salt and pepper to taste.

Mix well.

Form 2 balls per portion with hands moistened with water.

Cook vegetable stock, drain and add salt to liquid. Place balls in boiling liquid and cook on small fire for 20 min. Remove with draining spoon.

Serve on a round plate with horse-radish sauce and potatoes, or with tomato sauce and noodles.

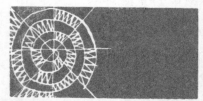

Codfish Patties

*2 lb. codfish * 1 medium onion * 3 tbs. fat * 2 oz. stale roll * 1/2 cup milk to soak roll * 1 tsp. potato starch * 1 egg * salt * pepper * 2 oz. bread crumbs * 5 tbs. fat for frying*

Cut onion and stew in fat. Soak roll.

Prepare ground mixture of fish, onion, roll, potato starch, egg, salt and pepper (see page 274).

Divide and form round or oval patties and dredge in crumbs.

Heat fat and fry patties in fat on a medium flame, until browned on both sides.

Serve with potatoes and raw salad, vegetable salad or cabbage.

Codfish and Pike Ministerial Schnitzel

*1 1/2 lb. codfish * 1 1/2 lb. pike * 2 oz. stale roll * 1/2 cup milk to soak roll * 2 oz. potatoes * 1 medium onion * 2 tbs. fat * 1/2 egg * * salt * pepper * 2 oz. stale roll for breading * 1/2 cup bread crumbs * * 1/2 cup fat for frying*

Clean and rinse codfish and pike. Remove skin. Fillet.

Soak roll in milk and squeeze out.

Peel potatoes and cook.

Brown onion lightly in fat.

Grind fish, roll, potatoes and onion. Add egg, salt and pepper to fish mixture and mix thoroughly.

Cut roll (for breading) into thin slices and then into small rectangles. Mix them with bread crumbs.

Form cutlets, dredge in the bread crumbs and roll mixture. The cutlets should have an oval shape.

Press the bread crumbs and roll mixture well, so that the breading does not fall off during the frying.

Heat fat and fry cutlets on a moderate flame, browning on both sides.

Serve with potatoes and lettuce or raw-vegetable salad.

Codfish Croquettes in Tomato Sauce

*2 lb. codfish * 2 oz. stale roll * 1/2 cup milk to soak roll * 2 oz. potatoes * 1 medium onion * 2 tbs. fat * 1/2 egg * salt * pepper * 4 tbs. flour for dredging * 3 tbs. fat for frying * tomato sauce*

Prepare meat mixture as for codfish schnitzel and divide into 10 parts. Shape small, oval croquettes in flour and fry. Prepare tomato sauce and place croquettes in hot sauce and heat on very small fire, being careful that they do not fall apart.

Serve with potatoes.

Codfish Cutlets in Greek Sauce

Fish mixture: *2 lb. codfish * 2 oz. stale roll * milk to soak roll * * 2 oz. potatoes * 1 medium onion * 2 tbs. fat * 1/2 egg * salt * * pepper * 4 tbs. flour for dredging * 4 tbs. oil for frying * Sauce: 3 oz. celery root (celeriac) * 3 oz. parsley * 3 oz. onion * 3 oz. carrot * * salt * paprika * bay leaf * allspice * 3 tbs. tomato paste * vinegar * * sugar * 1 tbs. mustard*

Prepare sauce. Clean celery root, parsley, onion and carrot and cut into long strips. Add salt, paprika, bay leaf, allspice, tomato paste and fry in oil until brown. Sprinkle with water and simmer until tender. Add vinegar, mustard and sugar to taste.

Prepare fish mixture as for codfish schnitzel and divide into 10 portions. Mold round, high cutlets in flour.

Heat oil and fry cutlets on both sides. Arrange in a bowl and cover with hot sauce and frying fat. Serve straight off the skillet, covered with hot sauce. Or store in cold place and serve cold on following day.

Codfish, Carp, Pike (Sauté)

*2 lb. codfish, or 2 1/2 lb. carp, or 3 lb. pike * vinegar * salt * pepper * * 4 tbs. flour * 5 tbs. fat*

Clean fish. Rinse and sprinkle with vinegar. Fillet fish and divide each fillet into portions. Sprinkle with salt.

Dust fish with pepper and flour before frying. Place on hot fat and fry on both sides on a medium flame.

Serve with potatoes and raw salad or vegetable salad, or with tomato, Greek, horse-radish or mushroom sauce.

Breaded Codfish, Carp, Pike

*2 lb. codfish, or 2 1/2 lb. carp, or 3 lb. pike * salt * 7 tbs. flour * * 2 1/2 eggs * 8 tbs. bread crumbs * 7 tbs. fat for frying*

Clean fish, rinse and fillet. Cut fillets into portions and salt. Arrange in porcelain dish and store in cold place.

Dry pieces of fish in clean towel.

Prepare flour and beat eggs slightly. Sift crumbs.

Pick up fish in two fingers of both hands and dredge in flour, then in egg and let excess drip off. Dredge in crumbs and press with hand.

Heat fat in skillet and fry fish on large flame. Complete cooking on small flame and brown to a light yellow.

Serve with horse-radish, potatoes and sauerkraut, vegetable salad, raw--vegetable salad.

Dredged Herring, Whiting or Flounder

*5 salted herrings or fresh herrings, or flounders, or other small sea fish * * salt * 7 tbs. flour * 1 1/2 eggs * 7 tbs. bread crumbs * 5 tbs. fat for frying*

Soak salted herrings on preceding day (change water several times).

Clean fresh fish, rinse and salt. Let stand.

Prepare flour, beat eggs lightly, sift bread crumbs.

Remove herrings (on the day of serving), squeeze out water well. Remove heads and tails; remove skin.

Fillet fish. Do not fillet flounders, but fry them whole.

Dip fillets or whole flounders in flour, then in egg and let excess drip off. Dip in bread crumbs and press crumbs to fish with hands, so that they do not fall off during cooking.

Heat fat and fry fish to a light yellow.

Serve with potatoes and raw or cooked vegetable salad.

Serve herrings with potatoes and sauerkraut or cabbage in roux.

Codfish Baked in Horse-Radish Sauce

*3 lb. codfish * vinegar * salt * 3 tbs. butter for dotting * H o r s e - -r a d i s h   s a u c e: 5 tbs. horse-radish * 3 tbs. butter * 5 tbs. flour * * 1 cup sour cream * salt * vinegar * sugar*

Rinse, clean and sprinkle codfish with vinegar. Salt fish and place in porcelain dish and let stand.

Prepare sauce. Grate horse-radish and let stand.

Melt butter, add flour and simmer. Dissolve mixture and dilute with cream. Bring to the boil stirring constantly. Add horse-radish, salt, vinegar and sugar to taste.

Dry fish in towel and fill cavity with edible entrails. Arrange on a fireproof dish, and bake partially, then cover with thick sauce, dot with butter and bake, browning the top of the sauce at the end.

Serve in the same plate garnished with potato balls boiled and sprinkled with browned butter and green parsley.

Codfish Bigos

*1 1/2 lb. smoked codfish or 3 lb. fresh codfish * 1 lb. sauerkraut * 1 lb. cabbage * 1 oz. dried mushrooms * 1 large onion * 5 tbs. fat * 2 tbs. flour * salt * paprika * marjoram * 3 tbs. tomato paste*

Clean codfish, removing skin and bones and divide into pieces.
Chop sauerkraut and cover with water. Cook.
Clean cabbage, rinse and shred. Add mushrooms. Mince onion and cook with cabbage.
Add to sauerkraut, when it is about ready.
Prepare roux with fat and flour and add to cabbage. Add salt and paprika to taste, add marjoram and tomato paste. Mix.
Add codfish to the cabbage, mix and bring to the boil.
Serve with potatoes.
Prepare bigos with fresh codfish in the same manner.

Smoked Codfish and Cereal Cutlets

*1 1/2 cups barley or millet cereal * 4 tbs. fat * 1 medium onion * 1 lb. smoked codfish * 1 egg * salt * pepper * marjoram * 7 tbs. bread crumbs * 7 tbs. fat for frying*

Rinse cereal.
Brown onion lightly in fat.
Boil twice as much water as cereal (2×1 1/2 cups). Add salt and onion with fat to the water and bring to the boil. Add cereal to boiling water and cook on low flame. When the water evaporates, stir and bake in oven. Cool.
Remove skin and bones from codfish and divide. Add to the cereal; add a raw egg and season with salt, pepper and marjoram to taste. Divide into 10 cutlets. Form cutlets in crumbs and fry on both sides to a light yellow.
Serve with raw salad.
Fresh codfish may be prepared in the same manner.

Smoked Codfish and Potato Cutlets

*1 lb. smoked codfish * 1 lb. potatoes * 3 tbs. fat * 1 medium onion *
* 1 egg * salt * pepper * marjoram * 7 tbs. bread crumbs * 7 tbs. fat
for frying*

Remove skin and bones from fish and cut meat.

Cook and mash potatoes.

Brown onion lightly in fat.

Add fish, onion with fat, egg to the potatoes and season. Divide into 5 cutlets. Form cutlets in crumbs and fry on both sides browning to a light yellow.

Serve with raw salad or vegetable salad.

Boiled Pike with Butter and Eggs

*7 oz. mixed vegetables without cabbage * 6 cups water * 1 medium onion * salt * allspice * bay leaf * vinegar * 2 1/2 lb. pike or carp * * 3 eggs * green parsley * 3 tbs. butter*

Rinse all vegetables, clean and cover with 6 cups of boiling water. Add onion, salt and seasoning and prepare stock. When the vegetables are tender, drain off stock, pour into pot for fish and bring to the boil. Add vinegar.

Clean fish and rinse thoroughly. Remove gills.

Place fish in boiling stock and cook slowly on a small flame for 25 min., taking care not to overcook it.

Cook hard-boiled eggs. Remove shells and dice.

Mince green parsley and brown the butter.

Remove cooked fish on to a rack, drain off and slip onto a heated plate. Sprinkle top with egg, green parsley and with browned butter.

Serve with boiled potato balls sprinkled with green parsley, Brussel sprouts and boiled carrot balls dotted with butter and arranged around the fish.

Pike à la Polonaise

*3 oz. mixed vegetables without cabbage * 5 cups water * 2 medium onions * salt * allspice * bay leaf * 2 tbs. 6% vinegar * 3 lb. pike * * 1 lb. potato balls * horse-radish sauce with sour cream * 2 egg yolks * * green parsley * 3 tbs. butter*

Clean and rinse vegetables, cook stock with 5 cups water. Add onions, salt, spices and vinegar. Drain off stock.

Clean pike (see page 273), rinse and place in pot on rack, with the back up.

Cover with boiling stock and cook slowly for 15 minutes.

Rinse, peel potato balls and cook in salted water.

Prepare horse-radish sauce with roux and sour cream (see page 317).

Mix with raw egg yolks.

279

Mince green parsley. Brown butter.

When the pike is about ready, remove with rack, drain and slide onto a long fireproof platter.

Cover fish with thick horse-radish sauce and dot with part of the browned butter. Place in oven for 20 min.

When the top of the sauce is browned, remove from oven and arrange potatoes on both sides of the fish. Pour rest of butter over potatoes and sprinkle with green parsley.

Garnish plate with shredded or grated horse-radish and serve immediately.

Pike Roll

*7 oz. mixed vegetables without cabbage * 6 cups water * 2 1/2 lb. pike * * 1 large onion * 4 tbs. butter * 2 oz. stale roll * milk to soak roll * * 1/2 egg * salt * pepper * bay leaf * allspice*

Prepare stock with vegetables and fish bones.

Rinse fish, cut off head and remove skin. Fillet.

Cut onion and simmer in fat until brown.

Soak roll in milk and squeeze out.

Grind together fish, roll and onion. Add egg, salt and seasoning, and mix well, adding 1/2 cup cold water.

Drain off liquid from stock and salt.

Moisten towel and spread with butter. Place on fish mixture and form into a roll. Roll up in towel and place in boiling, salted stock.

Cook fish roll on slow fire from 1 to 1 1/2 hours.

Remove carefully and remove from towel, cutting away with knife.

Cut in diagonal pieces of about 1/2 inch thick and serve hot with horse-radish, tomato or hot Greek sauce.

Boiled Carp with Butter

*7 oz. mixed vegetables without cabbage * 6 cups water * allspice * bay leaf * salt * 2 medium onions * 3 lb. carp * 6 tbs. butter * greens*

Cook stock with vegetables, seasoning, salt and onions. Drain off liquid.

Scrape fish, clean and rinse.

Place carp with the back up in a pot for cooking fish. Cover with hot vegetable stock and cook slowly for 45 minutes.

Remove fish when cooked, drain off liquid and arrange on plate. Pour melted butter over fish.

Serve with boiled potatoes (sprinkled with greens), carrots and turnips, green peas, string beans.

Carp in Polish Sauce

*2 1/2 lb. carp * salt * 3 oz. mixed vegetables without cabbage * 5 cups water * 3 tbs. butter * 2 tbs. flour * 1/2 cup red wine * 2 oz. gingerbread made with honey * lemon juice * 2 tbs. sugar caramel * 1 oz. raisins * * 1 oz. almonds*

Clean, rinse and salt fish. Let stand in a porcelain dish an hour before cooking.

Clean vegetables, add water, salt and cook. Drain off stock and pour into pot for cooking fish; bring to the boil. Add fish. Cook on a low flame for 20 minutes and drain off fish. Drain liquid and evaporate to 3 cups.

Melt butter, add flour and brown, stirring constantly. Remove from fire, Dilute roux with wine and fish stock to proper thickness.

Add crumbled gingerbread and cook until it dissolves.

Press sauce through sieve.

Season sauce with salt, lemon juice and sugar to taste. Color with caramel to a dark gold.

Clean raisins and scald almonds. Peel and shred. Add to sauce.

Place fish in sauce and keep in warm place until served.

Serve with łazanki or potatoes.

Carp in brown sauce may be prepared with fillets cut into portions, when there is no pot for boiling fish.

Baked Stuffed Carp

*2 1/2 to 3 lb. carp * salt * 5 oz. mushrooms (champignons) * 2 tbs. butter * pepper * 2 oz. stale roll * milk for soaking roll * 3 tbs. butter * * 2 egg yolks * green parsley * 2 egg whites * 5 tbs. butter for baking*

Clean, rinse and salt carp, and let stand for one hour.

Prepare mushrooms. Rinse and shred. Add salt, 2 tbs. butter and pepper. Sprinkle with water and simmer. When mushrooms are tender, brown stirring lightly. Soak roll in milk, and squeeze out.

Cream 3 tbs. butter, adding one yolk at a time. Mix with roll, salt, pepper and green, minced parsley. Cream. Mix with mushrooms and then with beaten egg whites.

Dry carp in towel and fill cavity with stuffing. Pin with sticks or sew.

Place part of the butter on a long fireproof dish and heat.

Place carp flat on the fat. Pour butter over the top and place in a hot oven.

During baking, 45 min., baste fish with sauce and sprinkle with water.

When the fish is pierced near the head and does not exude turbid juice, and is soft, remove from oven and serve on dish in which it was baked.

Royal Carp

Stock: *3 lb. carp * salt * 7 oz. mixed vegetables * 4 cups water * * 1 medium onion * bay leaf * allspice * 2 cups white wine * 1 tbs. butter * Sauce: carp's soft roe * vinegar * salt * 3 oz. mushrooms (champignons) * 2 tbs. butter * 2 tbs. flour * 3 egg yolks * salt * pepper * * Fish balls: 2 cups cooked and boned carp * 1 1/2 tbs. butter * * 2 eggs * 2 to 3 tbs. bread crumbs * green parsley * salt * pepper * * nutmeg*

Clean carp and rub cavity and exterior with salt and let stand for one hour.

Clean and rinse vegetables, and cook stock with 4 cups water, onion and seasoning. Cool.

Place carp on rack in pot and cover with boiling vegetable stock and white wine. Add butter and salt to taste.

Cover top of fish with greased paper and cook slowly for about 30 min. under cover.

Prepare sauce. Cook carp's soft roe in water with vinegar and salt. Drain and cut into large cubes. Clean and rinse mushrooms and cut into thin strips.

Sprinkle with water. Simmer. To finish brown lightly, stirring constantly and add cubed roe.

Prepare light yellow roux and dilute with fish stock. Combine with mushrooms. Add salt and pepper, and bring to the boil.

Before serving add raw egg yolks to sauce and immediately pour over fish.

Remove carp carefully from stock, drain and slide onto an oblong platter.

Arrange fish balls around carp and pour over with sauce. Serve remainder of sauce in sauceboat.

Prepare fish balls. Simmer pieces of fish covered with stock, or use remaining pieces of cooked or baked fish. Edible, cooked fish entrails may also be used. Remove bones from fish, grind or chop meat.

Cream butter, adding one yolk at a time. Mix fish with salt, nutmeg, pepper and green parsley.

Beat egg whites stiff, mix with fish mixture and crumbs.

Boil salted water and place in a spoonful of mixture. Boil and test if the mixture is not too fluffy.

If the mixture does not hold, then add crumbs.

Place mixture on floured board. Form a roll 2/3 inch in diameter. Cut into pieces and form each piece into a ball.

Before serving, cook balls in boiling, salted water. When they float to the top, bring slowly to the boil once.

Before removing from water, test by cutting one ball.

Remove cooked balls carefully with a draining spoon, place in sieve and allow liquid to drip off. Slide onto plate and pour butter or sauce over them.

Boiled Salmon

*2 lb. salmon * salt * 5 oz. mixed vegetables * 5 cups water * 1 medium onion * allspice * bay leaf * green parsley * 2 tbs. butter*

Remove scales, clean and rinse salmon. Salt.
Cook stock with vegetables, onion and seasoning. Drain off liquid. Bring liquid to the boil.
Place salmon in tight pot and cover with boiling stock. Cook liquid slowly for 30 min. Add salt if necessary.
Remove cooked salmon from water, drain and remove skin. Place on plate and sprinkle with green parsley and dot with butter.
Serve with Hollandaise sauce, boiled potatoes with browned butter and chopped green dill and parsley, or with French-fried potatoes.

Grilled Salmon

*2 lb. salmon * salt * 5 tbs. oil*

Clean salmon. Rinse and cut fish crosswise, into 5 thick portions.
Salt and let stand for one hour. Dry in towel and spread generously with oil on all sides.
Grease grill with oil and place salmon side by side. Grill and baste with oil and juice from fish.
When the fish is browned, turn and brown quickly on other side.
When baked, serve on long plate, arranging portions with the back turned in one direction and resting one against the other.
Serve with fried or boiled potato balls and Hollandaise sauce.

Crucian* in Sour Cream à la Polonaise

*2 to 3 (2 lb.) crucians * salt * 2 tbs. lard * 2 tbs. butter * 3 tbs. Ementhaler cheese * 1 cup sour cream * 1 1/2 tbs. flour * 2 tbs. bread crumbs*

Remove scales and clean fish (see page 273). Rinse and rub cavity and exterior with salt. Let stand for one hour.

---

* Crucian (*L. Carassius carassius*) is a fresh-water fish like the brown goldfish.

Dust with flour and brown on both sides in hot fat to a light yellow. When turning fish, add butter to brown with the fish.

Place browned fish on a fireproof dish.

Prepare sauce. Grate cheese. Mix cream with flour, add cheese, salt and frying fat and pour over fish. Sprinkle top with crumbs and bake. Serve with boiled potatoes sprinkled with green parsley.

Trout with Eggs

*10 medium trouts * salt * 1 large onion * allspice * bay leaf * pepper *
* 5 eggs * 6 tbs. butter * green parsley*

Rinse and clean trouts without cutting heads and tails. Remove scales. Salt.

Boil small amount of water with onion and seasoning.

Place trouts in boiling water and cook on slow fire. Add salt if necessary. Cook hard-boiled eggs. Remove shells and chop.

Brown butter.

Drain trouts well and arrange on hot plates. Sprinkle with eggs and green parsley. Pour over with butter and serve immediately.

Serve with boiled potatoes.

Stewed Trout

*10 trouts * salt * 4 tbs. butter * pepper * 1/2 cup white, dry wine *
* green parsley*

Rinse and clean trouts without cutting off heads and tails. Salt and let stand for one hour.

Take a shallow, fireproof dish and melt and heat butter. Do not brown. Dry trout in towel, sprinkle with pepper and place in butter.

Add wine and stew slowly until tender. Add finely-chopped parsley at end. Serve in the same dish in which the fish was cooked.

Boiled Crayfishes

*30 live crayfishes * water * salt * green dill*

Take each crayfish by the shell from the top and wash off mud very thoroughly. Scrub with a brush both top and bottom. Rinse thoroughly under running water.

Boil a large amount of water in a large pot on a very high flame. Salt. Add green dill.

Place crayfish in boiling water and cover, bring to the boil as quickly as possible. Cook on a lower flame.

When the crayfish turn red, serve in tureen with stock in which they were cooked.

Crayfishes à la Polonaise

*30 live crayfishes * water * salt * 3/4 cup butter * 1 cup sour cream * * 1 oz. bread crumbs * 5 tbs. chopped green dill*

Take each crayfish by the shell from the top and clean thoroughly with a brush. Clean both top and bottom and place in a large amount of boiling salted water. Bring quickly to the boil under cover and clean again more thoroughly. Dry in towel.

Melt butter in a round, fireproof dish. Place crayfish in dish and sauté until they turn red.

Add sour cream, salt to taste and simmer under cover for 10 to 15 minutes. Add crumbs toward end of cooking to thicken sauce. Add chopped dill at the end.

Serve in the dish in which crayfishes were cooked.

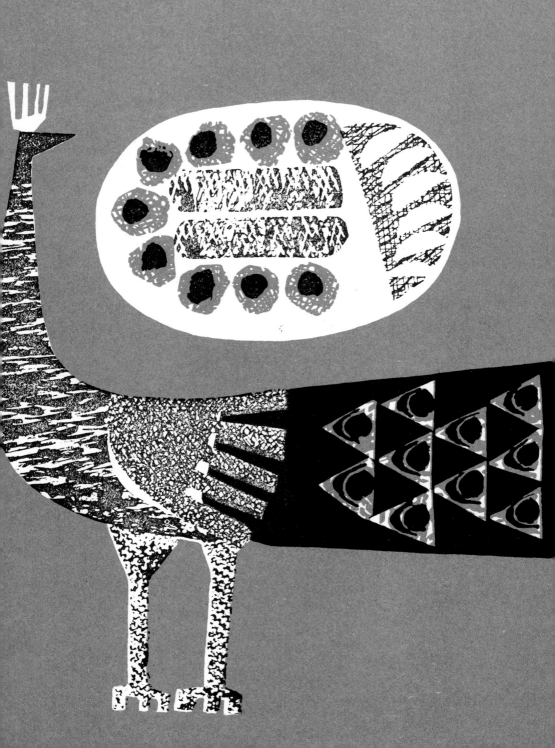

ECONOMY MEAT DISHES

Economy meat dishes consist mainly of vegetables with an addition of a small quantity of meat. The meat supplements the less valuable vegetable proteins. Economy meat dishes may be served as soups and second courses. The main ingredient of soups are the vegetables boiled with the meat. Soups prepared with meat are one-course dishes. Therefore a portion of soup for adults is from one to one and half pints. The basic products used to prepare economy second courses are vegetables; dough and cereals to which meat is added in various forms. They are prepared and served as one-course meals. The most nutritive and tasty is a combination of meat and vegetables. These dishes are very easy to make, take little time and work and are usually made in one pot. We use meat with bones to prepare these dishes. To improve their nutritive value they are served with potatoes, raw salad or lettuce. Sliced tomatoes with onion, dill pickles, sliced-cucumber salad with cream, lettuce, grated horse-radish with cream and apples, sliced beetroot relish with vinegar and grated horse-radish, onion relish with lemon and olive oil make an excellent addition to these dishes. Combination vegetable-meat dishes include: stewed meat with mixed vegetables, pork, bacon or sausage with cabbage and tomatoes, "bigos" (stewed sauerkraut with pork, ham, bacon, etc.), pork ribs with sweet cabbage, mutton or sausage with beans and tomato sauce, turnips with pork or sausage, stewed sausage with savoy cabbage and potatoes, and so on.

A portion of a one-course dish weighs approximately 3/4 lb.

In the second group of combination meat dishes, the basic ingredient is the dough or cereal instead of vegetables. The dough is cooked or fried, cereal is cooked fluffy and combined with meat. To this group belong dumplings (pierogi) with meat, potato dumplings with filling, baked macaroni with smoked meat or brain filling, vegetables stuffed with cereal and meat mixture, paprika stuffed with meat and vegetables, etc. Serve 2 to 3 pieces of stuffed vegetables or pancakes and 8 to 15 dumplings (pierogi) per person. Meat used to prepare these dishes has usually been previously cooked.

Cook meat for dumplings, pancakes with meat, baked macaroni. To the minced meat add a roll previously soaked, onion fried to a golden color, salt and pepper. To prepare combination meat-cereal dishes, the meat has to be stewed together with bones with the addition of onion and salt. When tender, drain the meat; the bones may be used for soup stock. Mince the mixture together with the sauce, then mix it with baked cereal, season with paprika and chopped parsley. These dishes require a spicy sauce with a distinct flavour, e.g., tomato, dill and mushroom sauce or a boiled vegetable with a tart taste like sauerkraut, sweet cabbage with tomatoes, potatoes and salad.

A different method is used to prepare combined minced-meat rolls. Add sweet boiled cabbage or cereal to the raw meat and mince it together with the meat. Very tasty and economical are minced-meat rolls with an addition of the same amount of potatoes. These rolls can be served with potatoes, various salads according to season.

Raw meat may also be used for stuffing cabbage, paprika or tomatoes and squash.

The stuffed vegetables should be stewed. They are served with tomato or mushroom sauce.

One portion of soup consists of 1 1/2—2 cups per helping. Each recipe serves 5 persons, thus there should be between 7—10 cups of liquid.

290

ONE-COURSE VEGETABLE AND MEAT SOUPS

Ukrainian Barszcz with Veal or Pork Meat

*1/2 cup dried white beans * 3/4 lb. veal breast or pork ribs * 10 cups water * 2 cups grated mixed vegetables * 2 cups grated beetroots * * 3 medium potatoes * 4 medium tomatoes or 2 tbs. tomato paste * * salt * 3 tbs. sugar * 2 cups sour cream * 3 tbs. chopped green dill * * 1 tbs. chopped green parsley * 1 tbs. chopped chives*

Pick over beans and soak overnight in cold, boiled water. Bring to the boil in the same water on the following day.

Rinse meat. Take 10 cups water, bring to the boil. Add meat, beans with water and cook over medium heat.

Clean vegetables and beetroots, rinse, drain and grate. When the meat and beans are almost tender, add the vegetables and beetroots, cook another 30 minutes.

Peel potatoes, cube and when the meat and vegetables are tender, cook them in the soup.

If necessary, add boiling water. Drain the meat, remove bones and cut finely, add to soup. Add tomato paste, salt and sugar to taste. Bring to the boil. Before serving stir in cream and sprinkle with chopped chives, green parsley and dill. Serve with bread.

Fresh tomatoes may also be used. Wash tomatoes, cut them into quarters and bring to the boil so that they are warm and not tender. Add to soup.

Vegetable Soup with Veal and Tomatoes

*1/2 cup dried white beans * 3/4 lb. veal breast or rib * 10 cups water * * salt * 4 cups grated mixed vegetables including cabbage * 1 medium onion * 4 tbs. flour * 4 tbs. butter * 1 cup sour cream * 3 medium tomatoes * green parsley and dill * D r o p p e d n o o d l e s: 2 eggs * * 3/4 cup flour * salt * water*

Select beans, soak overnight in boiled, cold water. Cook them on the next day in the same water.

Rinse the meat, pour boiling water over it, add salt and cook till tender. Drain, separate from bones and slice.

Rinse the vegetables, slice and put into meat stock. Add onion. Add the bean extract and cook on high flame. Stir in beans, add meat and bring to the boil.

Melt butter, add flour and prepare light yellow roux. Stir into the boiling soup, bring to the boil, and season with salt.

Prepare dough for the noodles (see page 101); cook the noodles in soup, add sour cream.

Rinse the tomatoes, cut them into quarters, put in the soup, heat well but do not bring to the boil.

Sprinkle each portion of soup with chopped green dill and parsley. Serve.

Vegetable Soup with Giblets and Cream

*Giblets of 2 hens * 10 cups water * 2 medium carrots * 1 medium parsley * * slice of celery root * 1 small cauliflower * 1 cup shredded cabbage * * 1 medium onion * 1 cup sliced string beans * (1/2 cup green peas) * * salt * 1 cup sour cream * 3 tbs. flour * 2 tbs. butter * green dill and parsley * D r o p p e d n o o d l e s: 2 eggs * 3/4 cup flour * salt * water*

Clean the wings, neck, legs, stomach and liver of the hens, rinse and cook until tender.

Clean vegetables. Cut the carrots, parsley and celery. Separate cauliflower. Slice the beans and cube the cabbage.

When the meat is tender, drain the stock, add salt, put the vegetables (first the cauliflower, beans and then the remaining vegetables) into meat stock and cook in an uncovered pot.

Separate the meat from bones, cut it, add to the soup, and bring to the boil. Prepare dough for the noodles (see page 101).

Stir flour into cream, mix thoroughly, add to the soup and bring to the boil. Season with salt. Cook the noodles in the soup, add fresh butter.

Sprinkle each portion with chopped parsley and dill. Serve with young potatoes sprinkled with chopped dill and melted butter.

Sauerkraut Soup with Pork and Potatoes

*3/4 lb. pork or 1/2 lb. sausage * 4 cups shredded sauerkraut * 10 cups water * caraway seeds * 1 medium carrot * 1 medium onion * bay leaf * * allspice * 3 tbs. fat back * 4 tbs. flour * 2 lb. peeled potatoes * salt*

Clean and rinse the pork.

Cut sauerkraut, rinse and grate carrot.

Boil water, add sauerkraut and caraway seeds, cook slowly in uncovered pot.

When the sauerkraut is almost soft, add meat, carrot, a part of sliced onion and spices and cook till completely tender.

When the meat is tender, separate it from bones and cut into portions.

Prepare roux: melt fat, add chopped onion and stew until tender, stir in flour and fry until light brown. Add the mixture to the boiling soup.

Add meat.

Cook potatoes separately in salted water. Add stock to the soup.

Salt if necessary. Bring to the boil. Put potatoes on plates. Pour soup over potatoes.

Barley Soup with Giblets and Potatoes

*1/2 lb. bones * giblets of 1 hen * 10 cups water * 7 tbs. fine or pearl barley groats * 2 cups grated mixed vegetables without cabbage * 1/2 lb. peeled potatoes * allspice * salt * 1 cup sour cream * green dill and parsley*

Rinse the bones and clean giblets. Put into boiling water and cook for a while.

Rinse the groats and when the meat is half cooked, add the groats to the soup.

Cook slowly in uncovered pot.

Rinse the vegetables and grate. Rinse, peel and cube potatoes. Drain cooked meat and giblets, slice. Add vegetables and potatoes to the stock, add allspice and boil. If necessary add boiling water to the stock. Before serving add cream, salt and sliced meat and heat well. Sprinkle each portion with chopped parsley and dill.

Serve with sliced bread.

Bean Soup with Meat and Pinched Noodles

*3/4 cup dried white beans * 1/2 lb. meat with bone or 5 oz. smoked bacon * 10 cups water * 1 cup mixed grated vegetables * 5 tbs. fat back * * 1 medium onion * salt * pepper * green parsley * N o o d l e s: 1 egg * * 1 1/2 cups flour * salt * water*

Select beans, rinse and soak in boiled water for a couple of hours, then bring to the boil in the same water.

Rinse the meat, add to the beans and cook slowly, adding some water.

Rinse the vegetables and grate. When meat and beans are tender, add the vegetables and cook quickly.

Prepare dough with flour, egg and water. Chop it with knife into tiny pieces and sprinkle with flour.

When the vegetables are tender, add the noodles with flour and bring the soup to the boil.

Remove the pot from the oven.

Chop onion, fry in fat until golden brown, add to the soup, sprinkle with salt, pepper and chopped green parsley.

293

Soup with Beef Tripe

*2 lb. beef tripe * 1 lb. beef and pork bones * 10 cups water * 1 medium carrot * 1 medium parsley * 1 slice of celery root * 1 medium onion * 5 tbs. lard * 4 tbs. flour * salt * pepper * marjoram * nutmeg*

Clean the tripe thoroughly with knife and rinse under running water.
Rinse the bones. Bring to the boil 10 cups of water; put bones and tripe into water and cook slowly (for about 4 hours). Add water if necessary. When the tripe is tender, drain; separate marrow from the bones, crush it gently and stir into the stock. Slice the tripe finely. Rinse vegetables, grate, add to the stock and cook together.
Melt fat in the frying pan, stir in flour and sauté over low flame until the mixture is golden brown. Dilute with stock. Pour into the boiling soup and add tripe. Season with salt, pepper, marjoram and nutmeg and bring to the boil. Sprinkle with chopped green parsley before serving. Serve with potatoes, suet balls or with sliced bread.

Cabbage Soup with Pork Meat and Tomatoes

*3/4 lb. pork meat with bones (ribs) * 10 cups water * 4 cups shredded cabbage * 1 medium onion * 5 medium tomatoes or 4 tbs. tomato purée * * 1 cup sour cream * 3 tbs. flour * salt * green dill and parsley*

Rinse meat, put into boiling water. Cook on low flame.
Rinse and shred cabbage, peel onion and chop finely.
When tender, drain the meat, separate from bones and cut thinly.
Add cabbage and onion to the stock and cook on medium flame in an uncovered pot. If necessary, add some water.
Rinse tomatoes, cut them into quarters, add to the cooked cabbage and bring to the boil.
Stir flour into the sour cream so that it makes a smooth mixture, add to the soup, bring to the boil, add salt and the sliced meat.
Sprinkle with chopped green dill and parsley. Serve with potato purée.

Leek Soup with Sausage

*1/2 lb. pork bones * 10 cups water * 1 cup grated mixed vegetables * 1 1/2 cups cut leek * 1 lb. peeled potatoes * 1/2 lb. sausage * 4 tbs. flour * 1 cup sour cream * salt * pepper*

Bring 10 cups of water to the boil, add rinsed bones and cook.
When ready, drain the stock.
Rinse, peel and grate the vegetables. Add to the stock and boil.

Clean and rinse the leek and potatoes, cut into small pieces.

When vegetables are almost tender, add potatoes and leek to the soup and cook. If necessary, add some water.

Skin sausage, cut into portions, put into soup.

Add cream mixed with flour, bring to the boil, season with salt and pepper to taste.

Serve with bread.

Potato Soup with Meat and Tomatoes

*1/2 lb. meat with bones * 10 cups water * 5 medium potatoes * 1 cup grated mixed vegetables * 3 tbs. lard * 1 medium onion * 3 tbs. flour * * 4 tbs. tomato paste * salt * paprika*

Rinse the meat, put into boiling water and cook slowly on moderate heat. When tender, drain, separate from the bones and cut into pieces.

Peel potatoes, cut into cubes. Clean vegetables, grate and add to the stock. If necessary, add some water.

Chop onion, stew in fat, add flour and brown to light golden color.

Add to soup. Add meat, tomatoes, salt and paprika and bring to the boil.

Potato Soup with Veal and Sour Cream

*1/2 lb. veal breast * 10 cups water * 5 medium potatoes * 7 oz. mixed vegetables * 1 cup sour cream * 4 tbs. flour * salt * green dill and parsley*

Rinse the meat and pour over with boiling water; cook slowly, drain; separate from the bones and cut.

Peel potatoes and cut into small cubes.

Clean vegetables, grate, add to the meat stock, add potatoes and cook together. Add some water if necessary.

When the vegetables are tender, add cream mixed with flour, add meat and salt and bring to the boil.

Sprinkle each portion with 1 tbs. of chopped green parsley and dill. Serve with bread.

COMBINATION VEGETABLE-MEAT MAIN COURSES

Sausage with Cabbage and Tomatoes

*2 1/2 lb. cabbage * 1 medium onion * 3 1/2 tbs. fat * 2 tbs. flour * 5 tbs. tomato paste or 5 medium tomatoes * salt * pepper * sugar * 9 oz. sausage*

Clean cabbage, cut into cubes, add a part of onion and some water, cook over hot flame in uncovered pot.

Prepare roux. Melt fat, stir in flour and the remaining chopped onion, fry to golden color; dilute with tomato paste and cabbage stock.

Pour roux into the cabbage, stirring constantly and bring to the boil.

Season cabbage with salt, sugar and pepper to taste.

Rinse sausage and cut into even pieces. Add to the cabbage and heat well (do not keep too long over the flame).

Serve with potatoes.

Sausage with Savoy Cabbage

*2 lbs. savoy cabbage * 5 medium potatoes * 5 tbs. fat * 4 tbs. flour * salt * * pepper * garlic * 9 oz. sausage or Vienna sausage*

Clean, rinse and cube cabbage, put into boiling water, heat on hot flame and drain.

Peel and cube potatoes.

Add potatoes to cabbage and boil in a small quantity of water on high flame.

Prepare roux. Melt fat, stir in flour and fry to yellow color; dilute with some cabbage stock.

When the cabbage and potatoes are tender, add roux, mix thoroughly and bring to the boil.

Season with salt, pepper and finally crushed garlic to taste.

Cut the sausage into 5 even portions, add to the cabbage and heat well.

Serve with black bread.

Turnips with Pork

*5 cups cubed turnips * 5 cups cubed carrots * 1 lb. pork with bones * 3 1/2 tbs. fat * 1 medium onion * 2 tbs. flour * salt * sugar * marjoram*

Peel turnips and carrots, rinse and cube or cut into balls.

Rinse meat and slice (2 slices per person). Melt part of the fat, brown the sliced meat on both sides, add to the turnips together with fat; add bones and cook on high flame in a small quantity of water in an uncovered pot.

Prepare roux with the remaining fat, chopped onion and flour. Fry to a golden color, dilute with the turnip extract.

When turnips and meat are tender, add roux and if necessary some water to thin the sauce. Season to taste with salt, sugar, marjoram. Serve with potatoes sprinkled with chopped parsley.

296

Bacon in Cabbage and Tomatoes

*2 1/2 lb. sweet cabbage * 5 thick slices of unsmoked bacon * 1 medium onion * 1 1/2 tbs. fat * 2 tbs. flour * 5 tbs. tomato paste * salt * sugar * * pepper*

Rinse, clean and cut the cabbage.
Fry bacon on each side, add to cabbage. Leave some fat for roux.
Chop onion finely; fry in bacon fat till golden brown. Add to the cabbage.
Add some water and cook in an uncovered pot.
When bacon and cabbage are tender, prepare roux with fat and flour; thin with some cabbage stock and pour into the cabbage.
Mix well. Add tomato paste, salt, pepper and sugar to taste. Bring to the boil.
Serve with potatoes sprinkled with chopped green parsley.

Segedin Goulash

*1 1/2 lb. pork meat with bones * 3 tbs. flour * 1 medium onion * 3 1/2 tbs. fat for frying * 5 cups sauerkraut * salt * ground paprika * 1 bay leaf*

Rinse the meat and slice (two slices per person), pound well and sprinkle with salt and flour. Fry on both sides. Fry onion to a golden color in the remaining fat.
Cut the sauerkraut.
Arrange in layers in a saucepan: one layer of sauerkraut, covered with one layer of meat, some onion and paprika. Boil in a small quantity of water in an uncovered pot. Add bay leaf.
When the cabbage is tender, thicken with the remaining flour; if necessary, add some salt and tomato paste.
Some sauerkraut juice may also be added before serving.
Serve with potatoes.

Stewed Pork with Vegetables

*3/4 cup dry beans or peas * 4 cups sliced cabbage * 2 medium carrots * * a slice of celery root * 3 small parsleys * 1 medium onion * 1 1/2 lb. pork meat * salt * 2 tbs. flour * pepper * 3 1/2 tbs. fat * 5 tbs. tomato paste * 3/4 cup sour cream*

Select beans, rinse and soak in cold, boiled water for a few hours.
Cook in the same water. Drain the beans.
Clean and rinse all the vegetables and slice them.

Rinse meat, cut into pieces, sprinkle with salt, flour and pepper, and brown in fat.

Arrange the vegetables and meat in layers in saucepan; add the fat left from frying, add bean stock, some water and cook under cover on high flame. When the meat and vegetables are tender, mix them with beans and tomato paste. Season with salt and pepper to taste.

Some sour cream may also be added.

Serve with potatoes, dill pickle, cucumber salad or lettuce.

(The same dish may be prepared with beef or veal).

Stewed Pork with Cabbage

*2 1/2 lb. cabbage * 1 lb. boneless pork * 3 1/2 tbs. fat * 1 medium onion *
* 2 tbs. flour * salt * pepper * vinegar*

Clean, rinse and cube cabbage.

Rinse the meat.

Melt fat, brown meat in fat on both sides, add to the cabbage; add chopped onion, add a little water and cook on medium flame uncovered.

Stir flour into fat left over from frying, mix it thoroughly.

Dilute with the cabbage extract and add to the cabbage and meat when tender.

Season with salt, pepper and vinegar to taste and bring to the boil.

Instead of vinegar you may use tomato preserve.

Serve with potatoes.

Pork Ribs with Cabbage

*1 1/2 lb. pork ribs * 2 1/2 lb. cabbage * 1 medium onion * 3 1/2 tbs.
fat * 2 tbs. flour * salt * pepper*

Rinse the ribs, chop the bones in several places, put into a small quantity of boiling water and cook until tender.

Rinse the cabbage, cut into cubes, add to the ribs, when they are nearly ready.

Add onion. Cook over high flame, leaving enough stock for the sauce.

Prepare sauce. Melt fat, stir in flour, brown while stirring.

Dilute it with the stock from cabbage, mix well; add to the ribs and bring to the boil. Season with salt and pepper to taste.

Serve with potatoes.

Stewed Pork Cutlets with Carrots

*5 medium carrots * 2 medium onions * 10 medium potatoes * 5 pork cutlets with bones * 3 1/2 tbs. cooking fat * salt * pepper * 1 cup strong bouillon*

Clean carrots, cut into about 1 inch thick slices.
Chop onions finely.
Peel potatoes, cut into quarters, and cut each quarter in half.
Beat the cutlets and if necessary cut off the bones, leaving only about 1 1/2 inches bone.
Melt the fat in a casserole, put a layer of carrots on the bottom, cover it with cutlets, sprinkle with pepper.
Cover the cutlets with one half of the onions, carrots and half of the potatoes; sprinkle with pepper and salt, and cover with the remaining cutlets.
Cover the meat with remaining onions and potatoes and sprinkle with salt and pepper.
Cover and cook over a medium flame.
After 10 minutes of cooking add the bouillon, cover and put on an asbestos plate or in the oven and cook.
When the meat is tender, serve it in casserole with lettuce.

Braised Lamb with Savoy Cabbage

*1 1/2 lbs. lamb breast * 1 cup sliced mixed vegetables * 1 medium onion * * 1 1/4 lbs. savoy cabbage * 3 tbs. butter * 3 tbs. flour * salt * pepper * * 2 cloves garlic*

Rinse lamb, cut in half and boil in a small quantity of water.
Clean vegetables and onion; peel and slice, add to the boiling meat and cook until tender.
When the meat is nearly ready but not quite tender, remove it from the stock and cut into 10 even pieces. Drain vegetables.
Clean the savoy cabbage and cut into segments. Put into boiling water, bring to the boil and drain.
Cover the meat and cabbage with the lamb stock and cook slowly in an uncovered pot until tender.
Prepare roux with butter and flour, add to the meat with cabbage, bring to the boil.
Season with salt, pepper and crushed garlic to taste.
Serce with potatoes.

299

Braised Lamb with Beans

*2 cups white, dry beans * 1 lb. lamb * 5 medium tomatoes or 5 tbs. tomato paste * 3 1/2 tbs. fat * 1 small onion * 3 tbs. flour * bean stock * salt * * vinegar * pepper * sugar*

Select beans, rinse and soak in cold, boiled water for a few hours.
Rinse the lamb, cut it into pieces and add to the soaked beans.
Cook together in the same water in which the beans were soaked. When tender, drain the meat.
Rinse tomatoes, cut into quarters and boil in a small quantity of water. Strain through a sieve when tender.
Chop onion, fry in fat, add flour, brown lightly. Dilute the roux with some bean stock and mashed tomatoes, bring to the boil stirring continuously. Pour the sauce over the beans and meat, season with salt, vinegar, pepper, sugar; stir and heat on medium oven.

Braised Lamb with Potatoes

*2 3/4 lb. lamb (leg shoulder or neck) * salt * pepper * allspice * bay leaf * * 10 medium potatoes * 1 medium onion * 3 medium carrots * 2 oz. fat back*

Rinse mutton, cut into portions (together with the bone), add some boiling water and seasoning. Cook on medium flame, make sure that meat is always covered with water.
Peel potatoes, cut into pieces, add to the meat. Add sliced onion.
Clean and rinse the carrots. Slice into about 1 inch-thick pieces, add to the meat and cook together.
Salt if necessary. If the lambs is lean, add rendered fat back.

Braised Lamb with Vegetables

*1 1/2 lb. lean lamb with bones * salt * 4 tbs. fat * 1 medium onion * 1 1/2 cups sliced carrots * 1 large slice of celery root * 3 small parsleys * * pepper * bay leaf * 4 cups cubed savoy cabbage * 5 medium potatoes * * 2 tbs. flour * 5 tbs. potato paste * garlic * sugar*

Rinse the meat, salt and fry on both sides over high flame.
Clean, rinse and slice all the vegetables except the cabbage and potatoes.
Put meat, onion and vegetables into a small quantity of boiling water, add pepper and bay leaf, stew slowly under cover.
Cube cabbage and add to the meat when almost tender.

Peel potatoes, cut into quarters, add to meat and vegetables, when they are tender, cook until the potatoes are tender. Stir flour into fat left over from frying, add to meat and vegetables, bring to the boil.

Stir in tomato paste; salt to taste, add a pinch of sugar and crushed garlic.

Fish with Vegetables in Tomato Sauce

*5 fish fillets * salt * 2 medium carrots * 1 1/2 cups string beans or 1/2 cup white beans * 2 medium parsleys * 1/2 medium celery root * 2 medium onions * 6 tbs. fat * paprika * bay leaf * allspice * nutmeg * 3 tbs. tomato paste or 5 medium tomatoes * 1 tbs. flour * 1 tbs. mustard * 1 tbs. sugar * * green parsley*

Bone the fillets, sprinkle with salt and set aside.

Clean vegetables and cut them into short but not too thick strips or cubes. Slice beans diagonally (if white beans are added, soak and cook separately).

Chop onions finely.

Heat fat, add vegetables and onion; fry stirring so that they do not burn. Add some water to the vegetables, cover the pot and let simmer on moderate oven until tender. When almost ready, season with salt, paprika, bay leaf, allspice and a pinch of nutmeg. Add tomato paste, mustard, flour and sugar and bring to the boil, stirring continuously.

Add the fillets to vegetables, cover and stew slowly.

Before serving, sprinkle with chopped green parsley.

Serve with potatoes or spaghetti.

Spinach with Sausage

*2 1/2 cups cooked spinach * 4 tbs. fat * 4 tbs. flour * 1 cup milk * salt * * garlic * sugar * 9 oz. sausage * eggs*

Rinse the spinach thoroughly and cut off stems.

Boil salted water, put spinach into it and bring to the boil over high flame. Drain immediately. Cool and put through the food chopper.

Prepare white roux with fat and flour. Thin with milk, add the spinach and, stirring constantly, bring to the boil.

Season with salt, garlic and a pinch of sugar.

Cut sausage into 5 thick slices, fry on both sides. On the same frying pan fry eggs.

Serve on a round platter with the slices of sausage and eggs placed alternatively around spinach. Sprinkle the eggs with green, chopped parsley.

Serve with potatoes or noodles.

Stuffed Summer Squash with Tomato Sauce

*3 lb. young, long summer squash * salt * Stuffing: 3/4 lb. pork without bones * 1 oz. stale roll * 1 small onion * 2 tbs. fat * 1 egg * salt * * pepper * Sauce: 3 tbs. fat * 3 tbs. flour * 3 tbs. tomato paste * salt * * sugar*

Peel and pit the squash, sprinkle with salt.

Prepare meat as for minced-meat cutlets (see page 211). Stuff the squash with meat.

Put into saucepan and pour over with a small quantity of water. Stew covered until tender.

Prepare light-yellow roux with fat and flour; thin with some stock from the saucepan; add tomato paste, salt and sugar to taste and bring to the boil.

Pour the sauce over the squash and let simmer over medium flame.

Serve with potatoes.

Cabbage Stuffed with Meat

Gołąbki

*2 large heads of cabbage * Stuffing: 3/4 lb. pork without bones * * 1 1/2 oz. stale roll * 1 small onion * 2 tbs. fat * 1 egg * salt * * pepper * Sauce: 3 tbs. fat * 4 tbs. flour * 3 tbs. tomato paste * salt * * paprika or pepper * sugar*

Clean cabbage and parboil whole in a large quantity of water. Do not cover.

When the leaves are tender, drain the cabbage, cool; select the 10 largest leaves; pound the midribs of the leaves with a meat hammer (shred the remaining cabbage and prepare it as usual).

Prepare stuffing. Soak roll in water, squeeze out, rinse the meat and put through food chopper together with the soaked roll; chop the onion finely and fry to golden color; add to the minced meat, add 1 whole egg, season with salt and pepper; mix thoroughly and divide into 10 even portions.

Spread the mixture evenly on the leaves; roll firmly, tucking the edges inside. Join the smaller leaves together (2 for one portion).

Put the stuffed cabbage tightly in a pan. Add small quantity of water (so as to make sauce), cover and let simmer on medium heat until tender.

Prepare golden roux with fat and flour. Dilute with tomato paste and stock from stuffed cabbage; bring to the boil.

Season the sauce with salt, pepper and a pinch of sugar to taste and let it simmer for a while. Add to cabbage.
Serve with potatoes.

Cabbage Stuffed with Rice and Meat
Gołąbki

*2 medium heads of cabbage * S t u f f i n g: 3/4 cup rice * 3 times as much water as rice * salt * 3/4 lb. pork without bones * 1 medium onion * * 3 tbs. fat * salt * pepper * 2 small dried mushrooms (1/3 oz.) * S a u c e: 3 tbs. fat * 3 tbs. flour * salt * pepper * (3 tbs. tomato paste)*

Clean the cabbage, remove the stalk; put the whole cabbage into boiling water and cook for a while. Take the 10 largest leaves, pound the midribs, prepare a soup or a side dish from the remaining cabbage.
Prepare stuffing. Rinse the rice and cook in 3 times as much water as rice; add salt and cook on medium heat until tender.
Rinse meat, put through food chopper.
Chop onion and fry to golden brown.
Cool rice, mix with onion and raw meat; season with salt and pepper. Divide the filling into 10 parts and spread evenly on the leaves.
Roll firmly, tucking the edges inside.
Arrange a layer of cabbage leaves on the bottom of the pan and on them place tightly stuffed cabbage with rinsed mushrooms.
Add some boiling water to the cabbage, sprinkle with salt and let simmer on medium flame or in the oven. If necessary add some water while cooking.
When the stuffed cabbage is tender, prepare the sauce.
Stir some flour into the melted fat and fry to a golden brown. Dilute with cabbage stock, bring to the boil, season with salt, pepper (tomato paste) and pour the sauce over the stuffed cabbage.
Serve with potatoes.
Tomato or mushroom sauce with sour cream may also be prepared.

Fresh Paprika Stuffed with Rice and Meat

*10 green or red paprikas * S t u f f i n g: 3/4 cup rice * 3 times as much water as rice * salt * 3/4 lb. raw boneless pork or 1/2 lb. cooked ham or sausage * 1 medium onion * 3 tbs. fat * pepper * S a u c e: 3 tbs. fat * * 3 tbs. flour * 3 tbs. tomato paste * salt * pepper * 1 tbs. sugar*

Rinse the paprika, cut off the stem ends and remove the seeds.
Prepare stuffing. Rinse the rice in hot water, cook in 3 times as much water as rice; add salt, and cook the rice till half tender. Cool.

Put meat through food chopper.

Chop onion finely, fry in fat till golden brown.

Mix cooled rice with onion and meat, season with salt and pepper, divide into 10 even parts and fill the paprikas.

Arrange the stuffed paprikas tightly in a pan, pour over with some boiling water and stew under cover until tender. Turn the paprikas in pan so that they are cooked evenly.

When the paprikas are tender, prepare the sauce. Stir flour into melted fat and fry till light brown; add some paprika stock and bring to the boil, stirring continuously. Add tomato paste, salt, pepper and sugar to taste. The sauce should be rather thin.

Add to the stuffed paprika and let simmer for a while.

Serve with potatoes.

Potatoes Baked with Smoked Ham or Fish

*10 medium potatoes * salt * 1/2 lb. ham or 1 lb. smoked codfish * 3 tbs. butter * 1 medium onion * 3 tbs. flour * 1 cup sour cream * pepper*

Peel, rinse and slice potatoes, add to boiling, salted water; boil a short while and drain.

Cube ham or fish (skin and bone the fish).

Prepare sauce. Chop onion finely, fry in butter till golden brown, stir in flour and fry a little. Add sour cream and bring to the boil, stirring constantly (if necessary thin sauce with milk). Mix with ham or fish. Add potatoes.

Place in a casserole, even the surface, sprinkle with butter, salt and pepper, put into very hot oven.

Serve in the same dish.

Meat Baked with Cabbage

*1 lb. pork or 1/2 lb. cooked left-over meat * 1 medium head of cabbage * * 2 oz. stale roll * milk for soaking * 2 tbs. fat * 1 medium onion * 1 egg * * salt * pepper * fat and bread crumbs for baking tin*

Rinse meat and boil in stock for soup (or use the left-overs of cooked meat).

Clean cabbage, cut, put into boiling water and cook in an uncovered pot, cool, drain in a towel.

Soak roll in milk, squeeze out.

Fry onion in fat till golden brown.

304

Grind meat in the food chopper together with cabbage and roll. Add to the mixture 1 whole egg, fried onion, salt and pepper to taste, and mix well. Grease baking tin, sprinkle with crumbs; add the mixture, even the surface, sprinkle with fat and bake in a hot oven.
Serve with potatoes and horse-radish or tomato sauce.

Minced-Meat and Potato Cutlets

*4 medium potatoes * 1 medium onion * 2 tbs. fat * 3/4 lb. pork without bones * 1/4 lb. beef * salt * pepper * 5 tbs. bread crumbs * 3 1/2 tbs. fat for frying*

Cook potatoes and when still hot, mash until smooth.
Chop onion, fry in fat till golden brown.
Rinse meat, grind, mix with potatoes, add fried onion, salt and pepper. Divide the mixture into 10 even parts. Form an oblong cutlet from each part, dip in bread crumbs and fry on both sides on moderate flame.
Serve with raw or cooked vegetable salad or with a side-dish of vegetables.

Minced-Meat and Cabbage Cutlets

*1 medium head of cabbage * 1 lb. pork without bones * 2 tbs. fat * 1 small onion * 1 egg * salt * pepper * 5 tbs. bread crumbs * 3 1/2 tbs. fat for frying*

Clean, rinse and cut cabbage into quarters; put into boiling water and cook uncovered over high flame. Drain the cabbage and let it cool.
Rinse the meat, grind together with cabbage.
Chop onion and fry to golden color. Add to meat mixture. Add egg, salt and pepper to taste and mix thoroughly.
Divide the mixture into 10 even parts and form round or oval cutlets, sprinkling generously with bread crumbs.
Heat fat in frying pan; fry cutlets on both sides over medium flame.
Serve with potatoes and spicy raw or cooked vegetable salads.

Minced-Meat and Cereal Cutlets

*2 tbs. fat * 1 medium onion * 1 cup millet or barley grits * 3/4 lb. boneless meat * 1 egg * salt * pepper * 5 tbs. bread crumbs * 3 1/2 tbs. fat for frying*

Chop onion and fry in fat until golden brown.
Bring to the boil three times as much of water as grits. Salt. Rinse the grits, put into boiling water and cook uncovered over medium flame.

Grind meat and grits in food chopper.

Add egg, salt and pepper to taste, mix thoroughly.

Divide the mixture into 10 even parts and form round cutlets; dip generously in bread crumbs.

Heat fat in frying pan, fry cutlets on both sides over moderate flame.

Potato Dumplings with Meat

S t u f f i n g: *1 small onion * 2 tbs. fat * 1 lb. cooked meat or haslet * * 1 large cooked potato * salt * pepper * * D o u g h: 7 medium potatoes * 2 1/3 cups flour * 2 tbs. potato starch * 1/2 egg * salt*

Prepare stuffing. Melt fat, fry finely chopped onion to light brown color, grind cooked meat and potato, add onion, salt and pepper and mix thoroughly.

Prepare dough. Cook potatoes in peels and cool a little. Peel, grind, add flour, potato starch, egg and salt and knead for a short time. The dough should be made, when the meat mixture is ready, since it softens, when it stands.

Divide the dough into even parts. Form flat rounds in hand, fill with meat mixture, press the edges firmly and shape into oval patties. Bring salted water to a boil and add dumplings. Do not add too many at once as they must float freely in the water. Cook over high flame.

When they come to the surface of water and boil once, remove one dumpling and test if done. Take out with draining spoon.

Serve sprinkled with rendered fat back or tomato sauce.

Pyzy à la Warsaw

Raw-Potato Dumplings with Meat

S t u f f i n g: *2 tbs. fat * 1 small onion * 1 lb. raw fat meat * marjoram * * pepper * salt * * D o u g h: 10 medium raw potatoes * 3 large cooked potatoes * salt*

Prepare stuffing. Chop onion finely and fry in fat till light brown.

Rinse meat and drain; grind, mix with onion and season.

Prepare dough. Grate the raw potatoes finely. Drain off the juice and set aside. Pour the juice off carefully, save the sedimented potato starch and add to the grated potatoes. Add the mashed and cooked potatoes and salt. Mix well.

Form oval cakes out of the dough, insert the stuffing and press the edges firmly; roll to the size of large oval nut.

Dumplings made of raw potatoes take a long time to cook, therefore it is better to form small pieces.

Bring salted water to the boil, add dumplings and cook slowly. Before draining take out one dumpling and cut it to test if ready. Take out with draining spoon on food strainer. Serve sprinkled with rendered fat back. The dumplings may also be put into the oven after sprinkling them with fat. Dry them slightly so that their surface is evenly browned.

Knedliki

Bread Dumplings with Bacon

*7 oz. smoked bacon * 5 oz. stale white bread * 1/3 oz. yeast * 3 1/2 cups flour * 3/4 cup milk * 1 egg * salt*

Cube smoked bacon finely and melt slowly on moderate oven.

Cut bread into cubes, mix with melted bacon, put into oven and brown to a golden color. Set aside to cool. Mix yeast, flour and some milk. When the mixture rises, add the remaining warm milk, egg and salt; mix thoroughly. Add the browned bread to the dough, mix once again and leave to rise. Bring salted water to the boil.

Form the knedliki with hands moistened in warm water; put them into boiling water and cook for about 15 minutes in covered pot.

Place the cooked knedliki in one larger baking tin. Pour over with some boiling water, bake in oven until they rise.

Pour over with tomato sauce or sprinkle with rendered fat back.

Meat Dumplings

S t u f f i n g: *1 lb. meat * 2 oz. stale white bread * 1 small onion * 2 tbs. fat * salt * pepper * D o u g h: 3 1/2 cups flour * 1 egg * salt*

Prepare stuffing. Rinse the meat, cook until tender. Drain.

Soak the bread. Squeeze out and grind together with meat. Chop onion, fry in fat till golden brown. Add to meat mixture. Mix and season with salt and pepper. If the filling is too dry, dilute it with hot bouillon (or water).

Prepare dough. Sift the flour, mix with egg, salt and water; knead well and divide into parts. Put up salted water to the boil.

Roll the dough until very thin and cut rounds.

Put the stuffing on the center of each round, press the edges firmly so that the stuffing does not get between the edges.

Put into boiling, salted water and cook on medium flame. When ready, remove with draining spoon, place in food strainer and pour over with hot water. Drain.

Serve on a warm platter, sprinkled with rendered fat back or butter. Cover and keep over a pot with boiling water.

Lithuanian Kołduny

Stuffing: *3/4 lb. fat leg of lamb * 1/4 lb. fat beef * 3 oz. white tallow from kidneys * garlic * salt * pepper * marjoram * D o u g h: 3 1/2 cups flour * 1 1/2 eggs * 6 tbs. water * salt*

Prepare stuffing. Remove membranes and tendons carefully from the meat. Clean the tallow from membranes, grind and mix carefully, adding 6 tbs. cold water gradually. Season the meat with garlic, salt, pepper and marjoram.

Prepare dough. Sift flour and mix it with egg and water in a bowl. Knead the dough carefully so that it becomes smooth and shiny. Strike against the flour board until springy and not sticky.

Divide the dough into parts and roll out each part until very thin. Form balls of the meat and place them in a row on the rolled-out dough. The balls should not be bigger than a hazelnut. Cover the rows of balls with another part of the dough. Press the edges round the meat balls firmly so that the meat does not get between the edges of the dough. Cut out the kołduny with a small round cutter (about 1 1/2 inches wide).

Cook the kołduny: bring salted water to the boil and add kołduny (not too many at once so that they float freely in the pot). Cook for about 3 minutes. Take out the cooked kołduny with draining spoon.

Drain well.

Serve in tureen with beef bouillon.

Baked Macaroni with Ham

*3/4 lb. boiled or canned ham * 1 medium onion * 8 tbs. smoked bacon * 1 lb. macaroni or spaghetti * salt * pepper * fat and bread crumbs for baking tin*

Grind the ham. Chop the bacon finely, render in the frying pan, but remember not to brown the cracklings. Set aside half of the fat and the cracklings. Chop the onion finely and fry to golden color with the remaining half of the fat.

Break the spaghetti (macaroni) into small pieces, cook in salted water and drain. Pour over with hot water and drain again.

Put the spaghetti (macaroni) into bowl, add the ham, fried onion, cracklings and pepper and mix well.

Grease a round tin, sprinkle with bread crumbs, add the macaroni, spread evenly and sprinkle the surface with the remaining fat.

Place into well-heated oven and bake for about 25—30 minutes, until brown and crispy.

Cut around. Put the macaroni on a serving dish, serve with tomato sauce or without sauce.

Pancakes with Meat or Brain

Meat stuffing: *3/4 lb. meat * 2 small potatoes * 1 small onion * * 3 tbs. fat * salt * pepper ** Brain stuffing: *1 beef brain or 2 calf's brains or 3 pork brains * 3 tbs. fat * 1 small onion * salt * pepper * * Batter: 1/2 cup milk * 1 egg * 1 1/2 cups flour * 3/4 cup water * * salt * rind or fat back to grease the frying pan*

Prepare meat stuffing. Cook the potatoes and meat. Grind.

Chop the onion, fry in fat, mix with meat mixture; add pepper and salt; if necessary add water or stock. The stuffing should be fluffy.

Prepare brain stuffing. Remove the membranes from the brain and chop. Fry chopped onion in fat to golden color.

Add chopped brain to the onion, season with salt and pepper and fry slightly.

Prepare batter. Mix egg and milk thoroughly, add flour and stir well; add water and salt and mix.

Heat two frying pans of the same size; place fat back on fork and grease the bottom of pan until it shines; pour batter into hot pan, pour off excess batter, fry over medium heat. When pancake stops steaming, turn on the other side, fry for a while and put on board.

Fry the remaining pancakes (15—17 pieces).

Spread the stuffing evenly on each pancake, fold two sides and roll firmly. Before serving fry the pancakes browning on both sides. The pancakes may be dipped in a beaten egg and sprinkled with bread crumbs before frying. Serve with raw or cooked vegetable salad.

Pancakes with Vienna Sausage

*1/2 cup milk * 1 egg * 1 1/2 cups flour * 3/4 cup water * salt * 5 Vienna sausages * fat back to grease the frying pan*

Prepare batter. Mix well egg and milk, add flour and stir to smooth paste, add water and salt and mix thoroughly.

Heat two frying pans of the same size, grease the bottom with fat back so that it shines. Pour batter into hot pan, cover the whole surface, pour off excess batter, fry on medium flame. When pancake stops steaming, turn on the other side and fry for a while, put the fried pancakes on board. Continue to fry the remaining pancakes (15—17 pieces) in the same way, stir the batter before pouring on the frying pan.

Rinse sausages in warm water, remove skin and cut into three pieces.

Put each piece on pancake, fold sides and roll firmly.

Fry on all sides to golden brown. The pancakes may be dipped in a beaten egg and sprinkled with bread crumbs before frying.

Serve with raw vegetable salad or tomato sauce.

Pancakes with Smoked Fish and Egg

B a t t e r: *1/2 cup milk * 1 egg * 1 1/2 cups flour * 3/4 cup water * * salt * fat back to grease the pan * * S t u f f i n g: 2 smoked herrings or 3/4 lb. smoked codfish * 2 eggs * 1 small onion * 2 tbs. fat * 1 raw egg white * salt * pepper*

Prepare batter. Mix thoroughly milk and egg, add flour and stir well to smooth paste. Add salt and water and mix well.

Heat two frying pans of the same size. Grease the bottom with fat back so that it shines. Pour the batter into the frying pan so that it covers the whole bottom, pour off excess batter. Fry over medium flame. When the pancake stops steaming, turn on the other side and fry for a while. Put the fried pancakes on a board. Fry the remaining pancakes in the same way (15—17 pieces).

Prepare stuffing. Bone and skin the smoked fish and cut into cubes.

Cook the hard-boiled eggs, shell and chop. Melt fat and fry chopped onion until tender (to a golden color).

Mix the onion with fish, eggs and raw egg white, add salt and pepper to taste.

Spread the stuffing evenly on the pancakes, fold two sides of the pancake and roll firmly. Fry the pancakes in hot fat on all sides.

Serve with vegetable salad, lettuce or tomato salad.

SAUCES

SAUCES FOR APPETIZERS

Horse-Radish in Vinegar

*2 cups grated horse-radish * 1/2 tbs. lemon juice powder * 1 cup water *
* 4 tbs. sugar * 4 tbs. 6⁰/₀ vinegar * 1/2 tbs. salt*

Dissolve lemon juice powder in water.
Add sugar to taste. The sauce should be very sour and sweet.
Rinse, peel and grate horse-radish. Cover with lemon juice solution so that it does not darken. Mix and spread on a plate and leave to stand for one hour. Combine the horse-radish with the vinegar, sugar and salt to taste. Place in a jar with a close-fitting cover. May be stored. Serve with meat appetizers.

Red-Bilberry with Horse-Radish

*2 cups red-bilberry jam (with apples or pears) * 2 tbs. grated horse-radish*

Clean horse-radish and grate. Add to jam and mix. Place in sauceboat.
Serve with poultry or game appetizers.

Horse-Radish Sauce with Mustard

*3 tbs. grated horse-radish * 1 cup sour cream * mustard to taste * salt *
* sugar*

Scrape horse-radish and grate. Mix all ingredients.
Serve with cold eggs and cold meats.

Sour Cream with Eggs and Chives

*1 cup sour cream * 2 eggs * 3 tbs. minced chives * salt * pinch of sugar*

Remove shells from and mince hard-boiled eggs.
Rinse chives and mince.
Mix all ingredients with the cream and add salt and sugar to taste (a pinch).
If the sauce is too thick add a small amount of milk.

Mayonnaise

*2 raw egg yolks * lemon juice or vinegar * 1 1/4 cups oil * cold water *
* sugar * salt*

Separate egg yolks and place in bowl.
Cream, stirring in one direction. Add several drops of lemon or vinegar
and stirring constantly continue to add oil by drops. When the sauce
becomes too thick, add lemon juice and cold water and continue to
add oil in a thin stream, stirring constantly.
At the end add sugar and salt to taste.
Use mayonnaise to mask appetizers or dilute and serve as sauce.

Economy Mayonnaise to Mask Appetizers

*2 tbs. margarine * 4 tbs. flour * stock (meat, fish or vegetable) * 1 egg
yolk * 1/2 cup oil * salt * sugar * vinegar * mustard*

Prepare white roux with margarine and flour. Combine with meat, fish
or vegetable stock (depending with what the sauce will be served). Stirring
constantly, bring to the boil. Stir until smooth. The sauce must be thick
so that it will adhere to the appetizers.

Remove sauce from fire and sprinkle with cold water. Cool.

Pour off water from the surface when sauce is cold, add egg yolk and cream like mayonnaise, stirring in one direction and adding oil gradually. When the oil is all used up, flavor with salt, vinegar, mustard and sugar to taste.

Sauce Vinaigrette

*3 raw egg yolks * 1 cup oil * vinegar * 2 tbs. mustard * 1/2 cup red wine * 2 tbs. minced chives * salt * 1 tbs. sugar*

Prepare mayonnaise sauce with egg yolks and oil. Add vinegar and mustard to sour taste. Add red wine to dilute sauce and mix with chives. Add salt and sugar to taste. Serve with appetizers.

Tartare Sauce

*4 hard-boiled egg yolks * 2 raw egg yolks * 1/2 cup oil * 1/2 cup meat or fish aspic * 3 tbs. gherkins * 3 tbs. mushrooms marinated in vinegar * * 1 small onion or 1 tbs. minced chives * salt * sugar * 1 to 2 tbs. mustard * * 1 tbs. mushroom vinegar*

Cook egg yolks and press through sieve. Place in bowl and cream, adding one raw egg yolk at a time.

When the eggs are well creamed, gradually add oil and vinegar. Chop gherkins, mushrooms and onion into fine cubes and combine with sauce. Add mustard, salt and sugar to taste.

Add heated fish or meat aspic to the sauce to desired consistency.

Broth without fat (or cold water) may be added to sauce instead of the aspic.

Serve with all varieties of appetizers.

Cumberland Sauce

*1 cup Madeira wine * 1/2 cup currant jelly or rose jelly * 1 lemon (juice) * 1 orange (juice) * paprika * ginger * 1 tbs. mustard * lemon peel * 3 tbs. orange peel — candied * 1 tbs. potato starch (cornstarch) * * salt * sugar*

Add jelly to the wine and bring to the boil. Combine with starch, paprika and ginger. Cool. Add to this cooled mixture — orange and lemon juice, mustard, thin strips of candied orange peel and small amount of grated lemon peel. Add salt and sugar to taste. Serve with game or poultry appetizers.

Rose Sauce for Meat

*1 cup red wine * 1 tbs. mustard * 1/2 cup rose marmalade * lemon juice * sugar*

Combine rose marmalade with mustard, lemon juice and sugar and add wine to dilute mixture.
Serve with game or poultry appetizers.

HOT SAUCES FOR MEAT AND VEGETABLES

Béchamel Sauce with Milk

*3 1/2 tbs. flour * 6 tbs. butter * 3/4 cup milk * salt * lemon juice * * 2 egg yolks*

Melt butter and combine with flour. Brown.
Dissolve mixture with milk and bring to the boil. Add salt and lemon juice to taste.
Mix with raw egg yolks.
Use for covering various meat, fish and vegetable dishes which are to be baked.

Béchamel Sauce with Sour Cream

*3 1/2 tbs. butter * 6 tbs. flour * 1 cup sour cream * salt * lemon juice * * 2 egg yolks * 2—3 tbs. Parmesan cheese*

Follow recipe for béchamel sauce with milk. Before serving combine with cheese. Serve with boiled beef, poached eggs and with baked meat, fish and vegetable dishes.

Horse-Radish Sauce with Broth

*2—3 tbs. horse-radish * 1 cup broth * 1 cup sour cream * 2 tbs. flour * * salt * vinegar * sugar * 1 1/2 tbs. butter * 2 egg yolks*

Rinse horse-radish, peel and grate.
Bring broth to the boil.
Combine flour with sour cream and pour into hot broth. Bring to the boil stirring constantly. Add horse-radish, salt, vinegar and sugar to taste. Bring sauce to the boil stirring constantly.
Cream yolks with butter. Add hot sauce slowly, stirring thoroughly.
Pour into sauceboat and serve immediately. This sauce cannot be reheated.

Horse-Radish Sauce with Roux and Sour Cream

*2—3 tbs. horse-radish * 3 tbs. butter * 3 tbs. flour * 1/2 cup broth *
* 1 cup sour cream * salt * sugar * vinegar * 1 to 2 egg yolks*

Grate horse-radish and sprinkle with vinegar so that it does not turn black.
Melt butter, add flour and heat without browning.
Dilute mixture with cream. Bring to the boil stirring constantly. If too
thick add some strong broth. Add horse-radish to taste. Bring sauce to
the boil stirring constantly.
Season sauce with salt, vinegar and sugar to taste. Before serving combine
with egg yolks.
Serve with boiled beef, boiled fish, or fish sauté, with vegetables and for
baking boiled meat and fish.

Mushroom Sauce

*1 1/2 cups mushrooms (champignons) * 1 small onion * 3 1/2 tbs.
butter * salt * pepper * 3 tbs. flour * 1 cup broth * 1/2 cup sweet
cream * 1/2 cup dry white wine * lemon juice * 2 egg yolks*

Clean mushrooms, rinse. Take skin off caps and cut into thin slices.
Add cut onion to mushrooms, add butter, salt and pepper. Sprinkle with
water and simmer.
When mushrooms are tender add flour and fry.
Dilute with broth. Boil, stirring constantly. Add cream, wine and lemon
juice. Add salt to taste. Bring to the boil.
Before serving mix in 2 egg yolks.

Mushroom Sauce (à la Nelson)

*1 oz. dried mushrooms * 1 cup water * 1/2 small onion * 3 tbs. butter *
* 3 tbs. flour * 1 cup sour cream * salt * pepper*

Wash mushrooms, and cook in covered pot. When mushrooms are tender,
drain off stock and chop.
Melt butter, add cut onion and brown lightly. Add flour and brown.
Dissolve mixture with stock from mushrooms and some sour cream. Bring
to the boil, stirring constantly.
Press through a sieve.
Add sour cream, chopped mushrooms, salt and pepper to taste and boil
a short while.
Serve with boiled beef, steak à la Nelson, fish sauté and vegetables.

Dill Sauce with Broth

*3 tbs. green dill * 3 tbs. butter * 3 tbs. flour * 3/4 cup sour cream *
* broth * salt*

Rinse dill, shake off water, pinch off feathery leaves and chop.
Melt butter, add flour. Brown lightly, stirring constantly. Set apart.
Add cream. Bring to the boil, stirring constantly. Add broth until desired
consistency. Beat and bring to the boil.
Add salt and dill to taste.

Tomato Sauce with Sour Cream

*1 lb. tomatoes * 1/2 small onion * 1 1/2 tbs. butter * 1 1/2 cups water *
* 1 cup sour cream * 2 tbs. flour * salt * sugar * 1 1/2 tbs. butter*

Rinse tomatoes and cut into segments. Add butter (1 1/2 tbs.), water and
onion. Cook. Press through sieve and bring to the boil.
Combine flour with cream and pour into hot stock. Bring to the boil,
stirring constantly. Add salt and sugar to taste.
Before serving mix sauce with 1 1/2 tbs. unmelted butter.

Tomato Sauce with Flour Garnish

*1 lb. tomatoes (or 4 tbs. tomato preserves) * 1/2 small onion * 3 tbs.
butter * 3 tbs. flour * 1 cup broth * salt * sugar*

Rinse tomatoes. Cut into segments. Add cut onion and small amount of
broth.
Cook on high flame in covered pot. Press through sieve.
Melt butter, add flour. Brown lightly, stirring constantly. Set aside. Add
the tomato purée to the garnish. Bring to the boil, stirring constantly.
If desired may be thinned with broth.
Add salt and sugar to taste.

Tomato Sauce with Sausage

*4 tbs. fat * 1 small onion * 4 tbs. flour * 4 tbs. tomato preserves * 5 oz.
sausage * salt * sugar * pepper * 1 cup broth*

Melt fat and brown lightly with finely cut onion.
Add flour and brown. Dilute sauce with broth (or water). Bring to the boil,
stirring constantly.

Add preserves to sauce. Stir. Add salt, sugar and pepper to taste.
Remove skin from sausage and cut sausage into large cubes. Add to sauce and cook for a while until sauce is permeated with sausage flavor.
Serve with potato dumplings, potatoes, cereal or macaroni.

Meat Sauce

*1/2 lb. meat * 2 medium onions * 1 cup broth * 4 tbs. flour * 4 1/2 tbs. fat * salt * bay leaf * allspice * coriander * 5 tbs. tomato preserves*

Rinse meat and cut into small cubes.
Add meat and cut onion into fat and brown. Add 1 cup of broth and stew with seasoning and salt.
When meat is tender, add flour to sauce and bring to the boil. If necessary add broth to dilute sauce.
Tomatoes may be added to meat sauce.

Brain Sauce

*3 tbs. butter * 1 small onion * 4 tbs. flour * 3/4 cup sour cream * * 1/2 cup milk * 10 oz. brains * salt * pepper * lemon juice*

Remove membrane from brains, dip in boiling water. When brains are firm, drain thoroughly.
Stew chopped onion in fat. Add flour and brown lightly. Add sour cream and milk.
Bring to the boil, stirring constantly.
Cut brains, add to sauce. Add salt, pepper and lemon juice to taste. Mix well and bring to the boil.

Brown Onion Sauce

*3 tbs. fat * 1 small onion * 3 tbs. flour * 1/2 cup cold broth or water * * salt * vinegar * sugar*

Cut onion and brown lightly in fat.
Add flour and brown until yellow. Set apart.
Add cold broth or water to garnish. Bring to the boil and press through sieve.
Add salt to taste. If necessary color with burnt sugar. Add vinegar and sugar to taste and pour into sauceboat.

White Onion Sauce (Soubise)

*3 medium onions * 3 tbs. butter * 1/2 cup broth * 3 tbs. flour * 2 cups sweet cream * salt * 1 tbs. sugar*

Peel onion, parboil. Drain and chop finely. Add butter and stew without browning. Sprinkle with strong broth. When onion is tender, press through sieve. Bring to the boil and garnish with flour mixed with one part of the cream. Boil, stirring constantly. Add remainder of cream, add salt and sugar to taste, mix well.
Sauce should be thick.
Serve with boiled beef or lamb chops.

Gherkin Sauce

*4 gherkins * 3 tbs. butter * 3 tbs. flour * 1 cup broth * (gherkin juice) * * salt * sugar*

Cut gherkins into small cubes.
Brown butter with flour until yellow. Dilute with broth and boil, stirring constantly.
Add gherkins and, if necessary, gherkin juice to sauce. Add sugar and salt to taste. Boil.

Madeira Sauce

*3 tbs. butter * 3 tbs. flour * 1 cup broth * 1 oz. buillon cube * salt * * pepper * 1/2 cup Madeira wine * 1 tbs. sugar * 1 1/2 cups mushrooms (champignons) * 1 1/2 tbs. butter*

Clean champignons, remove skin from caps and chop fine. Add butter, salt and pepper. Sprinkle with water and stew until tender.
Add buillon cube to broth and cook.
Melt butter and brown with flour.
Add buillon to flour garnish and boil, stirring constantly. Combine with cooked champignons.
Add salt, sugar and wine to taste.
Bring to the boil.

Mustard Sauce

*2 medium onions * 3 1/2 tbs. butter * 3 1/2 tbs. flour * 1 cup broth * * 1 1/2 tbs. mustard * salt * (sugar)*

Cut onion. Stew in butter, add flour and brown lightly.
Dilute garnish with broth. Boil stirring constantly. Add mustard, salt and sugar to taste.
Press sauce through sieve. Boil and, if necessary, dilute with broth.

Polish Sauce

*3 tbs. butter * 2 tbs. flour * 1/2 cup red wine * 3 cups fish or meat stock * 2 oz. gingerbread made with honey * salt * lemon juice * * caramel * 1 oz. raisins * 1 oz. almonds*

Melt butter, add flour and brown, stirring constantly. Remove from fire. Dilute roux with wine and fish (or meat) stock to proper thickness. Add crumbled gingerbread and cook until it dissolves. Press through sieve, season sauce with salt, lemon juice and sugar to taste. Color with caramel to a dark gold. Clean raisins and scald almonds. Peel and shred. Add to sauce. Boil a short while. Serve with boiled fish or boiled veal, beef or pork tongues.

Sauce Hollandaise

*1 cup broth (fish, poultry or meat) * 1/2 cup dry, white wine * nutmeg * * 6 tbs. butter * 5 egg yolks * salt*

Add wine and nutmeg to broth and boil (broth used depends on whether sauce is to be served with fish, meat or poultry). Cream butter and egg yolks. Beat over boiling water, adding broth with wine gradually. Add salt to taste. When thickened, pour into sauceboat and place in hot water. Stir so that sauce does not cool on top. Serve immediately.
Serve with fish, roast beef, asparagus, cauliflower.

Polonaise Topping

*3 tbs. fine soft or dry bread crumbs * 3—4 tbs. butter*

Method 1

Melt in a small skillet over law heat 3—4 tablespoons butter. Add the bread crumbs and cook over medium heat until bread crumbs are lightly browned, turning and moving mixture gently with a spoon.

Method 2

Brown bread crumbs in oven and mix with melted butter.

DESSERT SAUCES

Vanilla Sauce

*5 egg yolks * 1/2 cup sugar * 1/4 pod of vanilla * 2 cups milk*

Boil milk. Cream egg yolks and sugar and crushed vanilla. Add boiling milk gradually, stirring constantly.
When all the milk is poured, place mixture over boiling water and beat until sauce thickens. Be careful that the sauce does not curdle.
Cool, stirring constantly.

Cocoa Sauce

Prepare sauce according to the recipe for vanilla sauce. Add 1 1/2 tbs. of cocoa instead of vanilla.

Coffee Sauce

*5 egg yolks * 1/2 cup sugar * 3/4 cup full milk * 1/4 cup very strong coffee*

Prepare in same manner as vanilla sauce. Steam egg yolks with milk, remove from double boiler and cool. Mix with fresh, strong coffee.

Wine Sauce

*3 egg yolks * about 1 tbs. sugar * 2 cups white wine * lemon peel*

Cream egg yolks with sugar.
Boil wine.
Add wine gradually to creamed egg yolks, place over boiling water and beat until mixture thickens.
Flavor sauce with lemon peel and serve immediately when it is still foamy.

Punch Sauce

*5 egg yolks * 1 cup sugar * 1/4 tbs. lemon peel and orange peel *
* 1 lemon (juice) * 1 medium orange (juice) * 2 cups white wine *
* 1/2 cup water*

Cream egg yolks with sugar, add lemon and orange peel and drained juice and mix thoroughly.

Boil wine and water. Add half of the hot liquid, a spoon at a time, to the egg yolk mixture. Place over boiling water, and add remainder of wine. Beat well.

When the egg yolks lose their raw smell and thicken (i.e. when their temperature reaches 175°—182°F), remove sauce from water and cool, stirring occasionally. Add rum as final ingredient.

Apricot Sauce

*2 cups fresh, stoned apricots or 1/2 cup aried, stoned apricots * 1 tbs. potato starch (cornstarch) * 1 cup white wine * 1 cup sugar * 1/2 cup water*

Sprinkle fresh apricots with water and cook. Press through sieve. Soak dried apricots for a few hours. Cook in small amount of water and press through sieve.

Heat wine with sugar. Mix starch with water and add to hot wine. Bring to the boil, stirring constantly and mix with apricot pulp.

If the sauce is too thick add a few spoons of hot water.

The sauce may be prepared in the same manner using other aromatic fruit: raspberries, strawberries, wild strawberries. Do not cook strawberries and wild strawberries. Mix pulp with flavored wine when it begins to cool. The raspberry pulp should be added to the boiling wine since this helps to develop the proper raspberry aroma.

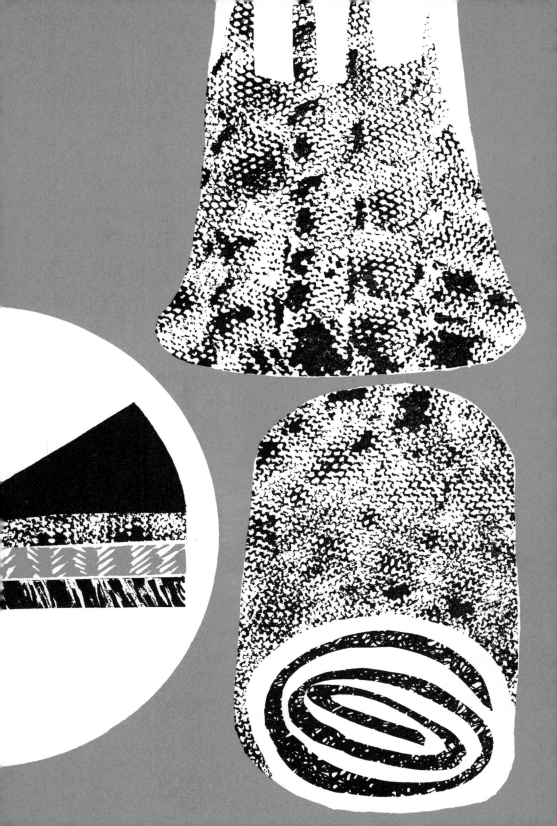

CAKES

PREPARATION OF INGREDIENTS FOR DESSERTS AND CAKES

Separation of Yolk and White of Egg

Eggs used for baking, especially for those cakes which call for creamed yolks and beaten egg whites must be fresh so that the yolks separate from the whites and do not spill over into them.

Cold-storage eggs may be used for baking yeast cakes, puffs, semi-crispy and ginger cakes.

Both fresh and cold-storage eggs should be free of any type of musty or unfresh odour.

As a rule, the egg yolks are creamed with sugar and the egg whites beaten stiff before being combined with the other ingredients of the dough. The creamed yolks and beaten whites create the fluffy texture made up of air bubbles.

Creaming of Egg Yolks with Sugar

Egg yolks should be creamed with sugar in a bowl with rough sides, with a wooden spoon until the mixture thickens, becomes light in color and fluffy (about 20 minutes). The yolk, thus creamed is added to the rest of the ingredients of the dough.

Creaming of Egg Yolks with Fat

Egg yolks creamed with fat are often used in dough or in cake fillings. The fat should stand at room temperature to soften, since it is difficult to cream when hard.

The fat should be placed in a bowl with rough sides and creamed with a wooden spoon in one direction, scraping the fat from the sides of the bowl with a knife to have a uniformly-creamed texture. When the fat begins to soften, the egg yolks should be added one at a time and combined with the fat. If other ingredients are to be added, especially fluids, they should be combined with the mixture a few drops at a time so that the mixture is not spoiled. Creamed fat and egg yolks are an emulsion which combine with liquid only in certain proportions. An excess of fluid causes curdling, that is, the separation of the fat from the other ingredients. The curdled mixture may be corrected. Take 1/4 of the original amount of fat used, melt the additional fat, and pour slowly (in a thin stream) to the curdled mixture, mixing slowly. When the mixture becomes smooth, the creaming should be discontinued.

Steamed Egg Yolks

Boil water in a saucepan big enough to hold the bowl in which the egg yolks are to be creamed.

Cream the yolks with sugar.

Heat the liquid for the steamed yolks (milk, wine, etc., depending on the recipe).

Place the bowl with the creamed yolks in the saucepan with boiling water, add the heated liquid slowly (in a thin stream) and beat until the egg yolks are completely combined with the added liquid and thickens.

Remove from steam and beat while chilling.

Egg yolks and sugar, without added liquid (steamed baba) may also be beaten in the same way being careful that not too much evaporates.

Mashed Hard-Cooked Egg Yolks

Since raw egg whites are extensively used in confectionary products, the hard-boiling of a whole egg, when only the hard-boiled egg yolk is to be used in the dough (for example crisp pastry), is not economical. The egg yolk must be hard-boiled, leaving the egg white raw.

Cook water in a saucepan. Separate egg yolk carefully from white, and drop into the boiling water, separating one egg yolk after the other. Cook until the egg is cooked through, drain, cool and mash through a thick sieve with a wooden spoon.

Beaten Egg Whites

Egg whites for beating must be fresh, very carefully separated from even the slightest traces of the yolk and placed in a clean dry bowl. They may be beaten with a wire whisk or with an egg beater. Raw egg whites are beaten most quickly with an egg beater, a wire whisk is used for beating over steam.

Egg whites are beaten best after being chilled and when beaten in a cool place. They should be beaten with a uniform motion, mixing the froth from time to time so that all layers are beaten uniformly.

When the whites stand up in peaks and separate from the beater, they are ready.

The whites should be beaten just before combining with the dough for if they stand, they fall, become watery and in course of time lose their stiffness.

Once the egg whites liquefy, they cannot be rebeaten.

The egg whites should be lightly combined with the other ingredients with a spatula or with a large spoon, and placed immediately into a well-heated oven. The heat causes the dough to increase in bulk within limits, later all ingredients are subject to transformation under the influence of rising temperature; the texture of the cake depends mainly on the congealing of the proteins and the gelatination of the starches. The rising of the dough is chiefly caused by air plus steam and other gases which are formed within the dough.

These increase their volume while being heated, fluffing the particles of the dough which is the basis of cake rising. The air in confectionery dough is mainly introduced by the beaten egg whites and creamed egg yolks.

Steamed Egg Whites

Boil water in saucepan large enough to hold the bowl for beating the egg whites.

Prepare a thick syrup (III stage) with sugar, water and vinegar.

Beat the egg whites and steam with half of the syrup adding the latter by spoonfulls and beating thoroughly with a wire whisk.

Place the bowl with egg whites in the saucepan with the boiling water, add the rest of the syrup by spoonfulls and beat until glossy and thick. When the egg whites separate from the wire whisk, combine with lemon juice, vanilla, etc., remove from heat and add immediately to dough.

Clarification of Butter

Melt butter slowly in saucepan and heat over low flame, remove scum from surface. Butter may also be clarified by cooking over very low flame until the scum drops to the bottom of the saucepan. Then pour the butter carefully into the dough, leaving the scum on the bottom of the pan. The second method is more economical and less troublesome.

Blanching and Skinning Almonds

Cover almonds with boiling water. Cover and leave in water until it becomes possible to remove skin without much effort. Test and skin almonds by pressing them out of skin between two fingers. Place shelled almonds on tin and dry in warm oven.

Browned Almonds

Place the shelled almonds in one layer on baking pan and brown to light golden color in hot oven, stirring them from time to time. Remove from oven when browned and place immediately on plate to cool.

Preparation of Almonds in Skins

Wipe dust off almonds with a clean towel and grind. Almonds in the skins are most often used for garnishing cookies, or for chocolate cakes where the dark skin is invisible.

Chopped Almonds

Almonds to be used for sprinkling should be soaked in cold water for an hour, then removed and cut into thin strips with a sharp knife. They may also be chopped either finely or coarsely with a knife. Almonds which are used as part of the ingredients of the dough should be ground.

Browned Hazelnuts

Hazelnuts become aromatic only after browning. They should be placed on a baking tin in one layer, placed in a hot oven, and turned a few times until they are a light golden color. Hazelnuts which are over-browned are untasty, bitter and harmful. Place the hot nuts on a towel and remove the skins. Separate the cleaned nuts.

Washing of Raisins and Figs

Pour warm water over raisins, wash, rinse, change water, drain and dry in clean towel.
Wash figs in warm water, rinse, drain.

Lemon Peel as a Flavoring

*2 tbs. grated lemon peel * 4 tbs. powdered sugar*
Rinse lemon, wipe dry.
Grate golden layer finely, combine with sugar into uniform consistency. Since lemons are often used in cooking, before squeezing out juice, grate the lemon peel, combine with sugar and add to jar, thus guaranteeing fresh supply.

Vanilla Sugar

*1 lb. powdered sugar * 5 vanilla beans*
Clean and dry jar with tight fitting cover.
Cut vanilla bean into 1/2 inch pieces.
Place the sugar in the jar in layers, placing pieces of vanilla bean between layers. Cover jar tightly. Use for sprinkling after 2 weeks. As the sugar decreases, press in vanilla to remaining sugar and add more sugar.

Chopped Vanilla Bean

Method 1

Place 2 pieces of vanilla bean between two lumps of sugar and grate. Combine with powdered sugar, place in sieve for sprinkling.

Method 2

Place 2—3 vanilla beans one on top of the other between the two first fingers of left hand, press at the edge and cut with sharp scissors into fine, small strips on the mixture or dough in which the vanilla is to be used. This method may also be used for preparing the vanilla for vanilla sugar.

Melting Chocolate

Chocolate may be chopped in nut chopper.
Chocolate for fillings or frostings should be softened by heating in oven, or steamed; the latter is recommended for it avoids burning which may happen easily.

Method 1

Place chocolate in saucepan, dampen with water and place in moderate oven. Remove when inside is soft. Avoid burning since it is then unusable.

Method 2

Place chocolate in plate or saucepan, and steam over boiling water. Remove when softened and while hot add gradually to filling or frosting, mixing vigorously.

Syrups for Saturating Torte and Cakes (Layers)

The syrups of drained preserves and candied orange peel are excellent for saturating tortes and cakes and are easy to prepare; they should be kept for this purpose.
Dilute the syrup with warm water so that it remains very sweet. Liquor, maraschino and rum may also be added and lemon juice. If preserves are not made at home, cook 1/4 cup of sugar in 1/2 cup of water, cool, add liquor or rum, vanilla sugar or a little lemon peel depending on the type of torte and then sprinkle on cakes.

Frostings

Many of the frostings consist of sugar boiled in water to form a syrup and small but very important additions of cream of tartar on which depends the correct texture of the frosting.

As different densities of syrup are needed for different recipes, they are classified into 5 stages of thickness as described below.

Syrup Stages and Their Uses

Stage I (thin syrup)

*1 1/4 cups sugar * 2 cups water*

Pour boiling water over sugar. Bring to the boil. Skim off scum on surface. Use for compotes, for saturating tortes, cakes.

Stage II (thread test)

*1 1/4 cups sugar * 1/2 cup water * 1/3 tsp. cream of tartar*

Pour boiling water over sugar, add cream of tartar, cook over medium flame covered. When a drop of the syrup dropped from a spoon forms a thread (thread test), the syrup is ready. Remove from heat. Use for frostings and preserves.

Stage III (feather test)

*1 1/4 cups sugar * 1/2 cup water * 1/3 tsp. cream of tartar*

Pour boiling water over sugar, add cream of tartar, cook over medium flame covered. When the syrup forms into "pearls" while boiling, or when a drop of syrup blown through a small wire ring forms a bubble which bursts in shreds, resembling feathers (feather test), remove from heat. Use for steamed, beaten egg whites, creams, cake decoration, candying orange peel.

Stage IV (thick blister)

*1 1/4 cups sugar * 1/2 cup water * 1/3 tsp. cream of tartar*

Pour boiling water over sugar, add cream of tartar. Cook longer than stage III. When the syrup boils and forms heavy blisters, remove from heat. Use for candies, for decorating tortes.

Stage V (caramel)

*4 tbs. sugar * boiling water for sprinkling sugar*

333

Sprinkle sugar with water. Cook until golden brown. Dilute with a little boiling water, adding very carefully. Dissolve, cook and thicken by reducing the liquid.

Use for coloring frostings, creams, sauces, kisiels, etc.

Boiled Frosting

*1 1/4 cups sugar * 1/2 cup water * 1/3 tsp. cream of tartar*

Pour boiling water over sugar, add cream of tartar, cook covered over high flame.

When a drop of the syrup dropped from the spoon forms into a thread (II stage syrup), pour syrup into bowl and stir.

If the syrup thickens too quickly and is already white, it may be diluted by adding a few drops of boiling water, lemon juice or black coffee, depending on the flavor of frosting.

Mix the frosting while still warm so that the frosting, thickening on top, does not become lumpy after mixing.

Boiled Creamy Frosting

*1 1/4 cups sugar * 1/2 cup water * 1/3 tsp. cream of tartar * lemon juice or coffee (vanilla)*

Measure sugar, place in saucepan, pour over with boiling water, add cream of tartar.

Prepare a thick, smooth syrup over high flame (III stage syrup).

Sprinkle surface of syrup with water, place in cold water to cool (to 140°F). While still warm, beat with flat wooden spoon until white; when too thick, dilute with lemon juice or cof.ee, depending on type of frosting. For vanilla frosting add vanilla. When finished, the frosting should have consistency of dumpling dough. The mixture may be used as a cream or diluted into thin frosting.

Heat part of creamed mixture over steam while stirring.

Dilute to desired thickness, ice torte with warm frosting.

The creamed mixture may be made in quantity and stored in a covered jar.

Chocolate Frosting for Mazurek or Gingerbread

*3 oz. chocolate * 3/4 cup sugar * 3 tbs. water * 3 tbs. butter*

Prepare a thick, smooth syrup from boiling water and sugar (III stage syrup).

Melt chocolate over steam; when soft, remove and combine with syrup. When the frosting begins to thicken, add butter gradually. Combine butter thoroughly with remaining ingredients.

Frosting with Steamed Egg Whites for Gingerbreads

*1 1/4 cups sugar * 1/2 cup water * 1/3 tsp. cream of tartar * 2 egg whites * 1 tbs. potato starch*

Prepare steamed beaten egg whites with a thick smooth syrup (III stage) as given above. Add potato starch to the beaten egg whites and mix while whipping egg whites over steam to avoid lumpiness. Divide frosting in several parts (for example, in 3 parts) and color one part with pink food coloring, the second part with caramel and leave the third snow white. Add a different flavour to each part: vanilla to the white, lemon peel to the cream-colored and a bit of rose-preserves to the pink, blend into the hot frosting and ice the gingerbread. Remove to dry place.

Powdered Sugar and Egg-White Frosting

*2 egg whites * 1 cup powdered sugar * 1 tbs. lemon juice * 2 tbs. butter*

Sift powdered sugar, place in a bowl, add egg whites and cream thoroughly with a spoon until the mixture is fluffy. Add lemon juice gradually. Add melted butter. Mix. For vanilla frosting — add vanilla at end, for lemon frosting — add lemon peel at end.

This frosting may be used to ice all small cookies, and cakes and also for gingerbread and placeks. Ice thinly and remove to dry place to avoid sogginess.

Icing and Handling Tortes

Place torte with even surface on top, even off sides, fill uneven sides carefully with filling and cut off pieces.

Brush crumbs from surface of torte.

Prepare same color frosting as filling.

Separate a few spoons of the warm frosting on a plate, dilute a little; pour the thin, warm frosting over all uneven parts of the surface of the torte, set aside to dry.

Ice the sides with the thick frosting, spreading with a table knife.

Remove hardened frosting from spatula each time and take frosting from the bowl with clean spatula.

When the top of the torte is dry, pour thick warm frosting over it, move torte with base and while turning, pour frosting over entire surface of torte, if necessary, spread with table knife.

Frost the sides again, the frosting should cover the torte with a thin, smooth layer.

When the frosting cools, decorate cake, loosen with knife from bottom of cake pan.

Place wide knives underneath on three sides, remove tort to cake plate or decorate bottom of cake pan with decorative paper.

YEAST BREADS AND CAKES

Yeast Dough

Leaven:

Crumble yeast. Place in a jug. Add small quantity of sugar. Mix.

Add small amount of warm milk and, if necessary, flour (according to the recipe). Mix well.

Cover with paper, place in warm place.

When the leaven rises to twice its size, pour into a bowl with flour and other ingredients.

Dough:

Sift flour.

Put flour to heat at room temperature.

Prepare leaven with yeast.

Render fat, prepare seasoning, warm milk.

Cream egg yolks with sugar (for dough with yolks), combine yolks with flour, seasoning and risen leaven, add salt, knead dough adding warm milk gradually.

When all the ingredients are combined, pour in warm fat gradually, knead with hands or spoon until the dough does not stick to hands or spoon, has bubbles on top and is elastic and smooth.

When the dough is finished, cover with cloth.

Place a bowl containing dough in a large pot of warm water, set aside to rise.

When the dough doubles in bulk, shape according to the recipe and place in greased pan.

Set aside to rise again, when double in bulk, smear with egg, fat or water with sugar, place in hot oven, bake small rolls or cakes 25—30 minutes, small baba — 3/4 hour, large loaf — 1—1 1/2 hours.

After removing from oven, leave in pan to cool slightly, ease out with a knife onto a towel (so that cake does not fall onto a hard table), let stand to cool slowly, shifting the cake when the spot on which it has been placed becomes too warm.

While the cake is still hot, sprinkle with powdered sugar with vanilla (or ice, when cooled). Serve the next day after baking.

Rye-Wheat Bread

L e a v e n: *1/3 oz. yeast * 1 tsp. sugar * 3 tbs. flour * 5 tbs. water **
D o u g h: *4 1/2 cups wheat flour * 4 cups fine rye flour * 2 cups water or milk or whey * 1 tbs. caraway seeds * salt * fat for greasing pan*

Prepare leaven, set aside to rise.

Combine wheat and rye flour in a bowl, add the risen leaven, salt, water or milk or whey.

Knead dough, add caraway seeds, set aside to rise.

Prepare a long narrow pan.

When the dough has doubled in bulk, place in pan, set aside to rise again. Brush with warm water, place in well-heated oven, bake for 3/4—1 hour.

Allow to cool for a while in pan, loosen from sides of pan, remove, place on flour board and cool.

Graham Bread

L e a v e n: *1 oz. yeast * 3 tbs. sugar * 2 cups milk * 1 lb. Graham flour ** *D o u g h: 1 lb. Graham flour * salt * milk * fat for greasing pan*

Prepare leaven with yeast, flour, sugar and milk, place in a bowl to rise. Prepare two long narrow pans, grease well.

Add the rest of the flour to the raised leaven and, if necessary, a little milk, add salt, knead into dough not too thick, shape in pans, level, set aside to rise.

Bake 1 1/4 hours, before removing brush with water, place back in oven for a while so that the top becomes glossy.

Loosen from sides of pan, remove, prop against side of flour board and cool.

White Wheat Bread

L e a v e n: *1/4 oz. yeast * 2 1/2 cups all purpose or cake flour * 2 cups milk * D o u g h: 7 cups all purpose flour or cake flour * salt * milk * * 1 tbs. fennel * fat for greasing pan*

Crumble yeast, dissolve with warm milk into smooth mixture.
Sift flour, pour the dissolved yeast into flour. Set aside to rise.
Add the rest of the sifted flour, salt and half the fennel to the leaven and knead until smooth to normal consistency (if necessary add milk), level the top and set aside to rise again.
Prepare long narrow pans, grease with fat. Shape dough in pans, level, set to rise again. Brush raised dough with a brush dipped in water or beer, or beaten egg, sprinkle with the fennel seed and bake for about 3/4 hour. Remove from pan, prop against side of flour board. Shift from time to time while cooling.

White Bread with Potatoes

L e a v e n: *2/3 oz. yeast * 1 tbs. sugar * 3 tbs. water * D o u g h: 9 cups flour * 3 medium potatoes * salt * about 3 cups water * fennel seeds * fat for greasing pan*

Prepare leaven, set aside to rise.
Wash and peel potatotes, cook, mash through a sieve.
Combine the potatoes and flour in a bowl, add the leaven, salt, tepid milk or water or whey.
Knead dough, add fennel seeds, set aside to rise.
Prepare a long, large narrow pan.
When the dough rises, place in pan, set aside again to rise.
Brush raised dough with tepid water, place in well-heated oven, bake for 3/4 hour.
Loosen from sides of pan, remove, place propped against side of flour board and cool.

Steamed White Bread

L e a v e n: *1 oz. yeast * 3 tbs. flour * 1/4 cup milk * D o u g h: 9 cups flour * about 3 cups milk * salt * caraway seeds * fat for greasing pan*

Put 3 level tablespoons of flour into a bowl, add boiling milk a little at a time and combine the flour and milk with a wooden spoon, dissolving carefully all the lumps which form during steaming flour; add milk to

338

form a thick gruel. Add the yeast diluted in milk, combine, cover and set aside for a few hours to rise.

Add 9 cups flour. Add salt and caraway seeds to the leavened dough, and knead to normal consistency, adding warm milk gradually. When the dough is no longer sticky, place in a greased pan, cover and set aside to rise.

When the dough doubles in bulk, brush the top with water, fat or egg white, place in hot, pre-heated oven.

When the dough begins to shrink from the pan, and is well-browned (about 3/4 hour) remove, loosen from sides of pan, remove and cool propped against side of flour board.

Shift the bread while cooling.

Bread made with steamed dough stays fresh for a long time.

Graham Rolls

L e a v e n: *1 3/4 oz. yeast * 2 tbs. sugar * 5 tbs. water ** D o u g h: 4 1/2 cups ground wheat * 2 1/2 cups flour * water * salt * fat for greasing pan*

Rinse whole ground wheat, pour over with cold water, soak for 12 hours. Put the soaked wheat through food chopper.

Prepare leaven with yeast, sugar and water, set aside to rise.

Pour the leavened mixture into the ground wheat, add flour, salt to taste and knead into normal consistency, set aside to rise.

Shape the raised dough into small long rolls, place in greased pan, set aside to rise again.

When the dough becomes puffy, brush with water and bake in hot oven (about half hour) guarding against drying out.

Sweet Yeast Buns

L e a v e n: *1 1/4 oz. yeast * 1 tbs. sugar * 5 tbs. milk ** D o u g h: 4 1/2 cups flour * 1 egg * 3/4 cup sugar * 1 cup milk * pinch of salt * 5 tbs. fat * vanilla sugar * lemon peel * fat for greasing pan*

Prepare leaven with yeast, set aside to rise.

Cream egg with sugar, add the leaven, flour, warm milk, salt, knead into rather thick dough.

When all the ingredients are well blended add melted fat, vanilla sugar, lemon peel, knead, set aside to rise.

When the dough has leavened, shape into small rolls and place on greased pan, set aside to rise.

Brush with egg, sprinkle with sugar or crumbs, set in hot oven, bake.
The same dough may be used to prepare a very tasty loaf and poppy-seed
cake.

Cheese Buns

L e a v e n: *2/3 oz. yeast* * *1 tsp. sugar* * *3 tbs. milk* * D o u g h: *2 egg
yolks* * *4 tbs. sugar* * *3 cups flour* * *1/2 cup milk* * *3 tbs. butter* * *salt* *
* *1/2 egg for brushing top* * *1 1/2 tbs. powdered vanilla sugar* * *fat for
greasing pan* * F i l l i n g: *1 cup cottage cheese* * *2 egg yolks* * *4 tbs.
sugar* * *lemon peel*

Prepare leaven with yeast, set aside to rise.
Prepare dough. Cream yolks with sugar, add the leavened mixture, add the
flour and milk, salt, knead into rather thick dough.
When all the ingredients are blended, add melted butter gradually, knead,
smooth and set aside to rise.
Prepare the cheese. Put through food chopper or grate cheese, add egg
yolks, sugar and lemon peel (or vanilla), cream thoroughly.
Place the leavened dough on floured board, roll out 3/4 inch thick and cut
out buns with cutter (diameter of 2 1/2 inches). Place buns on greased pan
far enough apart so they do not paste together during rising, cover with
napkin, and set aside to rise.
Make a well in the center of each bun after it has risen (1 1/2 inches in
diameter), place a tablespoon of cheese filling into well.
Brush the dough and the cheese with beaten egg, set in oven and bake for
about 30 minutes. After removing from oven, sprinkle with vanilla sugar.

Plum Buns

L e a v e n: *2/3 oz. yeast* * *1 tsp. sugar* * *3 tbs. milk* * D o u g h: *2 egg
yolks* * *4 tbs. sugar* * *3 cups flour* * *1/2 cup milk* * *3 1/2 tbs. butter* *
* *salt* * *1/2 lb. fresh blue plums* * *1/2 egg for brushing* * *butter for greasing
pan* * *2 1/2 tbs. powdered sugar for sprinkling* * *cinnamon*

Prepare dough according to recipe for cheese buns, set aside to rise, roll,
cut out buns, place on greased pan, cover and place to rise again.
Rinse plums, dry each one, slit in 4 but do not sever, remove pit.
Make a well in each bun, brush the surface with egg, place a plum in each
well, skin-side up, press so that the plum adheres to the dough and place
buns in well-heated oven; bake about 30 minutes.
After removing from oven, sprinkle buns with powdered sugar mixed with
cinnamon.

Vanilla Baba

Easter Cake

L e a v e n: *1 oz. yeast * 1 tbs. sugar * 5 tbs. milk * * D o u g h: 7 tbs. butter * 2 egg yolks * 1 egg * 1/2 cup sugar * 3 1/2 cups flour * 1/2 cup milk * salt * lemon peel * 2 1/2 tbs. raisins * buter for greasing mold * * powdered vanilla sugar for sprinkling*

Prepare leaven, set aside to rise.

Prepare the mold for baking the baba.

Cream the butter, add egg yolks one at a time, then the whole egg and sugar while continuing to cream.

Add flour to egg mixture, add the leaven, add a little tepid milk, salt, lemon peel and beat with a spoon; when the dough no longer sticks to the spoon, mix with raisins, place in mold, press raisins to the center of the dough, set aside to rise.

Bake in well-heated oven (3/4 hour), allow to cool for a while in mold, remove, sprinkle with vanilla sugar, cool, propped against edge of flour board.

Polish Baba

Easter Cake

L e a v e n: *3 oz. yeast * 2 1/2 tbs. sugar * 1 cup milk * * D o u g h: 30 egg yolks * 2 cups powdered sugar * salt * 1/2 vanilla bean * 4 tbs. raisins * * 3 bitter almonds * 9 cups flour * 2 1/2 cups butter * butter for greasing mold * vanilla sugar for sprinkling or vanilla frosting*

Prepare two Turk's head molds for the baba, grease with butter, sprinkle with flour.

Blanch and grind bitter almonds.

Prepare leaven, set aside to rise.

Beat the yolks in a double boiler without sugar, stir while cooling, add the raised leaven, powdered sugar, salt, vanilla, raisins, bitter almonds, blend in flour, knead. Melt the butter.

When all ingredients combine, add the melted butter gradually, knead the dough 1/2 hour for 2 lbs. flour (9 cups).

Set the dough aside to rise.

Place raised dough in molds (1/3 full), set aside again to rise slowly.

After rising place in well-heated oven, bake 3/4 hour.

Remove from oven and when it cools a little, remove carefully from molds, ice thinly by pouring over with creamy vanilla frosting (see page 334), or sprinkle with vanilla sugar, cool slowly, propped against the sides of the flour board.

Before serving cut into slanting round pieces, about 1/2 inch thick, then cut in half.

Steamed Baba à la Warsaw

Easter Cake

L e a v e n: *20 egg yolks * 1 1/2 cups powdered sugar * 2 1/2 cups flour * * 2 cups milk * 4 oz. yeast * D o u g h: 1 1/2 cups butter * 2 1/4 cups almonds * 12 tbs. raisins * 10 tbs. orange peel * 7 cups flour * salt * butter for greasing mold * V a n i l l a   f r o s t i n g: 1 1/4 cups sugar * 1/2 cup water * 1/3 tsp. cream of tartar * vanilla*

Cream the egg yolks with sugar.

Prepare leaven. Cook 2 cups of milk; sift 2 1/2 cups of flour into a bowl and while mixing pour over boiling milk in a thin stream, mix constantly so that no lumps are formed.

Combine flour and milk into smooth mass and cool.

Combine yeast with a small amount of milk into smooth mixture.

While the flour and milk mixture is still warm, add the yeast and creamed yolks, mix all ingredients, set aside to rise.

Prepare dough. Melt and clarify butter. Blanch almonds, grind.

Wash raisins in warm water, dry lightly in towel, sprinkle with flour.

Cube orange peel finely.

Grease deep ring mold (earthenware), sprinkle with flour.

Add the rest of flour to the leavened dough, add salt and knead, adding the clarified butter gradually.

Knead (1/2 hour for 4 cups flour).

When all the butter is added to the dough, sprinkle in the almonds, and during final stage add the raisins and orange peel.

Place the dough into the greased, heated mold about 1/3 full.

Place in a warm place to rise again, cover, allow to rise (it rises slowly).

When the dough doubles in bulk, place in a well and uniformly-heated oven, and bake about 1 hour.

Before removing, test with a caketester by piercing deeply into cake and if the caketester comes out dry, remove from oven and cool in mold.

Remove the cooled baba carefully from the mold with a long, narrow knife.

Cool slowly, shifting the position of the cake.

When completely cooled, ice thinly by pouring over with thin white creamy frosting (see page 334).

Yeast Cake with Crumb Topping

Silesian Easter Cake

L e a v e n: *1 oz. yeast * 1 tbs. sugar * 5 tbs. milk * * D o u g h: 2 egg yolks * * 1 egg * 5 1/2 tbs. sugar * 3 1/2 cups flour * 1/2 cup milk * lemon peel * * 3 tbs. orange peel * salt * 1/2 cup butter * 1/2 egg for brushing * vanilla sugar for sprinkling * butter for greasing pan * C r u m b t o p p i n g: 1/2 cup flour * 2 1/2 tbs. powdered sugar * 2 tbs. butter * (cinnamon)*

Prepare the baking pan.

Prepare leaven, set aside to rice.

Prepare crumb topping. Mix flour and sugar on a plate.

Melt butter, add to flour (add cinnamon), combine with spoon.

Prepare dough. Cream egg yolks and egg with sugar, add the raised leaven, blend in flour, add milk, lemon and orange peel, salt, knead.

When all ingredients are blended, add gradually the melted, warm butter. Knead, set aside to rise.

Set leavened dough into pan, fit to sides of pan, smoothen, brush with egg. sprinkle with crumb topping, by grating over the cake, set aside to rise.

Bake to golden color, while hot sprinkle with vanilla sugar.

Remove from pan on knives, cool on board.

Slice in squares or quadrangles (about 18 pieces).

Arrange on a platter.

Plum Yeast Cake

L e a v e n: *3/4 oz. yeast * 1 cup flour * 2 1/2 tbs. sugar * 1/2 cup milk * * D o u g h: 2 eggs * 2 1/2 tbs. sugar * 1 cup flour * (milk) * 2 tbs. butter * * lemon peel * salt * 1 lb. blue plums * 1/2 egg for brushing * butter for greasing pan * 2 1/2 tbs. powdered vanilla sugar for sprinkling*

Prepare leaven, set aside to rise.

Cream whole eggs with sugar, add raised leaven, add flour and knead; if necessary add a little milk.

When all ingredients are blended, add melted butter, lemon peel, salt and knead.

Set aside to rise.

Prepare plums. Wash, dry, slit into 4 parts but do not separate, remove pits.

Place leavened dough on greased pan, brush the top with mixed egg and place the plums on dough skin-side up, covering the entire surface of the cake. Press plums into dough so that they stick, place dough to rise again, cover.

Place leavened dough into hot oven, bake quickly so that the plums do not
dry up (about 3/4 hour).
Remove, cool a little, sprinkle with powdered sugar, cut into squares or
bars.

Makowiec (Strucla)

Poppy-Seed Roll

L e a v e n: *1 1/4 oz. yeast * 1 tbs. sugar * 5 tbs. milk * D o u g h: 4 1/2
cups flour * 1 egg * 3/4 cup sugar * 1 cup milk * pinch of salt * 5 tbs.
fat * butter for greasing pan * F i l l i n g: 3/4 lb. poppy seeds * boiling
water * 3/4 cup sugar * 3 bitter almonds * (lemon peel) * 2 tbs. butter *
* 2 1/2 tbs. raisins * 2 egg whites*

Pour boiling water over poppy seeds; when they can be crushed between
the fingers set aside in sieve to drain overnight, put through food chopper
the next day.
Add all ingredients to taste, combine.
Prepare dough as in recipe for buns (see page 339), set aside to rise.
Divide the leavened dough into two parts, roll out into rectangular shape,
place half the poppy seeds on the dough, spreading evenly, roll up tightly.
Place roll in greased pan (long, narrow shape), set aside to rise.
Prepare other roll.
When the roll in the pan doubles in bulk, place in well-heated oven, bake
for about 3/4 hour.
Remove carefully, cool resting on edge of board to avoid steaming.
The roll may be topped with powdered vanilla sugar or iced.
Serve the next day.

Makowiec, Polish Style

Christmas Cake

L e a v e n: *3/4 oz. yeast * 1 tsp. sugar * 3 tbs. milk * D o u g h: 2 egg
yolks * 1 egg * 3 tbs. sugar * lemon peel * 1 cup milk * 4 1/2 cups flour *
* salt * 1/2 cup butter * butter for greasing pan * F i l l i n g: 1 lb. poppy
seeds * 1 cup sugar * 4 1/2 tbs. butter * lemon peel * 8 tbs. orange peel *
* 5 tbs. raisins * cinnamon * 2 egg whites * F r o s t i n g: 1 1/4 cups
sugar * 1/2 cup water * 1/4 tsp. cream of tartar * vanilla*

Pour boiling water over poppy seeds; when they can be crushed between
the fingers, drain thoroughly on sieve.
Grease a narrow rectangular pan.

344

Prepare leaven, set aside to rise.

Cream egg yolks and egg with sugar, add raised leaven, lemon peel, milk, blend in flour, add salt, knead.

When all ingredients are blended, add melted butter gradually.

Knead, set aside to rise.

Put poppy seeds through food chopper 3 times.

Add sugar, fat, heat (evaporate), cool.

Combine with lemon and orange peel, raisins (or fruit from preserves), cinnamon and beaten egg whites.

Divide leavened dough in half, place half on board, roll out rather fine into rectangular shape, spread with half the poppy-seed mixture, roll up. Place roll in pan, seam side down, set aside to rise, prepare the second half of the dough in the same way.

When leavened, brush the top with tepid water, bake for about 3/4 hour. Remove from pan carefully, cool, propped against edge of flour board.

Prepare frosting. Make a thick syrup out of sugar and water, add cream of tartar, mix, when it whitens, add vanilla, mix, ice the roll with warm frosting.

Marmalade Yeast Roll

Christmas Cake

L e a v e n: *1/2 oz. yeast * 1 tsp. sugar * 3 tbs. milk * D o u g h: 2 egg yolks * 1/2 egg * 2 1/2 tbs. sugar * lemon peel * 1/2 cup milk * 2 cups flour * salt * 3 1/2 tbs. butter * 1 1/2 cups fine marmalade * 1/2 egg for brushing * a few almonds * powdered vanilla sugar for sprinkling * butter for greasing pan*

Prepare dough as for poppy-seed roll (see page 344), set to rise.

Grease a long narrow pan with butter.

If the marmalade is too thin, take more marmalade and cook a little to reduce the liquid.

Place leavened dough on floured board and roll out into square. Spread dough with marmalade, not too near the edges, wind up into tight roll, fold both ends to center. Fasten all edges brushing with egg white so that marmalade does not seep out during baking. Place roll into long narrow pan, with fastenings on bottom, set aside to rise again.

Brush the leavened dough with egg, sprinkle with thickly chopped almonds, place in well-heated oven and bake for 3/4 hour.

Remove from pan carefully, sprinkle the top with sugar and cool propped against higher edge of flour board.

Almond Yeast Roll

Christmas Cake

L e a v e n: *1/2 oz. yeast * 1 tsp. sugar * 3 tbs. milk * * D o u g h: 2 egg yolks * 1 egg * 2 1/2 tbs. sugar * lemon peel * 1/2 cup milk * 2 cups flour * salt * 3 1/2 tbs. butter * a few almonds for topping cake * powdered vanilla sugar for sprinkling * 1/2 egg for brushing * butter for greasing pan * F i l l i n g: 3 egg yolks * 1/2 cup sugar * 2 egg whites * 3/4 cup almonds * lemon peel*

Prepare dough in the same way as for poppy-seed roll (see page 344), set aside to rise.

Grease a long narrow pan with butter.

Prepare filling. Blanch almonds, skin, dry, grind.

Cream egg yolks with sugar.

Beat egg whites frothy, fold into yolks, add in ground almonds, add lemon peel, combine.

Roll out dough into rectangle 1/3 inch thick, spread with filling, roll up tightly into uniform thickness and place seam side down into long narrow pan, set aside to rise again.

Brush the leavened dough with egg, sprinkle with coarsely-chopped almonds, place in well-heated oven and bake for 3/4 hour.

Remove and allow to cool a little in pan, remove carefully and cool propped against high side of flour board.

Sprinkle generously with powdered vanilla sugar and then cool, or ice when cooled with vanilla frosting and while damp, top with coarsely chopped almonds.

Nut Yeast Roll

Christmas Cake

L e a v e n: *1/2 oz. yeast * 1 tsp. sugar * 3 tbs. milk * * D o u g h: 2 egg yolks * 1/2 egg * 2 1/2 tbs. sugar * lemon peel * 1/2 cup milk * 2 1/4 cups flour * salt * 3 1/2 tbs. butter * powdered vanilla sugar for sprinkling * 1/2 egg for brushing * fat for greasing pan * F i l l i n g: 3 egg yolks * 1/2 cup sugar * 2 egg whites * 1 cup walnuts * 4 tbs. orange peel*

Prepare dough as for poppy-seed roll and filling as for almond yeast roll. When cooled, ice with vanilla frosting or while still hot, sprinkle with powdered vanilla sugar.

Przekładaniec

Fruit Cake, Easter Cake

L e a v e n: *1 1/3 oz. yeast * 1 tbs. sugar * 5 tbs. milk * * F i l l i n g 1: 2 1/2 cups almonds * 3/4 cup powdered sugar * vanilla * juice of half lemon * F i l l i n g 2: 3 oz. figs * 3 oz. dates * 2 1/2 tbs. raisins * 8 tbs. orange peel * 1/2 cup walnuts * F i l l i n g 3: 3/4 cup rose jam * F i l l i n g 4: 1 cup strawberry jam * F i l l i n g 5: apricot jam * D o u g h: 5 tbs sugar * 5 egg yolks * 3 cups flour * salt * lemon peel * 1/2 cup milk * 1/2 cup butter * 1/2 egg for brushing * vanilla sugar for sprinkling * * butter for greasing pan*

Prepare the fillings a day before baking.

Drain each of jams separately by placing in sieve.

Prepare almond filling. Blanch almonds, grind.

Sift sugar, combine almonds, vanilla and the juice of half lemon; prepare into smooth mixture for easy spreading.

Prepare dried fruits. Rinse figs and raisins, dry in towel.

Cube figs and dates coarsely, cube orange peel, chop walnuts coarsely, mix all ingredients. If this filling does not hold together, add a spoon of syrup from orange peel or jam.

Prepare yeast dough. Prepare leaven, set aside to rise.

Cream yolks with sugar, add raised leaven, salt, flour, lemon peel and knead with milk into a thickness allowing for rolling out without flouring board.

When all ingredients are combined, add gradually warm, clarified butter, knead and set aside to rise.

When the dough is leavened, divide into 3 parts, place one part on the bottom of greased pan.

Divide each filling in half, arrange in rows alongside each other, place the almond mixture in the center, on one side of almonds — the rose jam, on the other — apricots, then the dried fruits, alongside the strawberry jam; the order may be changed according to taste.

Roll out the second part of the dough to the length and width of the pan, carry rolled up on rolling pin and place on the first layer of filling; seal sides well so that filling does not ooze out; arrange second layer of filling on the top of dough and cover with the third part of the dough as above, seal sides well; smoothen the top and set aside to rise.

Brush the top with egg and place in pre-heated oven. Bake 1 hour in moderate oven.

Let cool for a while in pan after baked, and then remove carefully. Cool leaning against the high side of flour board. After cooling, ice with vanilla frosting or, before cooling, sprinkle with vanilla sugar.

Pączki 1

Raised Doughnuts

L e a v e n: *1 3/4 oz. yeast * 2 tbs. sugar * 5 tbs. milk * * D o u g h*: *4 egg yolks * 2 eggs * 6 tbs. sugar * lemon peel * 7 cups flour * 1 1/2 cups milk * salt * 2 tbs. rum * 9 tbs. fat (butter) * 1 1/2 cups cherry jam * fat for frying * powdered vanilla sugar for sprinkling*

Prepare leaven, set aside to rise.

Cream egg yolks and eggs with sugar and lemon peel, add the leaven, flour, milk, salt, knead. Add rum, mix.

When all ingredients are combined, add gradually melted butter, knead, set aside to rise.

When the dough doubles in bulk, divide in 4 parts. Roll out each part on floured board to 1/3 inch thickness.

Drain jam on sieve, or use marmalade.

Cut rounds with small cooky cutter, place a bit of jam in center, cover with another round, pinch together with fingers, and then cut out again with cooky cutter (even the sides).

Place the doughnuts on sieve sprinkled with flour, leaving sufficient space between the doughnuts, cover with towel and set aside to rise.

When they rise, turn over on other side.

Put up fat for frying, test fat for temperature with piece of dough. If dough floats to top immediately, the fat is correct temperature.

Brush flour off the leavened doughnuts, place in hot fat, upper part down, the doughnuts should be able to float freely in the fat.

Fry covered on an asbestos plate over medium heat.

When half the doughnut is browned, turn over and fry through uncovered.

Remove with 2-tine fork onto absorbent paper; when drained, place on platter, sprinkle with vanilla sugar or pour over with punch frosting (see page 389).

Arrange hot doughnuts on long platter one beside the other. When completely cooled, they may be piled one on top of the other.

Pączki 2

L e a v e n: *1 3/4 oz. yeast * 1 tbs. sugar * 5 tbs. milk * * D o u g h*: *6 egg yolks * 5 tbs. sugar * 4 1/2 cups flour * 1 cup milk * salt * 2 tbs. rum * * 4 tbs. butter * 1 cup of cherry or rose preserves * fat for frying * powdered vanilla sugar for sprinkling*

Prepare as above.

348

COOKIES

Faworki (Chrust)

Carnival Cookies

*2 cups flour * 1 1/2 tbs. butter * salt * 1 tbs. rum * 5 egg yolks * fat for frying * powdered vanilla sugar for sprinkling*

Cut butter into flour, add salt, rum and as much egg yolk so that the dough does not stick to the flour board while kneading. Beat dough against the board.

If bubbles appear on the surface of the dough, cover and set aside for 1/2 hour.

Cut small amounts of dough at a time, roll out thin (1/8 inch), flour the board as little as possible.

Cut up in strips 1 inch wide by 3—4 inches long, cutting the ends diagonally.

Cut a slit lengthwise in the center of each strip (about 1 1/2 inches) and pull through one end of the strip through opening, level.

Fry the faworki while they are still damp. Heat fat, test for temperature, fry a few at a time in enough room so they float freely. Fry on both sides to light gold.

Remove with a fork, drain each piece, place on absorbent paper.

When the faworki cool a little, remove to a plate, sprinkle profusely with powdered vanilla sugar.

Rolled Cookies

Cut butter into flour with a long, evenly-wide knife, add sugar, blend.

Add eggs, sour cream or milk (according to recipe), mix with knife, knead with hands into dough stiff enough to be rolled out. Mixture should not be too thin.

When all ingredients are blended, place on floured plate and set aside in cold place.

Add baking powder to dough, combine.

Roll out not too thick, prick surface, cut out with cookie cutter, set on cookie sheet sprinkled with flour, spaced to allow for rising while baking.

If to be used as a cake, roll out thick to the size and shape of the baking pan, roll on rolling pin, unroll in pan, shape, complete according to recipe.

Place in heated, moderate oven, bake about 35 minutes.

After removing, brush flour off cookies.

349

After removing cake, cut with a sharp knife while hot.
Sprinkle cookies with sugar while hot or ice after they are cooled.

Vanilla Cookies

*3 1/2 cups flour * 7 tbs. fat * 3/4 cup powdered sugar * salt * vanilla *
* 1 egg * 3/4 cup milk * 4 1/2 tsp. baking powder*

Cut fat into flour, combine with sugar, add salt, vanilla.
Knead with egg and milk to a stiff dough, place in cold.
Add baking powder to dough, mix, divide in two parts.
Sprinkle the cookie sheet with flour.
Roll out thin, prick surface, cut out with small-size cookie cutter.
Arrange on cookie sheet, leaving room for rising during baking, bake to
light golden color in well-heated oven. After removing brush off flour.

Amoniaczki

*4 1/2 cups flour * 6 1/2 tbs. fat * 3/4 cup powdered sugar * vanilla *
* 1/3 ammonium carbonate * 3/4 cup milk * 2 eggs or 4 egg yolks*

Cut fat into flour, combine with sugar, add vanilla.
Warm 1/4 milk while stirring, dilute ammonium carbonate in milk. (Use
large saucepan because it rises quickly).
Knead the dough with eggs and diluted ammonium carbonate, add rest of
milk, knead to a dough thinner than for dumplings, place on plate
sprinkled with flour, cover, set in cold over night.
If the dough is to stiff the next day, dilute with milk, divide in two parts,
roll out, prick the surface, cut out with small cookie cutter.
Sprinkle the cookie sheet with flour, arrange cookies on sheet, space to
allow for rising during baking; bake to light yellow color in well-heated
oven.

Alberts

*2 tbs. butter * 1 egg * 3 tbs. sour cream * 2 cups flour * 6 tbs. potato
starch * 1/2 cup sugar * 1 tsp. baking soda*

Cream butter in bowl, add egg, blend with sour cream.
Sift flour and potato starch, combine on flour board, make a well, add
creamed mixture into well, add sugar and soda, knead thoroughly.
Roll out rather thin, prick surface, cut out with square or quadrangular
cookie cutter.

Sprinkle the cookie sheet with flour, arrange cookies one beside the other, bake to golden color.

Crispy Cookies

Cut butter into flour with a long, wide knife, add powdered sugar, mix. If almonds are to be used, blanch and grind, add together with sugar to dough.

Add raw or hard-boiled egg yolk which has been grated through a sieve (according to recipe).

Knead for a short time (butter melts quickly from hand temperature), knead only until all ingredients are combined. Set aside in cold place until firm.

Roll out on lightly floured board.

Complete according to recipe, remove cookies with spatula onto cookie sheet sprinkled with flour.

Bake to golden color, in a well-heated but moderate oven so that the dough bakes uniformly.

Star Cookies

*2 1/4 cups flour * 7 tbs. butter * 3 tbs. fat * 4 tbs. powdered sugar *
* vanilla * 1 egg * juice of 1/2 lemon * granulated sugar for sprinkling *
* vanilla sugar for sprinkling*

Cut butter and fat into flour, combine with sifted sugar and vanilla.

Add egg and lemon juice to flour, knead and set aside to chill for a few hours.

When the dough is firm, cut off a piece at a time and roll out to 1/8 inch thickness.

Cut out with star-shaped cookie cutter, arrange on cookie sheet sprinkled with flour. Brush with egg and sprinkle with granulated sugar. Bake in moderate oven to a golden color.

Remove carefully from cookie sheet, and sprinkle lightly with vanilla sugar.

Double-Decker Cookies

*2 hard-boiled egg yolks * 1 cup flour * 6 1/2 tbs. butter * 3 1/2 tbs.
powdered sugar * a few almonds * granulated sugar for sprinkling * 1 egg
white for brushing * vanilla sugar for sprinkling*

351

Prepare hard-boiled egg yolks, mash.

Cut butter into flour, add sugar, mashed egg yolks, knead, set aside.

Blanch and chop almonds, combine with granulated sugar.

Roll out dough to 1/8 inch thickness.

Cut out rounds with a fluted cookie cutter (about 40 cookies).

Divide rounds in two parts; make an opening in the center of half of them, brush the half without openings with egg white, press both rounds together.

Place on cookie sheet, brush with egg white, sprinkle with almond and sugar mixture, bake in well-heated oven to light gold.

After baking, sprinkle with vanilla sugar, garnish with jam.

Two-Colored Cookies

*2 cups flour * 10 1/2 tbs. butter * 1/2 cup powdered sugar * 3 egg yolks ** 1 tbs. hot water * 4 tsp. cocoa * vanilla*

Sift flour, cut butter into flour, combine with sugar, add raw egg yolks and boiling water, mix and divide dough in half.

Add cocoa to one half of dough, mix. Add vanilla to second half of dough, mix. Place both parts of dough in cold place until firm to avoid difficulties while shaping.

Different shapes may be made with the two-colored dough, by cutting with a cookie cutter, and placing the dark dough on top of light or vice versa.

The most popular designs are checker-board, double-decker, pinwheels or bars.

1. Pinwheels

Roll out light and dark dough separately to a thickness of about 1/4 inch, into a square of uniform size and thickness.

Brush the light dough with egg white, place dark dough on top, roll lightly. Brush top of dark dough with egg white, roll tightly, set aside to chill until firm.

Slice 1/4 inch thick with sharp, thin knife. Use sawing motion while cutting.

Arrange on cookie sheet, bake in well-heated oven until the light dough is light gold.

2. Checker-Board

Roll out dark and light dough separately into squares 1/4 inch thick; divide each piece into 3 strips of uniform size.

Brush two strips of the light and two strips of the dark dough with egg white, arrange in layers: a) white on bottom, center — dark, top — light, b) bottom — dark, center — light, top — dark.

Lightly press the dough, arranged in layers with rolling pin, set aside to chill until firm.

Cut with a thin knife into piece 1/4 inch thick.

Brush after slicing with egg white, arrange, changing the order of the color, 5 strips one on top of the other (chill).

Slice 1/4 inch thick, arrange on cookie sheet and bake in well-heated oven until the light dough is a golden color.

3. Double-Deckers

Roll out the light and dark dough separately to a thickness of 1/4 inch. Brush the light dough with egg white, cover with dark dough rolling up dough on rolling pin, roll lightly so that both layers adhere.

Brush the dark layer with egg white, cover with light dough, roll up on rolling pin, roll out lightly so that both layers adhere.

Slice into squares about 1/3 inch thick, 2 inches × 2 inches, place on cookie sheet, bake.

Almond Cookies

*1/3 cup almonds * 2 1/2 cups flour * 14 tbs. butter * 5 1/2 tbs. powdered sugar * 1 egg * vanilla sugar for sprinkling*

Blanch almonds, grind.

Cut butter into flour with knife, add sugar, almonds, egg and mix.

When all ingredients are blended, set aside dough for a while.

Press out rounds through pastry bag, arrange on cookie sheet.

Bake to golden color in well-heated oven.

After removing from oven, sprinkle with vanilla sugar.

Molded Almond Cookies

*1/3 cup almonds * 2 hard-boiled egg yolks * 4 cups flour * 1 cup butter * 1/4 cup powdered sugar * juice of half lemon * vanilla sugar for sprinkling*

Blanch almonds and remove skins, grind.

Hard boil and mash egg yolks through sieve.

Cut butter into flour, add sugar, mix with knife, add almonds, mashed egg yolks, lemon juice, knead, set aside.

Press dough through cookie press or pastry tube into long strip.

Cut into uniform lengths (about 45 cookies), arrange on cookie sheet not too close together, bake in a well-heated oven to light golden color.

Remove to plate when baked, sprinkle with vanilla sugar while hot.

Iced Cookies

D o u g h: *2 cups flour * 9 tbs. butter * 5 tbs. powdered sugar * 3 egg yolks * 2—3 tbs. water * salt * I c i n g: 1/2 cup powdered sugar * * 1—2 egg whites, or enough to make thick icing * 1 1/2 tbs. butter * * S p r e a d: 1 cup apricot marmalade or strained rose preserves*

Prepare icing. Cream powdered sugar with egg whites thoroughly in a bowl, combine with melted butter.

Prepare dough. Cut butter into flour, add sugar, beat raw egg yolks, add water to make the desired stiffness of dough, add salt, knead, roll out to 1/8 inch thickness.

Cut out with small round or square cookie cutter, spread icing on top, bake in well heated oven until light golden color.

Dilute marmalade so that it is easy to spread.

After removing cookies from oven, spread marmalade on uniced side, put two cookies together (about 25 cookies).

Cookie Rolls

*10 tbs. butter * 3 eggs * 14 tbs. flour * 3/4 cup powdered sugar * a few almonds * 2 tbs. raisins * 1/2 tbs. vanilla sugar for sprinkling*

Cream butter in a bowl, add 1 egg at a time, add sugar and flour gradually.

Blanch almonds, shred, rinse raisins, clean.

Spread dough fairly thickly in greased pan, sprinkle with raisins and almonds.

Bake quickly in well-heated oven to light golden color.

Cut the baked but still soft dough into pieces 1 1/2 inches × 5 inches, roll quickly on a rolling pin, pressing lightly with a napkin (raisins should) be outside).

Sprinkle the rolls with vanilla sugar and arrange on glass platter.

Or, cut baked dough into squares 1 1/2 inches × 1 1/2 inches, sprinkle with vanilla sugar (about 24 squares).

Coconut Cookies

*3 tbs. water * 3/4 cup sugar * 4 egg whites * 3/4 cup shredded coconut *
* (lemon) * butter for greasing cookie sheet*

Heat water for steamed egg whites (see page 330).
Make a thick syrup with water and sugar (III stage, see page 333).
Beat egg whites.
Steam egg whites with hot syrup, beat over steam.
When the egg whites separate from the beater add shredded coconut, (add
lemon juice), combine.
Drop from spoon onto greased cookie sheet or press through pastry tube.
Bake in heated but moderate oven until light golden color.

Almond or Nut Bars

*3/4 cup almonds * 3 egg whites * 1 cup granulated sugar * wafer*

Blanch almonds, cut in strips.
Beat egg whites, adding sugar gradually.
When the egg whites stand up in peaks, add almonds, combine.
Spread over wafer, slice into strips 4 inches × 3/4 inch.
Arrange on cookie sheet, place in moderate oven, bake until light golden
color.

Nougat

*1 lb. walnuts * 2 1/2 cups sugar * 1 cup water * 1 tbs. vinegar * 1/2 cup
honey * 6 egg whites * 4 wafers (11 inches × 8 inches)*

Put up water in saucepan to hold the bowl for beating the egg whites.
Select and chop walnuts.
Prepare a thick, smooth syrup from water, sugar and vinegar.
Add honey, heat again to third stage syrup, stirring constantly and carefully
since honey boils over easily.
Beat egg whites stiff.
Steam the beaten egg whites with half the syrup and honey, adding very
gradually.
Place the bowl with the steamed egg whites into saucepan with boiling
water, and beat over steam adding the rest of the syrup.
When egg whites stand up in peaks, remove from water, add the chopped
nuts, mix with spatula.

Divide mixture into two parts, spread each one on a wafer, even sides, place one piece on the other, cover with plain wafer and press by rolling the rolling pin over the surface, set aside to cool, weight lightly with flour board. Cut into 1 inch bars.

Coffee Meringues

*1/2 cup strong coffee * 2 cups sugar * 3 egg whites*

Prepare 1/2 cup strongly-brewed coffee.
Pour sugar into boiling coffee, cook to a thick, smooth syrup; when the syrup drops from the spoon in a heavy, slow stream, place over very low heat.
Beat egg whites stiff and steam gradually with the boiling syrup.
When half of the syrup has been poured in, place the bowl with egg whites on top of double boiler and add the rest of the syrup gradually, beating constantly.
When mixture separates from the beater, remove from heat.
Line tin with paper dampened in water and press mixture through pastry tube into round meringues of uniform size.
Place in warm oven, and allow to dry but do not brown.
When dry, remove from oven, remove paper carefully, cutting it off with a dampened knife, and join the two flat, moist sides of the meringues together.

Vanilla Nut Meringues

*1 cup walnuts * 1 cup sugar * 3 tbs. boiling water * 1/3 tsp. cream of tartar * 4 egg whites * vanilla*

Cut walnuts into strips.
Prepare a thick syrup with water, sugar and cream of tartar (III stage, see page 333).
Beat egg whites stiff, and continue to beat over steam while gradually adding half the syrup.
When the egg whites are combined with half the syrup, place on top of pot with boiling water, keep beating and add rest of syrup.
When the egg whites are somewhat thick, add the vanilla and nuts, remove from steam and while hot drop from a teaspoon onto greased cookie sheet.
Place in low oven and dry rather than bake.
Store in tightly-sealed jar so that they remain crisp.

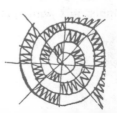

Helgoland Cookies

*a few almonds * 1 1/2 tbs. granulated sugar * 1 cup flour * 1 1/2 tbs. butter * 5 egg yolks * 1 tbs. rum * 1 egg white for brushing * vanilla sugar for sprinkling*

Blanch and chop almonds, combine with sugar.

Cut butter into flour, add egg yolks, rum, mix thoroughly, knead for about 20 minutes.

Roll out to fairly thick dough (as for dumplings), cut out with S-shaped cookie cutter, brush with egg white, sprinkle with granulated sugar and almonds. Bake in moderate oven, sprinkle with vanilla sugar.

Sponge Almond Fingers

*a few almonds * 1 1/2 tbs. granulated sugar * 3 eggs * 3/4 cup powdered sugar * 3/4 cup flour * lemon peel * 2 tbs. butter for greasing pan * * 1 1/2 tbs. vanilla sugar*

Cut almonds into strips, combine with granulated sugar.

Cream eggs thoroughly with sugar, adding flour gradually. Mix for about 20 minutes, add lemon peel last.

Grease pan with butter, pour in a layer of batter about 1/3 inch to 1/2 inch thick.

Sprinkle the almond and sugar mixture uniformly over surface, place in hot oven and bake to golden color.

Sprinkle with vanilla sugar immediately after removing from oven and cut into bars about 1/4 inch wide.

Remove from pan while hot and cool on board.

Serve immediately after baking or 2—3 days after baking for immediately after cooling they are hard and must stand for a few days to regain their softness.

Dried-Fruit Sponge Squares

*a few almonds * 1 tbs. raisins * 2 eggs * 1 cup powdered sugar * 1 cup flour * 1 tbs. butter for greasing pan * 1 1/2 tbs. vanilla sugar for sprinkling*

Cut almonds into long strips and combine with raisins.

Cream eggs with sugar, add flour gradually.

Grease pan, pour batter into pan 1 inch thick, sprinkle top with almonds and raisins, bake in hot oven, do not dry.

When brown, remove from oven, slice into squares 1 1/2 inches × 1 1/2 inches, sprinkle with vanilla sugar, remove carefully from pan, cool.

TARTS

Vanilla-Whip Tart

D o u g h: *1 cup flour * 4 1/2 tbs. butter * 3 tbs. powdered sugar * * 2 egg yolks * W h i p: 1 cup sugar * 3 tbs. water * 1/3 tsp. cream of tartar * 4 egg whites * vanilla * lemon juice*

Place 12 small tart molds one beside the other.
Cut in butter with flour, blend with sugar, add egg yolks, knead, set aside.
Roll out dough, roll up on rolling pin, put dough over molds, press dough tightly to bottom of molds, cut off edges, fasten to the molds, by pressing with fingers.
Knead scraps, roll out, fill rest of molds.
Place molds on baking sheet, set in hot oven, and bake until light golden color.
Prepare whip. Prepare a thick syrup (III stage) with sugar, water and cream of tartar, beat egg whites, steam with syrup and add vanilla and lemon juice to taste.
Invert molds on board, and when cool, tap lightly with knife and remove.
Fill with steamed whip just before serving.

Caramel-Whip Tart

D o u g h: *1 cup flour * 4 1/2 tbs. butter * 3 tbs. powdered sugar * * 2 egg yolks * W h i p: 1 cup sugar * 3 tbs. water * 1/4 tsp. cream of tartar * 4 egg whites * vanilla * lemon juice*

Prepare dough. Line molds and bake as in previous recipe.
Prepare whip. Prepare a thick syrup (III stage) with sugar, water and cream of tartar, brown to a light color, add a little water if too thick.
Beat egg whites, steam with caramel syrup, add vanilla and lemon juice to taste.
Remove tarts from molds as in previous recipe.
Fill with whip immediately before serving.

Rose-Whip Tart

D o u g h: *1 cup flour * 4 1/2 tbs. butter * 3 tbs. powdered sugar * * 2 egg yolks * W h i p: 1/2 cup sugar * 3 tbs. water * 1/3 tsp. cream of tartar * 4 egg whites * 1/2 cup rose preserves * lemon juice*

Prepare dough. Line molds and bake as in recipe for vanilla-whip tart.
Prepare whip. Prepare a thick syrup (III stage) with water, sugar and cream

of tartar, add rose preserves to syrup, combine, set aside. When cooled a little, add lemon juice to taste.

Beat egg whites stiff, adding syrup gradually while whipping, place over steam, beat until thick while gradually adding rest of syrup.

Remove and unmold tarts as above.

Fill with whip just before serving.

Whipped-Cream Tart

D o u g h: *1 cup flour * 4 1/2 tbs. butter * 3 tbs. powdered sugar *
* 2 egg yolks * Filling: 1 1/4 cups heavy cream * 2 1/2 tbs. powdered sugar * vanilla*

Prepare dough. Line molds and bake as in recipe for vanilla-whip tart.

Beat cream while cold.

Immediately before serving, sprinkle sugar with vanilla into cream and combine.

Fill tarts with cream just before serving and decorate with drained fruit preserves or fresh fruit.

Serve immediately.

Custard Tart

D o u g h: *1 cup flour * 4 1/2 tbs. butter * 3 tbs. powdered sugar *
* 2 egg yolks * Filling: 3 tbs. butter * 5 tbs. flour * 1 cup light cream * 3 egg yolks * sugar * vanilla*

Prepare dough. Roll out 2/3 of dough, line 8 tart molds as in recipe for vanilla-whip tart. Set aside remainder of dough.

Prepare a light roux, dilute with cream, stir while cooking, beat egg yolks, add to mixture, heat quickly, add sugar and vanilla to taste.

Roll out the rest of the dough, cut out rounds the size of the top of the tart molds, fill the tart (3/4 full), brush edges of rounds with egg white, cover tart; place on cookie sheet and bake to light golden color. When cool remove from mold, arrange on glass platter.

Almond Cream Tart

D o u g h: *1 cup flour * 4 1/2 tbs. butter * 3 tbs. powdered sugar *
* 2 egg yolks * Filling: 3/4 cup almonds * 4 egg yolks * 1/2 cup sugar * lemon peel * 4 egg whites*

Prepare dough. Line molds, place on cookie sheet as in recipe for vanilla--whip tart.

Prepare filling. Blanch and grind almonds.

Cream egg yolks with sugar. Add lemon peel.

Beat egg whites, add to creamed yolks, sprinkle with almonds, blend.

Fill tarts 3/4 full.

Bake in hot oven to light golden color.

When cool, remove from molds.

FLAKY FRENCH PASTRY

Cut butter into flour, add egg yolks and eggs, knead dough adding thick, sour cream and a pinch of salt.

When all ingredients are blended, remove to a bowl sprinkled with flour, smooth top of dough, cover and set in a cold place for 12 hours to ferment. The flakiness of the dough depends on the degree of fermentation, giving it its similarity to French pastry dough.

After 12 hours remove from a bowl, roll out to a thickness of 1/6 inch and shape according to recipe; work quickly so that it does not soften as a result of warm temperature.

Heat oven and place dough in very hot oven. Do not open oven during first ten minutes of baking. After baking, the pastry should be firm and should not crack, when pressed with the fingers; the top should be dry, of a light golden color, the sides of the pastry should also be firm.

If the pastry is still not baked and is browning too quickly, cover with paper and finish baking.

Sprinkle profusely with sugar after baking (or ice); this pastry is an economical substitute for French pastry, is easy to make, does not require skill, special processes; neither ice nor a refrigerator is necessary.

The indispensable requirements are: thick, fresh sour cream (not too sour), a cold place where the dough may ferment and an oven which heats to a high temperature.

Cheese Pastry with Apples

*1 1/3 cups flour * 1 cup butter * 1 1/2 cups bland cottage cheese * * 1 egg * 1/2 cup sour cream * salt * 4 medium apples * 1 egg white for brushing * 1/2 egg for brushing*

Cut butter into flour, combine with cottage cheese, knead with egg and sour cream. Add a pinch of salt.

Roll out to 1/8 inch thickness, cut out rounds with fluted cookie cutter (about 40 rounds).

Wash apples, peel, divide into 8 sections lengthwise, core.

Place a section of apple on each round. Fold over and shape into a half--open semicircle, fasten the edges of the apple and dough with egg white. Brush with beaten egg, bake in hot oven; while hot sprinkle with powdered vanilla sugar.

Serve the same day.

Flaky Semicircles with Apples

*3 1/2 cups flour * 1 1/3 cups butter * 2 egg yolks * 1 egg * 3/4 cup sour cream * salt * 1 lb. apples * 1 egg white for brushing * 1/2 egg for brushing*

Cut butter into flour, add egg yolks and egg, knead dough adding sour cream. Add a pinch of salt.

Prepare dough 12 hours before baking, and set in cold place (it can stand overnight).

Roll out to 1/6 inch thickness.

Cut out rounds with a fluted cookie cutter.

Rinse apples, peel, divide into several parts lengthwise, core.

Place a piece of apple on one half of round (border of apple to the border of the round), cover with the other half to form a half-open semicircle, fasten the edges of the apple and dough with egg white.

Place on cookie sheet, brush with egg.

Bake in very hot oven to a light golden color (about 30 minutes).

After removing from oven sprinkle with powdered vanilla sugar. Serve on the same day.

Flaky Semicircles with Marmalade

*3 1/2 cups flour * 1 1/3 cups butter * 2 egg yolks * 1 egg * 3/4 cup sour cream * salt * marmalade (or drained fruit preserves) * 1 egg white for brushing * 1/2 egg for brushing*

Prepare dough as above.

Roll out next day to a thickness of 1/6 inch.

Cut out rounds with a fluted large-size cookie cutter. Brush edges with egg white. Place marmalade on one half of round, cover with other half; fasten the edges with egg white to form a semicircle.

Set on cookie sheet, brush with egg and bake in very hot oven to a golden color; after baking sprinkle with powdered vanilla sugar.

Flaky Poppy-Seed Cakes

Dough: *3 1/2 cups flour * 1 1/3 cups butter * 2 egg yolks * 1 egg * * 3/4 cup sour cream * salt * 1 egg white for brushing * Filling: 1/2 lb. poppy seeds * 2 tbs. butter * sugar * lemon peel * 3 tbs. raisins * * 2 egg whites*

Prepare dough as in recipe for flaky semicircles with apples.

After 12 hours, prepare filling. Pour boiling water over poppy seeds, cover, set aside; when seeds crumble between the fingers, drain on sieve.

Put through food chopper 3 times, combine with sugar (to taste), add melted butter, lemon peel, raisins, cool, mix with egg whites.

Roll out dough to a 1/6 inch thick quadrangle.

Cut into squares 4 inches (about 15 pieces).

Place some poppy seeds in center of square, fold up 4 corners of square towards center, brush the edges with egg white, fasten in center and cover with a small square of dough.

Set on cookie sheet, bake in very hot oven to a light golden color.

Sprinkle with powdered vanilla sugar immediately after removing from oven.

Flaky Wild-Strawberry Cakes

Dough: *3 1/2 cups flour * 1 1/3 cups butter * 2 egg yolks * 1 egg * * 3/4 cup sour cream * salt * Filling: 2 1/2 cups sugar * 1/2 cup water * 2/3 tsp. cream of tartar * 8 egg whites * lemon juice * 2—3 cups wild strawberries * (red coloring)*

Prepare dough as in recipe for flaky semicircles with apples. Set aside in cold for 12 hours. Next day divide dough in two parts, roll out the shape of the baking sheets, roll up on rolling pin, line the sheets to edges with dough.

Brush surface of dough with cold water; bake in very hot oven to a light golden color, if necessary cover with paper to avoid burning.

Prepare filling. Prepare a thick syrup (III stage) from sugar, water and cream of tartar.

Beat egg whites, steam with syrup, beat over steam; when it thickens, remove from steam, add lemon juice to taste, wild strawberries and color to light pink, beating to a thick froth with the fruit. Put aside 1/3 of the fruit for decoration.

After the pastry is baked, place the filling on one piece, spread evenly, cut the second part into squares, 2 inches × 2 inches, and with a spatula place each square on the filling one close to the other so that the filling is completely covered.

362

Spread a thin layer of the filling on the surface, garnish with the rest of the berries.

Cut the entire cake into squares, in the places where the top layer has already been cut, dip knife in hot water to facilitate cutting.

Remove squares with spatula to a platter.

Serve on the same day.

Flaky Babkas with Fruit

D o u g h: *1 cup flour * 4 1/2 tbs. butter * 3 tbs. powdered sugar * * 2 egg yolks * F i l l i n g: 2 to 3 cups fruit (strawberries, wild straw-berries, apricots, peaches, grapes, oranges) * 1 cup sugar * 3 tbs. mara-schino or rum * 1 cup sweet heavy cream * 3 tbs. powdered sugar*

Prepare dough. Cut in butter and flour and mix with sugar. Knead dough with egg yolks.

Line 10 individual molds with the dough and bake in a moderate oven (330°F), browning to a light yellow.

Remove molds and place on board, bottom up. When cool, strike the bottom with a knife handle. When the shells are released, turn shells over and arrange on a plate.

Prepare fruit. Rinse fruit and drain off liquid. Remove stems from straw-berries. Scald apricots and peaches and remove skin. Cut in half and remove stones. Pick grapes off and peel oranges. Cut oranges into thick slices and cut each slice in four.

Sprinkle fruit with sugar and leave in cool place for 30 min. Before placing in shells, drain off juice through sieve. Place on plate and sprinkle with maraschino or rum.

Fill shells 3/4 full with drained fruit pressing lightly with spoon. Before serving, whip cream and mix with powdered sugar. Place whipped cream generously on the top of shells with fruit.

Egg-Yolk Filling in Flaky Crust

D o u g h: *2 cups flour * 1/2 cup butter * 5 tbs. powdered sugar * 1 egg yolk * F i l l i n g: 5 egg yolks * 1/2 cup sugar * lemon peel * 1 cup sour cream * 1 cup flour * vanilla * 5 egg whites*

Prepare dough. Cut in flour and butter and mix with sugar. Knead dough with egg yolk.

Use half of dough to line torte pan. Form a round from the second half to cover cake.

Prepare filling. Cream egg yolks with sugar and mix with lemon peel, sou.
cream, flour and vanilla. Whip egg whites and fold into egg yolk
mixture.

Pour mixture into pan lined with dough and cover with dough round. Bake
about 35 minutes in a moderate oven, until browned to a golden yellow.

Remove from oven. Remove ring, sprinkle with powdered vanilla sugar,
cut and serve immediately. Do not remove the bottom of the pan.

SPONGE CAKES

Sponge Babka with Potato Starch

Easter Cake

*2/3 cup butter * 4 egg yolks * 3/4 cup powdered sugar * vanilla * 1/2
cup milk * 1/2 cup potato starch * 1/2 cup flour * 2 1/4 tsp. baking
powder * 4 egg whites * a few almonds * 4 tbs. butter for greasing pan *
* 1 1/2 tbs. vanilla sugar*

Cream butter until fluffy, add yolks one at a time and the powdered sugar
and vanilla gradually, mix for 10 minutes, towards the end add milk, blend
with the mixture, add potato starch, flour and baking powder, mix.

Beat egg whites, fold into dough. Prepare pan (either round or loaf pan),
grease with butter and sprinkle with chopped almonds. Pour dough into
prepared pan.

Place in well-heated oven, bake (about 3/4 hour), test with caketester for
doneness.

Remove, invert carefully on cake platter; while hot, sprinkle with vanilla
sugar, cool slowly.

Cut after a few hours.

Almond Babka

Easter Cake

*1/2 cup almonds * 3 bitter almonds * 10 egg yolks * 1 1/4 cups powder-
ed sugar * 1 lemon (juice and peel) * 1 cup potato starch * 5 egg
whites * butter for greasing pan * vanilla sugar for sprinkling*

Blanch almonds, skin, dry, grind.

Cream egg yolks and sugar, add lemon juice and peel, potato starch and
mix for 10 minutes.

Beat egg whites and fold into dough and almonds.
Pour into greased pan, bake in well-heated oven.
Remove carefully and cool. Sprinkle with vanilla sugar.

Chinese Sponge Cake

*14 tbs. butter * 4 egg yolks * 9 1/2 tbs. powdered sugar * 2 1/4 tsp. baking powder * 2 level tsp. of ground coffee * 13 tbs. flour * 1 cup potato starch * 2 egg whites * butter for greasing pan*

Cream butter, add 1 egg yolk at a time and sugar gradually, combine with baking powder and coffee. Add flour and potato starch, mix.
Beat egg whites, fold into dough.
Set in a long, narrow, well-greased pan and bake in moderate oven.

Sponge Cake with Potato Starch

*5 egg yolks * 14 tbs. butter * 1 cup powdered sugar * 3 1/2 tsp. baking powder * vanilla * 5 egg whites * 1 cup flour * 11 tbs. potato starch * * butter for greasing pan*

Cream butter, add one egg yolk at a time and sugar gradually, add vanilla and baking powder.
Beat egg whites.
After mixing dough for 20 minutes, add egg whites, flour, potato starch, mix lightly, place in greased pan and bake in well-heated oven.
Cool for a while in pan after baking, then remove.
This dough may be used as a base for cakes with various fillings or may be iced.

Dried-Fruit Cake

*1/2 lb. dried fruits (raisins, figs, dates, walnuts or almonds, orange peel) * 5 eggs * 2 cups sugar * vanilla * lemon peel * 2 cups flour * * butter for greasing pan*

Clean raisins, clean and slice figs, slice dates, chop walnuts or almonds, cut up orange peel; dredge fruits dry with flour.
Cream egg yolks with sugar, add vanilla and lemon peel.
Beat egg whites, add to yolks, add flour, mixed fruits, pour into greased loaf pan, bake in well-heated oven 3/4 hour; if it browns too much, cover top with paper. After baking, remove from pan, cool propped against sides of flour board. Serve day after baking.

Chocolate Cup Cakes

D o u g h: *7 egg yolks * 5 tbs. powdered sugar * 9 egg whites * 1 cup flour * butter for greasing molds * flour for molds * * C h o c o l a t e f r o s t i n g: 4 oz. chocolate * 1 cup sugar * 1/2 cup water * 1/3 tsp. cream of tartar * * F i l l i n g: 1 cup heavy cream*

Prepare dough. Cream yolks with sugar.

Beat egg whites, fold into yolks, add flour, mix.

Grease bowl-shaped molds about 2 inches in diameter.

Sprinkle with flour. Pour dough into molds.

Bake to golden color in well-heated oven.

Prepare frosting. Melt chocolate over steam.

Prepare a syrup (II stage) from the sugar, water and cream of tartar, stir; when it begins to whiten, add small amounts of the melted chocolate, cream, dilute with a little boiling water if necessary.

Dip half the cakes in the hot frosting, using a skewer, set aside on platter to dry.

Prepare filling. Beat the cream, join two cakes together with the whipped cream in the middle. Take one frosted and one non-frosted cake.

Invert with frosting on top, arrange on glass platter.

Nut Roll

D o u g h: *5 egg yolks * 3/4 cup sugar * 5 egg whites * 8 tbs. flour * * F i l l i n g: 1/2 cup walnuts * 3 tbs. vanilla sugar * 1/2 cup heavy cream * * V a n i l l a f r o s t i n g: 3/4 cup sugar * 3 tbs. water * 1/3 tsp. cream of tartar * vanilla*

Line the bottom of rectangular pan with greased paper.

Prepare dough. Cream yolks with sugar.

Beat egg whites, place on yolks, add flour, blend, pour into pan about 1/2 inch thick, bake in well-heated oven.

Prepare filling. Clean nuts, grind together with vanilla sugar.

Beat cream, mix with nuts and sugar.

Place the baked cake on a towel, remove paper.

Cool the cake, spread with filling, roll so that the filling adheres to the cake, wrap in towel.

Prepare a syrup (II stage) from sugar, water and cream of tartar, stir; when it begins to whiten, add vanilla, dilute a little.

When the cake cools, frost, slice into pieces 1/4 inch thick, arrange on glass platter. The cake may be sprinkled with vanilla sugar instead of being iced.

Nut Cream Roll

D o u g h: *1/2 cup walnuts * 4 egg yolks * 1/2 cup powdered sugar * * 6 egg whites * 1 1/2 tbs. bread crumbs * C r e a m f i l l i n g: 1/4 cup heavy cream * 1 egg white * 4 tbs. powdered vanilla sugar * vanilla sugar for sprinkling or vanilla frosting*

Line the bottom of rectangular pan with greased paper.

Prepare dough. Clean nuts, grind.

Cream yolks with sugar.

Beat egg whites, place on yolks, add nuts and bread crumbs, blend, place in pan.

Bake in moderate oven (as for sponge cake).

Prepare filling. Whip cream, mix with beaten egg white, add powdered vanilla sugar. Invert the baked cake on towel, remove paper, cool.

After cooling, spread with cream, roll up.

Frost or sprinkle with vanilla sugar.

Cut with a sharp, thin knife into 1/3 inch slices.

Nut Coffee Roll

D o u g h: *1/2 cup walnuts * 4 egg yolks * 1/2 cup sugar * 6 egg whites * 1 1/2 tbs. bread crumbs * F i l l i n g: 2 eggs * 8 tbs. powdered sugar * 5 tbs. strong coffee * 1/2 cup butter * C o f f e e f r o s t i n g: 1 cup sugar * 1/2 cup water * 1/3 tsp. cream of tartar * coffee*

Line bottom of rectangular pan with greased paper.

Prepare dough. Clean nuts, grind.

Cream yolks with sugar.

Beat egg whites, place on yolks, add nuts and bread crumbs, fold, place in pan.

Bake in moderate oven.

Prepare filling. Cream eggs with sugar, beat over steam, adding coffee, cool while stirring.

Cream butter, add coffee-filling, mix; when combined, chill.

Turn cake onto board, remove paper, cool.

Spread with filling, roll.

Prepare frosting. Prepare a thick syrup (II stage) from sugar, water and cream of tartar, stir; when it whitens, add coffee.

Ice roll with a thin layer of coffee frosting.

Cut with a sharp knife into 1/3 inch slices, arrange in two rows on glass platter.

Chocolate Roll

D o u g h : *4 oz. chocolate * 1/2 cup almonds * 9 egg yolks * 4 1/2 tbs. sugar * 1 tbs. water * 10 egg whites * C r e a m f i l l i n g: 2 1/4 cups heavy cream * 1 egg white * 2 1/2 tbs. vanilla sugar * C h o c o l a t e f r o s t i n g : 3 oz. chocolate * 1/2 cup sugar * 1/3 tsp. cream of tartar * 3 tbs. water*

Line bottom of rectangular pan with greased paper.
Prepare dough. Melt chocolate over steam.
Wipe almonds, grind.
Cream egg yolks with sugar, add melted chocolate, sprinkle with water, mix thoroughly.
Beat egg whites, place on yolks mixture, add almonds, blend.
Pour into pan, spread evenly.
Bake quickly in moderate oven, being careful not to overbake.
When the surface of cake is dry, remove, place on board, remove paper, cool.
Prepare filling. Beat cream, combine with beaten egg whites and sugar.
Spread filling over cold cake, roll.
Sprinkle top with vanilla sugar or ice.
Prepare frosting. Melt chocolate on top of double boiler.
Prepare a thick syrup, mix. When it whitens, add chocolate gradually while stirring quickly.
Ice roll with warm frosting.
Slice with a thin, sharp knife.

Roll with Marmalade

D o u g h: *5 egg yolks * 3/4 cup powdered sugar * 5 egg whites * 7 tbs. flour * F i l l i n g: 1 cup jam or marmalade*

Line rectangular, low baking pan with greased paper.
Cream egg yolks with sugar until light.
Beat egg whites stiff and add to egg yolks. Add flour and mix.
Place dough in pan and spread with spatula to 1/2 inch thickness.
Bake quickly in very hot oven (350°F) — 20 min.
Cover board with clean towel.
When the cake is browned on top, remove from oven and place on towel. Remove paper. The cake should be baked, but should be soft and moist so that it may be rolled.
Spread thinned marmalade on cake and roll so that the layers of cake and marmalade adhere. Roll in towel and cool.

Before serving, remove towel and sprinkle roll with sugar. Cut in diagonal rounds about 1/2 inch thick and arrange in two rows on a glass plate.

Roll with Cream Filling and Walnuts

D o u g h: *5 egg yolks * 3/4 cup powdered sugar * vanilla * 6 egg whites * 6 to 7 tbs. flour * F i l l i n g: 1 cup heavy cream * 4 tbs. powdered sugar * vanilla * 1/2 cup walnuts*

Line low, three sided pan with greased paper.

Prepare cake. Cream egg yolks with sugar and vanilla. Beat egg whites stiff, add them to egg yolks, then add flour gradually and, while doing so, fold it in.

Place dough in pan and spread evenly to edges. Place in hot oven (350°F). Bake quickly so that it does not dry out for then it would be impossible to roll. When the cake rises, sets and falls a little and the top is browned (10 to 15 minutes), remove cake from oven, turn pan over and place cake on towel. When the cake falls out, remove paper. When the cake cools a little, spread with half of the filling and roll tightly so that the layers of cake and filling adhere. Roll in towel and cool. Cut cooled roll and place on glass plate. Garnish generously with remainder of cream filling and sprinkle with walnuts.

Prepare cream filling. Whip cream and just before spreading mix with sugar and grated walnuts and vanilla. Leave part of the walnuts to sprinkle on top.

Roll with Cream Filling and Wild Strawberries

D o u g h: *5 egg yolks * 3/4 cup powdered sugar * vanilla * 6 egg whites * 6 tbs. flour * F i l l i n g: 1 cup heavy cream * 4 tbs. powdered sugar * 1 cup wild strawberries*

Line low, three sided pan with greased paper.

Prepare cake. Cream egg yolks with sugar and vanilla. Beat egg whites stiff, add to egg yolks sprinkled with flour and fold in.

Place dough in pan and spread to edges of pan. Bake in hot (350°F) oven. The cake should be baked quickly so that it does not dry out and may be rolled.

When the cake rises, sets and falls a bit and the top is browned (10 to 15 minutes), remove cake from oven. Remove by turning pan bottom up. Place cake on towel, and when the cake falls out, remove paper quickly. Cool cake a little and spread with filling. Roll.

Prepare cream filling. Select berries, rinse and set apart the best looking berries for garnish. Whip cream on ice. Set three tablespoons aside for garnish. Mix cream with sugar and fruit and spread quickly on cake. Roll so that layers adhere. Cut the roll in diagonal slices and place on glass plate. Garnish with cream and best berries.

PUFF PASTRY

Boil water with fat or butter and salt. Place measured flour on a sheet of paper.
Pour flour out of paper into boiling water.
Remove from heat, mix with a flat wooden spoon to remove all lumps. Set the creamed mixture over medium heat so that the flour jellies and the water evaporates.
Stir constantly so that the dough does not stick to bottom of pan.
Keep over heat until the dough becomes translucent and thick.
Place dough in bowl, add eggs one at a time to the hot mixture, cream thoroughly (more eggs make the dough rise better, but use only enough eggs so that the dough may easily be shaped into balls).
Mix with a roller for about 20 minutes, set aside.
Shape puffs, either with a spoon or pastry tube, directly onto cookie sheet (all puffs are made in this manner except for soup puffs which may also be cut with a knife or pressed through cookie mold). Arrange puffs on greased tin not too close together since they rise greatly during baking. Bake in very hot oven. Do not open oven for the first 10 minutes of baking. Later open the door a little from time to time so that the steam may be released from the oven.
The sides of a well-baked puff are dry and firm, when touched with the fingers (puffs removed from oven too soon, fall).
After baking, cut and fill.

Cream Puffs

D o u g h: *4 1/2 tbs. fat * 1 cup water * salt * 1 cup flour * 3—5 eggs * * butter for greasing pan * F i l l i n g: 1 cup heavy cream * 2 1/2 tbs. powdered vanilla sugar * granulated vanilla sugar for sprinkling*

Boil water and fat with salt in quart-size saucepan.
Pour in flour, break up lumps stirring over low heat with a flat wooden spoon.

When the dough is sufficiently jellied and becomes translucent and thick, place into bowl, add one egg at a time and mix for 20 minutes. Set aside.

Drop dough with a spoon or press from pastry tube directly onto greased pan not too close together. Bake in hot oven. Do not open oven door at the beginning. When the puffs are firm and dry, remove, cut puffs after baking.

Beat cream, mix with powdered vanilla sugar. Fill the cooled puffs with whipped cream, sprinkle with granulated vanilla sugar.
Serve immediately after filling.

Coffee Éclairs

D o u g h: *4 1/2 tbs. fat * 1 cup water * salt * 1 cup flour * 3—5 eggs * * butter for greasing pan * * C o f f e e c r e a m: 3 1/2 tbs. butter * * 7 tbs. flour * 1/2 cup milk * 2 eggs * strong coffee * coffee frosting or sugar for sprinkling*

Heat water with fat and salt in one-quart saucepan.
Add flour, dissolve lumps and mix over low heat with a flat wooden spoon. When the dough is sufficiently cooked and is translucent and thick, transfer to a bowl, add 1 egg at a time and mix for 20 minutes, set aside.
Shape dough with spoon or press through a pastry tube into oblong shape directly onto greased pan not too close together. Bake in hot oven; do not open oven door at the beginning. When the éclairs are hard and firm, remove. Cut in half lengthwise.
Prepare cream. Melt butter, add flour, heat, dilute with milk, cook while stirring, add eggs, brewed coffee to taste, mix vigorously, add sugar to taste.
Fill the éclairs with cream, ice with coffee frosting or sprinkle with powdered sugar.

MAZUREKS (EASTER CAKES)

Mazurek with Chocolate Frosting

D o u g h: *2 1/4 cups flour * 9 tbs. fat * 1/2 cup powdered sugar * 2 egg yolks * 2 tsp. baking powder * 2—3 tbs. sour cream * * F r o s t i n g: 1 cup light cream * pinch of soda * 1 cup sugar * 2 1/2 tbs. butter * 2 1/2 tbs. cocoa*

Cut fat into flour, combine with sugar, add egg yolks, baking powder, knead with sour cream into rather thick dough.

Divide dough into 3 parts. Roll out 2/3 of dough into rectangular shape. Spread evenly in greased pan.

Shape the remaining 1/3 dough into uniform rolls, cut up to the exact size of the sides of the rectangularly-shaped dough.

Brush the edges of the dough with egg white, place the rolls of dough on top, press lightly so that they adhere.

Bake in well-heated oven to a golden color.

Prepare frosting. Heat cream, add soda, sugar, mix and cook on hot flame on asbestos plate; brown while stirring to avoid burning.

When the syrup is very thick (when dropped on plate, it maintains a round shape and does not spread), add butter, heat for a bit; add cocoa, mix, boil. If the frosting is too thick, add a few drops of boiling water, mix.

Pour the frosting over the mazurek immediately, spread evenly, cool. Decorate with preserved cherries, orange peel, almonds.

Crispy Mazurek with Crumb Topping

D o u g h: *3 1/2 cups flour * 1 cup butter * 1 cup powdered sugar * 2 tsp. baking powder * 3 egg yolks * 4—5 tbs. milk * * S p r e a d: *1 1/2 cups marmalade*

Cut butter into flour, add baking powder and sugar, mix, add egg yolks and milk, knead dough.

Roll out half the dough, place in greased pan, spread with marmalade.

Grate the rest of the dough over the mazurek, sprinkling evenly.

Bake to gold color; when it cools a little, cut into oblongs.

Day and Night Mazurek

D o u g h: *3/4 cups sugar * 5 tbs. fat * 1 egg * 1 cup milk * 2 1/4 cups flour * 4 tsp. baking powder * 2 1/2 tbs. cocoa * * F r o s t i n g: *2 egg whites * 1/2 cup powdered sugar * vanilla * lemon juice * 2 tbs. butter*

Cream fat, add sugar, egg and half the milk. Add flour and baking powder and combine with rest of milk.

Place half the dough on greased pan.

Add cocoa to the second half, blend thoroughly and pour over white dough, spread. Bake in moderate oven.

Cream egg whites with powdered sugar, add vanilla, lemon juice to taste, melted butter, mix.

When the cake cools, ice. Slice into oblongs 3/4 inch by 3 inches.

372

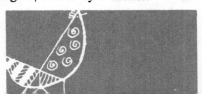

Poppy-Seed Mazurek

D o u g h: *2 1/4 cups poppy seeds * 1 1/2 cups powdered sugar * 1 1/3 cups butter * 3 eggs * 2 3/4 cups flour * 8 tbs. orange peel * a few bitter almonds * lemon peel ** F r o s t i n g: *1 egg white * 1/2 cup powdered sugar * vanilla * lemon juice * 1 1/2 tbs. butter*

Blanch poppy seeds, drain, grind in a food chopper.
Cream butter with sugar and eggs, add poppy seeds, flour, mix thoroughly.
Slice orange peel; blanch and chop almonds.
Add almonds, orange and lemon peel to dough, mix.
Place in greased pan, even top, bake in hot oven.
Prepare frosting. Mix egg white with sugar for 20 minutes; if too thick, dilute with few drops of water, add vanilla, lemon juice and melted butter. Mix.
Remove mazurek from oven; when cool, ice.
When frosting cools, cut into oblongs.

Almond Mazurek

D o u g h: *2 1/4 cups almonds * 2 1/4 cups flour * 1 1/2 cups butter * * 1 1/4 cups powdered sugar * vanilla * 6 egg whites ** F i l l i n g: *preserves (apricot, rose) *** F r u i t   f r o s t i n g: *3/4 cup sugar * 3 tbs. water * 1/4 tbs. cream of tartar * red food coloring*

Blanch and peel almonds, grind.
Cut butter into flour, mix with powdered sugar, almonds and vanilla.
Beat egg whites, combine with all ingredients.
Place dough in greased pan, bake in moderate oven to light golden color, leave in pan to cool.
When cool, remove from pan, cut in half, spread with rose preserves (or apricot marmalade), cover with the other half.
Ice with pink tart frosting.
Cut with sharp knife into oblongs 1×4 inches.

Flaky Mazurek

D o u g h: *2 1/4 cups flour * 1/2 cup butter * 2 egg yolks * 3/4 cup thick, sour cream * 1 egg white for brushing *** T o p p i n g: *1 1/2 tbs. raisins * * a few almonds * granulated sugar * vanilla sugar for sprinkling*

Cut butter into flour, add yolks and sour cream, knead.
Place in a bowl sprinkled with flour, cover and chill for 12 hours (overnight).

The next day, wash raisins and dry in towel, shred almonds into oblong strips.

Combine raisins and almonds with granulated sugar.

Roll the dough into thick, rectangular shape to fit the pan, roll up on roller and then roll out in greased pan.

Brush surface of dough with mixed egg white, sprinkle uniformly with almonds and raisins combined with granulated sugar. Prick with fork and bake in hot oven until brown.

Before removing from pan, slice into 2 inches squares, sprinkle with vanilla sugar.

Crispy Mazurek with Turkish Cream

D o u g h: *3 1/2 cups flour* * *1 cup butter* * *1/2 cup powdered sugar* * * *3 egg yolks* * *1/2 egg for brushing* * T u r k i s h   c r e a m: *3/4 cup coffee cream* * *pinch of soda* * *1 1/2 cups sugar* * *vanilla* * *8 tbs. butter*

Prepare dough. Cut butter into flour, combine with sifted sugar, beat yolks, and knead, set aside in cold place.

Divide dough into 3 parts. Roll out 2/3 of dough (on very lightly floured board) to fit a shallow rectangular baking pan.

Place dough in greased pan.

Make a uniform roll of the remainder of dough to fit around the sides of the pan.

Brush the edges of the dough with egg, place roll around and press lightly so that it adheres to the dough. Brush top of roll with egg, bake in moderate oven until golden color.

After baking, remove from pan.

Prepare Turkish cream. Boil the cream in a rather large saucepan, add the soda, sugar, and cook slowly on an asbestos plate stirring constantly so that it does not burn (the cream may also be baked).

When a bit of the cream dropped on a plate forms into a ball, add the vanilla and butter and heat until it is a golden caramel color. If the cream becomes too thick and begins to dry out, add a few drops of hot milk.

Spread the cream evenly over the mazurek and decorate with browned almonds and orange peel.

The Turkish cream should be cooked only long enough so that it does not crumble while being cut. If it evaporates, sprinkle with milk and mix. It should be moist and not brittle.

Crispy mazurek should be baked 3 to 4 days before eating so that the cake is rather moist, making it easy to slice.

Crispy Mazurek with Orange Spread

D o u g h: *3 1/2 cups flour * 1 cup butter * 1/2 cup powdered sugar *
* 3 egg yolks * 1/2 egg for brushing * S p r e a d: 2 oranges * 1 lemon *
* 1 1/2 cups sugar*

Prepare the dough and bake the mazurek as above.

Prepare spread. Wash orange and lemon and grate raw together with peel, remove pits.

Add sugar to grated fruit and heat slowly, stirring constantly.

When the marmalade falls from the spoon separating itself into lumps (or does not run when cooled but is solid and glossy), pour over the baked cake, spread and cool.

Garnish with orange peel and almonds.

Gypsy Mazurek

*5 egg yolks * 1 cup powdered sugar * lemon peel * vanilla * 7 oz. raisins *
* 2 1/3 cups walnuts * 3 bitter almonds * 5 egg whites * 1 cup flour *
* 2 wafers*

Cream yolks with sugar, add lemon peel and vanilla to taste.

Select, rinse and dry raisins. Shred walnuts and almonds in thin strips.

Beat egg whites stiff.

Place egg whites on yolks, add flour, raisins, walnuts and almonds, combine, place on wafers and bake.

After baking, remove from pan, cool and cut into oblongs (1×3 1/2 inches).

Chocolate Mazurek

*2 1/4 cups almonds * 1/2 lb. chocolate * 3 egg whites * 1 egg * 1 1/4 cups powdered sugar * 2 tbs. flour * 1 rectangular wafer*

Blanch almonds, shell, dry, grind.

Grind chocolate.

Cream egg whites, egg and sugar until white; when thickened add chocolate and mix, add almonds and flour (cream about 30 minutes).

Place the wafer on the bottom of a baking pan with 3 sides.

Pour the batter onto the wafer (or thin crisp pastry), spread to the edges of the pan and bake in well-heated oven for 15 minutes.

After baking, remove from pan, cool.

Cut into oblongs (1×3 1/2 inches).

375

Date Mazurek

*2 1/4 cups almonds * 1/2 lb. dates * 6 egg whites * 1 1/4 cups granulated sugar * vanilla * 2 tbs. flour * 1 rectangular wafer*

Wipe almonds, cut into thin strips.

Cut up dates into thin strips, remove pits.

Beat egg whites stiff, add sugar gradually, beat for 20 minutes, mix with vanilla.

Add the cut almonds and dates to the egg whites, sprinkle with flour, combine.

Line a rectangular shallow pan with wafer or thin pastry.

Spread batter on wafer, even and bake in well-heated oven for 3/4 hour. When the top of the mazurek dries and is lightly browned, remove from oven and remove immediately from pan.

Slice the next day with a sharp knife into bars (1×3 inches); heat knife, so that the cake does not stick.

Almond and Orange Mazurek

D o u g h: *6 1/2 tbs. butter * 2 eggs * 8 tbs. powdered sugar * 3 tbs. heavy cream * 10 tbs. potato starch * 5 tbs. flour * 1 tsp. baking powder * * S p r e a d 1: 1 3/4 cups almonds * 3/4 cup powdered sugar * 3 tbs. boiling water * lemon juice * vanilla * S p r e a d 2: 3 oranges * 1 1/2 cups sugar * 1/2 cup water * lemon juice*

Prepare dough. Cream butter; when foamy, add egg yolks one at a time, add sugar gradually and mix.

When all egg yolks are blended, add the cream gradually, then the potato starch and flour, mix, add baking powder last.

Beat egg whites stiff, fold into dough, mix lightly, pour on pan greased with butter and bake in well-heated oven (about 3/4 hour).

Remove from oven; remove from pan when a little cooled.

Prepare spread 1. Blanch almonds, skin, dry, grind.

Sift sugar, place in a bowl, combine with almonds, add a little boiling water, lemon juice, vanilla and mix thoroughly. Mix to thickness easy for spreading.

Prepare spread 2. Prick the skins of the oranges all over with a thick needle the depth of the peel, place oranges in boiling water and cook slowly until soft. Change water several times to remove bitterness.

Cut the soft orange into slices 1/3 inch thick with a sharp knife.

Prepare a thick syrup with sugar and 1/2 cup water, place sliced oranges into syrup and simmer in flat saucepan or deep skillet; when preserve is almost cooked, add a little lemon juice to make it tart. Before using drain the preserve. The day after the cake has been baked, spread the entire almond filling on top, even out sides. Decorate with the prepared orange slices.

PLACEKS (SHORT CAKES)

Placek with Marmalade

D o u g h: *4 1/2 cups flour * 3/4 cup fat * 8 tbs. sugar * 4 egg yolks or 2 eggs * salt * 4—5 tbs. sour cream * 3 1/2 tsp. baking powder * fat for greasing pan * F i l l i n g: 1 1/4 cups tart marmalade * F r o s t i n g: 1 1/2 cups sugar * 1/2 cup water * 2/3 tsp. cream of tartar * red food coloring * * lemon juice*

Cut fat into sifted flour, combine with sugar, make a well, add egg yolks, add salt, sour cream, knead into dough not too hard. When all ingredients are combined, set aside to chill.
Add baking powder to dough, mix, divide into two parts, place half in greased pan about the thickness of a finger, spread with marmalade.
Roll out second part of dough, cover other part in pan, fasten edges, even out, pieces top with fork, bake in well-heated oven.
Prepare a thick, smooth syrup from water, sugar and cream of tartar; when it whitens dilute, color pink, add lemon juice to taste.
Ice the cake. When the frosting cools, cut into smal squares (about 20).

Plum Placek

D o u g h: *4 1/2 cups flour * 3/4 cup fat * 8 tbs. sugar * 4 egg yolks or 2 eggs * salt * 4—5 tbs. sour cream * 3 1/2 tsp. baking powder * 1 egg white for brushing * fat for greasing pan * T o p p i n g: 1 lb. plums * * powdered vanilla sugar for sprinkling*

Cut fat into sifted flour, mix with sugar, make a well, add egg yolks, add salt, sour cream, knead into dough not too hard. When all ingredients are combined, set aside to chill.
Add baking powder to dough, mix, roll out to shape of pan, spread on greased pan, brush with egg white. Rinse plums, dry in towel, slice each plum in half, remove pits, slit each half into 2 parts lengthwise without severing. Arrange plums on dough, skin side up, press into dough, pierce

the dough between plums with fork, bake; slice into squares (about 16), sprinkle with powdered vanilla sugar.

Serve the day of baking to prevent sogginess.

Semi-Crispy Apple Placek

D o u g h: *4 1/2 cups flour * 3/4 cup fat * 8 tbs. sugar * 4 egg yolks or 2 eggs * salt * 4—5 tbs. sour cream * 3 1/2 tsp. baking powder * fat for greasing pan * 1 1/2 tbs. bread crumbs * 1/2 egg for brushing * 2 1/2 tbs. granulated sugar for sprinkling * powdered vanilla sugar for sprinkling * * F i l l i n g: 8 medium apples * 5 tbs. sugar * (cloves, cinnamon, lemon peel)*

Cut fat into flour, combine with sugar, make a well, add egg yolks, add salt, sour cream, knead into medium-hard dough. When all ingredients are combined, set aside to chill.

Add baking powder to dough, knead.

Clean apples, peel, grate into strips. Before arranging on cake, add sugar and spices, mix.

Divide dough into two parts; roll out one to the thickness of a finger and spread on bottom of greased pan and on part of the sides, sprinkle with bread crumbs, arrange apples on dough.

Roll out second half of dough and place over apples, press down, seal edges of cake, even top, brush with egg, sprinkle with granulated sugar, prick freely with fork, bake in well-heated oven (3/4 hour).

After baking, sprinkle with powdered sugar, cut into squares (about 20).

Serve on day of baking, for the cake becomes soggy.

Cheese Placek

D o u g h: *1 3/4 cups flour * 8 tbs. fat * 5 tbs. sugar * 2 egg yolks or 1 egg * 2 1/4 tsp. baking powder * salt * 2—3 tbs. sour cream * fat for greasing pan * 1/2 egg for brushing * powdered vanilla sugar for sprinkling * F i l l i n g: 1 medium potato * lemon peel * orange peel * 2 tbs. butter * 2 egg yolks * 1 1/2 cups cottage cheese (well drained) * sugar * * 2 egg whites*

Cut fat into sifted flour, mix with sugar, make a well, add egg yolks, add baking powder, salt, sour cream, knead into medium dough; when all ingredients are blended, set aside to chill.

Prepare filling. Boil potato, cut orange peel and grate lemon peel, strain cheese and potato through sieve.

378

Cream butter with egg yolks, combine with cheese and potato mixture, add sugar to taste, add orange and lemon peel, mix.

Beat egg whites, and blend with cheese mixture.

Divide dough into 3 parts. Roll out 2/3 of dough to spread on bottom and sides of pan. Spread with filling, even surface, brush with egg.

Roll out remaining dough, cut out even strips with pastry wheel, place criss-cross on cheese, brush entire cake with egg, prick freely, bake in well-heated oven, sprinkle with vanilla sugar while hot.

Meringue-Topped Placek

D o u g h: *1 cup flour * 6 tbs. butter * 3 tbs. sugar * 2 egg yolks * T o p - p i n g: 1 cup of apricot, rose or raspberry marmalade * 3 egg whites * * 1/2 cup granulated sugar * 1 tbs. sugar for sprinkling*

Prepare dough. Cut butter into flour, combine with sugar, add egg yolks, knead dough; when all ingredients are blended, set aside to chill.

Spread dough on bottom of cake pan and bake to very light gold color. Dilute marmalade with boiling water to spreading thickness, spread over cake.

Beat egg whites, adding sugar gradually (or steam egg whites with syrup — III stage, see page 333), place on top of cake, sprinkle with sugar, place in oven to brown.

When the meringue is dry and begins to brown, remove from oven. Serve on day of baking.

Cheese Cake (Sernik) on Crispy Crust

Easter Cake

D o u g h: *2 3/4 cups flour * 10 1/2 tbs. butter * 6 tbs. powdered sugar * * 2 egg yolks * C h e e s e m i x t u r e: 2 1/2 cups bland cottage cheese * * 1/2 cup butter * 4 egg yolks * 1 cup sugar * 12 tbs. orange peel * lemon peel * vanilla * 5 egg whites * F r o s t i n g: 1/2 cup water * 1 1/2 cups sugar * 2/3 tsp. cream of tartar * lemon juice*

Prepare dough. Cut butter into flour, combine with sugar and knead with egg yolks.

Roll out dough into two round sheets, place one in cake pan, bake.

Prepare cheese. Strain cheese through sieve. Cream butter, add one egg yolk at a time to butter, then add sugar, cream thoroughly. Add cheese to mixture, blend and mix for 10 minutes, add finely chopped orange and lemon peel, and vanilla at end. Beat egg whites, mix with chesse.

Place cheese on baked dough, spread, even out, cover with second round of raw dough, prick and place in well-heated oven. Bake for 1 hour.

After cooling, the cake may be iced or sprinkled while hot with vanilla sugar.

Vienna Cheese Cake

D o u g h: *3/4 cup flour * 4 tbs. butter * 2 tbs. powdered sugar * 1 egg yolk * C h e e s e   m i x t u r e: 2 1/2 cups bland cottage cheese * 1 cup butter * 5 egg yolks * 1 1/4 cups powdered sugar * lemon peel * vanilla * * 5 egg whites * 5 tbs. flour * 1/2 egg for brushing*

Prepare dough. Cut butter into flour, combine with sugar and knead dough with egg yolks; when all ingredients are blended, set aside to chill.

Place dough on bottom of cake pan and bake to light golden color.

Prepare cheese. Drain cottage cheese in towel, grind several times and strain through fine sieve. Melt butter, set aside, do not brown.

Cream egg yolks with sugar, add lemon peel and vanilla, and when the yolks thicken, add the cheese and melted butter gradually, creaming constantly, cream thoroughly for 3/4 hour.

Beat egg whites stiff, fold in cheese mixture sprinkling with flour.

Place cheese mixture on crust, even surface, brush with egg and place in moderate oven.

Bake for 3/4—1 hour, test by inserting thin caketester. If the tester is dry when removed, remove cake from oven, cool and remove carefully from cake pan.

The cake may be iced with lemon or vanilla frosting.

GINGERBREAD

Honey Kisses

Christmas-Tree Cookies

*3 tbs. honey * 4 whole cloves * 1/4 tbs. cinnamon * 1 tbs. water * 2 2/3 cups flour * 1 1/2 tbs. fat * 5 tbs. sugar * lemon peel * 1 egg * 1/3 oz. backing soda * 2 tbs. boiled water * fat for greasing cookie sheet * 1/2 egg for brushing*

Brown honey with cloves and cinnamon, add 1 tablespoon of water, cool. Cut fat into flour, combine with sugar and lemon peel, mix with honey, knead with egg, and combine thoroughly, chill for half an hour.

Chill 2 tablespoons of boiled water, mix with soda, add to dough, combine.
Roll out to 1/5 inch thickness, cut out with small cookie cutter, place on
greased cookie sheet not too close together.
Brush with egg, bake in very hot oven.
After cooling, the cookies may be iced with colored frosting.

Gingerbread without Honey

*3 tbs. water * 1 1/4 cups sugar * 1 cup water * 4 1/2 cups rye or wheat
flour * 1 egg * cloves * 1/2 tsp. cinnamon * 4 1/2 tsp. baking powder *
* fat for greaising pan*

Prepare a dark caramel with one half sugar and 3 tbs. water.
Dissolve the second half of sugar in 1 cup boiling water, combine carefully
with caramel, bring to the boil, cool.
Prepare dough with flour, diluted sugar, egg, add cloves and cinnamon,
knead dough.
Sprinkle baking powder into dough, blend.
Grease pan with fat, sprinkle with flour.
Place dough on greased pan and bake in well-heated oven (1 hour), remove
and cool propped against side of flour board.

Gingerbread with Carrots

*2 cups raw carrots * 4 cups wheat or rye flour * 1 cup sugar * 2 eggs *
* 1 tsp. cinnamon and cloves * 1 tsp. baking powder*

Clean carrots, grate finely.
Add flour, sugar, eggs, spices and baking powder, blend.
Grease pan, place dough in pan, even out, bake in well-heated oven. Turn
out of pan, cool.

Gingerbread with Browned Honey

*1 cup honey * cloves * cinnamon * nutmeg * 3 tbs. water * 5 oz. dried
fruits (raisins, nuts, orange peel, dates, figs, etc.) * fat for greasing pan *
* 3 tbs. fat * 5 egg yolks * 1 cup sugar * 5 egg whites * 4 1/2 cups flour *
* lemon peel * 1/3 oz. baking soda * 3 tbs. preboiled cold water*

Brown honey with spices, add 3 tablespoons of water, cool.
Rinse dried fruits, chop nuts, dates, figs and orange peel.

Cream fat with egg yolks, sugar and honey.

Beat egg whites.

Combine egg whites with yolk mixture, add flour, add lemon peel, mix, knead for 20 minutes.

Dissolve baking soda in preboiled cold water, add to dough, add dried fruits, mix with hands, place in greased pan (bake 3/4—1 hour in moderate oven).

When the cake begins to brown, cover with paper.

After an hour, test with caketester. If dry after removing from cake, remove cake from oven, allow to cool in pan for a while.

Then cut with knife from sides of pan, turn out carefully, and cool propped against the side of flour board.

The gingerbread may be decorated with chocolate icing.

Gingerbread Layer Cake

Christmas Cake

D o u g h: *1 cup honey * 1 tsp. cloves * cinnamon * lemon peel * 3 tbs. preboiled water * 3 tbs. fat * 5 egg yolks * 1 cup sugar * 5 egg whites * * 4 1/2 cups flour * 1/3 oz. baking soda * 3 tbs. preboiled water * fat for greasing pan * F i l l i n g f o r l a y e r 1: 10 oz. thick cherry or raspberry marmalade * F i l l i n g f o r l a y e r 2: 3 oz. figs *5 oz. raisins * 5 oz. orange peel * 1 cup drained fruit preserves * 1 cup walnuts * chocolate frosting*

Brown honey with spices, add 3 tablespoons of water, cool.

Prepare dough. Cream fat, add yolks, sugar and honey.

Beat egg whites.

Add flour and egg whites to creamed yolk and sugar mixture, mix and knead for 20 minutes.

Dissolve baking soda in preboiled cold water.

Add soda to dough, knead, divide dough in 3 parts, and bake in 3 rectangular greased pans of same size.

Prepare filling for layer 1. Heat up marmalade, mix.

Prepare filling for layer 2. Wash figs and raisins, dry in towel. Cube figs and orange peel, mix figs with peel, raisins and preserves into thick mixture, add coarsely-chopped nuts; if mixture is too dry, add a little syrup from the preserves.

Spread the first layer with hot marmalade, cover with second layer, fit carefully, then spread with second filling, spread evenly with knife, and cover with third layer.

Place flour board on top of gingerbread and some ligth weight (about 1 1/4 lb.) and set aside for a day so that the layers adhere to each other. Spread surface with thin layer of chocolate frosting.

TORTES

Spice Torte

D o u g h: *1 cup fat * 2 eggs * 1 3/4 cups powdered sugar * 1 cup milk * * 3 cups flour * salt * 4 1/2 tsp. baking powder * 1 tsp. cinnamon * 1/4 tsp. nutmeg * butter for greasing cake pan * S p r e a d: 4 1/2 tbs. butter (or cocoa butter) * 1 1/2 cups powdered sugar * 3 tbs. cocoa * 3 tbs. ground coffee (or 1 tbs. instant coffee dissolved in 4 tbs. water)*

Prepare dough. Cream fat, add one egg at a time, sugar, milk, blend thoroughly.
Add rest of ingredients, mix with spoon.
Pour into greased cake pan, bake in well-heated oven (1 hour).
Prepare spread. Cream buter, adding gradually sugar, cocoa and ground coffee.
Cool torte, spread filling over surface and sides of cake, remove to platter, decorate.

Cocoa Torte

D o u g h: *4 1/2 tbs. butter * 3 egg yolks * 1 cup sugar * 4 tbs. cocoa * * 1 cup milk * 3 egg whites * 3 cups flour * 4 1/2 tsp. baking powder * * butter for greasing cake pan * F i l l i n g: 1 1/4 cups sugar * 2 eggs * * 2 1/2 tbs. cocoa * 1 cup butter * 1 tbs. rum * few tbs. syrup from preserves * 2 tbs. boiling water*

Prepare dough. Cream fat with egg yolks and sugar, add cocoa, combine, add milk.
Beat egg whites, fold into yolk mixture, add flour and baking powder, mix, pour into greased cake pan, bake in well-heated oven (1 hour), be careful not to burn.
Prepare filling. Beat eggs and sugar over steam, add cocoa, remove from steam, mix while cooling.
Cream butter, add beaten, cooled eggs and rum, mix; divide filling in two parts.
Cut torte in two, pour preserve syrup diluted with warm watet and rum over cut sides of cake.

Spread half the filling over one half of the cake, cover with the second layer, even the sides of the cake.

Spread the second half of the filling over top and sides of torte, decorate, remove to a cake plate (use three knives).

Instead of butter filling, the cake may be filled with tart, aromatic marmalade.

Crispy Torte with Apricot Filling

D o u g h: *2 1/2 cups flour * 1 cup butter * 7 tbs. powdered sugar * 3 egg yolks * A p r i c o t f i l l i n g: 4 egg whites * 1 1/2 cups granulated sugar * 1 cup apricot marmalade * lemon juice*

Cut butter into flour, combine with sugar.

Add egg yolks, knead dough, set aside.

Divide dough into 5 parts, place in 5 greased cake pans of the same size and bake to light golden color.

Prepare filling. Beat egg whites, add sugar gradually, mix, adding hot apricot marmalade and lemon juice to taste, combine thoroughly.

Spread filling on layers and put one on another, spread on top and over sides, place on cake plate.

Serve in a few hours.

Crispy Torte with Coffee-Cream Filling

D o u g h: *1 1/4 cups almonds * 10 tbs. butter * 1 egg * 3/4 cup powdered sugar * 1 1/3 cups flour * F i l l i n g: 4 egg yolks * 1/2 cup sugar * 3 tbs. flour * 1/2 cup milk * a few spoons of strong coffee * C o f f e e f r o s t i n g: 1 1/4 cups sugar * 1/2 cup water * 1/3 cream of tartar * * coffee*

Prepare dough. Blanch almonds, peel, dry, grind finely.

Cream butter in bowl, add whole egg, and sugar gradually, combine with almonds, mix well, add flour, mix.

Divide dough in 3 parts and bake 3 cakes in the same size cake pans.

Remove on to board after baking.

Prepare filling. Cream egg yolks with sugar, mix with flour and beat over steam, adding boiling milk first and when the mixture begins to thicken, add hot coffee gradually, beat vigorously.

When the filling is the desired thickness, remove from steam and mix while cooling.

Spread filling over the baked layers and put one on the another. Ice with coffee-cream frosting the next day.

Crispy Torte with Chocolate-Cream Filling

D o u g h: *1 cup almonds * 1/2 cup butter * 3 egg yolks * 1/2 cup powdered sugar * 4 oz. chocolate * vanilla * 4 egg whites * 1 1/3 cups flour * F i l l i n g: 3/4 cup butter * 2 egg yolks * 1/2 cup powdered sugar * 5 oz. chocolate*

Wipe almonds and grind.

Cream butter, adding egg yolks one at a time and gradually adding the sugar, softened chocolate and almonds. Add vanilla last.

Beat egg whites, combine half with almond mixture. Then sprinkle with flour while mixing in the rest of the beaten egg whites.

Grease two cake pans and sprinkle with flour.

Divide dough in two parts and bake two cakes.

Prepare filling. Cream butter, adding egg yolks and sugar.

Add the softened chocolate gradually to the butter while mixing. Remove to cool place. Spread the filling on the cooled cake, cover with the other cake, even sides and spread chocolate filling on top.

Crispy Torte with Chestnut Filling

D o u g h: *5 oz. chocolate * 1/2 cup almonds * 10 tbs. butter * 4 egg yolks * 3/4 cup powdered sugar * lemon peel * 4 egg whites * 8 tbs. flour * butter for greasing pans * F i l l i n g: 2 lbs. chestnuts (unpeeled) * * 3/4 cup milk * 1 cup butter * 1 cup sugar * vanilla * V a n i l l a f r o s t - i n g: 1 1/4 cups sugar * 1/2 cup water * 1/3 tsp. cream of tartar * vanilla*

Prepare dough. Wipe almonds in a towel, grind together with chocolate.

Melt butter (do not brown). Cream butter adding egg yolks one at a time and then gradually add sugar, add lemon peel at end.

Beat egg whites stiff, fold into yolks, add flour, almonds and chocolate, mix all ingredients lightly.

Divide dough in two parts, pour into two greased cake pans and bake in slow oven (chocolate burns easily) for about 3/4 hour.

Remove layers after baking, cool.

Prepare filling. Rinse chestnuts, pour over with boiling water and parboil, drain off water when chestnuts are easy to peel.

Peel chestnuts, pour over with boiling milk and cook over very low heat (cooking over steam is recommended for they burn easily); when ready, the chestnuts must be the consistency of mashed potatoes but very fluffy. Strain chestnuts through sieve, cool.

Cream butter with sugar, add strained chestnuts gradually, add vanilla, mix thoroughly.

Spread chestnut filling over one cake, cover with other.
Spread filling over sides of torte and remove to cold place.
Ice torte with vanilla frosting, decorate.

Linzer Torte

*1 cup almonds * 1 cup butter * 3 1/4 cups flour * 1/2 cup powdered
sugar * 6 egg yolks * lemon peel * a pinch of crushed cloves * nutmeg *
* 1 cup red-currant or raspberry jelly*

Prepare dough. Wipe almonds in a towel, grind.
Cut butter into flour, combine with sifted sugar, almonds and hard-boiled
egg yolks, lemon peel, cloves, nutmeg, knead dough, and when all ingredients are combined, remove to cold place. Grease bottom of rectangular pan with three sides.
Divide dough in 2 parts, roll out to fit pan, roll up on rolling pin, roll out
on bottom of pan, even out, brush with egg.
Divide the rest of the dough into a few parts, shaping them into thin rolls,
and place criss-cross on top, brush with egg.
Place in moderate oven and bake to light gold.
Remove from pan and cool on board.
Immediately before serving, spoon red current jelly into hollows formed
by criss-cross design.

Poppy-Seed Torte

D o u g h: *1 cup flour * 6 1/2 tbs. buter * 3 tbs. sugar * 2 egg yolks *
* P o p p y - s e e d t o p p i n g: 10 oz. poppy seeds * egg yolks * 1 1/2
cups sugar * lemon peel * 8 tbs. orange peel * 8 egg whites * 3 tbs. bread
crumbs * F r o s t i n g: 1 1/4 cups sugar * 1/2 cup water * 1/3 tsp. cream
of tartar * lemon juice*

Prepare crispy dough. Cut butter into flour, combine with sugar, add egg
yolks, knead.
When all the ingredients are combined, set dough aside.
Place the dough on the bottom of a cake pan, bake in moderate oven
browning lightly.
Pour boiling water over poppy seeds, cover.
When the poppy seeds break when preseed between the fingers, drain
through sieve thoroughly.
Grind poppy seeds 3 times in food chopper.
Cream egg yolks with sugar until white, add lemon and orange peel, the
ground poppy seeds, mix.

Beat egg whites, fold into yolks, add bread crumbs, mix lightly.
Place mixture on crispy layer, place in moderate oven, bake (3/4 hour).
Prepare frosting the next day. Make a thick, smooth syrup from sugar, water and cream of tartar, cream; when it whitens, add lemon juice.
Pour warm frosting over torte, decorate.

Sponge Cake (Torte Layers)

Line bottom of springform cake pan with paper.
Separate egg whites from yolks, squeeze lemon juice.
Cream yolks with sugar until white, add lemon juice.
Beat egg whites until stiff, place on top of yolks, add flour, blend entire mixture carefully so as not to break up egg whites.
Batter should only reach halfway to top of pan.
Preheat oven and bake in slow oven. Dough should not shrink from sides of pan nor should the top be dry.
Place on board, when removed from oven, loosen sides of cake from cake pan with a knife, place cake and cake pan on small inverted pot, push out cake together with bottom of cake pan, remove ring, cover with bottom of another spring cake pan, invert, remove bottom and paper, set aside to cool.
After cooling, invert once again on to bottom of spring cake pan, set aside until the next day.
Cut in half or in three parts on the next day with a sharp knife or cord, spread with filling, frost and decorate.

Sponge-Cake Torte with Vanilla-Cream Filling

*60 lady fingers * a few spoons of red currant or other jelly * C r e a m f i l l i n g: 5 egg yolks * 1/2 cup sugar * 1 cup boiling milk * vanilla * *1 cup butter * F r o s t i n g: 3/4 cup powdered sugar * 1 tbs. boiling water * 1 1/2 tbs. butter * lemon juice*

Beat egg yolks and sugar over steam, steam with boiled milk and beat until thick, add vanilla, cool.
Cream butter, add the cooled egg yolks gradually while creaming.
Place lady fingers in cake pan, arrange so that the entire bottom and sides of the pan are covered, cut fingers where necessary, spread jelly over lady fingers.
Place a layer of cream alternately with a layer of lady fingers, spreading thinly with jelly, place a layer of lady fingers on top.

Press the torte with a disc, weight lightly, chill for a few hours.
Prepare frosting. Pour boiling water over sugar, mix thoroughly with butter and lemon juice, pour over torte, decorate.

Coffee Sponge Torte

D o u g h: *8 egg yolks * 1 1/2 cups sugar * juice of 1 lemon * 9 egg whites * 1 1/2 cups flour * F i l l i n g: 1/2 cup strong coffee * 4 egg yolks * 1 cup sugar * 1 cup butter * C o f f e e   f r o s t i n g: 1 1/4 cups sugar * 1/2 cup water * 1/3 tsp. cream of tartar * coffee*

Prepare dough. Line bottom of spring cake pan with paper.
Cream egg yolks with sugar. Add lemon juice.
Beat egg whites, place on yolks, add flour, mix, pour into cake pan, bake in moderate oven (about 3/4 hour); remove from cake pan, remove paper.
Prepare filling. Brew coffee (about 1/2 cup).
Beat egg yolks and sugar over steam; when it thickens, add coffee, mix, and evaporate a little, beating over steam. Remove steamed, thickened yolks from steam, cool while mixing.
Cream butter until fluffy, add the cooled yolks gradually, combine (if the aroma of the filling is too bland, add a few drops of coffee or a little instant coffee).
Cut cake into 3 layers, sprinkle liberally with the diluted sweet-coffee brew, spread filling between layers, even sides, dust off crumbs, spread sides with filling.
Prepare frosting. Make a thick, smooth syrup of sugar, water and cream of tartar, cream; when it turns white, tint with coffee.
Pour the warm frosting over the cake, set aside to cool.
Remove torte next day to cake plate, decorate.

Sponge Torte with Hazelnut Filling

D o u g h: *8 egg yolks * 1/4 cup sugar * juice-of 1 lemon * 9 egg whites * * 1 1/2 cups flour * F i l l i n g: 1/2 lb. hazelnuts (shelled) * 1 1/4 cups powdered sugar * vanilla * 1/2 cup thick sour cream * V a n i l l a   f r o s t - i n g: 1 1/4 cups sugar * 1/2 cup water * 1/3 tsp. cream of   tartar * * vanilla*

Line cake pan with paper.
Prepare dough. Cream yolks with sugar, add lemon juice.
Beat egg whites, place on yolks, add flour, fold in lightly.
Place in cake pan, bake to light gold color, remove from cake pan, remove paper. Set aside till next day.

Prepare filling. Brown nuts to golden color, clean off peel in towel, grind with sugar.

Cream nuts in a bowl, add vanilla and enough sour cream to make spreading easy.

Cut cake in 3 parts, spread 2 layers with filling, put one on another, spread filling on sides, brush off crumbs.

Prepare frosting. Make a thick, smooth syrup from sugar, water and cream of tartar, cream until white, add vanilla.

Ice the torte with warm frosting, spread frosting on sides.

Remove to cake plate, decorate.

Sponge Torte with Walnut Filling

D o u g h: *8 egg yolks * 1 1/4 cups sugar * juice of 1 lemon * 9 egg whites * 1 1/2 cups flour * Filling: 1 cup powdered sugar * 2 1/3 cups walnuts * 1 cup butter * vanilla * Vanilla frosting: 1 1/4 cups sugar * 1/2 cup water * 1/3 tsp. cream of tartar * vanilla*

Line cake pan with paper.

Prepare dough. Cream egg yolks with sugar, add lemon juice.

Beat egg whites, place on egg yolks, add flour, fold in lightly.

Place dough in baking pan, bake in moderate oven, remove from pan, remove paper.

Prepare filling. Select walnuts, grind together with sugar.

Cream butter until fluffy, add grated nuts and vanilla.

Cut each cake into 3 parts. Spread with filling, place one on top of the other, even sides, dust off crumbs.

Prepare frosting. Prepare a thick, smooth syrup from sugar, water and cream of tartar, cream and when it turns white, add vanilla.

Ice the torte with warm frosting, spread around sides, decorate.

Remove to cake plate.

Sponge Punch Torte

D o u g h: *8 egg yolks * 1 1/4 cups sugar * 1 lemon (juice and peel) * 9 egg whites * 1 1/2 cups flour * syrup for sprinkling layers * Filling: 2 1/4 cups almonds * 1 1/4 cups powdered sugar * 3 tbs. rum * lemon juice * *Punch frosting: 1 1/2 cups sugar * 1/2 cup water * 1/3 tsp. cream of tartar * juice of 1 lemon * 1 tbs. rum*

Line cake pan with paper.

Prepare dough. Cream yolks with sugar, add lemon juice.

Beat egg whites, place on yolks, add flour, fold in lightly.

389

Place dough in cake pan, bake in moderate oven, remove from cake pan, remove paper.
Prepare filling. Blanch almonds, peel, dry (do not brown).
Grind finely together with sugar.
Cream the almonds with sugar in a bowl, add rum and lemon juice, if necessary add a little boiling water so that filling is not too thick.
Cut cake in 3, sprinkle layers with syrup, spread thin filling between layers, even sides, brush off crumbs.
Prepare frosting. Prepare a smooth, thick syrup from sugar, water and cream of tartar, cream, add lemon juice and rum.
Ice torte with warm frosting, spread around sides.
Remove to cake plate, decorate.

Dobosz Torte

Stefanka

D o u g h: *8 egg yolks * 1/2 cup sugar * 8 egg whites * 1 cup potato starch * butter for greasing cake pans * * F i l l i n g: 4 egg yolks * 3/4 cup sugar * 4 oz. chocolate * 3/4 cup butter*

Prepare dough. Cream egg yolks with sugar.
Beat egg whites, place on yolks, add potato starch, fold in.
Grease 2 shallow rectangular baking pans with butter. Place dough in pans. Bake.
Remove from pans. Cool.
Prepare filling. Cream egg yolks with sugar, add melted chocolate gradually, cool.
Cream butter until fluffy, combine with chocolate mixture.
Spread chocolate filling between layers, spread over sides and on top.

Sacher Torte

D o u g h: *3/4 cup butter * 10 egg yolks * 1 1/2 cups sugar * 12 tbs. cocoa * 10 egg whites * 1 cup flour * butter for greasing cake pan * * S p r e a d: 1 cup raspberry or red currant marmolade * C h o c o l a t e g l a z e: 7 1/2 oz chocolate * 3 tbs. butter * 3 tbs. boiling water*

Prepare dough. Melt butter, clarify and cream in bowl, adding egg yolks one at a time and sugar gradually, combine with cocoa, mix thoroughly.
Beat egg whites until stiff, place on yolks, add flour and fold in lightly, pour into greased cake pan and bake in slow oven. Bake slowly. If necessary, cover top of cake with paper during baking to avoid burning.

Remove baked tort, cool and spread with thick, well-heated marmalade.
Prepare glaze. Melt chocolate together with butter in a double boiler.
Add water gradually to heated chocolate, creaming vigorously. When the
mixture has a uniform texture, cook over low heat to thread stage; stir
constantly while cooking.
When the glaze begins "to pull", remove from heat and pour over the
torte. Decorate torte.

Macaroon Dough (Layers for Tortes)

Line bottom of cake pans with paper, bake cake in 2 or 3 cake pans; ma-
caroon layers cannot be cut after baking, since they crumble.
Blanch almonds, peel, dry and grind.
If chocolate is to be one of the ingredients of the dough, grind.
Separate whites from yolks, cream yolks with sugar until white.
Beat egg whites stiff, place on yolks, sprinkle in almonds, bread crumbs,
ground chocolate, fold in carefully with spatula, do not break.
Place in cake pans, dividing dough in even parts.
Place in pre-heated, slow oven; dough should not shrink from sides of
cake pan nor the top be dry.
Place baked layers on board, loosen sides from cake pan, place the cake
in cake pan on a small pot, push out cake together with bottom of cake
pan, remove ring from spring cake pan, place the bottom of another cake
pan on top, invert, remove bottom and paper.

Brown-Bread Torte

*3/4 cup almonds or nuts * 3 oz. chocolate * 3—4 tbs. brown rye
bread * 4 tbs. orange peel * 8 egg whites * 4 1/2 tbs. butter * 8 egg
yolks * 3/4 cup sugar * lemon peel * chocolate frosting or raspberry
jelly * grated chocolate for sprinkling*

Prepare dough. Wipe almonds in a towel, grind together with chocolate.
Slice rye bread into thin slices, dry, brown, crush and sift.
Dice orange peel.
Beat egg whites stiff.
Cream butter, adding one egg at a time and sugar gradually, at the end
combine with lemon and orange peel.
Place egg whites on yolks, sprinkle with almonds and grated chocolate
and the bread, combine with a spatula.

Place dough in greased pan lined with paper, even out and place in oven. Bake until cake shrinks from sides of pan and springs back when pressed with finger, remove from oven. Remove from pans, cool.

Ice with chocolate frosting or spread with raspberry jelly and sprinkle with grated chocolate.

Hazelnut Torte

D o u g h: *3 oz. hazelnuts * 3/4 cup almonds * 8 egg yolks * 1 1/4 cups sugar * 10 egg whites * 3 tbs. bread crumbs * F i l l i n g: 1/2 cup strong coffee * 1 cup butter * 2 egg yolks * 3/4 cup powdered sugar * * C o f f e e f r o s t i n g: 1 1/4 cups sugar * 1/3 tsp. cream of tartar * * 1/2 cup water * coffee*

Line 3 pans of uniform size with paper.
Prepare dough. Grind almonds and nuts.
Cream egg yolks with sugar.
Beat egg whites stiff, place on yolks, combine with almonds, nuts and bread crumbs.
Place in cake pans, bake in slow oven, remove from pans and remove paper.
Prepare filling. Prepare strongly-brewed coffee (1/2 cup).
Cream butter until fluffy, add egg yolks and sugar, cream, adding coffee gradually. Spread filling between layers, even, brush off crumbs.
Prepare frosting. Prepare a thick, smooth syrup from sugar, cream of tartar and water; when it begins to whiten, tint with coffee.
Ice the torte with frosting, spread on the sides.
Arrange on cake plate. Decorate.

Walnut Torte

D o u g h: *5 egg whites * 3 tbs. orange peel * 1 1/2 cups walnuts * * 5 egg yolks * 12 tbs. sugar * 1 tbs. bread crumbs * N u t f i l l i n g: 1 1/2 cups walnuts * 1 1/2 cups powdered sugar * vanilla * 3—4 tbs. sour cream * V a n i l l a f r o s t i n g: 1 1/4 cups sugar * 1/2 cup water * 1/3 tsp. cream of tartar * vanilla * C o f f e e f i l l i n g: see page 395 * C o f f e e f r o s t i n g: 1 1/4 cups sugar * 1/2 cup water * * 1/3 tsp. cream of tartar * coffee*

Beat egg whites until stiff.
Select nuts, grind.
Dice orange peel fine.
Cream egg yolks with sugar, add orange peel, place beaten egg whites on yolks, combine egg yolks with egg whites, nuts and bread crumbs.

Pour into cake pan lined with paper, place in moderate oven for 3/4 hour.
Prepare filling the following day. Grind walnuts and sugar together, add
vanilla and enough sour cream to make the filling easy to spread.
Cut the torte in three, spread filling between layers.
Prepare vanilla frosting, ice the top and sides of the torte. Sprinkle
coarsely-chopped walnuts on the sides.
Coffee or chocolate-cream filling may be used to fill the torte.
Ice the torte with the suitable frosting (coffee or chocolate).

Great-Grandmother Torte

D o u g h: *2 1/4 cups almonds * 8 egg yolks * 1 1/4 cups sugar * 10 egg
whites * 3 1/2 tbs. bread crumbs * F i l l i n g: 1/2 lb. hazelnuts * 1 1/4
cups powdered sugar * vanilla * 1/2 cup sour cream * V a n i l l a
f r o s t i n g: 1 1/4 cups sugar * 1/2 cup water * 1/3 tsp. cream of
tartar * vanilla*

Line 3 cake pans with paper.
Prepare dough. Blanch almonds, skin, grind.
Cream egg yolks with sugar.
Beat egg whites stiff, place on yolks, add almonds and bread crumbs,
combine.
Pour into cake pans, bake in moderate oven.
Prepare filling. Brown hazelnuts, wipe in towel, peel, grind twice together
with sugar.
Cream nuts with sugar in a bowl, add vanilla and enough cream so that
the mixture is easy to spread.
Turn cake out of cake pan, remove paper, cool.
Spread filling between layers, even edges, fill uneven edges with filling.
Prepare frosting. Prepare a thick, smooth syrup, cream; when it begins to
turn white, add vanilla.
Frost the torte, spread over sides.
Remove to cake plate on three knives, decorate.

Chocolate Torte

D o u g h: *1 3/4 cups almonds * 5 oz. chocolate * 4 tbs. orange peel *
* lemon peel * 12 egg yolks * 1 cup sugar * 8 egg whites * fat for
greasing pan * C h o c o l a t e f r o s t i n g: 1/2 cup sugar * 3 tbs.
water * 1/3 tsp. cream of tartar * 3 oz. chocolate*

Wipe almonds in towel, grind with skin.
Grind chocolate.

Chop orange peel, grate lemon peel.

Grease a long mold thoroughly (if posible with semicircular bottom).

Cream egg yolks with sugar, combine with lemon and orange peel.

Beat egg whites stiff, place on yolks, fold in all ingredients using a spatula.

Pour into pan, bake in low oven, remove carefully, cool.

Prepare frosting. Prepare a thick, smooth syrup, cream; when it begins to, turn white, add melted chocolate gradually; if necessary, dilute with water. Pour the warm frosting over torte; when dry, decorate with chopped almonds in two rows — lengthwise.

Two-Color Almond Torte

D o u g h: *2 1/4 cups almonds * 10 egg yolks * 1 1/4 cups sugar * * 10 egg whites * 4 oz. chocolate * S p r e a d: 1 1/4 cups almond, raspberry or red currant marmalade * C h o c o l a t e   f r o s t i n g: 1 cup sugar * 1/2 cup water * 1/3 tsp. cream of tartar * 4 oz. chocolate*

Line cake pan with paper.

Blanch almonds, peel, grind.

Cream egg yolks with sugar.

Beat egg whites stiff, place on yolks, add almonds, combine all ingredients. Pour half the dough into cake pan, mix the other half with the ground chocolate, place the latter on top of light layer, spread evenly, bake 3/4 to 1 hour.

After baking, loosen cake from sides of cake pan with thin sharp knife, invert pan, remove paper, cool.

Spread thick hot marmalade on top of torte.

Prepare frosting. Prepare a thick, smooth syrup with sugar, water and cream of tartar, cream; when it begins to turn white, add melted chocolate gradually, stir. If necessary dilute with a few drops of boiling water.

When the marmalade cools, pour warm chocolate frosting over torte.

Place on cake plate (with the help of 2 or 3 knives), decorate.

Polish Chocolate Torte

D o u g h: *2 1/4 cups almonds * 7 1/2 oz. chocolate * 12 egg yolks * * 1 cup sugar * 12 egg whites * 3 tbs. water * F i l l i n g: 2 1/4 cups almonds * 1 1/4 cups sugar * 1/2 cup water * juice of 1 1/2 lemons * * vanilla * C h o c o l a t e   f r o s t i n g: 1 cup sugar * 1/2 cup water * * 1/3 tsp. cream of tartar * 4 oz. chocolate*

Grease two cake pans, line with paper.

Prepare dough. Wipe almonds in towel, grind with skins.

Grind chocolate.

Cream egg yolks with sugar.

Beat egg whites stiff, place on yolks, combine all ingredients, sprinkling in the water.

Pour dough into two cake pans, bake in well-heated oven, cover cake with paper while baking so that it does not brown too much.

Prepare filling. Blanch almonds, dry, grind. Prepare a thick, smooth syrup from sugar and water.

Add almonds to boiling syrup, mix, place in a bowl, stir with stick until cool, add vanilla, and lemon juice to taste.

Filling should be easy to spread. Spread filling between layers (when cooled), even edges, brush off crumbs.

Prepare frosting. Prepare a thick syrup from sugar, water and cream of tartar, cream; when mixture begins to turn white, add melted chocolate gradually. If necessary, add a few drops of boiling water to dilute syrup.

Pour warm frosting over torte, spread on sides.

Place on cake plate, decorate.

Mocha Almond Torte

D o u g h: *4 1/2 cups almonds * 12 egg whites * 2 1/3 cups powdered sugar * C o f f e e   f i l l i n g: 1 1/2 cups powdered sugar * 2 egg yolks * * 1 1/2 cups strong coffee * 1 1/3 cups butter * C o f f e e   f r o s t i n g: 2 cups sugar * 3/4 cup water * 5 tsp. cream of tartar * coffee*

Line 3 cake pans with paper, grease paper.

Prepare dough. Blanch almonds, peel, dry, grind.

Beat egg whites stiff, add sugar gradually, combine with almonds using a spatula.

Pour dough into cake pans, bake in moderate, well-preheated oven, do not overbrown.

Turn out of pan, remove paper.

Prepare filling. Cream egg yolks with sugar, beat over steam, adding brewed coffee gradually, cool.

Cream butter, when foamy add egg-yolk mixture, mix.

Spread filling between layers, even sides, brush off crumbs.

Prepare frosting. Prepare a thick, smooth syrup from sugar, water and cream of tartar, stir; when it begins to turn white, dilute with coffee.

Frost torte, spread on sides.

Sprinkle the ground almonds on the damp sides of the torte.

Place on cake plate, decorate.

Gâteau de Provence

Dough: *1 3/4 cups almonds * 5 egg yolks * 1 cup sugar * 5 egg whites * Filling: 3 1/2 cups almonds * 2 1/4 cups butter * 2 1/2 cups powdered sugar * vanilla * Vanilla frosting: 1 1/4 cups sugar * 1/2 cup water * 1/3 tsp. cream of tartar * vanilla * lemon juice*

Line rectangular cake pan with paper, grease.
Prepare dough. Blanch almonds, grind.
Cream egg yolks with sugar.
Beat egg whites stiff, place on yolks, add almonds, mix.
Pour into cake pan, spread about 1/3 inch thick, bake in slow oven, cover with paper so that the cake does not brown too much. After baking, turn out cake on board, remove paper.
Prepare filling. Blanch almonds, brown to light golden color, cool, grind.
Cream butter, add sugar, almonds, vanilla, mix, set aside.
Cut cake in two, spread filling between both parts, spread filling on sides, brush off crumbs from top.
Prepare frosting. Prepare a thick, smooth syrup from sugar, water and cream of tartar, cream; when it begins to turn white, add vanilla and lemon juice, mix.
Pour the frosting over top of torte, allow frosting to run over on the sides, forming a festoon with the frosting.
Place on cake plate, decorate.

Chestnut Torte

Dough: *2 1/4 cups almonds * 1 1/4 cups granulated sugar * 12 egg whites * 2 tbs. butter for greasing pan * 3 tbs. bread crumbs for pan * * Filling: 2 lbs. chestnuts * 3/4 cup milk * 1 cup sugar * 1 cup butter * vanilla * Punch frosting: see page 389*

Prepare dough. Blanch almonds, peel, dry in slow oven, grind.
Beat egg whites stiff, adding sugar gradually; when all sugar has been added, mix with almonds.
Grease two cake pans with butter, sprinkle with bread crumbs.
Divide dough in two. Pour into cake pans, bake but do not brown.
Rinse chestnuts, pour over with cold water, and cook. When they begin to burst, drain, cover and place over steam so that they burst further. Remove one at a time and shell thoroughly.
Mash the shelled chestnuts, add milk to the chestnuts, and stir while cooking. Be careful not to burn the mixture as it is very thick. (Use an asbestos plate).

When the chestnuts are very soft, add sugar to taste, strain through sieve, cool.

Cream butter; when foamy, add chestnuts gradually, add vanilla and mix well.

Divide the filling into three parts. Spread two parts between the layers. Place a light weight on top so that the layers stick together. Add 2—3 tablespoons of cream to the rest of the filling, mix and spread over the top and sides of the torte or ice with punch frosting.

Decorate with colored decorations, sprinkle coarsely-chopped almonds on the sides.

Fedora Torte

D o u g h: *1 cup almonds * 6 egg whites * 1 1/4 cups powdered sugar * * juice of 1/2 lemon * F i l l i n g 1: 9 oz. chocolate * 2 1/4 cups butter * 1 1/4 cups powdered sugar * vanilla * F i l l i n g 2: 1 1/4 cups sugar * 1/2 cup water * 1 cup almonds * vanilla * lemon juice*

Line cake pan with paper.

Blanch all almonds, peel, dry, grind and divide in two parts.

Beat egg whites stiff, combine with part of almonds (1 cup), sugar and lemon juice with a spatula.

Place dough into cake pan, bake in slow oven; cover after a while so that the cake does not overbrown.

Prepare filling 1. Melt chocolate over steam.

Cream butter till foamy, add melted chocolate gradually, add sugar and vanilla, mix and chill.

Prepare filling 2. Prepare a syrup from sugar and water, add almonds (1 cup), mix, place in a bowl; mix, adding vanilla and lemon juice so that the filling spreads easily.

Divide chocolate filling in half.

Spread half the chocolate filling on torte, cover with the almond filling, then cover with the other half of chocolate filling. Spread chocolate filling on sides.

Remove to cake plate, chill.

Decorate with almonds and orange peel.

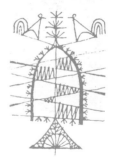

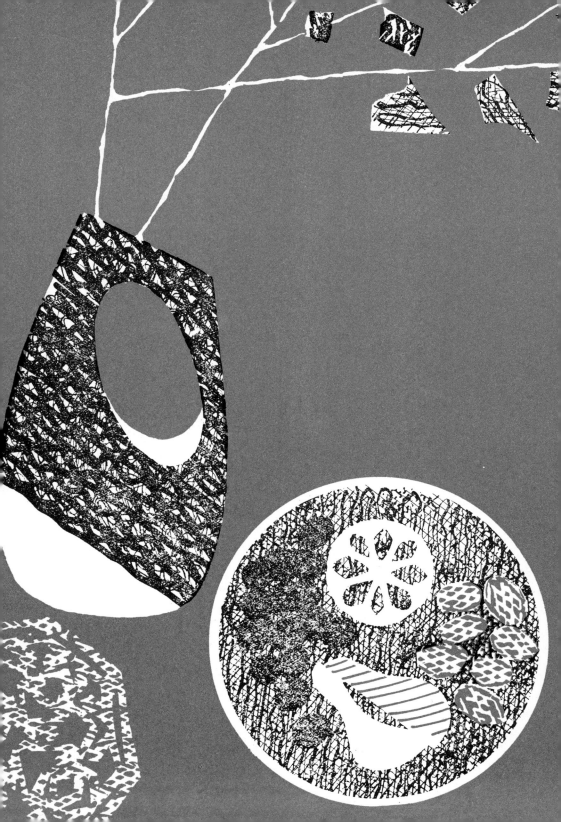

DESSERTS

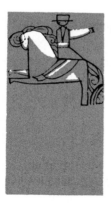

Products used in the making of desserts as well as the methods of their preparation are very varied. In general, desserts may be divided into two main groups: cold or hot.

Cold desserts are usually prepared, in Poland, with fruits, milk, sweet and sour cream and eggs. Some of these are served after chilling. They are made with gelatine or their firm texture is achieved by other thickening agents. They will be described in a separate group of recipes.

Hot desserts are usually made with dough, with the addition of egg yolks and beaten egg whites. The beaten eggs combine during intensive heat (steamed, baked or fried) giving the dessert the desired light and fluffy texture.

Dishes made with rice, farina and tapioca used for preparing cold and hot, sweet desserts are very cheap and nourishing when cleverly combined with fruits. We achieve the same results with hot desserts by using cooked or fried pastries filled with fruits, marmalade, cheese or sweetened poppy seeds, etc.

We are also acquainted with and use other desserts which are more complicated to prepare, such as puddings, soufflés and various lightly-baked products which are made up of costly ingredients with a large amount of eggs and butter.

Many of these widely-used sweet dishes are known as "traditional cooking", and are connected with various holidays and celebrations. The recipes are included in the book with adequate notes and descriptions on how to serve them.

FRESH FRUIT

Fresh fruit make the simplest and healthiest dessert. Most popular in Poland are raw berries, aromatic and beautiful in color, which may be served with sweetened whipped cream, sour cream or vanilla sauce. Fruit salads are not particularly recommended, as cut fruits when in contact with air swiftly lose their color and aroma as well as their nutritious value. This may be counteracted by sprinkling the cut fruit with lemon juice and mixing with the juice, with syrup made of sugar or with cream.

Strawberries with Cream

*2 cups strawberries * 4 tbs. powdered sugar * 1 cup sweet cream * 3 tbs. powdered sugar for cream * uncooked strawberry juice*

Rinse strawberries, drain and remove stems.
Place in refrigerator.
Beat chilled cream and mix with sugar. Arrange in portions at the center of a round, glass plate, forming into mounds.
Sprinkle strawberries with sugar and arrange on plate around the cream. Pour chilled strawberry juice on cream. Serve immediately as a chilled dessert.

Wild Strawberries with Cream

Prepare as strawberries.

Raspberries with Cream

Prepare as strawberries.

Pasteurized Apricots with Cream

*20 halves of pasteurized apricots * 1 cup juice of pasteurized apricots * * 1 cup powdered sugar * lemon juice to taste * 2 cups sweet cream * * 3 tbs. powdered sugar for cream*

Drain off juice from pasteurized apricots and mix with sugar. Place halves of apricots in mixture and store in refrigerator for a few hours.
Before preparing dessert, remove apricots from syrup. Add lemon juice to syrup if necessary.
Whip chilled cream and mix with sugar. Place in portions in center of a round, glass plate, arranging in mounds.
Arrange apricots on plate around the mounds of cream.
Pour chilled syrup over cream.

Pasteurized Peaches with Cream

Prepare in the same manner as apricots.

Pasteurized Cantaloupe with Cream

Prepare in the same manner as apricots. Add two liqueur glasses of maraschino or rum to the syrup.

Strawberries in Vanilla Sauce

*2 to 3 cups strawberries * 5 tbs. powdered sugar * 1 cup sweet light cream * 3 egg yolks * 1 egg * 3/4 cup powdered sugar for sauce * vanilla*

Rinse strawberries, remove stems, drain and place in a large compote dish. Sprinkle with sugar and let stand.
Prepare sauce. Cream egg yolks and egg with sugar and vanilla until fluffy. Bring cream to the boil, add to egg mixture one spoon at a time, beating mixture over boiling water. When sauce begins to thicken remove from water and cool, stirring so that it does not congeal on top.
Pour cold sauce over strawberries in the compote dish.

Pear Salad in Vanilla Sauce

*3 medium juicy pears * 2 cups sweet light cream * 3 egg yolks * 1 egg * * 3/4 cup sugar * vanilla*

Cream egg yolks and egg with sugar and vanilla until fluffy.

Bring cream to the boil and add to egg mixture one spoon at a time, beating over boiling water.

When sauce begins to thicken remove from boiling water and cool, stirring so that it does not congeal.

Wash and peel the pears and slice into thin pieces very quickly.

Mix with sauce immediately and serve.

Cantaloupe Salad

*2 cups sliced cantaloupe * 3/4 cup sugar * vanilla * lemon juice to taste * * 2 liqueur glasses maraschino or rum * 1/2 cup water*

Cut cantaloupe into segments, remove skin and seeds and shred into thin slices across each segment.

Arrange the cantaloupe in layers in a glass compote dish, sprinkling each layer with sugar and vanilla, and then with lemon juice, water and maraschino or rum.

Chill the salad and serve immediately.

COMPOTES AND BAKED FRUIT

A compote is a cold dessert·composed of fruit cooked in syrup and served in the syrup when cooled. Second quality fruit may be used for a compote, that is ripe fruit that is not perfect in appearance.

The fruit may be crushed, somewhat shaken and moist though without mildew and not spoiled.

Fruits with a sour and refreshing taste and a strong aroma are used for a compote. However, not all fruits that fit this description look well after they have been cooked, though the taste and aroma may be good. Strawberries may be taken as an example. They lose color when cooked and do not look delicious though the juice is very tasty. Therefore, a compote made of strawberries is prepared by covering the carefully washed fruit with cold syrup and placing them to cool for one hour. Strawberries of a dark color are used for this purpose. Raspberries add an excellent and refreshing taste and smell to dishes. We do not use them for compote for not only do they lose color when cooked, but disintegrate into an unappetizing pulp full of small seeds. Not all varieties of apples are suitable for a compote for some lose their aroma or grow discolored or have a flat taste.

Therefore, fruit suitable for a compote:
1. should possess a specific aroma,
2. should be sufficiently sour,
3. should be of a strukture which does not lose form when cooked,
4. should possess a strong color which does not change when cooked in syrup.

The most commonly used fruit in a compote are: apples, pears, sweet and sour cherries, greengage plums, blue plums. The berries used are: blueberry, bilberry, strawberry, currant, gooseberry.

Fruit which lacks color and has a flat taste, without aroma or with a bitter or too sour taste is usually combined with fruit which will offset this, thus resulting in a mixed compote. An example of a good combination are bilberries and apples or pears, currants with the juice of raspberries, etc.

We select fruit not only for its taste but also due to the vitamin content, combining fruit with a low vitamin content with fruit that are rich in vitamin C. This is highly recommended, particularly as regards plums, pears, apples and cherries which have a low vitamin content but are widely used. In order to increase the vitamin C value, it is best to select fruit that are in season simultaneously. For instance a cherry compote may be supplemented with pulp of black currants, a pear or plum compote with shepherdin berries.

Black currant pulp should be used carefully due to its specific taste and aroma. Fresh shepherdin berries creamed with sugar or covered with water give a light yellow color and should be prepared for light colored compotes.

A compote is cooked in a wide and low pot with a tight fitting cover which is not used for preparing rich foods. A pot assigned for this purpose should be made of a material which will not detract from the vitamin C content nor influence the color of the fruit.

The first step is the preparation of a syrup or a liquid of water and sugar. The second step is to prepare the fruit.

Place one layer at a time of cleaned and quartered fruit in boiling syrup with froth removed. If all fruit is placed at the same time the fruit will become pulpy for the time is too long from the moment when the fruit is placed in the water to that when it comes to the boil.

All fruit in compote should be cooked slowly in the boiling syrup. Some fruit, like apples with a delicate tissue, should be heated on a high flame when placed in the syrup, then covered, removed from the fire and left to stand for half an hour. The fruit will get done in the heat of the syrup, the apples will soften but will not fall apart and will look delicious.

Mixed fruit compote is prepared by cooking each variety of fruit separately in the same syrup. When cooked, the fruit is removed from the syrup and arranged according to variety in a compote dish. When all the varieties have been cooked they are covered with syrup and cooled. Fruit arranged according to variety looks better than mixed.

When preparing fruit that requires long cooking, or when we cook fruit in several portions, attention must be paid to the liquid in which the fruit is cooked. Remember to supplement the evaporated liquid with boiling water.

Apple Compote

*3 cups water * 1/2 cup sugar * 5 medium compote apples * lemon peel*

Rinse apples and peel. Cut apples in halves and larger apples in quarters. Core the apples. Bring water and sugar to the boil. Place one layer of apples and boil slowly, turning the quarters during cooking. Cook the apples each layer separately. If necessary add water to syrup, bring to the boil and add lemon peel.
Place apples in a compote dish, cover with syrup and cool.

Pear Compote

*3 cups water * 1/2 cup sugar * 5 medium pears * lemon juice * vanilla*

Rinse pears and peel. Cut in halves and core.
Bring water and sugar to the boil and add one layer of pears. Cook on a medium flame until tender. Turn the halves during the cooking. Cook the pears each layer separately.
At the end add lemon juice, vanilla and some boiled water to the syrup. Place pears in a compote dish, cover with syrup and cool.

Pear and Cherry Compote with Currants

*3 cups water * 3/4 cup sugar * 3 medium pears * 1/2 cup dark cherries *
* 1/2 cup black currant pulp*

Bring water and sugar to the boil.
Rinse fruit thoroughly. Peel the pears, cut in halves, core and place in boiling syrup. Place cooked pears in a compote dish.
Place cherries in syrup in which the pears were cooked. Add 3 tbs. water and cook slowly so that the fruit does not crack. Remove cherries with a draining spoon and place in compote dish with pears.

Remove stems from currants and press through sieve. Place in syrup, mix and pour over the cooked fruit.

Cool the compote and serve immediately. It is rich in vitamin C and may not be kept if the vitamin is to be preserved.

Skinned Black Plums in Compote

*3 cups water * 1/2 cup sugar * 25 black plums * lemon peel or pinch of cloves and cinnamon*

Rinse plums and place in sieve several at a time. Bring water and sugar to the boil. Dip sieve with plums in boiling water for a while. When the skin begins to pucker remove sieve from water. Remove skin immediately and then scald the next portion. Bring syrup with skins and seasoning to the boil, drain. Place one layer of plums and cook slowly. Cook plums each layer separately.

Place plums in a compote dish, cover with syrup and cool.

Prune Compote

*4 cups water * about 1/2 cup sugar * 25 prunes * lemon juice and lemon peel*

Wash prunes carefully in warm water and place in porcelain dish. Bring water to the boil and cool slightly. Cover prunes with boiled, warm water and soak for 5 to 12 hours, depending on how dry the prunes are. When the fruit swells and is soft, drain off water in which prunes were soaked and bring to the boil. Add sugar and prunes and bring to the boil. Flavor with lemon juice and lemon peel. Pour into compote dish and cool.

All compotes made of ripe greengage plums and other plums as well as of prunes may be supplemented with pasteurized black currant pulp, (1/4 to 1/2 cup) depending on how sour the fruit is.

Apricot Compote

*3 cups water * 1/2 cup sugar * 10 apricots*

Rinse thoroughly ripe, medium-sized apricots and drain. Cut in half lengthwise and remove stones. Pour hot water over sugar, bring to the boil and skim froth.

Place separately layers of apricots in boiling syrup and cook slowly. Turn over so that they cook evenly. Place in a compote dish and cool.

Morello-Cherry Compote

*3 cups water * 3/4 cup sugar * 2 cups cherries*

Pour hot water over sugar and bring to the boil in a flat pan. Select cherries and rinse under running water. Remove stems and place in syrup. Cook slowly and remove from fire. Place in a compote dish and cool.

Cherry Compote with Currants

*3 cups water * 3/4 cup sugar * 1 1/2 cups dark sweet cherries * 1/2 cup black currants*

Bring water and sugar to the boil.
Wash cherries thoroughly and rinse. Place in boiling syrup and cook slowly so that skin does not split. Place drained cherries in a compote dish. Rinse currants and remove stems. Press through sieve. Pour pulp in syrup, stir and pour over cherries. Serve as soon as possible for the high vitamin value is lost when compote stands too long.

Blueberry Compote

*3 cups water * 1/2 cup sugar * 1 1/2 cups blueberries*

Select blueberries, rinse and drain. Bring water and sugar to the boil, add fruit to syrup and bring to the boil on a slow flame several times. When fruit is cooked, place the compote in a compote dish and cool.

Strawberry Compote

*2 1/2 cups water * 3/4 cup sugar * 2 cups strawberries*

Rinse strawberries thoroughly and remove stems. Drain and place in a compote dish.
Bring water and sugar to the boil and cool.
Pour cold syrup over strawberries and place in cool place for 1/2 or 1 hour and serve. Do not keep strawberry compote longer.

Pears in Vanilla Sauce

*5 large pears * 2 cups water * 1/2 cup sugar * lemon juice*

Rinse pears, pare and cut in halves. Core. Bring water with sugar to the boil. Add pears to syrup so that they cover the surface and cook slowly until tender. Cook pears in separate portions. Towards end add lemon juice to syrup.

Cool pears in syrup, remove, place on bottom of compote dish and cool. Prepare vanilla sauce (see page 322). Cool. Pour cool sauce over pears.

Apples in Vanilla Sauce

*5 large compote apples * 2 1/2 cups water * 3/4 cup sugar * lemon peel*

Prepare vanilla sauce to pour over fruit (see page 322). Cool. Rinse apples, pare and divide in halves or quarters. Core. Bring water and sugar to the boil.

Add lemon peel. Place apples in syrup until they cover the surface. Bring to the boil on a high flame and cook on a slower flame (or remove from fire and keep under cover until done). Cool.

Remove cooled apples from syrup, drain and place in compote dish. Cover with cold vanilla sauce.

Baked Apples

*5 large compote apples * 1/2 cup sugar * lemon peel * 2 1/2 tbs. butter * butter for greasing pan*

Select large apples of the same size. Wash. Core apples beginning with end of the stem.

Mix sugar and grated lemon peel and fill in cavities.

Arrange stuffed apples on a greased baking pan. Dot apples with butter, place in medium oven and bake until tender.

Serve apples on separate dessert plates. Sprinkle with powdered sugar before serving. Serve hot.

Apples Baked in Froth

*10 medium compote apples * 1/2 cup powdered sugar * preserved fruit * * 1/2 cup sugar * 3 tbs. water * 3 egg whites * lemon juice *. butter for greasing pan*

Rinse apples, core. Be careful not to pierce apples through.

Drain preserves and mix with powdered sugar to form a thick mixture.

Prepare steamed egg-white froth. Cook a thick syrup using water and sugar.

Beat egg whites stiff and scald with syrup. Let steam slightly over boiling water, beating constantly. Flavor with lemon juice.

Fill apple cavities with preserves and arrange on a fireproof plate greased with buter. Cover with froth and bake in a medium oven. Sliced almonds may be sprinkled on top.

Serve on the same plate immediately when taken from the oven.

Baked Apples in Cream

*10 medium compote apples * 3/4 cup sugar * 1 cup water * 1/2 cup morello cherry preserves * 4 egg yolks * 4 tbs. powdered sugar * lemon peel * 4 egg whites * 2 tbs. bread crumbs * butter for greasing platter*

Wash apples, rinse, peel and core. Bring water and sugar to the boil. Place apples in boiling syrup, parboil, remove.

Drain and arrange on a fireproof, round platter greased with butter. Fill apples with drained preserves.

Cream egg yolks with powdered sugar and grated lemon peel.

Beat egg whites and combine with creamed yolks and bread crumbs. Cover apples with this cream and place in medium oven. Bake. Remove from oven and serve immediately.

JELLIED DESSERTS

Jellied desserts are: jellies, mousses, creams, kisiels and custards.

A jelly is made with liquid and a substance necessary for jelling. The jelly sets more quickly in colder temperature.

Kisiel is based on the swelling and gelatination of potato starch (potato flour).

Jelly is made with the addition of gelatine or agar-agar which also soak in fluids and swell.

Jellies are chilled desserts which are set with gelatine.

Fruit jellies or milk jellies may be prepared for dessert. The basis of a fruit jelly is a clear, sweet extract of fruit. A milk jelly is prepared with full pasteurized milk, sweet or sour, with an addition of sour cream. Besides this the jelly consists of sugar, dissolved gelatine and in some cases flavoring. We begin work at a jelly dessert by preparing the gelatine.

Gelatine leaves are added to the ingredients after having been soaked in cold water, drained and dissolved in hot water into a uniform mixture of

medium thickness. Powdered gelatine is prepared by dissolving it in a few spoons of hot water. The mixture is placed over boiling water, stirred constantly until dissolved completely.

In order that the thick gelatine mixture does not congeal it must be kept over hot water.

The main factor that decides on the consistency of the gelatine is the **relation of the gelatine to the liquid.** 4 cups of liquid for a fruit jelly with sugar to 2 1/2 tbs. (or 1 oz.) dry gelatine will give the desired consistency. The same amount of milk mixture for a milk jelly can be jellied with 2 tbs. of dry gelatine. The amount of gelatine must be increased during hot weather and the time of setting must be extended. Jellies should be prepared several hours before serving.

Most popular in the daily menu are fruit jellies. These are prepared with ripe fruit which are very aromatic. Since only the fruit extract is used for the jelly, fruit of inferior quality may be used though it should be fresh not over-ripe, selected and rinsed.

Fruit used for the jelly should be cooked slowly until tender. It should be placed in boiling water. The cooked fruit and liquid should be left to cool and then carefully drained through a sieve lined with a double thickness of cheesecloth to which the small particles of fruit will cling. A clear jelly is made only when the fruit is cooked slowly and not boiled too long. The drained-off liquid should be measured, and hot water should be added when necessary to the full amount needed. Add sugar and the dissolved gelatine, and stir thoroughly so that all the ingredients are well mixed. Cool. A certain variation of a jelly is fruit in jelly. This is prepared with such fruit as strawberries, pears, apricots, plums, greengage plums (peeled), grapes, oranges, pineapple slices. This dessert is made of prime fruit cooked in compote, arranged in a compote dish and covered·with jelly made of the same fruit. Strawberries, orange and lemon slices and grapes are not cooked but fresh fruit is covered with the jelly. Before arranging on plate rinse and drain thoroughly.

Milk jelly is very suitable because it is a very light and nutritious dessert. Milk jellies are prepared with flavoring like vanilla, roasted almonds or hazelnuts. Crushed ingredients are added to fresh milk and brought to the boil. Milk absorbs aromas easily and is colored by the ingredients placed in it. Almonds or nuts, cooked in the milk, are drained or left in the milk and the nut meats are mixed with sugar and dissolved gelatine. Vanilla jelly is colored by an addition of egg yolk which imparts a light cream color; sour-milk jelly is colored with a piece of red gelatine which is dissolved with the white gelatine and imparts a light pink color to the jelly.

When the jelly sets each portion is garnished, matching colors to the color of the jelly. The jelly may be garnished with fruit from which the jelly had been prepared and combined with contrasting colors.

Jelly of Cooked Fruit Syrup

*3 1/2 cups water * 1 1/2 cups cooked fruit syrup * lemon juice * * sugar * 1 1/2 tbs. gelatine * 3 tbs. hot water*

Soak gelatine for an hour.
Measure water, add fruit syrup and bring to the boil. If necessary add sugar and lemon juice to taste. Dissolve gelatine in 3 tbs. hot water. Add to the liquid, stirring constantly. Pour into compote dish, cool and garnish.

Currant Jelly

*3 cups water * 2 cups currants (half red, half black) * about 3/4 cup sugar * 2 1/2 tbs. gelatine * 3 tbs. hot water*

Soak gelatine for an hour.
Rinse currants, drain, remove stems and cover with boiling water. Cook and pour into a cloth bag and leave to let liquid drip, pressing lightly so that the juice remains clear.
Add sugar to the juice. Dissolve gelatine in 3 tbs. hot water and stirring add to the syrup.
Cool the jelly a bit and then pour into a compote dish, let set and garnish.

Lemon Jelly

*3 cups water * about 1 cup sugar * synthetic lemon powder * lemon peel * 2 1/2 tbs. gelatine * 3 tbs. hot water * 1 lemon*

Soak gelatine for an hour.
Bring water with sugar to the boil and add the synthetic lemon powder and lemon peel to taste. Dissolve gelatine in 3 tbs. hot water and stirring add to the syrup. Cool.
Rinse lemon, cut in thin slices or half slices and garnish the compote dish. Using a spoon pour some setting jelly on the bottom of the dish to set the lemon.
When the jelly sets pour the remaining jelly to the compote dish and let set.

412

A clear lemon jelly may be made only with synthetic lemon powder. A jelly made of real lemon or orange juice is not clear but more nutritious.

Morello-Cherry Jelly

*3 cups water * 2 1/2 cups morello cherries * 1 cup sugar * 3 tbs. gelatine * 4 tbs. hot water*

Soak gelatine for an hour.
Rinse cherries and cover with boiling water. Cook fruit and drain.
Add sugar to the cherry juice and bring to the boil.
Dissolve gelatine in 4 tbs. hot water.
Add the dissolved gelatine to the juice and mix thoroughly so that the gelatine is uniformly stirred into the juice. Pour into a compote dish and allow to set.

Raspberry Jelly

*3 1/2 cups water * 2 cups raspberries * about 3/4 cup sugar * lemon juice * 2 1/2 tbs. gelatine * 3 tbs. hot water*

Soak gelatine for an hour.
Select best raspberries; rinse and drain the rest. Bring water and sugar to the boil, add the rinsed raspberries and bring to the boil several times. Drain through a fine sieve.
Flavor syrup with lemon juice.
Dissolve gelatine in 3 tbs. hot water and stirring add to the syrup. Cool.
Pour a few spoons of cooling jelly into a compote dish and allow to set.
Arrange fresh raspberries on set jelly, add some cooling jelly and let set. When the fruit is set, place remaining thickening jelly in the compote dish and let set. Garnish.

Almond Jelly

*3 cups milk * 1/2 cup almonds * 3 bitter almonds * vanilla * 3/4 cup sugar * 2 egg yolks * 2 tbs. gelatine * 3 tbs. hot water*

Soak gelatine for an hour.
Scald almonds and remove peel. Dry and grind the almonds.
Bring milk to the boil, add almonds and cook slowly for a few minutes.
Add sugar and vanilla. Dissolve gelatine in 3 tbs. hot water,
Add the dissolved gelatine to the mixture, stirring constantly.

413

Remove from fire and cool slightly. Add raw egg yolks and mix.

Pour into compote dish and let set. Garnish.

The jelly may be prepared in a somewhat different manner.

The almonds may be boiled in milk a little longer, drained and squeezed out well in a linen bag and put aside. Then the remainder of the ingredients may be added to the jelly liquid.

Sour-Milk Jelly

*3 cups of full, young, sour milk * 1 cup sour cream * 3/4 cup sugar *
* vanilla * 2 egg yolks * 2 tbs. gelatine * 3 tbs. hot water*

Soak gelatine for an hour. Stir the milk and sour cream with a rotary beater until smooth. Mix with sugar, vanilla and egg yolk.

Dissolve gelatine in 3 tbs. hot water. Pour the dissolved gelatine slowly into the milk, beating the mixture thoroughly so that the gelatine is mixed in uniformly.

Pour the jelly into a compote dish, chill and garnish.

Apple Jelly

*2—3 cups water * 5 medium apples * 1 cup sugar * lemon peel * 3 tbs.
morello cherry or strawberry preserves or candied orange peel * 2 tbs.
gelatine * 3 tbs. hot water*

Soak gelatine for an hour.

Rinse apples, peel, cut in halves and core.

Cook syrup in flat pot, place one layer of apples and cook slowly until tender and retaining their form. Turn over during cooking. Apples with delicate tissue should be removed from the fire at the appropriate moment and get done under cover. Cook each portion separately and cool in syrup so that they become plump.

When the apples cool, drain off syrup and place apples in portions in the individual compote dishes and fill in cavities with drained preserves.

Measure drained syrup and supplement with boiled water to 2 cups (if necessary).

Dissolve gelatine in 3 tbs. hot water. Add to the syrup.

Bring to the boil with the syrup. Add water to the syrup and flavor with lemon peel, cool. Pour a few spoons of cooling jelly over the arranged apples and allow to set.

When the fruit, has set, add jelly so that it covers the fruit and preserves and then allow to set.

Pear Jelly

Prepare in the same manner as apples.

Strawberry Jelly

*2 cups water * 2 1/2 cups strawberries * 3/4 cup sugar * lemon juice *
* 3 tbs. gelatine * 4 tbs. hot water * food coloring*

Soak gelatine for an hour.
Remove stems from strawberries, rinse carefully and drain thoroughly. Select about 1 cup of inferior strawberries and use for the juice. Choice fresh strawberries are to be used for jelly. Bring water and sugar to the boil, add strawberries, cook and flavor with lemon juice. Add coloring. Let the compote and fruit cool so that the maximum elements are absorbed by the juice. Drain the juice and bring to the boil.
Dissolve gelatine in 4 tbs. hot water. Add to the juice, stirring constantly. Bring to the boil and cool. If necessary supplement with hot water to measure 2 cups.
Arrange the choice, drained strawberries at the bottom of the compote dish, cover with a few spoons of cooling jelly and let set. When the strawberries at the bottom of the compote dish have set, fill the compote dish with the jelly liquid so that the fruit is covered. Allow to set.

Apricot Jelly

*2 cups water * 1 1/2 cups apricots * 1/2 cup sugar * 2 1/2 tbs. gelatine *
* 3 tbs. hot water*

Soak gelatine for an hour.
Rinse the apricots, place in sieve and dip sieve in boiling water for a short while. When the skin begins to pucker, remove the apricots and peel. Split in half without cutting the apricots through and remove stones.
Bring water and sugar to the boil. Add the apricots and cook slowly until tender. Remove the tender apricots, drain and arrange on the bottom of individual compote dishes (3 halves per portion) with the split part face down. Drain the syrup, bring to the boil. Dissolve gelatine in 3 tbs. hot water and stirring add to the syrup. Cool. Pour three spoons of cooling jelly into each compote dish and let apricots set in the jelly.
When the jelly is set, add the rest of the liquid and allow to set. Serve the jelly garnished with sweet cream.

415

Peach Jelly

*2 cups water * 8 ripe peaches * 1/2 cup sugar * 2 1/2 tbs. gelatine * 3 tbs. hot water*

Prepare in the same manner as apricot jelly.

MOUSSES

Mousse and custard are two other types of dessert, in addition to jelly, that are thickened with gelatine.

The basis of a mousse is egg white or sweet cream and fresh, cooked or baked fruit pulp. Sugar and gelatine are also added to mousse. Since one of the main ingredients of a mousse is beaten egg white, it is a light and fluffy dessert.

A mousse is prepared with sour and aromatic fruit. Fruit like wild strawberries and strawberries are added raw. They must be thoroughly rinsed and lightly crushed (not mashed). Apricots and cantaloupe are cooked in a very small amount of water and pressed through a sieve. Apples for mousse are baked and pressed through a sieve. Since the fruit is principally sour the mousse is rarely flavored with lemon juice, as for instance a cantaloupe mousse. The fruit pulp may be cooked with sugar before mixing in the egg whites.

The aroma may be improved or enhanced by adding vanilla, lemon peel or candied orange peel, as is usually the case in apple mousse made of non-aromatic apples.

Gray-colored fruit pulp may be colored with red food coloring.

The preparation of mousse is very simple and requires usually very little work. The first step is to soak and dissolve the gelatine. Then the fruit pulp should be prepared. Now beat egg whites stiff, add sugar and fruit pulp gradually.

Add the dissolved gelatine, beating constantly. Divide the mixed and uniform mass into portions.

A variety of a mousse is a dessert made of whipped sweet cream or sour cream with the fresh pulp of strawberries or wild strawberries with sugar, set with gelatine.

Apart from small, dry cookies served with a mousse, one may also serve vanilla sauce, cooked fruit syrup, fresh raspberry juice, fresh wild strawberries or strawberry juice.

Apple Mousse

*3 medium, sour apples * 3 egg whites * 1/2 cup powdered sugar * (lemon juice) * lemon peel * 1 tbs. gelatine * 3 tbs. water*

Soak gelatine in cold water.

Wash apples, arrange in an enameled pan and bake in medium oven until tender. Press hot apples through sieve.

Heat the softened gelatine in a small pot. Stirring, dissolve and place over hot water so that gelatine does not cool. Beat egg whites stiff and add apple pulp and sugar gradually, beating constantly. Flavor the mixture with lemon juice and peel and mix with the dissolved gelatine, adding it gradually. Place the mousse in compote dish with a spoon and allow to set. Garnish the top with candied orange peel and whole cranberries or slices of red rhubarb.

Raspberry Mousse with Cream

*1 cup raspberries * 3 egg whites * 1/2 cup powdered sugar * (lemon juice) * 1 tbs. gelatine * 3 tbs. water * 1/2 cup sweet heavy cream*

Soak gelatine in cold water.

Select the raspberries and rinse carefully. Put aside best raspberries for garnish, drain off the rest.

Heat the softened gelatine in a small pot.

Stirring, dissolve and place over hot water so that it does not cool.

Whip cream and set aside in cool place.

Beat egg whites stiff and add sugar, raspberries and the dissolved gelatine gradually, beating constantly. When the mousse becomes pink from the crushed raspberries and when all the ingredients are well mixed, add the whipped cream and fold in. Leave three tablespoons of whipped cream for garnish. Place the cooling mousse in individual compote dishes with a spoon. Garnish the top of mousse with whole raspberries and whipped cream.

Wild-Strawberry Mousse with Cream

*1 cup wild strawberries * 3 egg whites * 1/2 cup powdered sugar * (lemon juice) * 1 tbs. gelatine * 3 tbs. water * 1/2 cup sweet heavy cream*

Soak gelatine in cold water.

Select berries and rinse carefully, separate the best-looking fruit and drain off the rest.

27 Polish Cookbook

Heat the softened gelatine in a small pot.

Stirring, dissolve and place over hot water so that it does not cool.

Whip cream and set aside in cool place.

Beat egg whites until stiff, then add sugar, crushed berries and the dissolved gelatine gradually, beating constantly. When the mousse becomes pink from the crushed berries and when all the ingredients are well mixed, fold in the whipped cream. Leave a few spoons of whipped cream for garnish. Place the cooling mousse in individual compote dishes with a spoon. Garnish the top with whole berries and whipped cream.

Strawberry Mousse with Cream

*1 1/2 cups strawberries * 3 egg whites * 3/4 cup powdered sugar * (lemon juice) * 1 1/2 tbs. gelatine * 4 tbs. water * 1/2 cup sweet heavy cream*

Prepare as in recipe above.

CREAMS

Creams are cold desserts and belong to the group of desserts thickened with gelatine and made light with whipped cream or beaten egg whites. The basin of creams are egg yolks creamed with sugar and whipped cream (sometimes with an addition of egg whites). The creamed egg yolks and the whipped cream give the creams their fluffy and light texture.

Added to the creams may be: fruit pulp or juice or some other ingredient with a strong aroma and taste, like strong coffee or tea, caramel, rum, vanilla, browned hazelnuts, etc.

These ingredients add taste and aroma to the cream. The name of the cream comes from the principal ingredient (coffee, punch, lemon, etc.). Gelatine is the thickening ingredient. The manner of preparing creams is quite complicated and requires a lot of work. Steps in preparing creams: prepare fruit pulp or juice or other ingredients (like strong coffee, caramel, browned and ground hazelnuts); dissolve gelatine; whip sweet cream (beat egg whites); cream egg yolks with sugar until fluffy; mix egg yolks with fruit pulp or other ingredients and the dissolved gelatine, beating constantly; when the mixture begins to thicken fold in the beaten egg whites and the whipped cream and divide into portions immediately before it starts to set.

The creams may be spoiled when the setting egg yolk mixture is combined with the egg whites. If the whipped cream or beaten egg whites are mixed with the egg yolks when they are still not thickened, the cream, after having set, will separate into two layers. The lower layer is created by the egg yolks creamed with sugar and the gelatine set into a solid jelly. The top layer, the beaten egg whites, will rise at first but it will begin to disappear, not having been set by the gelatine and egg yolks.

Adding the egg whites to the egg yolks, when they have already set with the gelatine, the cream cannot be mixed into a uniform texture. In cross section there will be lumps of egg white with lumps of the set egg yolk. The correct thickness of the egg yolk mixture before adding the egg whites may be tested by drawing a creaming spoon through the bottom of the bowl. The groove should not overflow with the liquid but should disappear gradually.

After this test has been made, when the egg yolks are sufficiently set, the whipped cream and egg whites should be added quickly and folded in with a spatula until smooth. The mixture will begin to set immediately on coming in contact with the cold egg whites. The mixing and dividing into portions must be completed quickly.

Lemon Cream

*2 lemons * 1 tbs. gelatine * 3 tbs. water * 4 egg yolks * 1/2 cup sugar * * 5 egg whites*

Grate lemon peel and squeeze lemon juice.
Dissolve gelatine and leave over boiling water.
Beat egg whites until stiff.
Cream egg yolks with sugar, add lemon juice and the dissolved gelatine and stir until as thick as sour cream.
Quickly mix the beaten egg whites with the thickening egg yolk mixture.
Place cream in individual cups or glasses and allow to set.
Prepare a few hours before serving.
Serve with cookies.

Orange Cream

*1 tbs. gelatine * 3 tbs. water * 1/2 cup sugar * 4 egg yolks * 2 lemons * * 2 oranges * 2 egg whites * 1 cup sweet heavy cream*

Dissolve gelatine. Place over boiling water.
Squeeze lemon and orange juice.
Clean the orange peel of the remaining pulp and cut out ridges.

Beat egg whites until stiff. Whip cream.

Cream egg yolks with sugar and mix with lemon and orange juice.

Add the dissolved gelatine and stir until as thick as sour cream. Mix the thickening mixture with the whipped cream and egg whites.

Place in the orange peel shells (when there are more at hand) or into low cups. Allow to set.

Prepare a few hours before serving. Serve with cookies.

Punch Cream

*1 lemon * 1 orange * 1 tbs. gelatine * 3 tbs. water * 4 egg yolks * 1/2 cup sugar * 2 tbs. Jamaica rum * lemon peel * orange peel * 3 egg whites * 1 cup sweet heavy cream*

Dissolve gelatine and place over boiling water.

Pound lemon and orange peel together (1/2 tsp. each).

Beat egg whites until stiff. Whip cream. Retain 3 spoons of whipped cream to garnish the dessert.

Cream egg yolks with sugar and mix with rum juice, lemon and orange juice and lemon and orange peel. Add the dissolved gelatine and stir slowly.

When the mixture becomes as thick as sour cream, fold in the beaten egg whites and then the cream. Place immediately in cups or compote dishes and allow to set.

Before serving, garnish with whipped cream and fresh slices of lemon and orange.

Wild-Strawberry or Strawberry Cream

*3 cups fresh strawberries or wild strawberries * 1 tbs. gelatine * 3 tbs. water * 1 cup sweet heavy cream * 3 egg whites * 1/2 cup sugar * (red food coloring)*

Select the berries, rinse and drain. Remove stems and crush berries but do not cream for the crushed seeds are bitter.

Dissolve gelatine and place over boiling water.

Beat egg whites until stiff. Whip cream.

Mix all the ingredients with the cream and egg whites and beat.

If necessary add coloring.

When the cream thickens place in cups or glasses and allow to set.

Prepare a few hours before serving.

Serve with small cookies.

Vanilla Cream

*1 1/2 tbs. gelatine * 3 tbs. water * 1 cup milk * 1 cup sweet heavy cream *
* 2 egg whites * 4 egg yolks * 1/2 cup sugar * vanilla*

Dissolve gelatine and place over boiling water.

Cream egg yolks with sugar and vanilla, scald with boiling milk and beat over boiling water.

Whip cream. Beat egg whites until stiff.

Combine egg yolks with the dissolved gelatine, stirring until as thick as sour cream.

Mix the thickening egg yolk mixture with the cream and egg whites and place in suitable dish. Allow to set.

Prepare a few hours before serving.

Serve with small cookies.

Caramel Cream

*1/4 cup sugar for caramel * 1/2 cup water for caramel * 1 1/2 tbs.
gelatine * 3 tbs. water * 1/2 cup milk * 1 cup sweet heavy cream * 2 egg
whites * 4 egg yolks * 1/2 cup sugar * vanilla*

Brown sugar to a dark golden color, dissolve with hot water, cook and cool.

Dissolve gelatine and place over boiling water.

Whip cream and beat egg whites until stiff.

Cream egg yolks with sugar and vanilla and scald with boiling milk. Beat over boiling water.

Combine the egg yolk mixture with the dissolved gelatine and caramel and mix until as thick as sour cream. Mix the thickening mixture with the cream and egg whites. Place in cups or glasses and allow to set.

Prepare a few hours before serving.

Serve with small cookies.

Coffee Cream

*1 oz. ground coffee * 1/2 cup water for coffee * 1 1/2 tbs. gelatine *
* 3 tbs. water * 1/2 cup milk * 1 cup sweet heavy cream * 2 egg whites *
* 4 egg yolks * 1/2 cup sugar*

Make coffee (1/2 cup).

Dissolve gelatine and place over boiling water.

Whip cream and beat egg whites until stiff.

Cream egg yolks with sugar and scald with boiling milk, beating over boiling water.

Combine egg yolks with coffee and the dissolved gelatine and mix until as thick as sour cream. Mix the thickening egg yolk mixture with the whipped cream and egg whites and place in cups. Allow to set.
Prepare a few hours before serving.
Serve with small cookies.

Tea Cream

Prepare as the coffee cream, substituting 1 1/2 tbs. tea (1/2 cup) for the coffee.

Chocolate Cream

*1 1/2 tbs. gelatine * 3 tbs. water * 4 egg yolks * 1/2 cup sugar * 3 1/2 oz. chocolate * 1 cup milk * 3/4 cup almonds * 3 egg whites * 1/2 cup sweet heavy cream*

Melt chocolate.
Wipe almonds in towel and grind with skins.
Dissolve gelatine and place over boiling water.
Beat egg whites and whip cream.
Cream egg yolks with sugar; gradually add the softened chocolate intermittently with a few spoons of boiling milk and beat over boiling water. Add the dissolved gelatine to the egg yolk mixture and stir.
When the egg yolk mixture begins to thicken add the egg whites, whipped cream and almonds. Retain some whipped cream for garnish.
Place cream in compote dish and allow to set.
Garnish with roasted almonds that have been chopped and with whipped cream.

KISIELS

Kisiel is a very popular dessert. It is tasty, inexpensive and easy to prepare.
It belongs to thickened desserts. Potato starch is the thickening agent that gives the dessert the consistency of a jelly.
Due to the principal ingredient, the kisiel may be divided into two groups: fruit and milk kisiel. The basis of a **fruit kisiel** is the juice and pulp, or the boiled syrup of sour and aromatic fruit. The other ingredients are

sugar and potato starch. Fruit kisiel may be served throughout the year with due consideration paid to the fruit in season.

Fruit kisiel is made of white or red or black currants, raspberries, Morello cherries, strawberries, cranberries, lemon, apples, fruit syrup, etc. From this choice of fruit we see that those used for kisiel are quite sour and have a strong aroma. The fruit should be ripe, for only this has the proper taste and smell.

Milk kisiel is prepared on the base of full milk. The most frequent flavor added to the milk kisiel is browned caramel of a dark golden color, coffee, cocoa, vanilla, roasted almonds, etc., these aromatic ingredients give it taste, aroma and its name. Other ingredients of a milk kisiel are sugar and potato starch. A small amount of butter is added to a caramel and vanilla kisiel. Butter makes the kisiel moist. Instead of butter, egg yolks may be added to a vanilla kisiel. This improves not only the consistency but also the color.

In order to escape streaks and lumps, the kisiel should be prepared in the following manner:

1. Heat the liquid which is to be thickened (sweetened juice and fruit pulp or sweetened milk) and remove from fire.

2. Mix potato starch with a small amount of cold liquid (water or milk).

3. Pour the potato starch mixture into the hot liquid immediately and mix thoroughly.

4. Place the kisiel on heat and mixing thoroughly bring it to the boil. Kisiels set very easily and are ready when cooled. To avoid film from forming on top, sprinkle surface with a few drops of cold water.

The consistency of the kisiel depends on the amount of starch used to the amount of liquid. Fruit kisiel is most often served with sweetened cream or sweetened milk mixed with egg yolk. Milk kisiel may be garnished with fruit syrup, vanilla sauce or whipped cream. Caramel kisiel is covered with dissolved, rather thick caramel sauce, browned to a golden color.

Cranberry Kisiel

*1 1/2 cups cranberries * 2 1/2 cups water * about 3/4 cup sugar * 6 tbs. potato starch * 1/2 cup cold water*

Rinse the cranberries and cover with hot water. Cook and press through a sieve, pouring juice over the cranberries in the process. Add sugar to the pulp and heat. Remove from fire. Mix the potato starch with cold water and pour slowly into the pulp. Stirring constantly bring to the boil. Allow to set. If necessary add sugar. Divide into portions and sprinkle with a few drops of cold water. Cool.

This kisiel may be served with sweetened milk and egg yolk.

Currant Kisiel

*1 1/2 cups red and black currants * 2 1/2 cups water * about 3/4 cup sugar * 6 tbs. potato starch * 1/2 cup cold water*

Select the currants and rinse thoroughly under running water. Remove stems.

Place the currants in boiling water and bring to the boil several times. Press through a sieve, pouring juice over them. Add sugar to the pressed fruit and bring to the boil. Remove from fire.

Mix the potato starch with cold water and pour slowly into the juice. Stirring constantly, bring to the boil. Allow to set. Divide into portions and sprinkle with a few drops of cold water. Cool.

May be served with sweetened milk.

Morrelo-Cherry Kisiel

*1 cup morello cherries * 2 1/2 cups water * about 3/4 cup sugar * 6 tbs. potato starch * 1/2 cup cold water*

Rinse the cherries and stone. Bring water to the boil and add the cherries. Cook on high flame. Press through a sieve, pouring juice over the cherries. Add sugar to the mixture and bring to the boil. Remove from fire.

Mix the potato starch with cold water and pour into the hot fruit juice. Stirring constantly, bring to the boil. Remove from fire and cool a little.

Divide the kisiel into portions and sprinkle the top with a few drops of water. Cool. May be served with sweetened milk and egg yolk.

Raspberry Kisiel

*1 1/2 cups raspberries * 2 1/2 cups water * about 3/4 cup sugar * 6 tbs. potato starch * 1/2 cup cold water * (red food coloring)*

Select the raspberries carefully, put into sieve, rinse and drain. Bring water to the boil and add the raspberries. When the raspberries have boiled several times, press through a sieve, pouring juice over them. Add sugar to the juice and bring to the boil. Remove from fire.

Mix the potato starch with cold water and add to the hot juice.

424

Stirring constantly, bring to the boil. Mix the kisiel with coloring. Remove from fire and cool a little.
Divide the cooling kisiel into portions and sprinkle the top with a few drops of cold water. Cool.
Serve with sweetened milk.

Apple Kisiel

*4 large compote apples * 1 1/2 cups water * about 3/4 cup sugar * * 5 tbs. potato starch * 1/2 cup cold water * lemon peel*

Wash the apples and remove stems. Arrange tightly in a pot, cover and bake in a moderate oven, being careful not to let them brown. Press the baked apples through a fine sieve. Bring water and sugar to the boil, add the apple pulp and heat.
Mix the potato starch with cold water and add to the hot pulp.
Stirring constantly bring to the boil. Remove from fire and cool a little. Flavor the warm kisiel with lemon peel and then divide into portions. Cool.

Fruit-Syrup Kisiel

*1 1/2 cups fruit syrup (morello cherry or raspberry) * 1 cup water * * 5 tbs. potato starch * 1/2 cup cold water * lemon juice to taste * * (sugar to taste) * red coloring*

Bring water to the boil. Remove from fire. Mix the potato starch with cold water and add slowly to the hot water. Stirring constantly, bring to the boil. Mix with the syrup and lemon juice. Add sugar if needed. Add coloring to the kisiel, remove from fire and cool a little.
Divide the cooling kisiel into portions and sprinkle the top with a few drops of cold water. Cool.
May be served with sweetened milk.

Caramel Kisiel

*3 tbs. sugar for caramel * 1/2 cup water for caramel * 1 1/2 cups milk * about 3 tbs. sugar * vanilla * 4 to 5 tbs. potato starch * 1/2 cup cold milk * 1 tbs. butter*

Prepare caramel. Brown sugar to a dark golden color, dissolve with hot water, stirring while cooking.

Heat the milk with sugar and vanilla. Add the caramel. Mix the potato starch with cold milk and pour slowly into the hot mixture. Stirring constantly, bring to the boil. Add sweet fresh butter to the hot milk. Mix and remove from fire. Cool a little. Divide the cooling kisiel into portions, sprinkle with caramel and cool.

Caramel kisiel may be served with vanilla sauce or sweetened cream.

Vanilla Kisiel

*1 1/2 cups milk * 4 to 5 tbs. potato starch * 1/2 cup cold milk * about 1/2 cup sugar * vanilla*

Heat the milk.

Mix the potato starch with cold milk. Pour into the hot milk. Stirring constantly, bring to the boil. Add vanilla and sugar to taste. Mix.
Divide into portions and allow to set.

Serve with whipped cream, vanilla sauce or fruit juice.

Cocoa Kisiel

*1 1/2 cups milk * 4 to 5 tbs. potato starch * 4 tsp. cocoa * 1/2 cup cold milk * about 1/2 cup sugar * vanilla*

Heat the milk.

Mix the starch and cocoa in cold milk and pour into the hot milk. Bring to the boil, stirring constantly. Add vanilla and sugar to taste. Mix and divide into portions. Allow to set. Serve with whipped cream, sweetened milk or vanilla sauce.

CUSTARDS

Custards are cold thickened desserts. Since the principal ingredients are milk and eggs, they are prepared in the spring and summer when milk and eggs are of great nutritional value.

A jelly constituting a custard differs somewhat from one made with gelatine, since the milk sets for different reasons. When we mix an appropriate amount of liquid with raw eggs, added in a given ratio to the liquid and heated for a certain time, then a jelly forms. Moreover, when the egg white congeals or shrinks, the liquid pushed out by the congealing egg white is again absorbed.

From the description above it is apparent that the most important factors in a custard of a delicate consistency are:

1) a specific amount of liquid,

2) an addition of raw eggs in a specific ratio to the liquid,

3) a specific, closely defined temperature and time of heating the mixture out of which the custard is formed.

The proportions of ingredients in a custard are as follows:

*4 cups of full milk * 4 to 5 fresh eggs * about 1/2 cup sugar * flavoring*

The most frequent flavorings are vanilla, caramel, coffee, cocoa, etc. The flavoring gives the name to the custard.

In making a custard the mixture must be heated under specific conditions. The most delicate consistency in a custard, with a correct structure, that is fluffy, smooth and sufficiently springy, is attained at a temperature of 178—185°F.

The time of heating the custard is also important. The heating must be stopped at the appropriate moment, when the custard becomes of a gelatinous consistency and smooth. The custard sets at moderate temperature in about 30 to 40 minutes.

We achieve a constant temperature during cooking by placing the custard, divided into cups or special porcelain dishes in a large pan. The custard cups are covered with waxed paper. The pan is placed on the flame and filled with warm water. The water in the pan should be at a lower level than the custard in the cups. The pan is then covered with a cover or another pan and the custard simmered on a low flame for about 30 to 40 minutes. Do not allow the water to boil.

When the custard has reached the appropriate consistency, the cups are removed from the pan and cooled. The custard is served in baking dishes.

The cooled custard should be covered with waxed paper so that the surface does not dry.

Custards are very nutritious desserts. If particularly desired, the custard may be served with cooked syrup (as raspberry syrup with cocoa custard) or sweetened cream.

Caramel Custard

*4 cups milk * 4 or 5 eggs * 2 tbs. sugar * vanilla * 2 tbs. sugar for caramel * 1/4 cup water for caramel * 3 tbs. sugar and 1/4 cup water for caramel as a garnish*

427

Prepare caramel. Brown 2 tbs. sugar to a golden color. Add a small amount of hot water and cook, making a thick syrup.

Mix the eggs with sugar and milk. Add the cooked caramel and vanilla. Mix the custard and pour into cups.

Place the cups in a pan with hot water, cover with waxed paper and cover the pan. Simmer until the mixture thickens (3/4 of an hour). Remove from fire and cool under cover. Prepare the caramel out of the second portion of sugar and pour in a thin stream over a marble slab moistened with oil. When it cools, remove and break.

Sprinkle the top of the custard with the crushed caramel. Serve in cups on saucers.

Vanilla Custard

*4 cups milk * 4 or 5 eggs * about 1/2 cup sugar * vanilla*

Prepare as above without the caramel.

Coffee Custard

*2/3 oz. ground coffee or 2 tsp. instant coffee * 1/5 cup water for coffee * * 4 cups milk * about 1/2 cup sugar * 4 or 5 eggs*

Prepare small amount (3 tablespoons) of strong coffee.

Add eggs and sugar to the milk and mix thoroughly. Add the coffee. Mix and pour the custard into cups. Place the cups in a pan with hot water. Cover with waxed paper and cover the pan. Simmer for about 45 min. When the liquid sets into a gelatinous consistency, remove the cups and cool under cover.

CEREAL AND PASTRY DESSERTS

Kutia

Christmas-Eve Dessert

This is a traditional Christmas-Eve dessert, which originated in the dim past when the people ate cereal stews, and the food was garnished with poppy seeds and poppy oil and sweetened with honey. Kutia has a specific taste and is considered by some people to be better than any other Christ-

mas-Eve dish. It is very simple to prepre. One must only have cleaned, whole polished wheat, fresh poppy seeds and honey.

*1 1/2 cups wheat grain * 4 cups water * 2 cups poppy seeds * 3 to 5 tbs. sweet cream * honey to taste * (almonds or walnuts)*

Rinse the polished wheat grain and place in boiling water. Bring to the boil and drain. Bring to the boil 4 cups of fresh water, add the wheat and cook slowly on an asbestos pad until tender (it takes about 2 hours). If it is too thick add boiling water. Remove the cooked wheat grain from the fire and cool. Drain if necessary.

Cover the blue poppy seeds with boiling water and allow to soak without heating. When the poppy seeds become soft and break between the fingers, drain through a fine sieve.

Grind the dry poppy seeds through a fine grinder, several times.

Add a few spoons of sweet cream to the poppy seeds and mix with the cooled wheat and sweeten with honey, or honey and sugar. Kutia should be moist but the liquid should not seep to the bottom.

Serve as a cold dessert during the Christmas-Eve supper. Kutia must be stored in a cold place since it ferments very quickly.

Rice with Whipped Cream

*3/4 cup rice * 3 to 4 cups water with milk in equal proportions * 1 tbs. butter * pinch of salt * about 1/2 cup sugar * vanilla * 1 to 1 1/2 cups sweet heavy cream*

Rinse the rice in warm water, changing the water several times. Drain. Bring the milk and water to the boil. Add butter and salt. Add the drained rice, stir thoroughly and bring to the boil.

Parboil the rice on a small fire. Add sugar and vanilla. Cover the rice, place in a moderate oven and bake until tender.

Place the rice on a round plate. Level the surface with a spoon dipped in milk and cool the rice.

Before serving, cover with cream (mixed with sugar and vanilla to taste) and garnish generously with preserved fruit and juice.

Rice with Fresh Apples

*3/4 cup rice * 3 to 4 cups water with milk in equal proportions * 1 tbs. butter * pinch of salt * about 1/2 cup sugar * 2 tbs. candied orange peel * 4 medium compote apples * 1 cup sweet heavy cream * lemon peel*

Rinse the rice in warm water, changing the water several times. Drain off the rinsed rice.

Bring the milk and water to the boil. Add butter, salt, rice and bring to the boil, stirring thoroughly. Parboil the rice on a low flame. Add sugar.

Cover the rice, place in a moderate oven and bake until tender. Cut the orange peel into small cubes.

Rinse apples, pare and grate coarse (add sugar and lemon peel to taste).

Moisten the mold with water and sprinkle with powdered sugar. Mix the cooked rice with orange peel. Arrange in mold with layers of apples in between. Arrange a layer of rice on top. Place the mold with the rice in a cool place and chill.

Place the rice on a plate and garnish with whipped cream (mixed with sugar and vanilla to taste) and preserved fruit (sour cherries, strawberries, cornel).

Punch Rice

*3/4 cup rice * 3 cups water with milk in equal proportions * pinch of salt * 1/2 cup sugar * 1/2 cup water for syrup * 2 tbs. candied orange peel * 2 tbs. Jamaica rum * lemon juice * 2 tbs. maraschino liqueur * * 1 cup sweet heavy cream*

Rinse the rice in warm water, drain and add to boiling milk and water. Add a pinch of salt and cook slowly.

When the milk and water is absorbed by the rice, place in a double boiler and steam until grains are separated.

Cook a thick syrup with the sugar, add to the cooked rice. Mix and leave until absorbed by the rice. Then remove rice from double boiler and cool. Add rum, lemon juice to taste and candied orange peel to the rice. Mix the rice and place in a mold moistened with water and sprinkled with powdered sugar. Press tightly with a spoon and chill.

Before serving, remove the rice from the mold and sprinkle with maraschino liqueur. Surround with whipped cream with sugar. Garnish with preserved fruit.

Rice Baked with Apples

*3/4 cup rice * 3 cups water with milk in equal proportions * 2 1/2 tbs. butter * pinch of salt * cinnamon * about 1/2 cup sugar * 2 eggs * * 3 medium compote apples * butter for mold * bread crumbs for mold * * 4 tbs. powdered sugar*

Add salt and cinnamon and part of the butter to the boiling milk and water. Add the rinsed and drained rice and cook until semi-puffed. Cream the remainder of the butter. Add egg yolks and sugar, creaming constantly. Add warm rice to the yolks and mix. Add well-beaten egg whites and fold in.

Wash apples, peel, core and shred.

Grease a shallow mold with butter and powder with bread crumbs. Arrange alternately one layer of rice and one of apples, sprinkling them with powdered sugar and placing the rice as the first and last layers.

Level out the rice, cover and place in a hot oven for 30 minutes.

Remove from oven and leave under cover for several minutes.

When the rice is no longer steaming, pry up the edges and remove from mold.

Serve sprinkled with sugar and cinnamon.

Rice Pudding with Chocolate Sauce

*1 cup rice * 1 cup water * 2 cups milk * pinch of salt * 1 tbs. butter *
* 4 egg yolks * 1 1/2 cups sugar * 5 oz. chocolate * vanilla * 5 egg
whites * butter for mold * bread crumbs for mold*

Rinse the rice in warm water. Bring the water and milk to the boil. Add rice and a pinch of salt and cook rice slowly on very slow flame. When rice is tender, remove from flame and cool.

Melt chocolate over boiling water.

Cream butter adding one egg yolk at a time, a little sugar, vanilla and the melted chocolate. When creamed, mix with rice. Beat egg whites stiff and fold in the rice mixture. Place in mold, greased and powdered with bread crumbs. Bake (1/2 hour) in a moderate oven (320°F).

Cracow-Groats Pudding Baked in Cream

*2 cups Cracow groats (fine buckwheat meal) * 1 egg * 1 1/2 tbs. butter *
* 1 cup milk * pinch of salt * about 1/2 cup sugar * 3/4 cup sweet
medium cream * vanilla * butter for mold * bread crumbs for mold *
* 1 cup sweet heavy cream*

Sift the groats and cream thoroughly with the egg. Dry in moderate oven. Bring milk to the boil with butter and salt and add the cooled groats. Mixing thoroughly, bring to the boil. Cover the pot and place in hot oven for 30 minutes.

Add sugar, cream and vanilla to the baked warm groats and mix. Place the prepared mixture in a low pot, greased with butter and powdered with bread crumbs. Level out the surface, cover the pot and place in hot oven for one hour.

Leave covered after removing from oven for a few minutes until there is no more steam. Then loosen around edges and remove.

Serve hot with cooked fruit syrup or whipped cream with sugar and vanilla.

Knedle

Dumplings with Plums, Apples, Strawberries or Marmalade

*2 cups flour * 4 cups cooked potatoes * 1 egg * pinch of salt * 2 1/2 cups plums or 3 medium apples or 2 cups small strawberries * salted water * 2 1/2 tbs. butter*

Wash potatoes, cook, peel, mash and cool.

Wash plums and wipe with a clean towel, remove stems (peel apples, cut in quarters and core).

Mix potatoes with sifted flour and salt. Knead dough with an addition of one egg. Knead only long enough to mix ingredients. Form dough into a long roll (1 inch thick) and cut into 1/2 inch pieces. Form small rounds with fingers and fold into them plums, strawberries or parts of apple. Seal, forming into a round knedel (ball).

Bring salted water to the boil and place knedles into boiling water so that they float freely.

At first cook knedles on a high flame, then reduce flame to medium so that fruit is cooked. Test if ready by cutting one knedle in half. Remove with a draining spoon, drain and place on a heated plate. Cover with browned butter.

Serve sprinkled with powdered sugar.

Noodles with Poppy Seed

Christmas-Eve Dessert

*1 cup poppy seeds * sugar or honey to taste * 4 cups flour * 1 egg * about 1/2 cup water * pinch of salt * salted water * 3 1/2 tbs. butter.*

Prepare poppy seeds. Scald with boiling water, cover and let stand until · the seeds can be crushed between the fingers. Drain through a fine sieve and drain off well. Grind through a grinder three times.

Prepare dough. Sift flour and mix with salt, egg and 1/2 cup water. Knead well. Roll out dough to a thickness of 1/5 inch and leave to dry. Bring salted water to the boil.

Cut even strips and place one upon another. Move to the edge of the board and cut noodles with a sharp knife, pushing noodles off with a knife. When cut, scatter noodles on board.

Place noodles in boiling salted water and when they rise to the top, drain. Pour hot water over noodles and let it drain off.

Place noodles into a bowl and mix with butter and poppy seeds. Add sugar or honey to taste. Place on a heated plate, cover and heat over boiling water.

Pierożki (Filled Dumplings) with Blueberries

*5 cups blueberries * 4 cups flour * 1 egg * 1/2 cup water * pinch of salt * * salted water * 3 tbs. butter * 4 tbs. powdered sugar * 1 cup sour cream*

Select blueberries, rinse and drain.

Prepare dough. Sift flour, mix with salt, egg and water and knead well. Roll out thin and cut out rounds.

Place one tablespoon of blueberries in each round and seal edges, pressing thoroughly.

Bring salted water to the boil and place in dumplings. Cook on a medium flame.

When the dumplings float to the top, remove with a draining spoon and rinse with warm water. Place on a heated plate and pour butter on top. Serve with powdered sugar and sour cream.

Prepare raspberry and blackberry dumplings in the same way.

Fruit dumplings may be served hot or cold.

Pierożki (Filled Dumplings) with Prunes

*1 1/2 lb. prunes * 4 cups flour * 1 egg * 1/2 cup water * pinch of salt * * salted water * 3 tbs. butter * 4 tbs. walnuts * 4 tbs. powdered sugar*

Rinse prunes in warm water, soak for a few hours. Bring to the boil, drain and remove pits.

Prepare dough. Sift flour and mix with salt, egg and water. Knead well. Roll out dough thinly and cut out rounds.

Place a prune on each round and seal, pressing edges.

Bring salted water to the boil and put dumplings into boiling water. When they float to the top, remove with draining spoon. Rinse with warm water and drain. Place on a heated plate and mix with butter.

Serve ground walnuts mixed with powdered sugar to sprinkle over the dumplings.

Pierożki (Filled Dumplings) with Cherries

*3 cups sour or sweet cherries * 4 cups flour * 1 egg * 1/2 cup water *
* pinch of salt * salted water * 3 tbs. butter * 4 tbs. powdered sugar * 1 cup
sour cream*

Rinse cherries and remove stems. Wipe.
Prepare dough. Sift flour and mix with salt, egg and water. Knead well.
Roll out dough quite thin and cut out rounds.
Place two cherries into each round and seal, pressing edges firmly.
Bring salted water to the boil and place dumplings in water. When they
float to the top, remove with a draining spoon and rinse warm water.
Place on a heated plate and pour butter over dumplings. Serve powdered
sugar for sprinkling.
Serve with sour cream.

Naleśniki (Pancakes) with Cheese Filling

B a t t e r: *1 1/2 cups flour * 4 egg yolks * 1 cup milk * 1/2 cup water *
* pinch of salt * 4 egg whites * fat back for greasing griddle ** F i l l i n g:
*1 1/2 cups cottage cheese * 2 egg yolks * 4 tbs. butter * sugar * vanilla*

Cream egg yolks, milk and flour and beat well. Add water and salt. Beat
egg whites stiff. Add batter to the egg whites and mix a beater.
Grease hot griddle with fat back (held on a fork) until surface gleams.
Pour batter on hot griddle and spread over whole surface by moving the
griddle. Pour off extra batter.
Fry quickly on an even fire. When the batter no longer steams, turn over
with a spatula.
Fry pancakes on both sides and place on upturned plate.
Cream egg yolks with butter, add grated cheese, sugar and vanilla to
taste. If necessary add sour cream so that mixture will spread.
Spread pancakes with cheese filling and fold over in half then once again,
to form triangles. Heat in oven or fry on butter.
Serve sprinkled with sugar and vanilla.

Naleśniki (Pancakes) with Preserved Fruit

*2 cups flour * 2 eggs * 1 cup milk * 1 cup water * pinch of salt * fat back
for greasing griddle * 1/2 cup preserved fruit*

Prepare batter. Add eggs to milk and beat well. Add flour and beat until
all flour lumps disappear.

When mixture is smooth, add water, salt and mix.

Grease hot griddle with fat back (held on a fork) so that the whole surface gleams and fry pancakes as above.

Fold pancakes into triangles.

Serve covered with preserved fruit or syrup.

These pancakes may be also stuffed with cheese as given above.

Naleśniki (Pancakes) with French Cream

B a t t e r: *1 cup flour * 1 egg * 1/2 cup milk * 1/2 cup water * pinch of salt * fat back for greasing griddle * C r e a m: 2 egg yolks * 5 tbs. sugar * * 2 tbs. potato starch * 1 cup sweet medium cream * lemon peel * vanilla * * 1 1/2 tbs. butter * 2 eggs whites*

Prepare batter. Add egg and milk to flour. Mix until smooth and lumps disappear. Add salt. Add water to make batter thin and beat well. Heat griddle (about 6 inches in diameter) and grease surface with fat back held on a fork. Pour batter on hot griddle and moving griddle spread batter evenly. Pour off excess batter back to the bowl. Fry pancakes quickly on both sides, browning lightly.

Prepare French cream. Cream egg yolks with sugar, lemon peel and vanilla. Mix potato starch with sweet cream, bring to the boil and pour slowly to egg yolk mixture. Place over boiling water and beat constantly. Add the dissolved butter to the heated mixture. Beat. When the mixture thickens and the dissolved butter is mixed in, remove from steam and cool stirring constantly. Beat egg whites stiff and mix with cooled cream.

Place pancakes on board and spread cream.

Roll each pancake.

Before serving heat pancakes on butter.

Naleśniki (Pancakes) with Sour Cream

B a t t e r: *4 egg yolks * 3 tbs. sugar * 1 1/2 cups sour cream * pinch of salt * 4 egg whites * 1 to 1 1/2 cups flour * 3 tbs. butter for frying * * F i l l i n g: powdered sugar * vanilla * rose preserves*

Cream egg yolks with sugar. Add sour cream, salt and flour and mix. Beat egg whites stiff and mix with batter. The batter should flow off the spoon.

Heat butter on the griddle and place in batter with a spoon. Spread thickly so that there is one pancake per person.

Fry pancake slowly under cover only on one side.

Place pancakes one on top of another with the uncooked side up. Sprinkle sugar with vanilla on each or spread with rose preserves.

Serve immediately on a round plate.

Naleśniki (Pancakes) with Yeast

L e a v e n: *1 oz. yeast * 1 tsp. sugar * 3 tbs. milk * * D o u g h: lemon peel * * about 3/4 cup milk * 2 cups flour * 5 egg yolks * 4 tbs. sugar * 3 tbs. butter * salt * 3 tbs. fat for frying * F i l l i n g: marmalade or jam*

Prepare leaven. Crumble yeast and mix with warm milk. Add one teaspoon of sugar and place in warm place under cover to allow to rise, being careful not to allow to become too hot.

Prepare dough. Cream egg yolks with sugar and lemon peel and mix with raised leaven, melted butter and a pinch of salt. Add flour to the egg yolks and enough milk to form dough which would be thicker than that used usually for pancakes. Beat dough thoroughly. When bubbles appear, remove spoon and place dough in pot. Cover and place in warm place to rise slowly. Place one teaspoon of fat on two griddles of equal size. When griddles are hot, pour 1/2 cup of raised dough and fry over an asbestos plate on both sides until brown. Spread fried pancakes with marmalade or jam, fold in half and sprinkle with sugar.

Serve straight off the griddle, freshly fried and hot.

Blinki

Griddle Cakes

L e a v e n: *1/2 oz. yeast * 3 tbs. milk * 1 tbs. sugar * D o u g h: 2 egg yolks * 2 1/2 tbs. sugar * lemon peel * 2 egg whites * 1 1/2 cup flour * * about 3/4 cup milk * salt * 2 tbs. butter * 1 tsp. alcohol * 6 tbs. fat for frying * 1/2 to 1 cup jam for spread * 2 tbs. powdered sugar * vanilla*

Prepare leaven and alow to rise. (See above).

Prepare dough. Melt butter and beat egg whites until stiff. Cream egg yolks with sugar and lemon peel.

Pour raised leaven into egg yolk mixture, add flour, pinch of salt, egg whites and milk and beat dough with flat spoon.

When bubbles appear, gradually add melted butter and alcohol. Mix well. Place dough in warm place under cover and allow to rise. Be careful that dough does not become overheated. When dough is double its size, begin to fry. Heat part of the fat in griddle or egg griddle. Place dough in hot fat with a spoon. Form round, thick cakes. Place cakes on griddle, leaving space between so that they do not stick together as they rise during the frying. Fry over a medium flame. Turn and brown on both sides. Add a little fat to the griddle and fry following portions of blinki.

Seal two cakes with jam when fried and sprinkle with powdered sugar and vanilla. Serve hot.

Racuszki

Sour-Milk Pancakes

*2 cups sour milk * 2 eggs * about 3 cups flour * 1/4 tsp. soda * 6 tbs. fat for frying * powdered sugar*

Mix milk thoroughly, add eggs, flour and soda.

Place some fat on griddle and heat. Pour dough on griddle and spread into small round cakes. Fry on both sides until brown.

Place fried cakes on a round plate and sprinkle with powdered sugar.

Fry all racuszki in similar manner. Serve hot off the griddle.

A few teaspoons of sliced rhubarb or apples may be added to the dough. Mix thoroughly and fry.

Apples Fried in Batter

*1 1/2 cups flour * 1/2 cup cold water * 1 egg * 2 tbs. oil * salt * 3 medium compote apples * 1/2 cup fat for frying * 4 to 5 tbs. powdered sugar * * vanilla*

Prepare batter. Add egg and oil to the flour and mix thoroughly until all flour lumps disappear and batter is smooth. Add water and salt. Mix.

Rinse apples, peel and cut into round slices 1/3 inch thick, with 3 slices per serving.

Place part of the fat in griddle and heat. Pierce apple slices with fork and dip each in batter. Lift out of batter and when it has flowed off a bit arrange slices on griddle with spaces in between so that they do not stick together and lose shape. Fry apples slowly. When browned on one side, turn and brown quickly.

When the apples are tender and the batter is browned, remove from griddle and place on a heated dessert plate. Sprinkle generously with powdered sugar and vanilla.

Serve immediately, as the cake grows limp when the steam from the apples saturates it.

Mądrzyki

Cheese Pancakes

*2 1/2 cups cottage cheese * 4 egg yolks * 4 tbs. sugar * 4 egg whites * 1 cup flour * salt * 6 tbs. fat for frying * vanilla * powdered sugar*

Press cheese through a sieve, or grind and cream.
Add one yolk at a time alternately with the sugar and cream.
Add flour and salt and mix well.
Beat egg whites and fold into cheese.
Roll out 1/3 inch thick and cut out small rounds.
Heat part of the fat in griddle. Place cakes and fry until browned on both sides. Fry in batches. Place pancakes on a heated plate and sprinkle generously with sugar and vanilla.
Serve while hot.
Whipped cream may be served with the pancakes.

Baked Macaroni and Apples

*2 1/2 cups flour * 3 to 4 eggs * salt * 6 medium apples * about 3/4 cup sugar * 3 tbs. butter * butter for greasing pot * bread crumbs for pot * * 2 tbs. butter for dotting * powdered sugar * cinnamon*

Prepare dough. Break eggs into flour. Add a pinch of salt and knead dough well.
Roll out dough very thin. Dry on board and roll. Cut as thin as possible with a sharp knife.
Scatter macaroni on the bottom of a baking pan, place in oven and brown to a light golden color.
Prepare apples. Wash apples and bake. Put through sieve. Add sugar to taste, add 3 tbs. butter and simmer, stirring constantly.
Grease pot well with butter and dust with bread crumbs.
Divide macaroni into three parts. Arrange first part on bottom of pot, dot with butter, sprinkle with powdered sugar and spread with half of the apple marmalade. Place second layer of macaroni dot with butter and sprinkle with sugar and spread with apples. Cover this layer with a third part of macaroni.
Pour the remaining butter over the top and place in very hot oven for 15 minutes.
Place macaroni on a round plate and sprinkle generously with sugar and cinnamon.
Serve while hot.

Baked Macaroni and Walnuts

*2 1/2 cups flour * 3 to 4 eggs * salt * 3/4 cup walnuts * 4 egg yolks *
* 1/2 cup sugar * vanilla * 2 tbs. butter * 4 egg whites * butter for greasing
casserole*

Prepare dough. Break eggs into flour. Add a pinch of salt and knead
dough thoroughly without water. Roll out into two thin sheets.
Dry dough and roll out. Cut very thin strips. Scatter macaroni over board
to dry.
Bring salted water to the boil, add the macaroni. When it floats to the top,
drain and rinse with cold water. Drain off.
Grate walnuts.
Cream egg yolks with sugar and vanilla. Melt butter. Beat egg whites.
Add butter to egg yolks. Cream and add macaroni and egg whites. Mix.
Add walnuts at very end.
Place macaroni in a greased casserole and place in oven for 15 minutes.
Serve hot with vanilla sauce.

Steamed Omelet

*4 egg yolks * 4 1/2 tbs. sugar * 4 egg whites * 4 tbs. flour * 1/2 cup
preserved fruit with syrup*

Heat water in pot in which a bowl with egg yolks can be placed. Cream egg
yolks with sugar and place in boiling water and heat, creaming constantly.
Cool.
Beat egg whites stiff and add to yolks. Add flour and mix.
Place in small torte pan and bake in a hot oven.
Remove baked omelet from pan, fold in half and garnish with preserves
or cover with wine sauce.

Strawberry Pie

D o u g h: *7 tbs. flour * 4 1/2 tbs. butter * about 1 1/2 tsp. cold water *
* 1 egg white * * C r e a m: *1 egg yolk * 1 egg * 4 1/2 tbs. powdered sugar *
* 2 tbs. flour * vanilla * 8 tbs. milk * 1 tbs. butter * * T o p p i n g: *2 cups
strawberries * 3/4 cup strawberry purée (sherbet) * 1 1/2 tsp. gelatine *
* 2 tbs. hot water*

Prepare dough. Cut butter into flour. Sprinkle with water and cut in and
mix until dough forms into a roll. Knead lightly, forming into a ball, place
on plate and store in cool place for 2 or 3 hours.

Divide chilled dough into three parts: roll out 2/3 of the dough and line the bottom of small cake pan. Form 1/3 of the dough into a roll. Spread dough in pan with egg white. Arrange a dough roll around the bottom layer near the sides of the pan and press down with fingers so that it is sealed with the bottom round. Flatten it out, pressing to the sides of the pan. In this manner sides are formed which will contain the layer of filling. Bake in hot oven until a golden yellow. Remove from oven and cool.

Prepare cream. Cream egg yolk and whole egg with sugar. Add flour, vanilla and add boiling milk gradually, creaming mixture constantly over boiling water. When the mixture thickens and the flour loses its raw smell, add butter and mix. Cool in cold place.

Prepare strawberries. Select large, first-grade, ripe strawberries. Rinse and drain. Remove stems.

Prepare sherbet. Rinse the remaining strawberries, remove stems and press through sieve. Sift sugar, press lumps and add to strawberry purée. Mix and place in cool place. Soak gelatine.

Dissolve gelatine in 2 tbs. hot water, stirring constantly. Add to strawberry purée, mix and cool.

Finish pie. Place cold cream in pie shell, spread. Arrange whole strawberries on cream.

When the purée begins to set, fill in spaces between the strawberries arranged on the cream. Place pie in cool place. Serve when the top sets.

Grape Pie

D o u g h: *7 tbs. flour * 4 1/2 tbs. butter * about 1 1/2 tsp. cold water * * 1 egg white * * C r e a m: 1 egg yolk * 1 egg * 4 1/2 tbs. powdered sugar * * vanilla * 2 tbs. flour * 8 tbs. milk * 1 tbs. butter * T o p p i n g: 1 lb. Malaga grapes * 1/2 recipe for lemon jelly without lemon peel (see page 412)*

Prepare dough. Cut in butter and flour, sprinkle with water and cut in, forming into a ball.

When dough is formed, knead lightly with hand and place on plate. Smooth out and place in cold place for a few hours.

Divide the chilled dough into three parts: roll out 2/3 of the dough and line the bottom of cake pan. Form a roll out of the remaining 1/3 of the dough.

Spread egg white over the dough in the pan. Arrange dough roll around the bottom layer near the sides of the pan and press down with fingers so that it adheres to bottom round. Form a ridge around which the filling will hold.

Bake shell in hot oven until a light golden yellow (about 40 min.). Remove from oven and cool.

Prepare cream. Cream egg yolk and whole egg with sugar, vanilla and flour. Bring milk to the boil.

Place mixture in double boiler and mix, adding boiling milk. When the cream thickens and loses the smell of raw flour, add butter, mix and remove from double boiler. Cool and stir so that the top of the cream does not dry.

Prepare lemon jelly without lemon peel (using half the recipe for lemon jelly).

Rinse grapes′and remove stems. Drain off water.

Place egg yolk cream in pie shell and cover top with fresh grapes. Pour setting lemon jelly over the grapes and allow to set. Serve on the day of baking so that it does not become soggy.

Orange or pineapple pie may be baked in a similar manner.

Cut pineapple into thin slices and divide each into four parts and arrange on the cream in rows with the top of the triangles all turned in the same direction. Pour pineapple jelly which has been prepared out of the pineapple stock, gelatine, sugar and lemon juice.

Apricot or Peach Pie

D o u g h: *7 tbs. flour * 4 1/2 tbs. butter * about 1 1/2 tsp. cold water * * 1 egg white * C r e a m: 1 egg yolk * 1 egg * 4 1/2 tbs. powdered sugar * * 2 tbs. flour * vanilla * 8 tbs. milk * 1 tbs. butter * T o p p i n g: 20 apricots or peaches in compote * 3/4 cup compote syrup * 3 tbs. sugar to taste * 1—1 1/2 tsp. gelatine * lemon juice * (yellow-orange or light pink food coloring)*

Prepare dough and cream as for strawberry pie (see page 439). Drain apricots taken out of the compote.

Prepare jelly. Soak gelatine. Bring compote syrup and sugar to the boil. Add gelatine and dissolve, stirring constantly.

If necessary add lemon juice to syrup and food coloring.

Remove to cool place so that the jelly begins to set.

Finish pie. Spread egg yolk cream over bottom of pie shell. Arrange drained apricots. When the jelly begins to set, pour some over the fruit. (This should be repeated two or three times. When the first portion of the jelly sets, pour more jelly, being careful that the jelly does not overflow).

Łamańce (Triangles with Poppy Seed)

Christmas-Eve Dessert

D o u g h: *2 1/2 cups flour * 3 1/2 tbs. butter * 1/2 cup powdered sugar * * 1 egg yolk * salt * about 1/2 cup sour cream * P o p p y - s e e d m i x - t u r e: 2 cups poppy seeds * honey or sugar * 1/2 cup medium cream * * 3 tbs. almonds * 3 bitter almonds * lemon peel*

Prepare dough. Cut in flour and butter. Mix with sugar and knead with egg yolk, salt and sour cream. Add only enough sour cream so that the dough does not adhere to the board.
Knead well, pounding on board. Rool out quite thin and cut into small triangular cakes. Arrange on a greased sheet and bake until a light golden. Scald almonds, remove peel and grind.
Cover poppy seeds with boiling water.
When poppy seeds can be crushed between fingers, drain in fine sieve. Drain off and grind poppy seeds several times through a fine mesh until smooth and moist.
Add honey, or honey and sugar to taste, to ground poppy seed. Add almonds, lemon peel and enough cream to form a thick sauce. Place poppy-seed mixture in compote dish and before serving add the triangle cookies. Serve remaining łamańce on a plate. Łamańce with poppy seed are a traditional cold dessert for Christmas Eve.

Buchty

Yeast Rolls

L e a v e n: *1/2 oz. yeast * 1 tsp. sugar * 3 tbs. milk * D o u g h: 3 egg yolks * 1 egg * about 1/2 cup sugar * lemon peel * salt * 3 1/2 cups flour * 1/2 cup milk * 6 tbs. butter*

Prepare leaven and set in warm place to rise. Be careful that it is not overheated.
Cream egg yolks and egg with sugar. Add lemon peel and pinch of salt. Add leaven to egg-yolk mixture, add flour and mix dough with a flat spoon, adding warm milk. When all the ingredients are mixed, gradually add warm butter and beat dough with spoon until bubbles of air appear. Then even out dough, cover and let stand in warm place to rise.
Grease deep pan. When dough is double its bulk divide into 15 even portions. Moisten hands with butter and knead out round rolls. Arrange tightly one beside another and let stand to rise. Place rolls in hot oven (350°F) and bake (about 40 min.).

Remove from oven and allow to cool a little in pan. Take out of pan and separate rolls.

Serve while still warm with fruit syrup or sweet sauce — for instance vanilla sauce.

PUDDINGS AND SOUFFLÉS

Pudding is a light dessert prepared in steam in a special tightly-covered container.

The pudding is usually prepared on a base of egg yolks creamed with sugar (with an addition of butter or without butter), beaten egg whites, a flour ingredient or nuts and almonds. The cake is also composed of a variety of flavors and aromas.

Soufflé (from the French) is a baked desert which is prepared of ingredients very much like those in a pudding. A second variety of soufflés, more generally known, are fruit soufflés composed of egg white, sugar and fruit pulp.

Puddings may be divided into two groups, depending on their ingredients. The first group is composed of pudding prepared with egg yolks creamed with sugar, a dry ingredient, which together with the egg yolks constitutes a batter, and flavorings. This light cake is made fluffy with beaten egg whites. As an example walnut or poppy-seed puddings belong to this group. The second group is composed of puddings with a more compact batter, though also fluffed with beaten egg whites. These cakes are composed not only of egg yolks creamed with sugar, flour and beaten egg whites, but also of a large amount of butter creamed with egg yolks until fluffy. Dried fruit or chesse puddings may serve as an example.

Puddings are cooked in steam in special pudding molds.

The cooked pudding is elastic, springs back under pressure of the finger. The top is dry and does not adhere. The sides should be shrunk back from the pan. Pudding may be tested with a sharpened wooden stick. If the stick comes out dry the pudding is done.

When the pudding is overdone, the cake falls and is too dry, more compact and smaller in yield than a cake that has been properly cooked. An underdone pudding falls when taken out of the pan and cooled. That is why it is necessary to follow recipes in baking and to make the test with wooden stick.

Pudding is a hot dessert (with a few exceptions as for instance cheese or poppy-seed pudding), and is usually served with sweet sauces, some with cooked fruit juice or syrup. The following sauces are most often used: vanilla sauce, wine chaudeau, chocolate, apricot sauce, etc.

Very aromatic fruit syrups are selected for puddings (raspberry, cherry, strawberry).

Cocoa Pudding

*4 1/2 tbs. fat. * 1 egg * 3/4 cup sugar * 1 cup milk * 3 tbs. cocoa ** 2 cups flour * baking powder * salt * butter and flour for mold*

Prepare pudding mold and heat water.

Cream fat, add egg, sugar, cocoa and dilute with part of the milk. Cream. Add remainder of milk to the creamed mixture. Combine with flour, baking powder and pinch of salt. Mix well and pour into greased mold sprinkled with flour. Steam for 1 to 1 1/4 hours.

Turn out pudding on round plate and cut into portions.

Serve with cocoa sauce or cooked fruit juice.

Poppy-Seed Pudding

*5 oz. poppy seeds * 3 tbs. candied orange peel * lemon peel * 4 egg yolks * 1/2 cup sugar * 4 egg whites * 1 tsp. bread crumbs * butter and flour for mold*

Scald poppy seeds and drain off well. Grind through fine mesh into smooth paste. Prepare pudding mold and heat water. Chop orange peel.

Cream egg yolks with sugar. Add poppy seeds, orange peel and lemon peel. Cream.

Beat egg whites and combine with egg-yolk mixture and bread crumbs. Place in greased mold sprinkled with flour and steam for 45 minutes.

Remove pudding to round plate and cut into portions.

Serve with vanilla or wine sauce.

Poppy-Seed Pudding with Almonds

*1/2 cup poppy seeds * 4 egg yolks * 4 1/2 tbs. sugar * 1/2 cup almonds * lemon peel * 3 1/2 tbs. candied orange peel * 2 to 3 tbs. bread crumbs * 4 egg whites * butter for mold*

Cover poppy seeds with boiling water and let soak until steeped and may be crushed between fingers (about 1 hour). Pour into fine sieve and allow to drain off. Grind 2 or 3 times through a fine mesh.

Place almonds in boiling water, scald and remove skin. Dry in oven and grind.

Cut orange peel into fine cubes.

Cream egg yolks and sugar until fluffy. Add lemon peel, orange peel, poppy seeds and cream mixture.

Beat egg whites stiff and add to mixture. Add almonds and bread crumbs and fold in.

Prepare pudding mold and heat water.

Pour mixture into greased mold and steam (45 minutes).

Serve with vanilla or chocolate sauce.

Roll Pudding

*3 oz. stale roll * 1 cup milk * 1 tbs. raisins * 1 oz. almonds * 3 bitter almonds * 3 tbs. candied orange peel * lemon peel * 3 tbs. butter * * 4 egg yolks * 1/2 cup sugar * 4 egg whites * butter for mold*

Prepare pudding mold and heat water.

Soak roll and squeeze out milk.

Rinse raisins and remove stems. Scald almonds and chop; chop orange peel. Cream butter, add egg yolks one at a time, add sugar gradually, and cream. Add squeezed roll, cream.

Whip egg whites, place in egg-yolk mixture, add almonds, orange peel and lemon peel. Mix. If necessary add bread crumbs (batter should have the consistency of sponge batter). Place in greased mold and steam 3/4 of an hour.

Remove pudding to round plate and cut into portions.

Serve with wine sauce or cooked fruit juice.

Walnut Pudding

*1 1/2 cups walnuts * lemon peel * 3 tbs. candied orange peel * 6 egg yolks * 1/2 cup sugar * 6 egg whites * 1 tsp. bread crumbs * butter and flour for mold*

Prepare pudding mold and heat water.

Grind walnuts.

Chop orange peel.

Cream egg yolks with sugar, add lemon and orange peel.

Beat egg whites stiff and mix with egg yolks, walnuts and bread crumbs. Place in greased mold sprinkled with flour and steam for 45 minutes. Remove pudding to round plate and cut into portions. Serve with vanilla sauce or wine sauce or with whipped cream.

Chocolate Pudding

*2 1/2 oz. chocolate * 3/4 cup almonds * 5 egg yolks * 1/2 cup sugar *
* 6 egg whites * 3 tbs. flour * butter for mold*

Melt chocolate in double boiler.
Prepare pudding mold and heat water.
Wipe almonds in a towel and grind.
Cream egg yolks with sugar, add melted chocolate and cream. Beat egg
whites stiff. Place in egg-yolk mixture. Sprinkle with almonds and flour.
Mix lightly. Place in greased mold. Steam for 45 minutes. Remove pudding
to round plate and cut into portions. Serve with vanilla, apricot sauce
or with whipped cream.

Cheese Pudding

*1 medium potato * 7 tbs. candied orange peel * 3 bitter almonds *
* 1 3/4 cups white cheese * 3 tbs. butter * 4 egg yolks * 1/2 cup
sugar * vanilla * 5 egg whites * butter for mold*

Rinse potato, peel and cook. Mash.
Chop orange peel fine.
Scald almonds and chop fine.
Grind cheese and potato.
Prepare pudding mold and heat water.
Cream butter, adding one egg yolk at a time and a little sugar. Add vanilla,
cheese and potato. Cream thoroughly. Combine with orange peel and
almonds at the end.
Beat egg whites stiff and fold into cheese mixture. Place in greased mold
and steam for 45 minutes.
Remove pudding to round plate. Mark portions and sprinkle with sugar
and vanilla.

Puff Pudding

*1 cup milk * 5 tbs. butter * 1 cup flour * 6 egg yolks * 1/2 cup sugar *
* vanilla * 6 egg whites * butter and flour for mold*

Prepare pudding mold and heat water.
Bring milk and butter to the boil. Add flour to boiling milk and beat well.
Steam on a medium flame until batter becomes translucent. Remove from
fire.
Cream egg yolks with sugar and vanilla, add gradually to the hot batter.

Beat well. Beat egg whites and add to mixture. Place in greased mold sprinkled with flour and steam for 45 minutes.

Remove pudding to round plate. Cut into slices. Serve with wine, vanilla, coffee sauce or cooked fruit juice.

Pudding with Preserved Fruit

*1 cup mixed fruit preserves * 2 tbs. rose preserve * 6 egg whites * * 3/4 cup sugar * 2 tbs. butter * 2 tbs. bread crumbs * butter for mold*

Place fruit preserves in sieve for several hours to drain. Prepare pudding mold and heat water.

Beat egg whites and mix with sugar. Cream for 30 minutes. Add drained preserves and bread crumbs gradually. Add butter at end and mix well.

Place in greased mold, cover and steam for 45 minutes. Remove pudding to round plate.

Serve immediately with vanilla sauce or cooked fruit juice.

Buckwheat-Flour Pudding

*6 egg yolks * 1/2 cup sugar * vanilla * 3 cups buckwheat flour * 3 cups sour cream * 6 egg whites * butter for mold * 1 cup sweet heavy cream * 4 tbs. sugar * vanilla*

Cream egg yolks with sugar and vanilla.

Add sour cream to flour and mix thoroughly.

To fluffy mixture add a spoon of egg yolks (with sugar and vanilla) at a time and cream 20 minutes.

Beat egg whites stiff and mix with creamed ingredients. Place mixture into greased mold and bake in a medium oven for 45 minutes. Whip sweet cream and mix with sugar and vanilla. Remove pudding to round plate. Serve warm with whipped cream or cold with lemon frosting.

Steamed Apricot or Raspberry Soufflé

*10 apricots * a few spoons of hot water * 1 cup sugar * 4 egg whites * * lemon juice * butter for dish*

Rinse apricots, stone and cover with a small amount of water. Cook until tender. Press fruit through sieve. Evaporate liquid from fruit pulp.

Add sugar to thick pulp and cook over asbestos plate as marmalade burns easily. When mixture has been reduced to about 10 tbs., begin to whip egg whites.

447

Add one spoon of cooking marmalade at a time and a few drops of lemon juice (to taste) to whipped egg whites.

Grease a round fireproof dish. Place the beaten egg-white mixture in greased dish.

Cover top with granulated sugar and place in moderate oven.

When the soufflé rises and the top is browned and dry, remove and serve immediately for a cold soufflé falls.

Serve with vanilla sauce.

Apple Soufflé

*5 medium compote apples * 1 cup sugar * lemon peel * juice of 1/2 lemon * 4 egg whites * butter for dish * 1 1/2 tbs. granulated sugar to sprinkle*

Rinse apples and arrange tightly in pan. Bake in a moderate oven. Remove apples and immediately press through sieve. Add sugar to fruit pulp and lemon peel and cook a little.

Beat egg whites stiff, combine with hot marmalade, beating with egg beater constantly. When mixed, remove from flame and flavor with lemon juice.

Grease a fireproof dish.

Place mixture in fireproof dish using a spoon or through tube to form mounds. Place in hot oven (350°F).

When the soufflé rises and the top is browned, remove from oven and serve immediately.

The soufflé should be baked just before serving, otherwise the soufflé falls.

Serve with vanilla sauce.

Steamed Soufflé

*1 1/2 cups milk * 4 1/2 tbs. butter * 1 cup flour * 4 egg yolks * 1/2 cup sugar * 6 egg whites * butter for dish*

Bring milk to the boil, add butter and when it melts add flour. Beat quickly and thoroughly with a spoon until smooth.

When the batter becomes translucent place in a bowl. Add one egg yolk at a time to hot batter beating constantly and add sugar gradually. Beat egg whites stiff and add to batter.

Mix and place batter immediately in greased, fireproof dish. Bake 25 minutes in very hot oven.

Serve with vanilla sauce or wine or apricot sauce.

Steamed Soufflé with Orange Peel

*8 egg yolks * 1/2 cup sugar * 2 tbs. candied orange peel * 2 cups milk * 3 tbs. butter * 1 cup potato starch * 8 egg whites * butter and flour for dish*

Cut orange peel into small pieces.
Cream egg yolks with sugar and mix with orange peel.
Heat 1 cup milk and butter until butter melts.
Mix second cup of milk with potato starch and pour into hot milk, and without removing from fire beat quickly and well until smooth. Stir mixture and bring to the boil. Remove from fire.
Add one spoon of creamed egg yolks at a time and beat constantly. Beat egg whites and fold into batter. Place in greased plate that has been dusted with flour. Bake in a moderate oven for 30 minutes. Serve immediately.
Serve with hot vanilla sauce or wine or apricot sauce.

Lemon Soufflé

*2 lemons * 4 egg yolks * 3/4 cup sugar * lemon peel * 4 egg whites * * 2 tbs. bread crumbs * butter for dish*

Prick lemons very lightly so as not to harm the fruit and bring to the boil twice, pouring off the whole water twice.
Press cooked lemons through sieve and cool.
Cream egg yolks with sugar, adding gradually the cooked lemon pulp and fresh lemon peel.
Beat egg whites stiff.
Add egg whites to egg-yolk mixture, sprinkle with bread crumbs and mix.
Place batter in greased, fireproof dish and place in hot oven. Bake 25 min.
Serve immediately before soufflé falls. Serve with vanilla sauce.

BEVERAGES

COFFEE, TEA AND COCOA

The most popular drinks in Poland are coffee and tea. Neither cocoa nor chocolate have ever been extensively used.
Tea in Poland is served in glasses or in teacups.

Turkish-Style Black Coffee

*2 1/2 cups brewed coffee (2 oz. pulverized coffee per person) * 4 tbs. powdered sugar * 4 tbs. sugar*

Use pulverized coffee; sift powdered sugar. Place coffee and sugar into saucepan, pour in exact amount of water and place on asbestos plate over gas or electric burner. Heat three times until coffee begins to rise, but do not allow it to boil. Cover and serve immediately from saucepan into demitasse cups.

Serve the rest of the sugar separately so that coffee may be sweetened to taste. Turkish-style coffee is served very hot and drunk immediately after pouring and sweetening, together with grounds.

Viennese-Style Coffee

*2 1/2 cups strong coffee * 3/4 cup whipped cream * 1 1/2 tbs. powdered sugar for cream * about 10 lumps of sugar*

Prepare very hot, strong coffee, pour immediately into cups or glasses, place some slightly sweetened whipped cream on top.
Serve lump sugar separately. The coffee is sweetened individually to taste, and while stirring, the whipped cream is mixed with the coffee.
Viennese-style coffee is served with small sweet cakes or torte.

Coffee with Milk or Cream

*2 1/2 cups strong coffee * 2 1/2 cups milk or cream * about 10 lumps of sugar*

Pour brewed coffee and hot milk or cream into separate silver or porcelain pitchers.
Serve sugar on the side.
Allow each person to pour coffee and milk according to his own taste. Coffee with milk or cream is most generally used as a breakfast drink and served very hot. It is served with fresh wheat or Graham bread, butter, choice smoked meats, honey or sweet yeast buns.
Viennese-style breakfast consists of coffee with milk or cream, fresh wheat bread, butter, ham and soft-boiled eggs.

Iced Black Coffee

*2 1/2 cups strong coffee * 10—12 lumps of sugar * 3 ice cubes for each portion*

Sweeten brewed coffee, pour into vessel which can be tightly sealed, cover and cool. Serve in tall glasses, add 3 ice cubes and serve with a straw.

Mazagran

*2 1/2 cups strong coffee * 1/2 cup sugar * 3/4 cup vodka (45 proof) * * 4 tumblers of rum * 3 oz. ice*

Prepare strong coffee, pour into vessel, sweeten, close tightly and chill. When coffee is chilled, add vodka and rum, mix, serve in tall glasses, add 2 ice cubes and serve with a straw.

Frozen Coffee

*1 1/2 cups strong coffee * 4 tbs. sugar * 1 1/4 cups heavy cream * * 3/4 cup whipped cream*

Mix brewed coffee with sugar, cool in covered vessel, add cream, place in ice-cream freezer. When the coffee freezes, forming a thick but not completely frozen mass of large crystals with fluid in between, remove from freezer and serve in tall glasses.

Frozen coffee is served with sweetened whipped cream.

Iced Tea

*2 1/2 cups tea * 1/2 cup sugar * 2 1/2 cups sweet cream * 3 tumblers of rum*

Add cream and sugar to brewed tea, cover and chill thoroughly.

Mix with rum before serving.

Serve in tall glasses with a straw.

Cocoa

*1 quart milk * cocoa to taste * sugar to taste*

Boil milk, mix cocoa with sugar, pour a little boiling milk into sugar and cocoa mixture, stir vigorously. When cocoa is smooth and combined with the milk, pour into boiling milk and stir while heating.

Cocoa may be served with whipped cream.

Iced Cocoa

*6 tbs. sugar * 4 eggs * 4 cups milk * 8 tbs. cocoa * 3/4 cup sweet cream*

Cream eggs with sugar until fluffy. Prepare cocoa with milk. Add half the boiling cocoa gradually to eggs while beating constantly. Place the mixture over steam and beat until it loses its raw aroma. Remove from steam, combine with rest of cooked cocoa, cool and place in ice-cream freezer. When cooled, cover tightly, crank on dasher and turn as for ice cream. When the cocoa begins to form crystals but is not completely frozen, add sweet cream and turn in machine for a short time. Remove from freezer, spoon cocoa into tall glasses and serve immediately.

455

FRUIT AND HERB DRINKS

Lemonade

*2 cups water * 1 1/2 cups granulated sugar * lemon peel * lemon slices with peel * lemon juice to taste * 2 cups soda water*

Boil water with sugar in an enamel saucepan, pour into jar. Dice lemon peel finely, add to hot syrup and cool together. Rinse lemon, dry thoroughly, slice fine, cutting enough for two slices per portion Add soda water to cooled syrup and add lemon juice to taste. Divide into tall glasses, add slices of lemon and ice cubes or cracked ice. Serve with a straw.

Currant Cooler

*1 1/2 cups red or black currants * 4 cups water * 1/2 cup granulated sugar * (red food coloring)*

Clean currants, drain and stem. Heat water in enamel saucepan. Add currants to boiling water, bring to the boil a few times, drain and press out juice on sieve. Add sugar to hot liquid, dissolve while stirring; if necessary add food coloring to color liquid. Pour drink into jar and chill.

The drink may be served with ice cubes or crackel ice and should then be served with a straw.

The above recipe may be used substituting strawberries or raspberries for the currants.

Cranberry Cooler

*3 cups water * 1 1/2 cups cranberries * 1 cup sugar * lemon peel*

Boil water in enamel saucepan. Rinse cranberries, drain, place in boiling water and cook, strain, press out juice on sieve. Add sugar to hot liquid (if necessary, add food coloring). Add lemon peel to taste. Pour into jar and chill.

The cooler may be served with ice cubes or cracked ice, and should then be served with a straw.

Carrot and Cranberry Cooler

*1 lb. sweet carrots * 6 cups water * 2 1/2 cups cranberries * 2 1/2 cups sugar * (lemon peel)*

Clean carrots, grate finely, pour over with boiling water.
Mix carrots and water thoroughly to secure the maximum amount of juice.
Drain off pulp, press out juice and water.
Select cranberries, rinse, crush with spoon into a pulp, strain and add juice to drink, add sugar to taste; add a little lemon peel. This drink may be made with lemon juice and carrots instead of cranberries.
Chill thoroughly.

Honey Beverage

*5 cups water * honey to taste * lemon, currant or cranberry juice*

Heat water, add honey and dissolve.
Prepare pure juice from currants, cranberries or lemon. If necessary add a little sugar.

Linden-Blossom Cooler

*5 cups water * 6 tbs. dried linden blossoms * 6 tbs. honey * sugar*

Add dried linden blossoms to boiling water, set aside covered.
When the dried herbs drop to bottom, filter, add honey and sugar to taste.
Chill.
Serve in tall glasses.

Mint Cooler

*5 cups water * 3 tbs. dried mint * 3 oz. sugar * 1/2 cup cracked ice*

Boil water, drop in mint, cover and place on low heat to brew.
When mint leaves fall to bottom, filter, sweeten, and chill in covered vessel so that aroma is not lost.
Serve in tall glasses with cracked ice and straw.

MILK BEVERAGES

Sour Milk

*5 cups milk * 3 tbs. sour cream*

The milk should be soured in glasses or porcelain cups, preferably at room temperature. Souring takes from 24—28 hours depending on the freshness of the milk and the temperature. The milk should be mixed with the sour cream and then poured into cups or glasses and left to stand until soured. The most tasty sour milk is made with fresh milk, and should not be kept too long. On hot days, the sour milk may be chilled in a refrigerator before serving.

Serve sour milk with boiled or fried potatoes, fluffy cereals, especially groats, or with rye or Graham bread with butter and chives, radishes, tomatoes, etc.

Roztrzepaniec

*5 cups sour milk * 1/2 cup sour cream*

Milk for roztrzepaniec is soured in a large crock, used only for this purpose. Immediately after the milk is soured, beat thoroughly into smooth, uniform consistency, combine with fresh sour cream, and chill.

Serve in tall glasses with straw.

Spring Beverage

*1 bunch of radishes * 2 tbs. chopped chives and green dill * 4 1/2 cups sour milk * salt to taste*

Clean radishes, cut off leaves and root, slice finely or chop. Rinse chives and dill, drain off water, chop finely.

Stir milk thoroughly, combine with greens, salt lightly, chill and serve immediately.

Lithuanian Beverage

*1 cup sour beet liquid * 1 tbs. chopped green dill and chives * 3 cups sour milk * 1/2 cup sour cream * salt * sugar*

Prepare beet liquid. Scrub beets, peel, rinse several times, cut into small pieces, place in a jar and pour over with warm pre-boiled water, add 1 tbs. of sugar. Cover jar with gauze, set aside in warm place to sour. After 4—5 days, when the liquid sours, pour into bottle. Do not keep for too long a time, avoid over-souring, as then it cannot be used for the drink.

Rinse dill and chives thoroughly, drain off water, chop fine.

Stir sour milk to smooth consistency, add sour cream, beet liquid, salt, sugar to taste, combine with dill. Cool.

Serve in glasses.

Whey Beverage

*1 cup chopped cucumber * 2 tbs. chopped green dill * 4 cups fresh whey * salt*

Rinse cucumber, peel, chop finely.
Rinse dill, drain, chop finely.
Add dill and cucumber to whey. Salt to taste. Mix. Chill.
Serve in glasses with spoon for cucumber.

Buttermilk

*2 tbs. chopped chives or green dill * 5 cups fresh buttermilk * salt*

Rinse chives or dill, drain, chop finely, add to buttermilk, salt to taste.

Vanilla Milk with Egg Yolks

*3 egg yolks * 3 tbs. sugar * vanilla * 5 cups fresh milk*

Cream egg yolks with sugar and vanilla. Boil milk. Place creamed yolks in pot with boiling water, steam with 1 cup of boiled milk, beat until the yolks lose their raw aroma.
Remove yolks, mix with rest of milk. If the milk is to be served cold, stir while cooling to avoid skin on milk.
Serve either hot or cold.

Caramel Milk

*1 cup caramel (dissolved) * 4 cups fresh milk * 4 tbs. sugar*

Prepare caramel. Brown 2 1/2 tbs. sugar to dark golden color, add boiling water carefully, bring to the boil while stirring.
Boil milk, add dissolved caramel, combine with milk, add sugar, cool.
The drink may be served hot or cold.

Cocoa Milk

*4 cups fresh milk * 1/2 cup sweet cream * 1/2 cup cocoa * 1/2 cup sugar*

Boil milk with sweet cream. Add cocoa to 2 cups of boiled liquid, mix quickly, add to the rest of liquid while stirring, cook, add sugar to taste.
Serve hot or chilled (in summer).

Milk with Fruit Syrup

*4 1/2 cups fresh milk * 1/2 cup strawberry or raspberry syrup * sugar*

Combine milk with syrup; if necessary add sugar to taste, mix, chill.

Wild-Strawberry and Cream Cocktail

*2 cups wild strawberries * 8 tbs. sugar * 1/2 cup cracked ice * 3 cups sweet cream*

Rinse wild strawberries, drain, sprinkle with sugar and set aside for an hour in a cool place. Place strawberries and juice, ice and cream into mixer. Beat.

When thoroughly combined, serve immediately.

Fruit Cocktail with Cream

*2 cups fresh or frozen raspberries or apricots fresh or canned, or fresh sour cherries * 8 tbs. sugar * 1/2 cup cracked ice * 3 cups sweet cream*

Select fruit, clean, drain. Slice apricots in parts, pit the cherries.
Sprinkle fruit with sugar, set aside in cold place for an hour.
Place fruit with juice, ice and cream into mixer, beat.
Serve in glasses with vanilla wafer.

Nut Cocktail with Cream

*2 cups shelled hazelnuts * 8 tbs. sugar * 1/2 cup cracked ice * 3 cups sweet cream*

Brown nuts, wipe in towel, grind. Place nuts, sugar, ice and cream into mixer, beat.

When thoroughly blended, serve cocktail in mug placed on saucer with teaspoon and vanilla wafer.

Coffee Cocktail with Cream

*1 cup brewed coffee * 1/2 cup sugar * 1/2 cup cracked ice * 3 1/2 cups sweet cream*

Cool strong coffee, place in mixer, add sugar, ice and cream, beat.
When thoroughly blended serve cocktail in mug placed on saucer with teaspoon and vanilla wafer.

POLISH HOME-MADE VODKAS, LIQUEURS AND CORDIALS

VODKAS

Vodka is between 42 to 45 proof. It is chilled two hours before serving and served iced.

Kminkówka

Caraway-Seed Vodka

*4 cups spirits 96 proof * 1/2 cup cold water * 2 oz. caraway seeds * * 3 1/2 cups water for syrup * 8 oz. sugar*

Pour 1/2 cup of cold pre-boiled water and 4 cups of spirits into bottle, add caraway seeds, cork the bottle and set aside for four days.
Boil water for syrup, add sugar, cook slowly, skim.
Filter the spirits and caraway mixture, add carefully to hot syrup, mix thoroughly with spirits, pour into bottle, close hermetically.

Dried-Herbs Vodka (Vespestro)

*16 cups water * 3 lb. sugar * 16 cups spirits 96 proof * juice and peel of two lemons * 1 oz. angelica root * 1 oz. coriander * 1/2 tsp. anise*

Boil water, add sugar, bring to the boil slowly and skim.
Add spirits carefully to syrup.
Wash lemons, remove fine yellow layer of lemon peel.
Press out juice.
Pour the spirits with syrup into large narrow-necked bottle, add lemon juice and sliced lemon peel and all the herbs. Cork the bottle and set aside to steep in a dark place for four weeks.
After 4 weeks filter the vodka, pour into bottles, close hermetically.

Żubrówka

Bison-Grass Vodka

*1 bunch of dry Żubrówka (Herba Hierochloe) grass * 2 cups spirits 96 proof * 2 cups cold pre-boiled water*

Rinse the blades of żubrówka grass, shake off water, place in bottle and pour over with spirits. Cork bottle carefully, place in a cold, dark place for seven days. After seven days, filter the spirits.

Pour the cold pre-boiled water into the bottle, add the filtered spirits. Cork bottle carefully and set aside for 24 hours; żubrówka can be served immediately.

Śliwowica

Prune Vodka

*5 oz. dried prunes * 4 cups water * 4 cups spirits 96 proof*

Rinse prunes, dry and crush together with pits.
Boil water and cool.
Mix spirits with cold water, pour into large bottle, add prunes, cork and set aside for four weeks.
After four weeks have passed, filter, pour into bottles, close hermetically, place in a cold dark place.
Use after one year.
Before serving, chill.

Tarniówka

Sloe-Plum Vodka

*1 cup frozen sloe plums * 1 cup spirits 96 proof * 1 cup water * 3—5 oz. sugar*

Gather the sloe plums right after the first frost, when they are a little less tart, crush together with pits, place in bottle and pour over with spirits. Cork bottle and set aside for 7 days. After seven days, filter the spirits. Boil 1 cup of water, add sugar, cook slowly, skim. Add the filtered spirits to the hot syrup, mix, pour into bottle, close hermetically and place in dark, cold place for one month.

Orange or Lemon Vodka

*The peel of 2 oranges or lemons * 4 cups spirits 96 proof * 4 cups water * 1/2—1 lb. sugar (the vodka can be sweet or semi-dry)*

Rinse oranges or lemons, pare off thin surface of golden peel.
Pour spirits into bottle, add peel and place in spirits for a few hours, closed well.

462

Boil water, add sugar, cook slowly, skim, set aside and cool slightly. Add spirits to the warm syrup, mix thoroughly and pour back into bottle. Leave peel in vodka for two more days, after which filter the vodka and pour into bottles, close hermetically. Store in dark, cold place for a few months (6—8).

Lemon Vodka Made with Milk

*1 lemon * 1 vanilla bean * 4 cups milk * 10 oz. sugar * 2 cups spirits 96 proof*

Rinse lemon, cut in half, remove pits carefully, place in 2-quart jar.
Cut vanilla bean lengthwise, place in jug.
Boil milk, dissolve sugar in it, cool, pour into jug.
Add spirits at end. Close jug hermetically and place in a cool, dark place to steep for six weeks.
At the end of six weeks, filter, pour into bottles. Close bottles hermetically. This vodka may be served immediately.

Porter Vodka

*1 cup water * 1/2 lb. sugar * 2 cups porter * 2 cups spirits 96 proof * * 1/2 vanilla bean*

Boil water, add sugar, cook slowly, skim, pour in porter and bring to the boil.
Set syrup on table, cool for five minutes and add spirits gradually.
Add vanilla bean last.
Pour into bottles, close, cool and place in dark, cool place for four weeks.

Krupnik

Vodka with Honey

*1 lb. sugar * 2 cups boiling water * 0.1 oz. cinnamon * 15 cloves * * about 50 allspice berries * about 20 pepper seeds * 1 1/2 stars or about 8—10 segments of star-anise (Fructus Anisi Stellati; Illicium verum) * 1 lb. honey * 2 cups spirits 96 proof*

Sprinkle a little water over the sugar, mix and caramel to rather dark golden color, pour in 2 cups of boiling water gradually, add spices, parboil and strain.

Add honey to dissolved caramel, stir and bring to the boil, remove from heat, set aside on table, and add spirits gradually to hot mixture, stirring constantly. Strain and serve while hot. May be served cold too.

Eiercognac

*6 egg yolks * 10 oz. sugar * 2 cups heavy cream * 2 cups spirits 96 proof * * 1—2 tbs. Jamaica rum*

Cream egg yolks with sugar, steam, pouring boiling cream over them gradually, beat over steam until thick.
Remove yolks from steam, cool while stirring.
Add spirits gradually to warm mixture, stirring constantly so that the eggs do not curdle. Add rum.
Pour when cold into bottles, close and set aside for 14 days.

LIQUEURS

Liqueurs are sweet drinks with an alcohol content up to 60 proof.

Angelica Liqueur

*2 oz. angelica seeds * 1/4 oz. fennel seeds * 1/4 oz. anise * 1/5 oz. coriander * 4 cups spirits 96 proof * about 1 1/2 cups water * 1 lb. sugar*

Crush spices, place in large bottle, add spirits, cork and set aside for 7 days to steep in a cold, dark place.
After 7 days boil water, add sugar, cook slowly, skim and remove from heat.
Filter spirits, add gradually to warm syrup. Pour liqueur into bottles, close hermetically. Keep in dark, cold place for a few months.

Portuguese Liqueur

*Peel of four oranges * juice of two oranges * 4 cups spirits 96 proof * * 4 cups water * 2 lb. sugar*

Pare thin layer of peel from 4 oranges, cut into narrow strips.
Press juice from 2 oranges.
Place peel and juice into large bottle, add spirits, close and set aside to steep for one day (24 hours).

Boil water, add sugar, cook slowly while stirring continuously, skim and remove from heat.

Add the spirits and orange peels gradually to syrup while still hot, mix thoroughly, filter.

Pour into bottles, close hermetically and set aside in a cold, dark place for two months.

Tangerine Liqueur

*4—5 ripe tangerines * 4 cups spirits 96 proof * 3 cups water * 2 lb. sugar*

Remove thin layer of golden peel from tangerines, press out juice.

Place juice and peel into large bottle, pour in spirits, cork and set aside to steep for 24 hours.

Boil water, add sugar, cook slowly while stirring, skim, remove from heat and cool a little.

Add spirits carefully to syrup while hot, filter and pour into bottles. Close hermetically and place in cold, dark place for a few months (6—8).

Coffee Liqueur

*1/2 lb. quality coffee (hot ground) * 2 cups spirits 96 proof * 4 cups water * 3 lb. sugar * 4 cups spirits 96 proof*

Place coffee in a jar with tight-fitting cover, add 2 cups of spirits, seal jar, set aside for a week to steep.

After one week, strain the spirits.

Boil water, add sugar, dissolve while stirring, bring to the boil, skim and remove from heat.

Add 4 cups of spirits to syrup while still hot, then the coffee-flavored spirits. Filter, pour into bottles. Close hermetically, and set aside in dark place for a few months.

Vanilla Liqueur

*2—3 vanilla beans * 1 cup spirits 96 proof * 4 cups water * 3—4 lb. sugar * 4 cups spirits 96 proof*

Cut vanilla beans in the length and width, place in screw-top jar, add 1 cup of spirits, seal, place in dark place to steep for 1 week.

After one week boil water, add sugar, cook while stirring, skim and remove from heat.

Add vanilla and spirits to syrup while hot and then 4 cups of spirits, filter and pour into bottles. Close hermetically and keep in a dark place for a few months (6—8).

FRUIT CORDIALS

Cordials may be prepared with all types of aromatic fruits. Their alcoholic content is between 50—60 proof.

Wiśniak [Dry]

Cherry Cordial

*2 lb. dark, late sour cherries (Griotte) * 3 portions of sugar — 2 oz. each * * 1 cup pre-boiled warm water * 4 cups spirits 96 proof*

Rinse cherries, stem, and place in large bottle, add the first portion of sugar, mix by shaking the bottle, add water with a temperature of 68°F. Seal bottle with cork and cotton and set aside for one day in a dark place. After one day add second portion of sugar and set aside for 2 days. After the 2 days have elapsed, add the 3rd portion of sugar, and set aside for 2 more days. The fruit, sugar and water should be allowed to ferment for a total of 5 days.
The fruit should be kept in a dark place during the entire time.
After the last fermentation add spirits to the fruit and set aside for 36 hours. Then pour all the liquid (fruit juice and spirits) into second bottle, cork tightly and set aside for 6 weeks to clarify in a dark cold place.
Then filter carefully and pour into bottles.
The cherries which remain may be used to make a lighter vodka.

Wiśniówka [Sweet]

Cherry Cordial

*2 lb. dark, late sour cherries (Griotte) * 3 portions of sugar — 5 oz. each * * 1 cup warm pre-boiled water * 4 cups spirits 96 proof*

Prepare the same as wiśniak.

Vodka Made with Cherries Left from Cordial

*Cherries remaining after preparing wiśniak or wiśniówka * 3 oz. sugar * * 1 cup spirits 96 proof * 1 1/2 cups water*

Add sugar to the cherries remaining after straining the wiśniak, mix with cherries shaking the bottle, set aside for 1 week. Pour off juice which has formed, mix with spirits and pre-boiled water, filter and pour into bottles. Close hermetically and keep in dark, cold place.

Cordial of Aromatic Fruits

*1/2 lb. of sugar for each lb. of fruit * spirits 96 proof*

Add cleaned and drained ripe fruit (wild strawberries, strawberries, raspberries, pitted apricots, etc.) to a large gallon bottle and add spirits 96 proof so that the fruit is covered (about 3 cups of spirits to 2 lb. of fruit). Cork bottle and set aside in dark place for about 4 days.

After 4 days have elapsed, pour fruit-flavored spirits into bottles, cork and keep in dark place.

Add sugar to the fruit remaining in the bottle, mix thoroughly with the fruit, shaking the bottle. Cork the bottle and keep in dark, cold place for 3—4 weeks so that juice is formed.

After 3—4 weeks have elapsed, pour the juice into fruit flavored spirits, mix thoroughly, filter and pour back into bottles. Close hermetically and keep in cold, dark place for a few months or longer.

MISCELLANEOUS

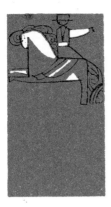

Sour Beet Juice for Barszez

*6 medium beets * warm water * 2 1/2 tbs. sugar * rye bread crust*

Clean and pare medium-size beets, remove root, cut into cubes.
Place in jar, pour over with warm water, add sugar and rye bread crust, cover jar with perforated paper or a cloth, set aside in a warm place for 5—8 days.
When the juice is fermented, pour off and set in cold place.
Pour water once more over beets, after souring mix with juice from the first fermentation, pour into bottle, close, keep in cold place.
Use to beet soup (barszcz).
The 5-day juice may be used as a nourishing drink with the addition of a small amount of sugar.

471

Oat or Rye Żur

Żur — a Type of Sour Soup

*2 cups of coarse oat or rye flour * 4 cups warm water * 1 tbs. leavening (fermented żur or a little leavened rye dough) or crust of rye bread * * 3 cloves garlic*

Place flour in jar, combine with part of water, add leavening (or crust of rye bread), crushed garlic, mix.

When the emulsion settles, add water — 3 inches over top of flour — cover with perforated paper or cloth, set aside in warm place for 3 days.

Make just enough żur so that it may be used up quickly; when over-fermented it has an unpleasant taste and aroma.

Pickled Lettuce Stalks

Remove leaves from young lettuce stalks, remove woody layer together with skin, cut up into stalks about 2 inches, place in earthenware crock or jar.

Boil water, salt and cool. Pour water over stalks, add garlic and dill stems (dried), cover with cloth and set aside to pickle.

Pickle in small amounts, as it spoils easily.

They may be used for soups, especially to sour beet soups.

Parzonka Sauerkraut

Steamed Sauerkraut

Shred cabbage finely and salt. When juice begins to form, press into earthenware crock and pour over with boiling liquid drained from cooked potatoes. Cover crock with a cloth and set aside in warm place for a few days to sour. After three days, remove to cold place, press with a saucer turned upside down, weigh down a little. After several days use for cooking like ordinary sauerkraut.

Sauerkraut for Salads

*10 lb. white cabbage * 1 lb. cooking apples * 4 oz. carrots * 2 bay leaves * * (1 tbs. allspice) * caraway seeds * 4 oz. salt*

Rinse apples and cabbage (after removing wilted leaves), drain off water. Cut cabbage in half, slit heart lengthwise. Shred cabbage finely. Cut apples in quarters, core and shred coarsely. Clean carrots, shred finely.
Crumble bay leaves.
Crush allspice.
Place cabbage in large earthenware crock in layers. Press each layer down tightly with palm. Place first layer of cabbage, sprinkle with spices and salt, arrange half of apples and carrots on top. Add a similar layer of cabbage on top of first one, press firmly, sprinkle with spices and salt, add apples and carrots. Cover with third and last layer of cabbage, sprinkled with spices and salt. Cover with wooden board and weigh down with 5-pound weight (non-metallic). Let stand in kitchen for one day.
Remove weight, pierce down cabbage to bottom in few places with a strong sharpened stick and set aside for two days to change the gases. After two days, weigh down once more.
After a few days remove wooden board, place clean linen napkin on cabbage and place in cellar (or in a dark, cold place), weigh down again.
Skim off skin from cabbage weekly and wash napkin. The cabbage should be covered with juice. If the cellar is too dry and the juice evaporates, add a little salted water.
The cabbage may be used together with the apples and carrots for salads.

Dill Pickles, Polish Style

Wash cucumbers and place in jar, adding dill stems (dried), a few oak or cherry leaves, a few cloves of garlic. When the jar is full, pour over with warm, salted water (using about 1 oz. salt for 4 cups of water) and let stand in warm place.
Place the cucumbers in cold pantry the following day, cover and weigh down lightly so that they do not float to surface.
After 4—6 days, depending on temperature of atmosphere, the cucumbers sour.
Both the dill pickles and juice should be used, for the latter makes a delicious ingredient for various soups and salads. It may also be used as a drink.

Dill Pickles in Bottles (for Winter Use)

Rinse and pare fresh, young cucumbers, slice thickly or cut lengthwise in thin strips.

Fill sterilized bottles with cucumbers and crumbled dill stems (dried).

Boil water salted to taste (using about 1 1/2 oz. salt for 4 cups of water), cool and pour over cucumbers.

Close bottles immediately, keep in a dark, cold place.

Use from January on.

Pickled Green Peppers for Immediate Consumption

*20 sweet green peppers * water * salt * dried dill (stems and seeds) * * 3 cloves of garlic*

Rinse peppers, remove peduncle with core and seeds. Do not remove seeds from one of peppers, cut this one in half.

Boil water, salt (using about 1/3 oz. salt for 4 cups of water). Cool.

Place peppers in earthenware crock, add dill and garlic, pour over with salted water.

Cover with double piece of gauze, set in kitchen to ferment for they ferment most rapidly in heat.

Pickled Tomatoes

Tomatoes for pickling should be fresh, hard, only slightly red — not completely ripe, otherwise they burst during pickling and fall apart.

Rinse the tomatoes, place in vessel close together, bottoms down. When the vessel is filled, pour cold salted water over the tomatoes (using about 2/3 oz. salt for 4 cups of water). Cover tomatoes with a plate (if they are in a pot) or with wooden disc (if pickled in keg) and weigh down lightly, so they do not float to top.

Make sure that while being pickled, they are always covered with juice.

Remove mold which is formed. Tomatoes may be used for soups. While they are still hard, they may be used for salads.

Pickled Mushrooms

*2 lb. mushrooms (champignons or red agaric) * pepper * allspice * a few bay leaves * 2 oz. salt*

474

Select mushrooms, clean, cut off stems. Place mushrooms in jar or wooden keg, adding spices. Salt each layer of mushrooms freely.

When all mushrooms are in jar, cover with plate and weigh down heavily with stone, set aside in cold place. When the mushrooms begin to give off juice and settle, add fresh mushrooms to fill jar, and weigh down once more. If there is too little juice, add very salted water so that the mushrooms are completely covered with liquid.

Keep in cold place.

They should be looked at often, removing the mold as it forms and adding pre-boiled salted water when necessary (using 2 oz. salt for 4 cups of water).

Tomato Sauce for Appetizers

*14 lb. tomatoes * 2 cups vinegar (4⁰/₀) * 2 oz. salt * 1—2 cups sugar *
* 1 tsp. allspice * 1 tsp. pepper * 1 tsp. cinnamon * 1 tsp. cloves * 1 tsp.
coriander * 1 tsp. nutmeg * 1 tsp. crushed bay leaves*

Select high quality, ripe yet firm, fresh tomatoes.

Wash tomatoes, cut in segments, sprinkle with water and cook slowly so they do not burn.

When the tomatoes soften, strain to remove pits, pour juice into saucepan and cook slowly, reduce to one half.

Add salt and sugar to vinegar and bring to the boil; crush finely all spices, wrap spices in thin gauze or linen, tie well and add to the vinegar; cover and cook vinegar slowly for about one-half hour; before pouring vinegar into tomatoes, remove spices.

When the tomatoes are cooked, pour over with boiling vinegar and cook slowly, stirring constantly.

Cook, clean and heat the bottles, pour the hot sauce into the bottles, close tightly.

Keep in a dark, cold place.

Gherkins or Small Cucumbers in Vinegar

*10 lb. gherkins or small cucumbers * 2 medium carrots * 1 root horse-
-radish * 1 1/2 cups small onions * 4 tbs. mustard seeds * 1/2 tbs.
allspice * 6 cloves * 10 bay leaves * 12 cups vinegar (4⁰/₀) * 2 oz. salt *
* 1/2 cup sugar*

Clean gherkins, pierce lightly with a fork, dry, place in pot and pour over with boiled salted water.

475

Clean carrots and horse-radish the following day. Dice horse-radish finely, slice carrots into rings or strips. Peel onions, rinse.

Pour off water after 24 hours, place the gherkins in jars, together with carrots, horse-radish, onions and spices.

Boil vinegar, add 2 oz. salt and 1 cup sugar, pour hot vinegar over gherkins in jar, cool.

Close jars tightly.

The gherkins should be checked often while being stored. If the fluid begins to ferment, the jars should be opened, the juice poured off, and a fresh solution of 4⁰/₀ vinegar substituted.

Small cucumbers may be pickled in the same manner.

Mizeria of Seed Cucumbers in Vinegar

*10 lb. very ripe seed cucumbers with yellowing peel * 2 medium carrots * * 1 root horse-radish * 1 1/2 cups small onions * 4 tbs. mustard seeds * * 1/2 tbs. allspice * 6 cloves * 10 bay leaves * 12 cups vinegar (4⁰/₀) * * 2 oz. salt * 1/2 cup sugar*

Wash cucumbers, peel, slice lengthwise into 4—6 slices, remove seeds and withered parts of cucumber with spoon. Place cucumbers in crock, pour over with boiled salted water.

After 24 hours, pour off water, place cucumbers in jars together with carrots, horse-radish, onions, and spices, the same as for gherkins.

Boil vinegar with salt and sugar, pour boiling vinegar over cucumbers. Cool cucumbers and close tightly.

Mushrooms in Vinegar

*2 lb. mushrooms (small red agaric or edible boletus) * 1 cup water * * 1 cup small onions * 1/2 tbs. allspice * 5 bay leaves * salt * sugar to taste * 2 cups vinegar (4⁰/₀)*

Peel onions, rinse.

Clean mushrooms and rinse quickly but thoroughly in water, place in saucepan, add a little water, onions and spices, simmer slowly covered until tender. When the mushrooms are tender, add salt and sugar to taste, add vinegar, cook slowly and place in small jars. When the mushrooms are cooled, close jars.

The mushrooms should be covered with a thick fluid (when fluid evaporates, add vinegar).

Mushrooms are widely used as an addition to salads and cold courses.

Plums in Vinegar

*2 lb. purple plums * B r i n e 1: 2 cups vinegar (6%) * 2 cups water * * B r i n e 2: 2 cups vinegar (6%) * 2 cups water * 2 1/2 cups sugar * * a few cloves * cinnamon to taste*

Boil vinegar and water, pour boiling brine over plums and let stand, until it cools. Strain brine, cook again, and pour boiling over plums once more, allow plums to cool in brine and drain off.
Cook second brine with sugar and spices, pour boiling brine over plums, cool and drain off brine.
Bring brine with sugar to the boil, cool.
Place plums in jars, pour over with cold brine to cover plums, close jars tightly.
Serve as a side-dish to meat appetizers.

Sherbet of Strawberries or Raspberries

*2 lb. berries * 2 1/2 lb. sugar*

Rinse fresh berries, drain thoroughly, strain through sieve.
Add sugar gradually to juice and cream in sterlized bowl with wooden spoon or rolling pin.
When the sugar dissolves completely, pour through sterillized funnel into clean, sterilized bottles to the top; close bottles tightly.
The sherbet may also be poured into a narrow jar and closed hermetically.

Sherbet of Black and Red Currants

*3 lb. red currants * 1 lb. black currants * 5 lb. sugar*

Wash fresh berries, drain thoroughly, remove stems, strain through sieve, squeeze rest of juice from pits through linen, combine the juice and thin mass with sugar.
When the sherbet begins to jell during mixing, pour quickly into sterilized narrow jars or bottles, close hermetically.

Sherbet of Currants and Raspberries

*3 lb. red or red and black currants * 1 lb. raspberries * 5 lb. sugar*

Prepare same as above.
Sherbets made of fresh fruits are used as garnishes for desserts and cold drinks.

Red-Bilberry Jam with Pumpkin and Blackberries

*11 cups bilberries * 2 1/2 cups pumpkin * 6 cups blackberries * 4 cups sugar * 1/2 cup water*

Select bilberries, rinse under running water in a sieve, drain.
Peel pumpkin, drain, cut into thin strips. Rinse blackberries, drain.
Place bilberries and pumpkin in saucepan, add sugar, add 1/2 cup boiling water and cook slowly over medium flame. When it begins to bubble and forms a foam, add blackberries, place in medium oven.
Bake to normal consistency so that the berries remain soft and juicy.
Place hot preserve into jars (crocks) and when cool close tightly.

Red-Bilberry and Apple Jam

*12 cups bilberries * 4 cups sugar * 5 medium tart apples*

Select bilberries, rinse, drain, place in saucepan, mix with sugar, and cook slowly while stirring. Place in oven and cook slowly. Stir from time to time. While mixing skim off scum on top with spoon. Reduce liquid to 3/4 of its original volume.
Rinse apples, peel, cut into 5 parts, remove seeds and core, add to bilberries and cook slowly until apples are translucent.
The berries should remain juicy and soft.
Place while hot in hot sterilized crock and close tightly.
Bilberry and apple jam is used as a relish with poultry and game.

Red-Bilberry and Pear Jam

*12 cups bilberries * 4 cups sugar * 4 medium pears*

Cook bilberries as in the previous recipe.
Peel pears, cut lengthwise into 4, remove seeds and core. Boil 1 cup of water, add pears and cook until half done.
Add the pears to the par-cooked bilberries in the oven, and cook through together. Finish as in previous recipe.
Bilberry and pear jam is used as a relish for poultry.

Cranberry and Apple Jam

*12 cups cranberries * 5 cups sugar * 5 medium tart apples*

Prepare the same way as red-bilberry and apple jam.

Raspberry and Currant Jam

*10 cups raspberries * 4 cups sugar * 2 1/2 cups red or red and black currants * 5 cups water * 1 1/4 cups sugar*

This jam is prepared rather differently from other fruit jams and takes a little more work.

Select dry raspberries, place in a bowl and sprinkle over with 4 cups sugar, set in cold place.

When the raspberries begin to secrete juice, place in saucepan and cook slowly, shaking the pan and skimming off scum. Dip spoon in cup with boiling water and skim off surface again with spoon until it settles.

Rinse currants, pour over with water, cook and strain.

Cook the currant juice with 1 1/4 cups sugar, skimming off scum.

Pour the curant syrup into raspberries, cook a little longer still skimming off the surface. The jam should be perfectly clear. Be careful while skimming not to take up too much of the syrup.

When the jam falls off the spoon in flakes, remove from flame and pour while hot into hot jars. Close jars tightly.

Use for filling cakes.

Candied Orange Peel

*2 lb. orange peel * 7 1/2 cups sugar * 5 cups boiling water * 2/3 tsp. cream of tartar*

Pour cold water over fresh peel and soak for 3 days, changing the water twice daily; at end of three days drain off water.

Prepare a syrup with sugar and boiling water, add cream of tartar, drop the skins into this syrup and cook a little daily for a few days until a drop of syrup dropped on a plate forms a ball; the cooked peels should be soaked through with the syrup until soft and vitreous. Cook slowly and cool by placing the vessel in cold water after each batch is cooked.

Then place peels in jars, pour over with syrup, close tightly.

Candied orange peel has varied uses.

INDEX

485

486

MEAT

489

SAUCES

Sauces for Appetizers, Meat and Vegetables

491

LIST OF PHOTOGRAPHS

Photographs by J. Czarnecki: 1, 3, 4, 5, 7, 8, 11, 13, 16, 17, 20, 21, 24, 25, 27, 28, 32

Photograph by J. Proppe: 31

Photographs by J. Styczyński (Lay-out: A. Grochowska, M. Iwaszkiewicz): 2, 6, 9, 10, 12, 14, 15, 18, 19, 22, 23, 26, 29, 30

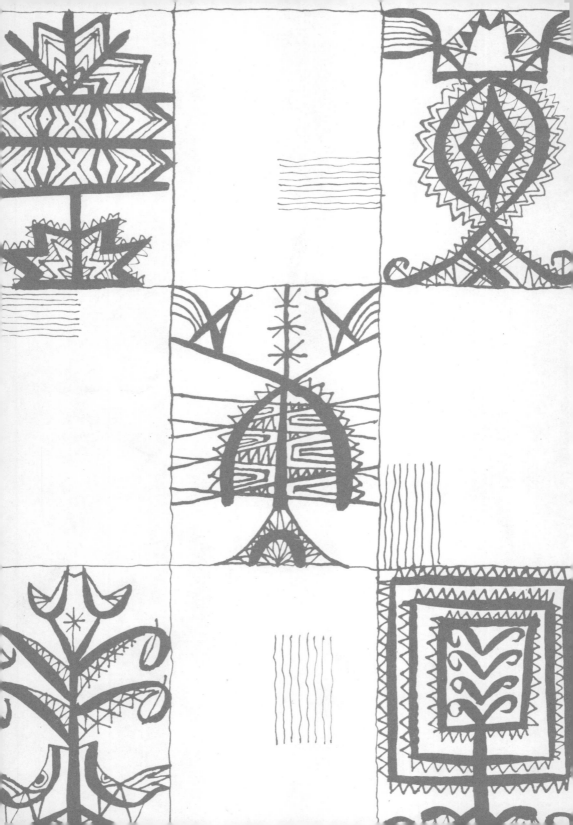